Multiple Exposures
Allen Jones & photography

presented by
Philippe Garner

ACC ART BOOKS

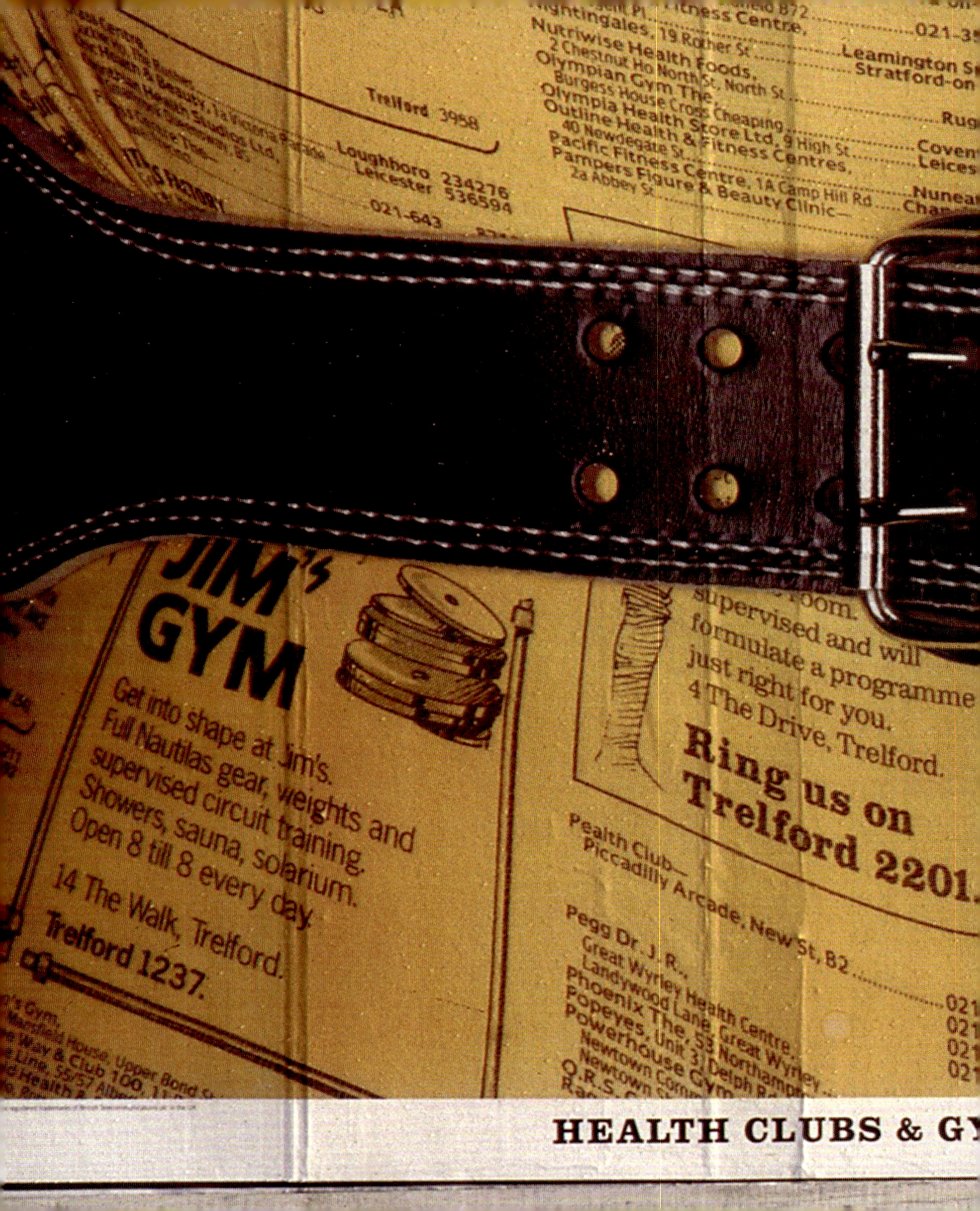

Nightingales, 19 Rother St
Nutriwise Health Foods,
2 Chestnut Ho North St, North St
Olympian Gym The,
Burgess House Cross Cheaping
Olympia Health Store Ltd, 9 High St
Outline Health & Fitness Centres,
40 Newdegate St
Pacific Fitness Centre, 1A Camp Hill Rd
Pampers Figure & Beauty Clinic—
2a Abbey St
Trelford 3958
Loughboro 234276
Leicester 536594
JIM'S GYM
Get into shape at Jim's.
Full Nautilas gear, weights and supervised circuit training.
Showers, sauna, solarium.
Open 8 till 8 every day.
14 The Walk, Trelford.
Trelford 1237.
supervised and will formulate a programme just right for you.
4 The Drive, Trelford.
Ring us on Trelford 2201.
Piccadilly Arcade, New St, B2
Pegg Dr. J. R.,
Great Wyrley Health Centre,
Landywood Lane, Great Wyrley
Phoenix The, 55 Northampton
Popeyes, Unit 3, Delph Rd
Powerhouse Gym
HEALTH CLUBS & GY

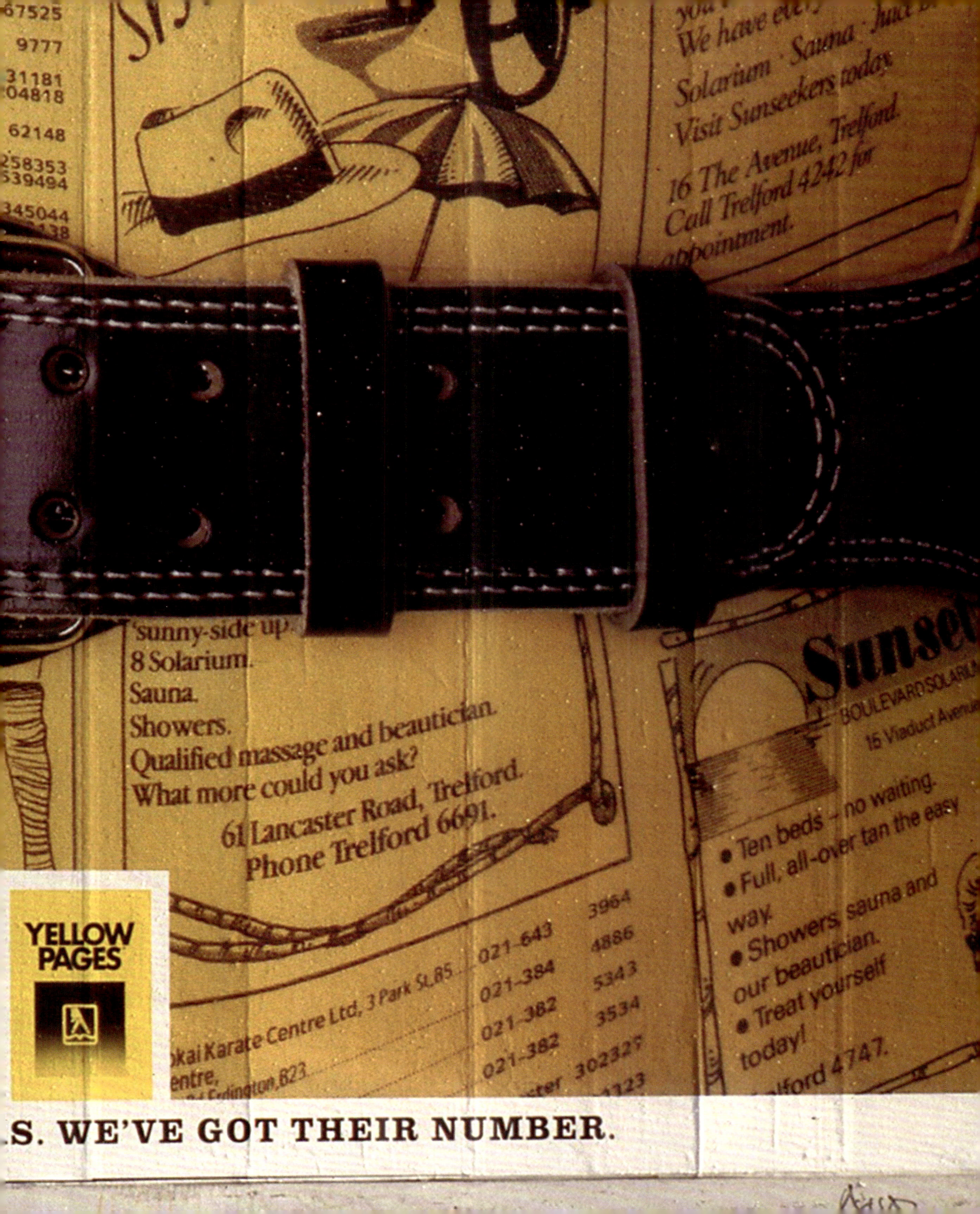

We have every
Solarium · Sauna · Juice Bar
Visit Sunseekers today.
16 The Avenue, Trelford.
Call Trelford 4242 for
appointment.
'sunny-side up.'
8 Solarium.
Sauna.
Showers.
Qualified massage and beautician.
What more could you ask?
61 Lancaster Road, Trelford.
Phone Trelford 6691.
Sunset
BOULEVARD SOLARIUM
16 Viaduct Avenue
• Ten beds – no waiting.
• Full, all-over tan the easy
way.
• Showers, sauna and
our beautician.
• Treat yourself
today!
Trelford 4747.
Karate Centre Ltd, 3 Park St, B5 021-643 3964
021-384 4886
021-382 5343
021-382 3534
302327
YELLOW PAGES
S. WE'VE GOT THEIR NUMBER.

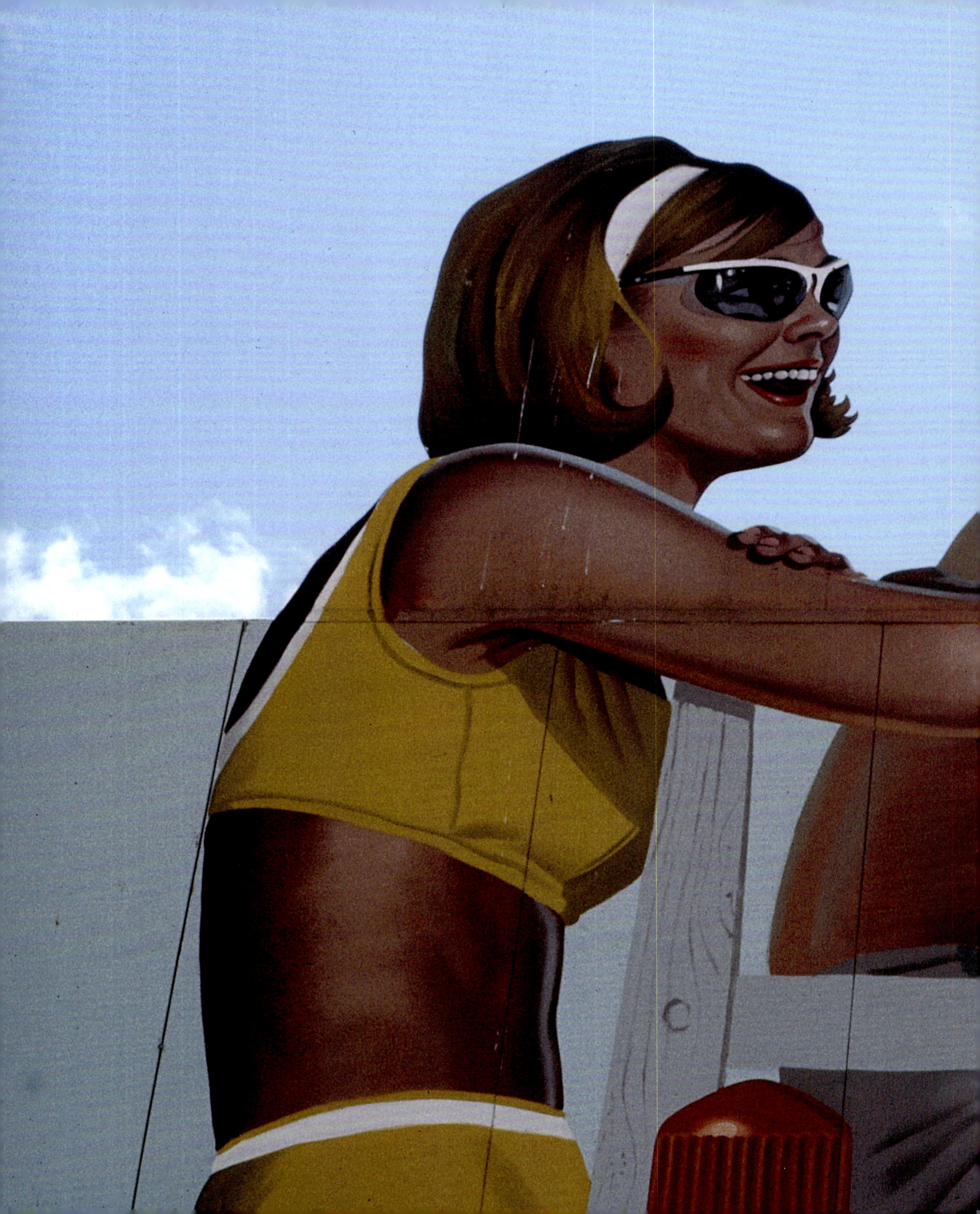

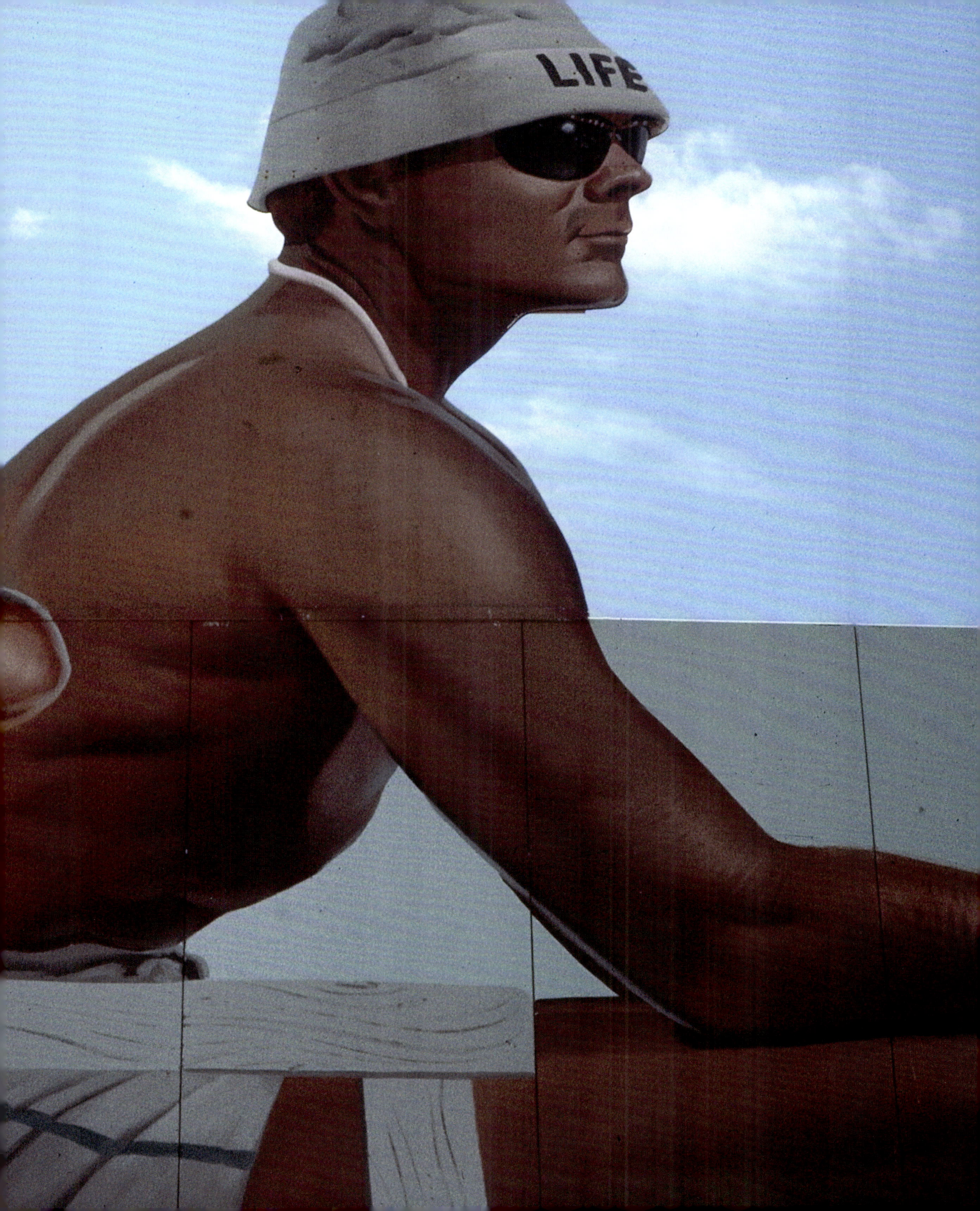
LIFE

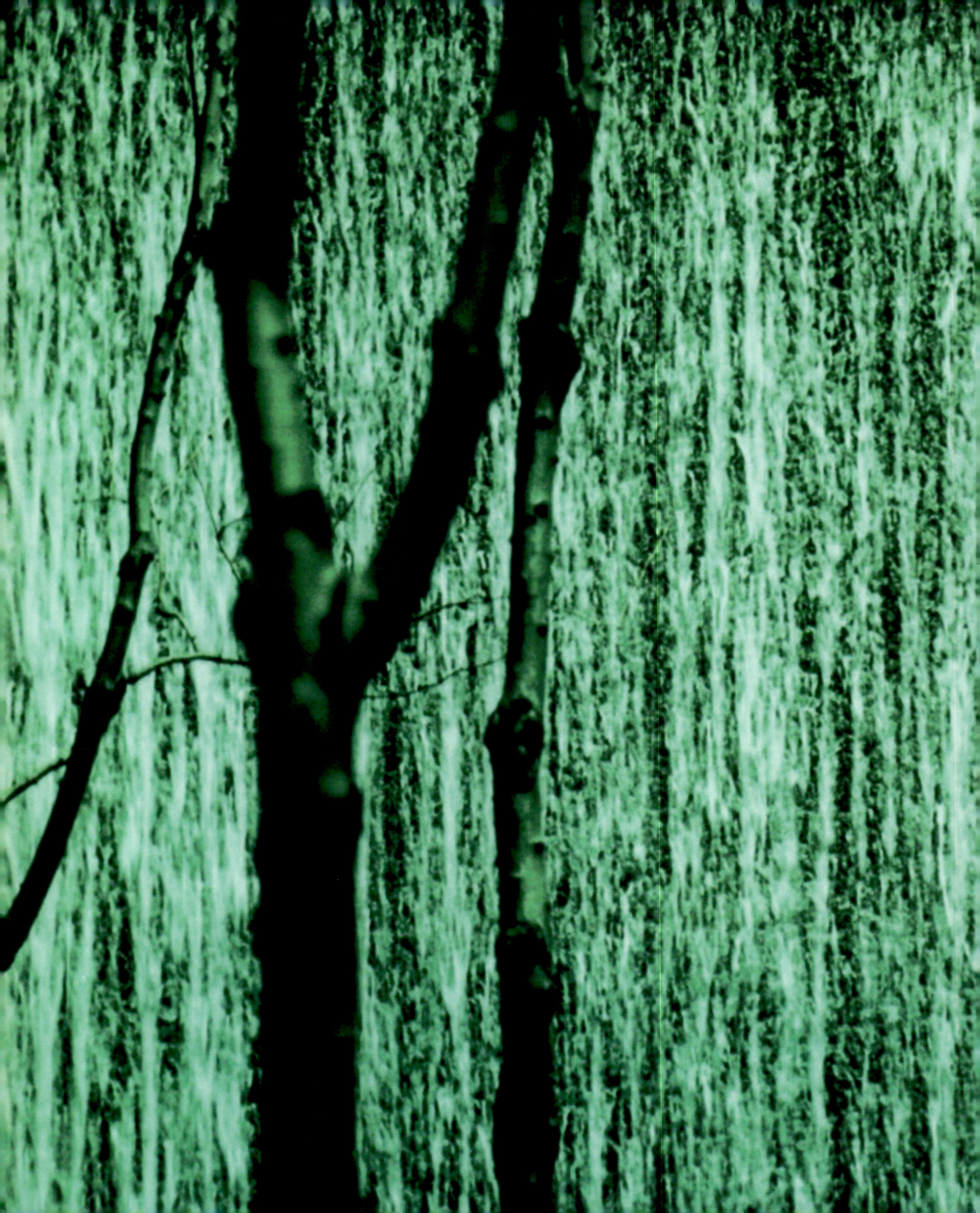

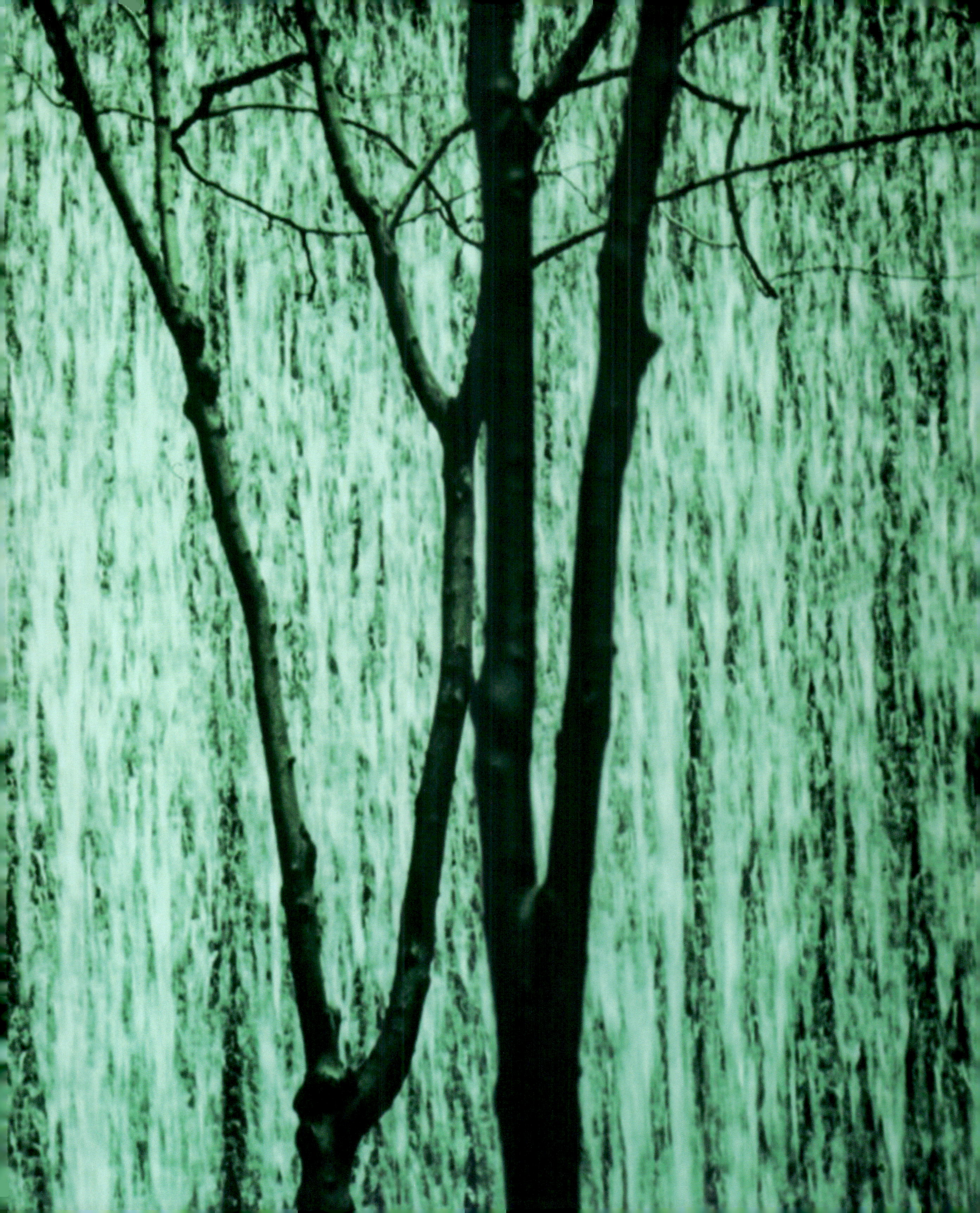

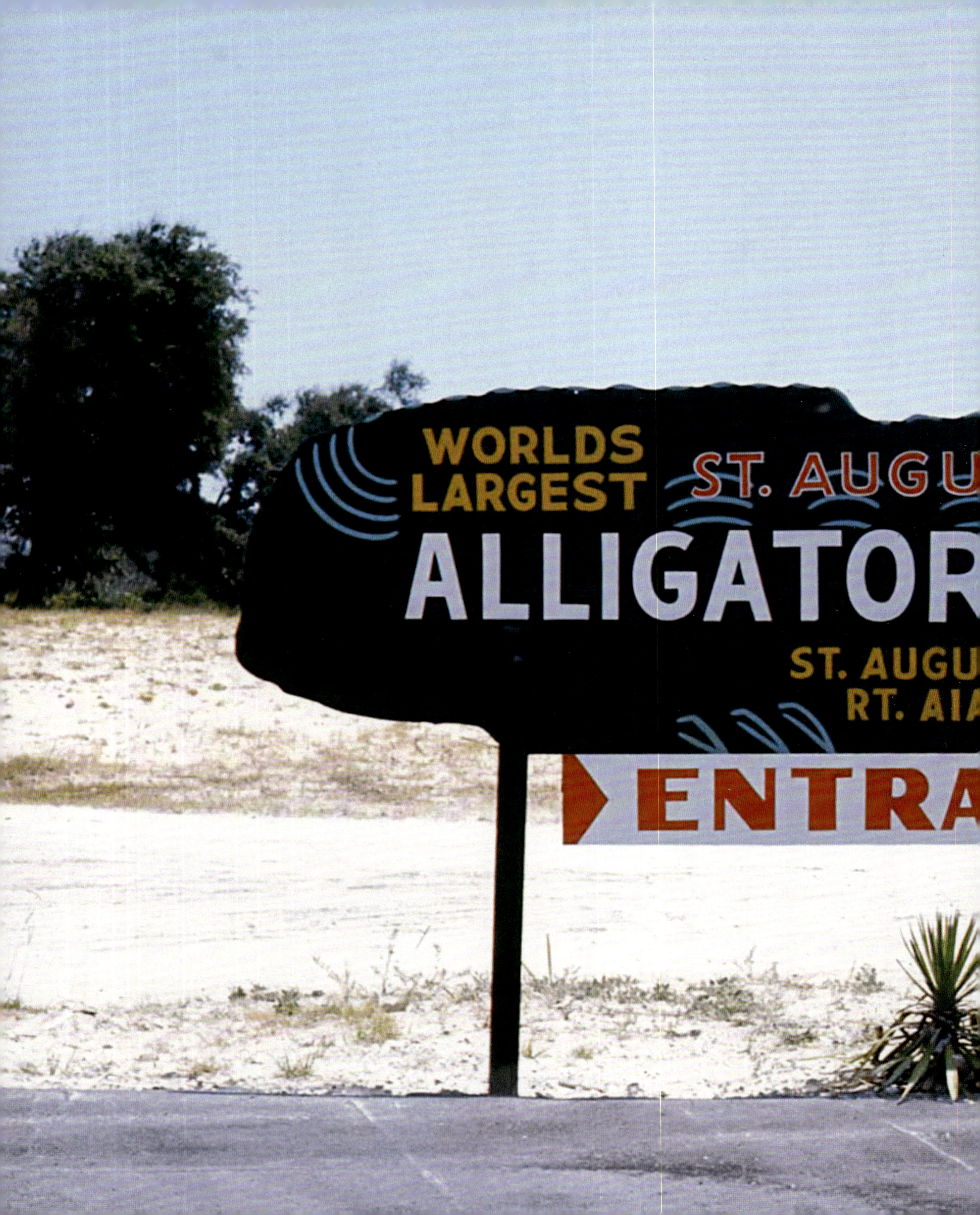
WORLDS
LARGEST
ST. AUGU
ALLIGATOR
ST. AUGU
RT. AIA
ENTRA

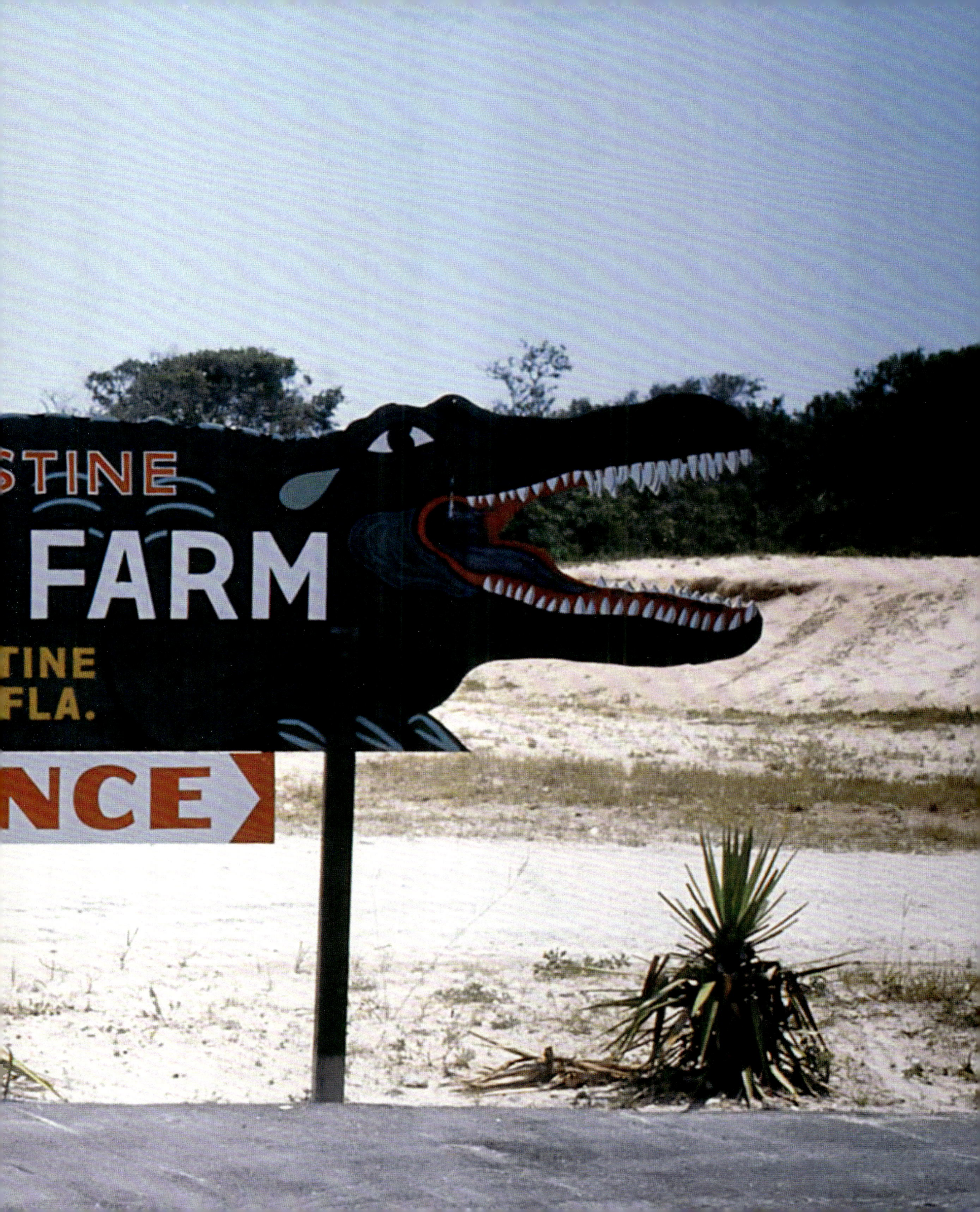

STINE
FARM
TINE
FLA.
NCE

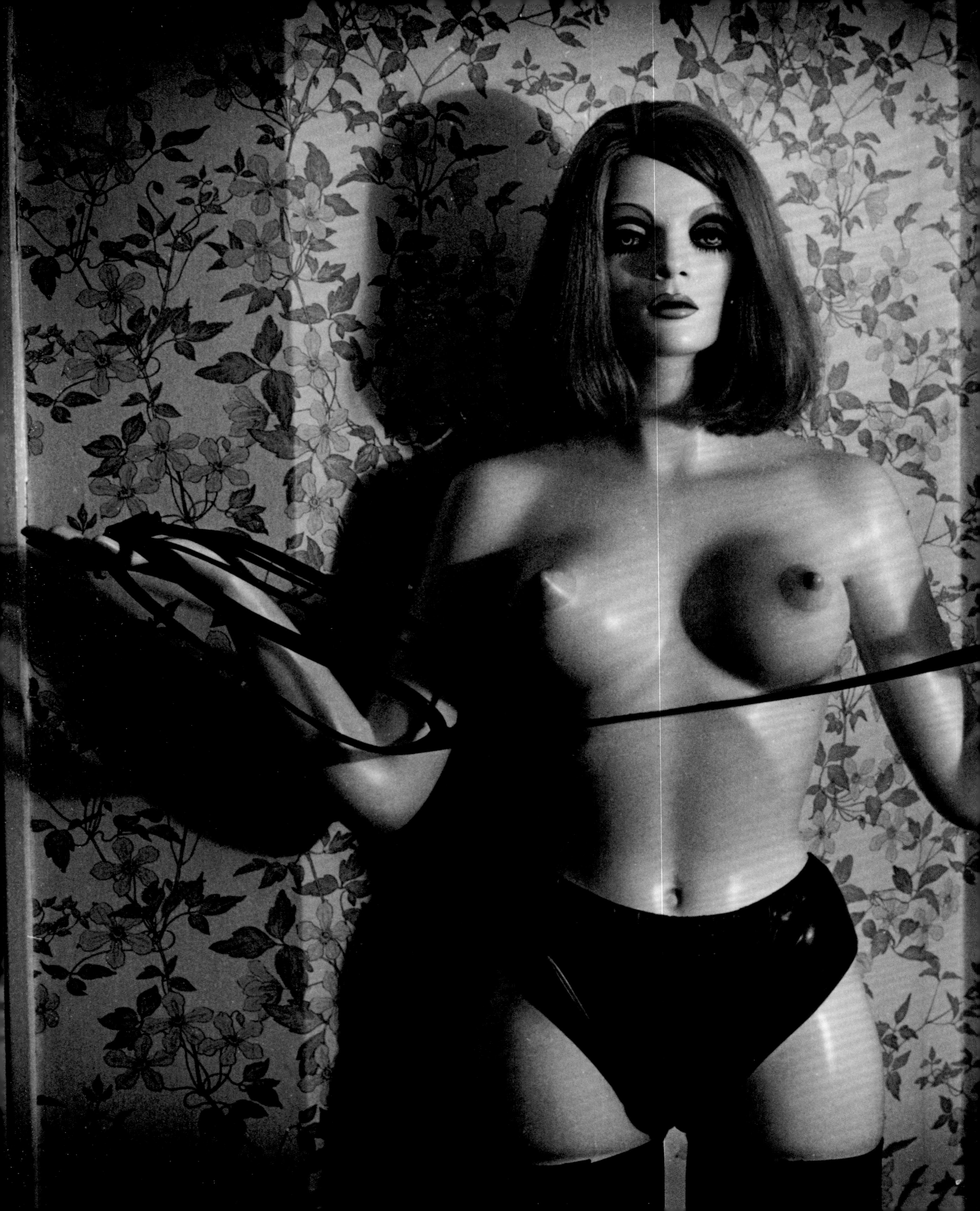

Left 'Hatstand', Edith Grove, London, 1969
Overleaf 'Get a Grip', Ledwell, Oxfordshire, 2019
Page 18 Ledwell, Oxfordshire, 2014

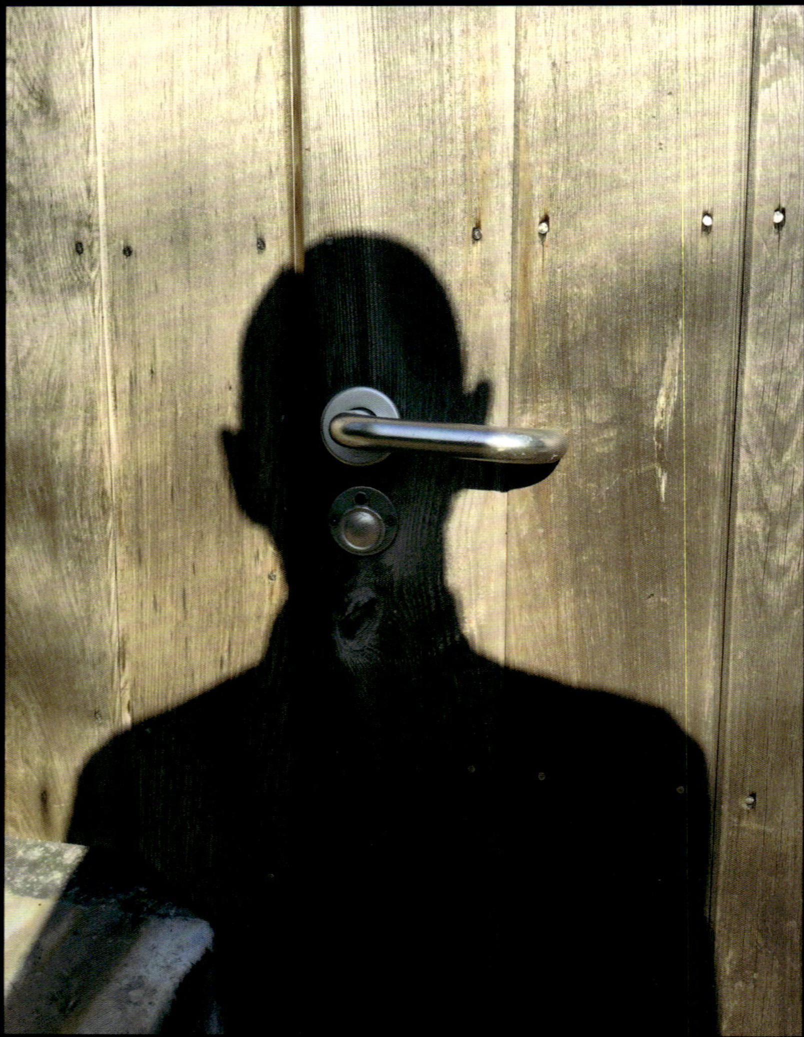

Multiple Exposures

Allen Jones & photography

presented by
Philippe Garner

Allen Jones's vision as an artist situates the female figure as its most insistent motif. This vision has been significantly informed and inflected by his exposure to the popular photo-imagery of the post-war age of mass visual communication in which he grew up. Allen's sensibility has always been quintessentially urban, fuelled by the rich visual tapestry of the city – by the signage and the advertising, by the ubiquitous proliferation of magazines and newsprint, and by the flashes of vivid colour and the constantly shifting patterns of people in movement.

An informal portrait of Allen from the early 1960s by his friend, photographer Michael Cooper, shows him, smiling, before a wall covered in photographs of alluring women. These pictures, cut from magazines, are dominated by Brigitte Bardot, notably by a fold-out of this emblematic idol published in the Royal College of Art journal *Ark* in the autumn of 1959, the semester of Allen's enrolment. He is integrated by Cooper within a collage of mediated images of actresses and models as symbols of desire, images that herald a life-long engagement with this performative theme – the constant thread that runs through his paintings, his sculptures, his photographs, and the mass of images that he has collected and assimilated into his personal image bank. Among Allen's most telling early works are photo-collages that echo those of the Dadaists – the generation of Paul Citroen, Hannah Höch, and Kurt Schwitters – while marking their own contemporaneity with topical iconography and radical new painterly elements.

Allen's art is at once highly accomplished in the most traditional sense and vitally connected to tropes of popular culture. As a painter, he is a thoughtful and technically skilled master of colour, tonal gradation, line, and pictorial structure; he can speak admiringly of such specifics as the clever compression of planes and the effects of transparency in Lord Leighton's 'Flaming June', and just as deliberately deconstruct the stylisations of curiously compelling newsprint cuttings or magazine tear-sheets of glamourised figures. Allen has marked out his signature territory in the conjunction – at once obsessional and ironic – of his high technical skill and the provocative visual codes of his subject matter.

The present anthology, pieced together from so many strands of Allen's archive and oeuvre, reveals, in words and in images, his lasting fascination with photographs and the multi-faceted nature of his relationship with this medium. We discover the various ways in which photographs – collected in one form or another, artful and artless, or made by Allen either as aide-mémoire references or as works in their own right – have enriched his creative imagination and expression.

Allen's earliest photographs are black and white. His study in Finsbury Park underground station, an image vibrant with splashes of light, is a precocious indicator of his sharp eye, inspired by the 'Action' paintings of Jackson Pollock he had just seen exhibited at the Whitechapel Gallery in 1958, and in the best experimental tradition of Man Ray or László Moholy-Nagy. His early close-ups of lollipops and of a girlfriend licking one stand out as impactful explorations of colour and of proto-'Pop' imagery. Allen's first figure studies involving fetishistic symbols, materials, and poses anticipate a career-long investigation. Trips to the USA – the Promised Land to a generation seduced by the consumerist fantasies of the post-war boom years – have provided rich opportunities to make pictures. In Manhattan,

Miami, Los Angeles, and many cities and sites in between, Allen has recorded neon cowboy signs, giant billboards, cars, cops, sunbathers, a brass band, a row of fibreglass dinosaurs, and many other intriguing subjects. On his home turf in London, he is drawn to local equivalents such as a picturesque shopfront or a traffic-stopping poster for Wonderbra. Wherever he goes, Allen has also found pictorial potential in the most mundane subjects – in debris and detritus and in his abstracted details of road markings that can remind him of Dadaist concrete poetry or of the paintings of Barnett Newman.

The camera has played a crucial role in a number of Allen's projects – as a tool to better prepare for making painted portraits; in the commission to create a suite of images for Pirelli's 1973 calendar; and, forty years later in 2013, in his representations in various media of Kate Moss. More recently, Allen has used photography to propose a fresh experience of his sculptures. These intriguing images – made with camera, iPad, and iPhone – play with layering, light, and shadows and invite us deep into his unique imaginative universe.

Philippe Garner

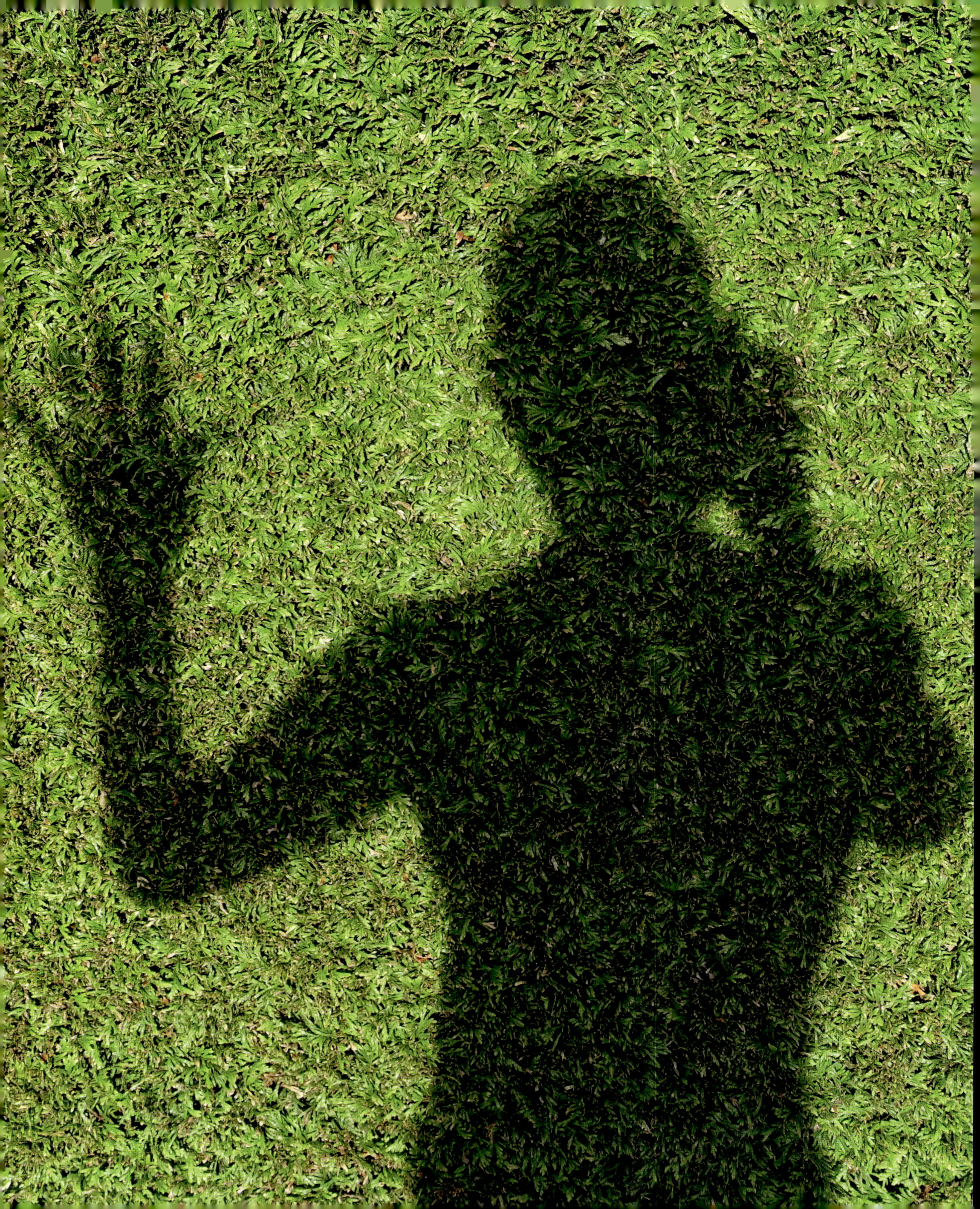

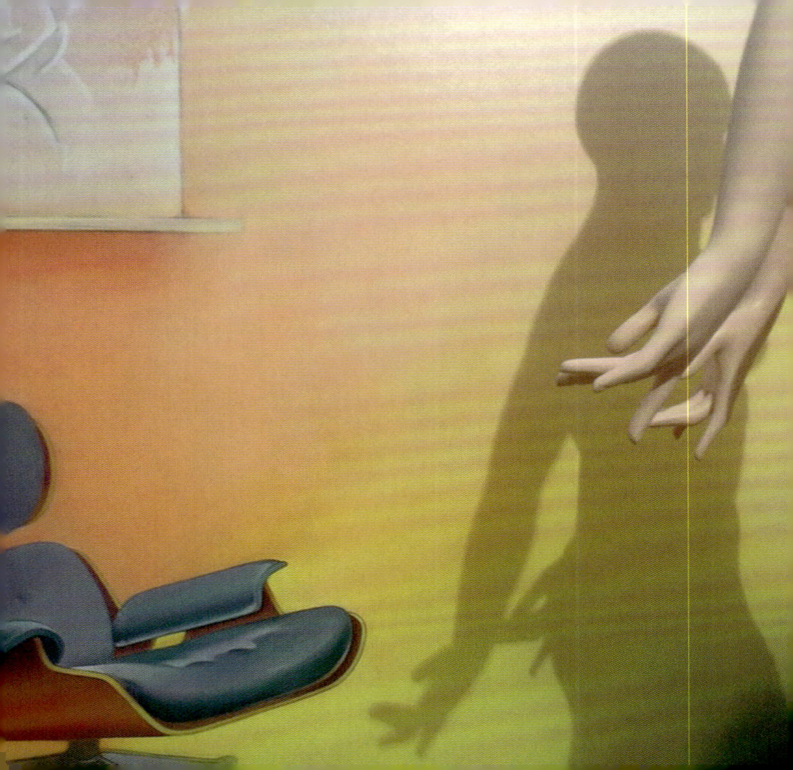

3D into 2D

For some time, I have been making different sculptures using casts of the same figure. I am intrigued by how different the figure can be, simply by the different colours used and varied ways they are painted.

Sculptures, like furniture, can gather dust, and so I use commercial paint that makes the surface easy to clean. It was necessary to develop a new technique with the brush to achieve the subtle gradations I am used to creating in oil paint.

I can spend several hours painting some detail of the figure that the viewer's eyes will skim over whilst looking at the sculpture. The camera, however, can fix on this detail and make it an entity in itself worthy of contemplation.

With the facility of today's digital cameras, iPads, and iPhones, taking pictures has become an extension of my thought process as much as making notes in pencil.

Opposite 'Bystander' (detail), Ledwell, Oxfordshire, 2015

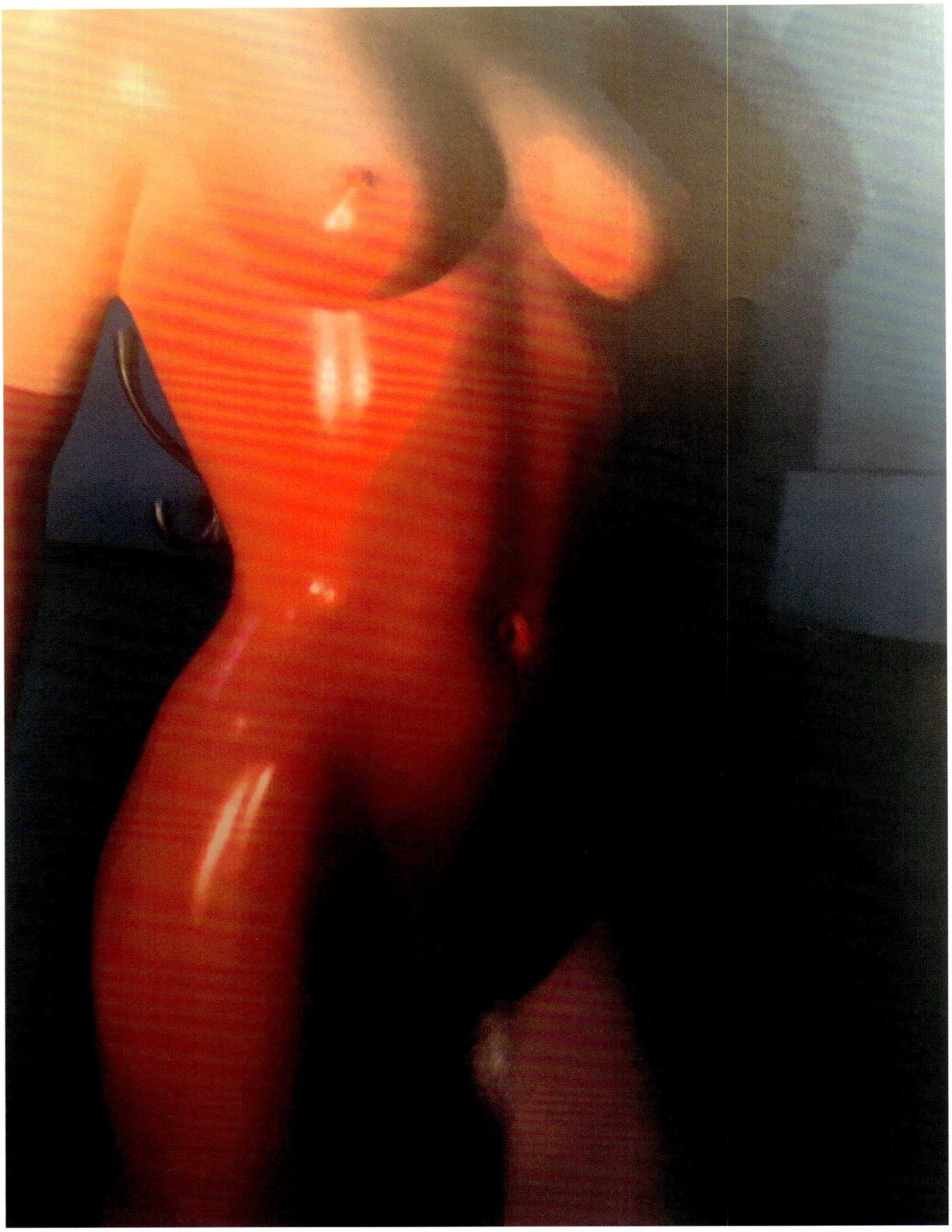

Above and opposite
Ledwell, Oxfordshire, 2019

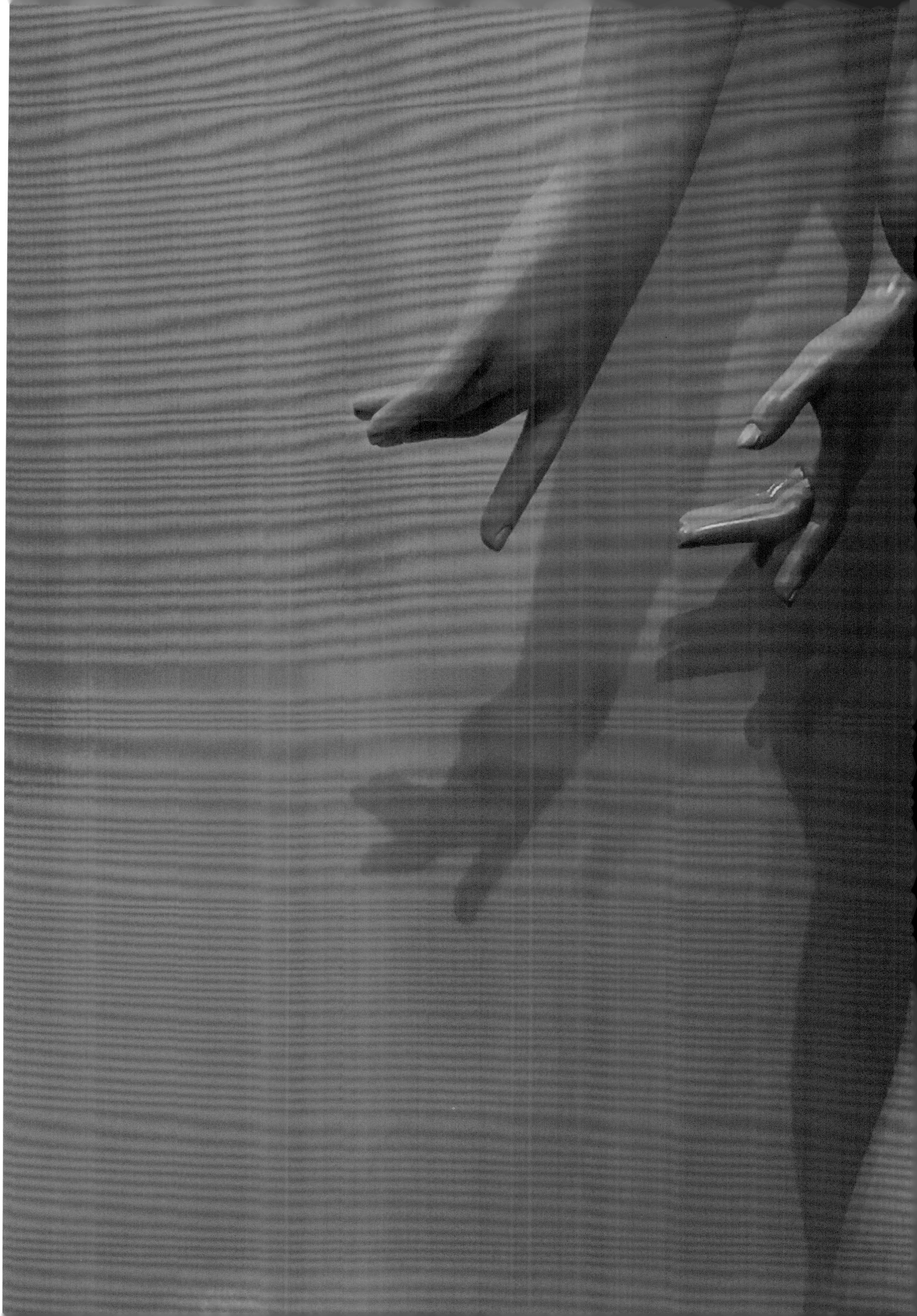

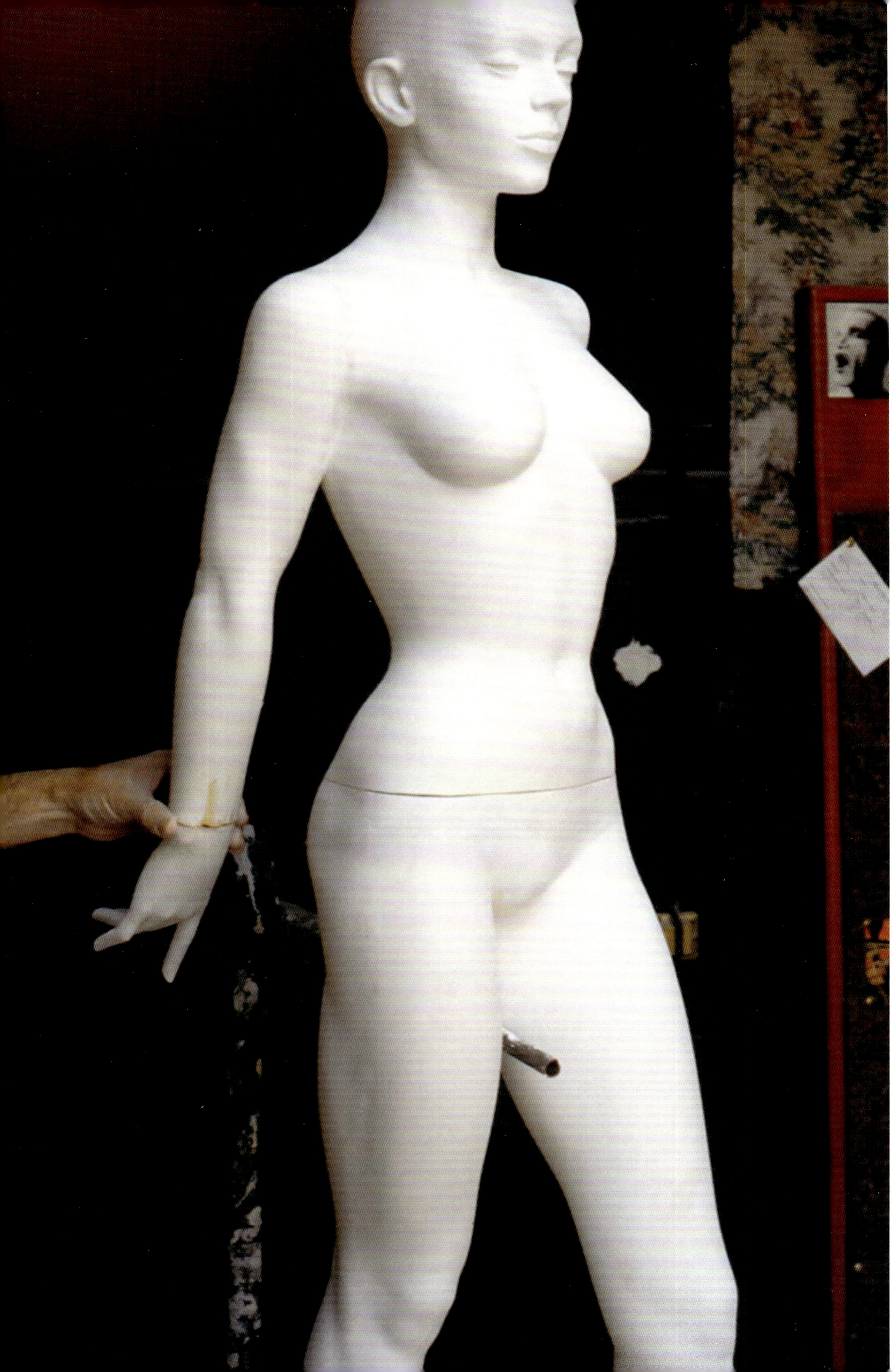

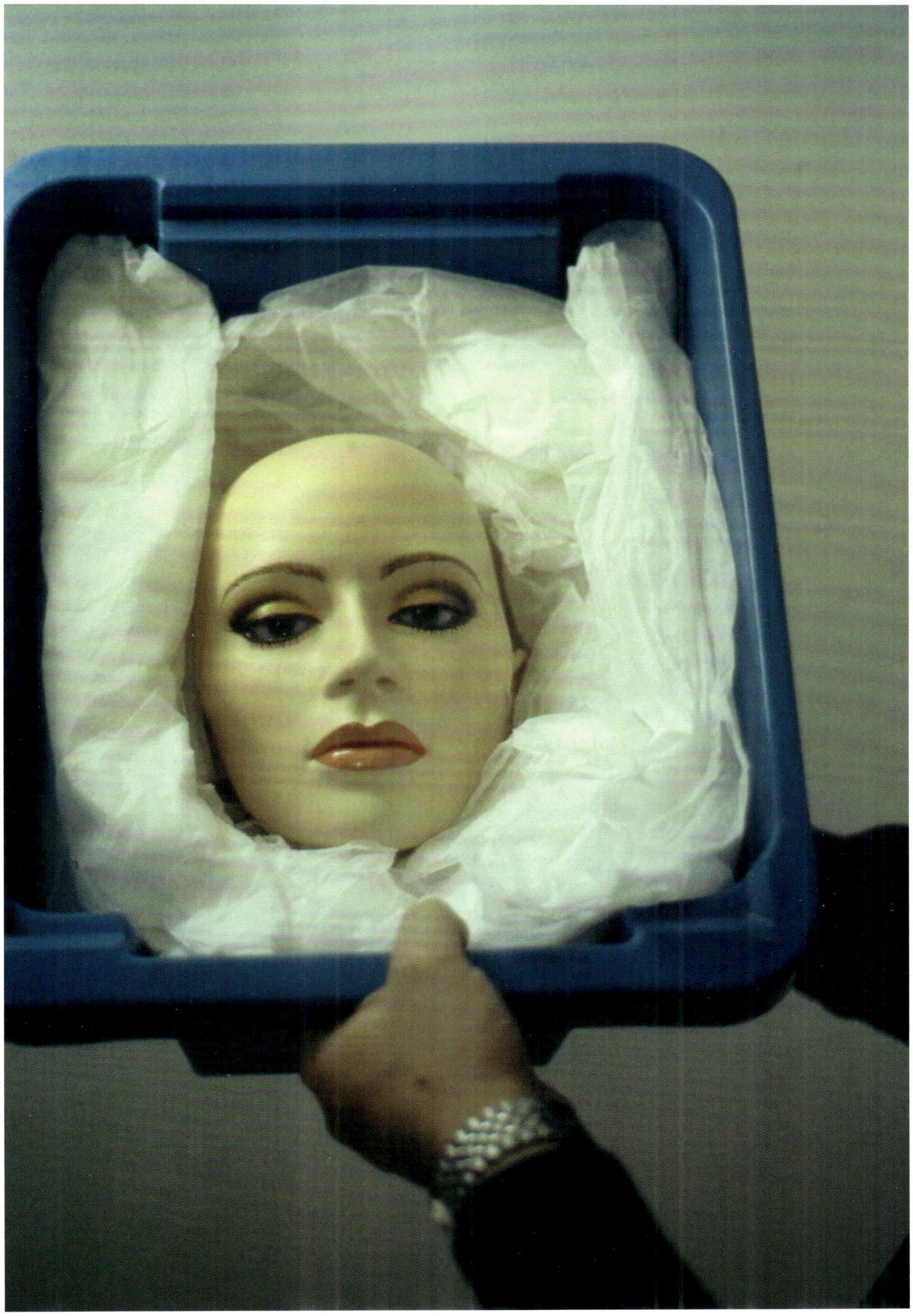

Opposite In Dik Beech's workshop, London, 1987
Above Charterhouse Square, London, 2002
Overleaf Dik Beech's hands, London, 1987

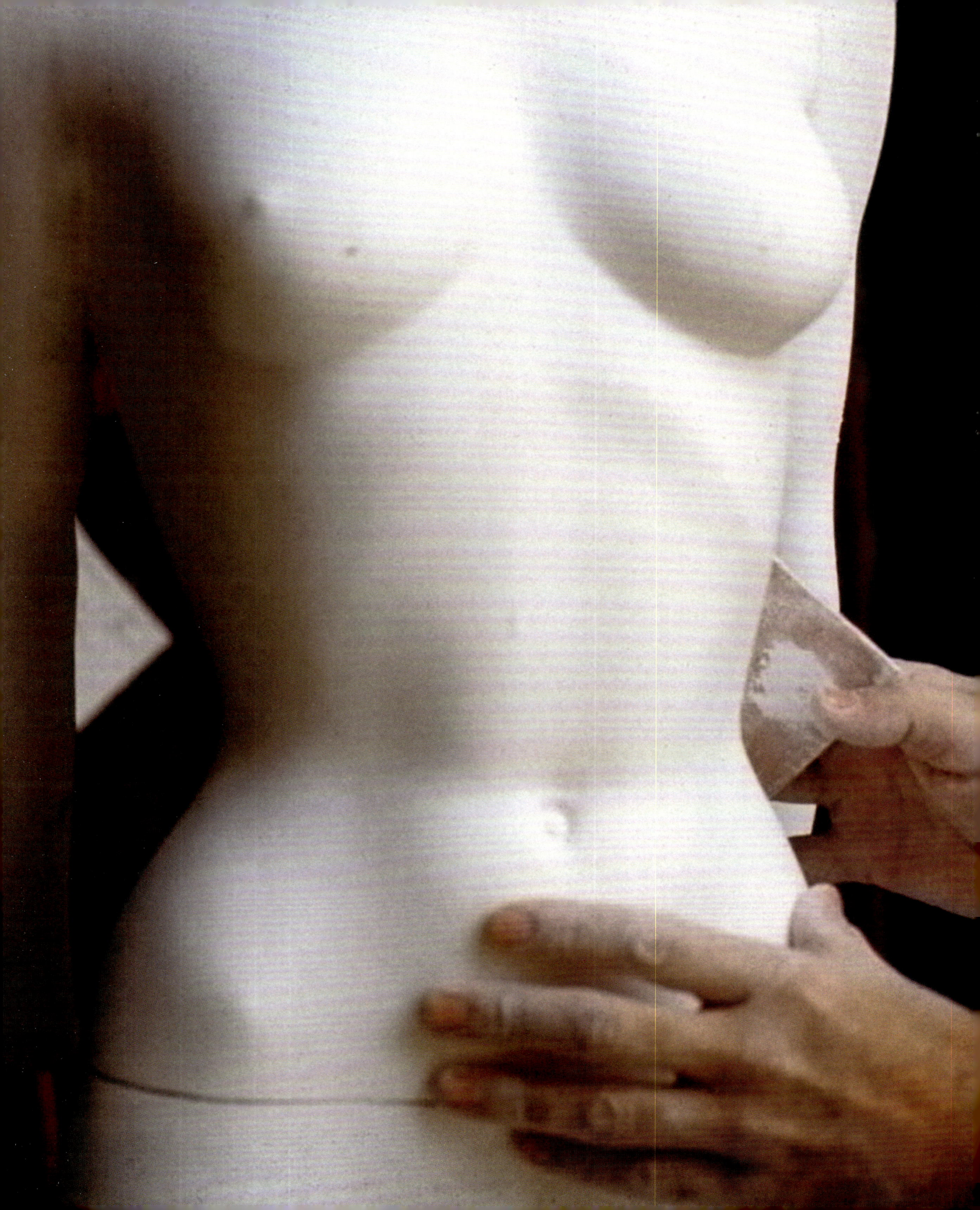

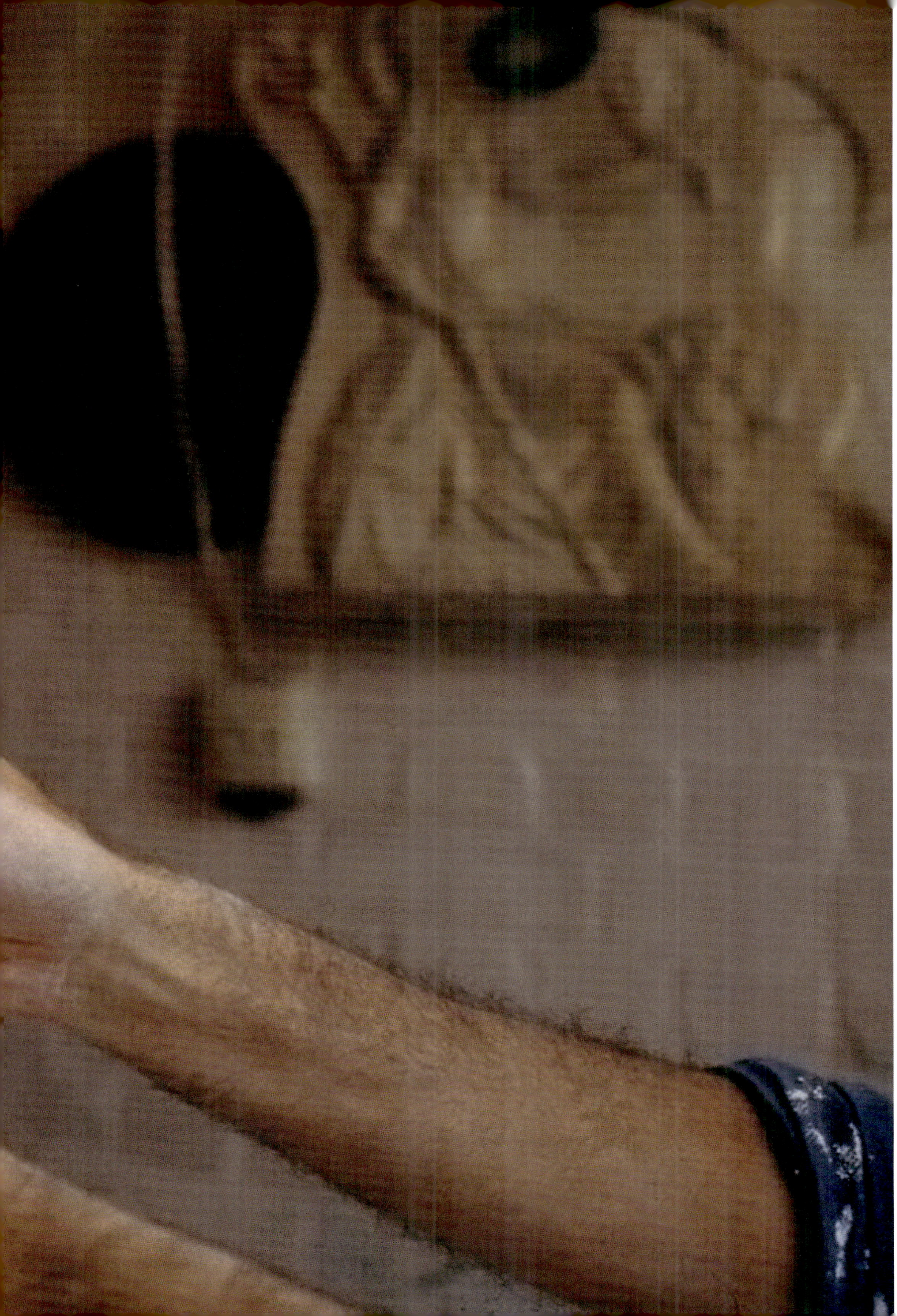

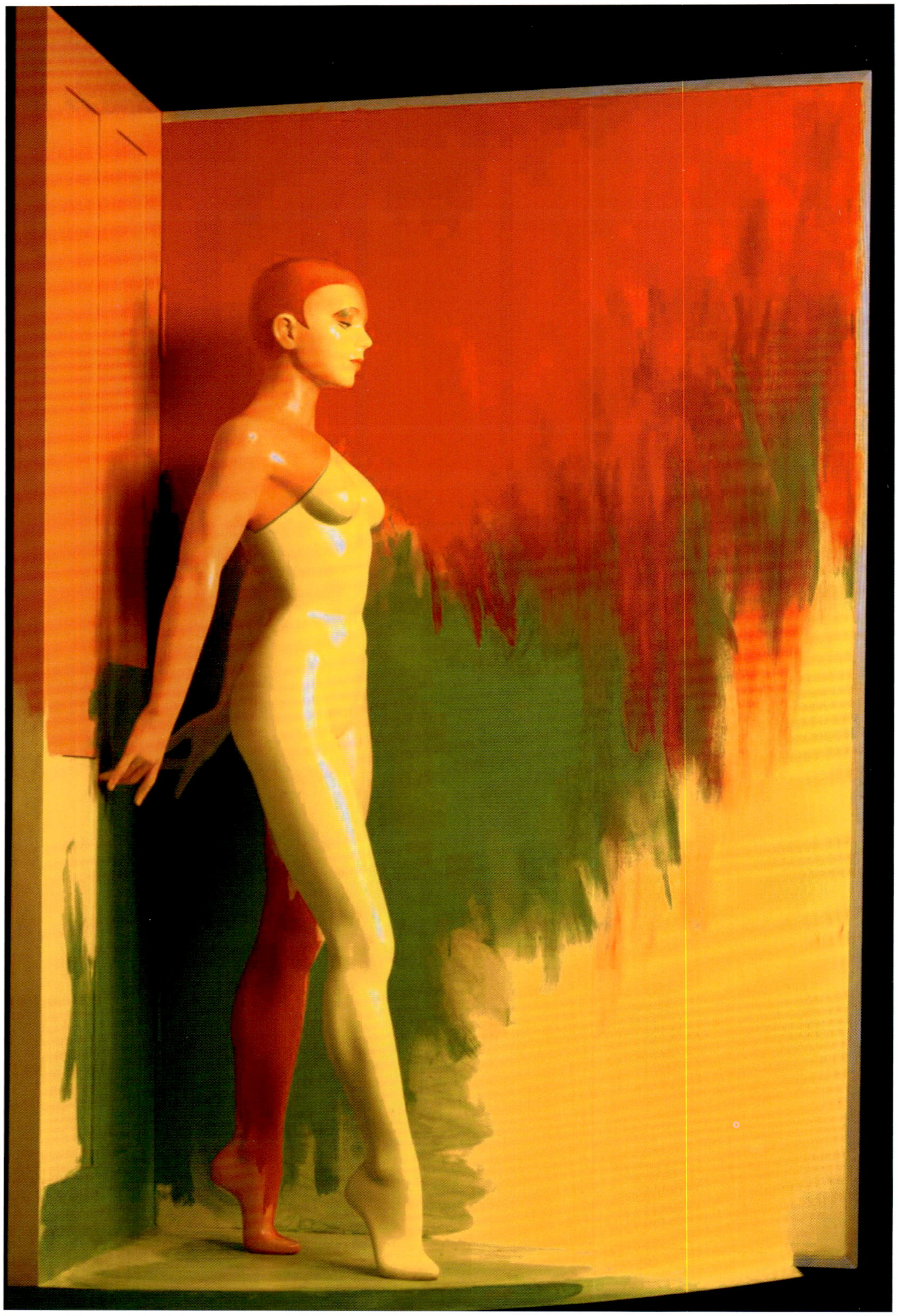

Above 'Stand Out', 1992
Opposite 'Enchanteresse' (detail), Ledwell, Oxfordshire, 2016

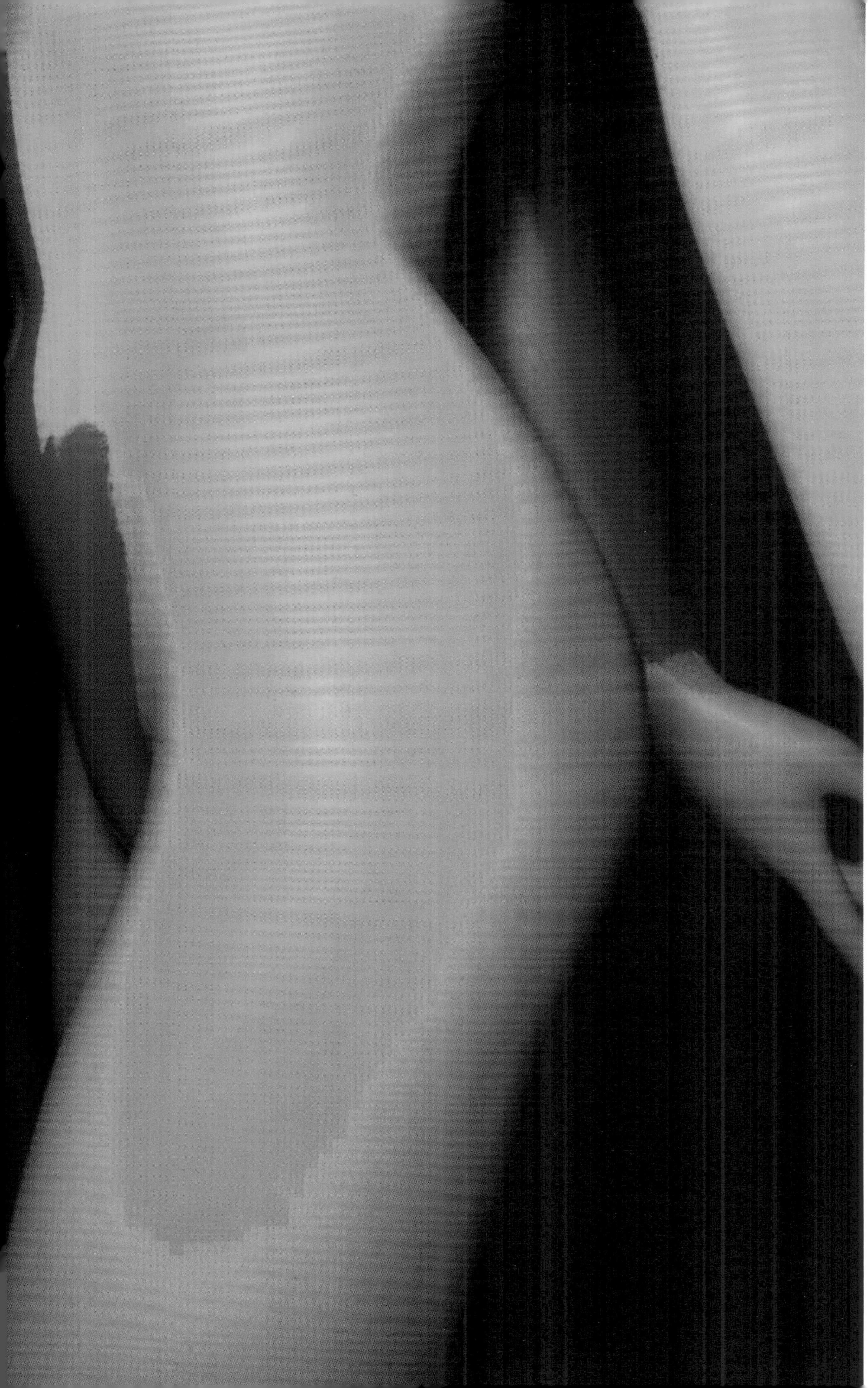

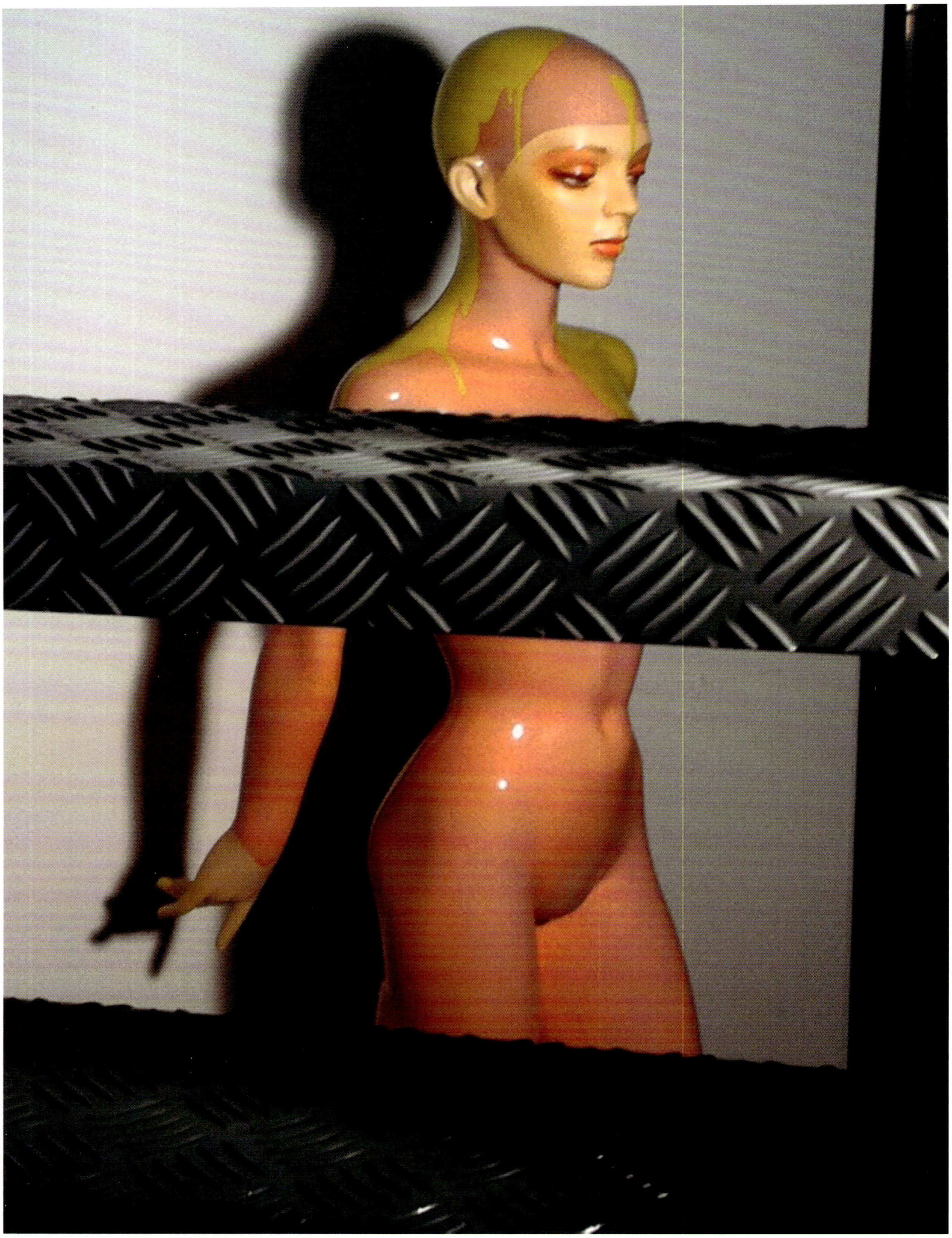

Above and opposite Works in progress, Ledwell, Oxfordshire, 2015

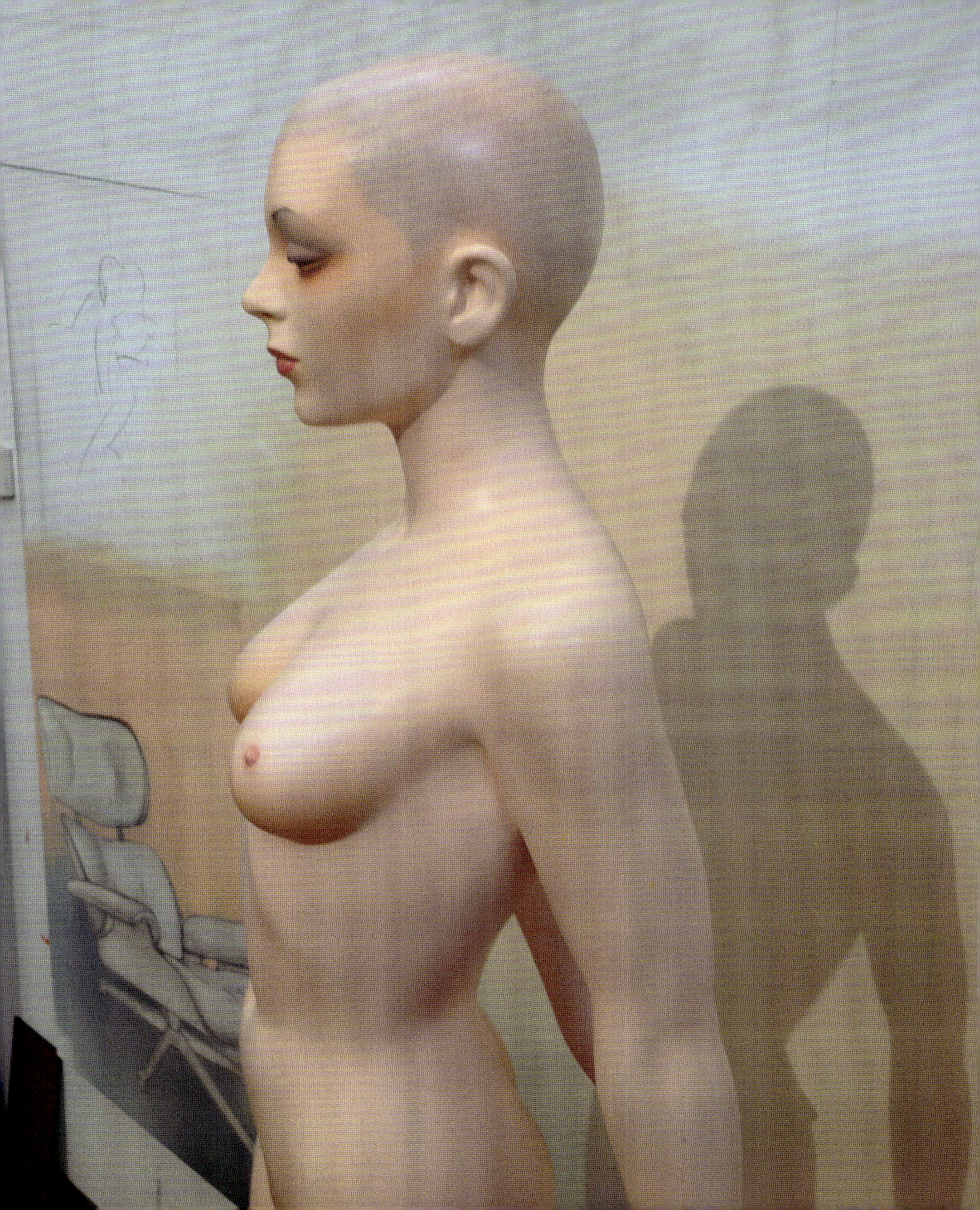

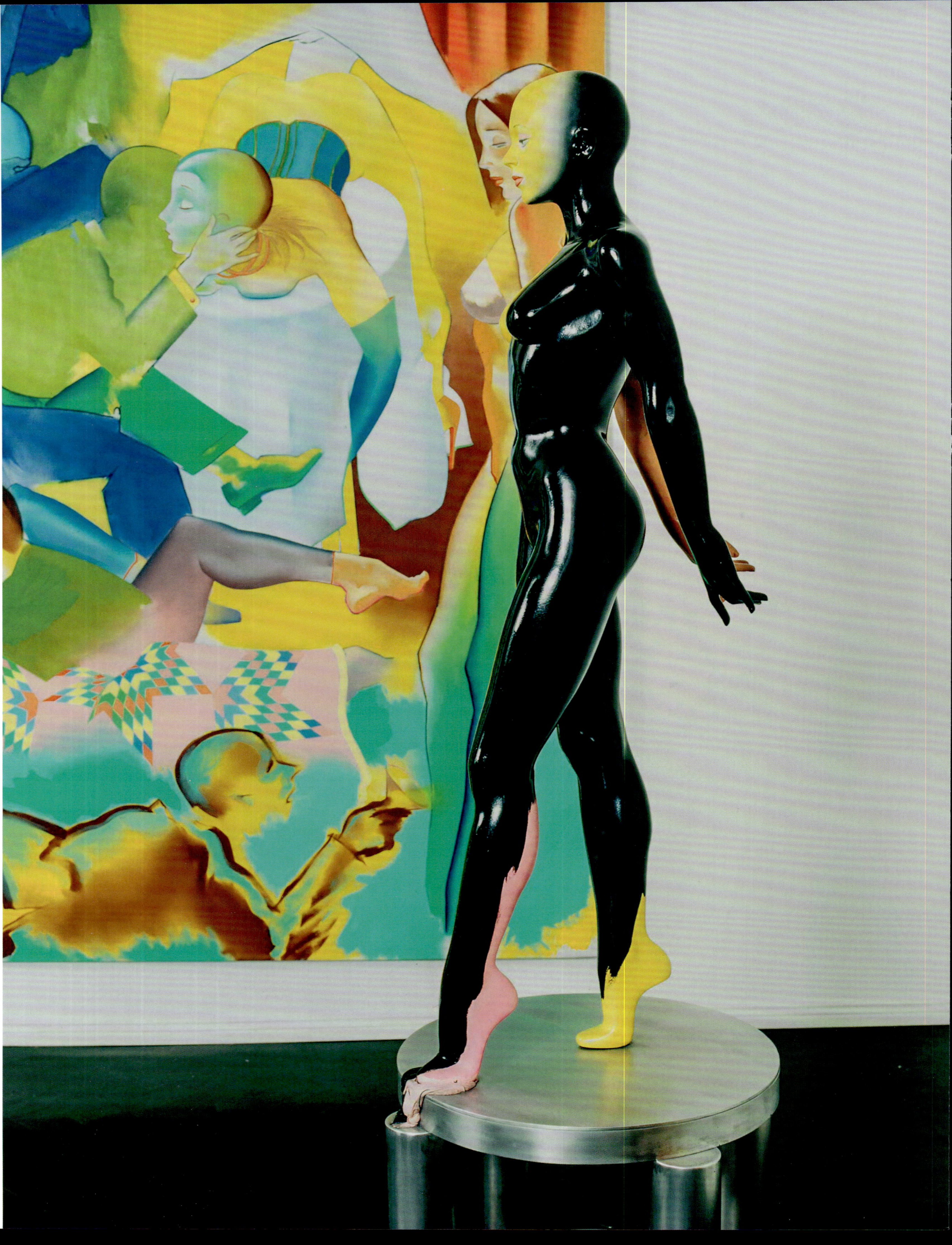

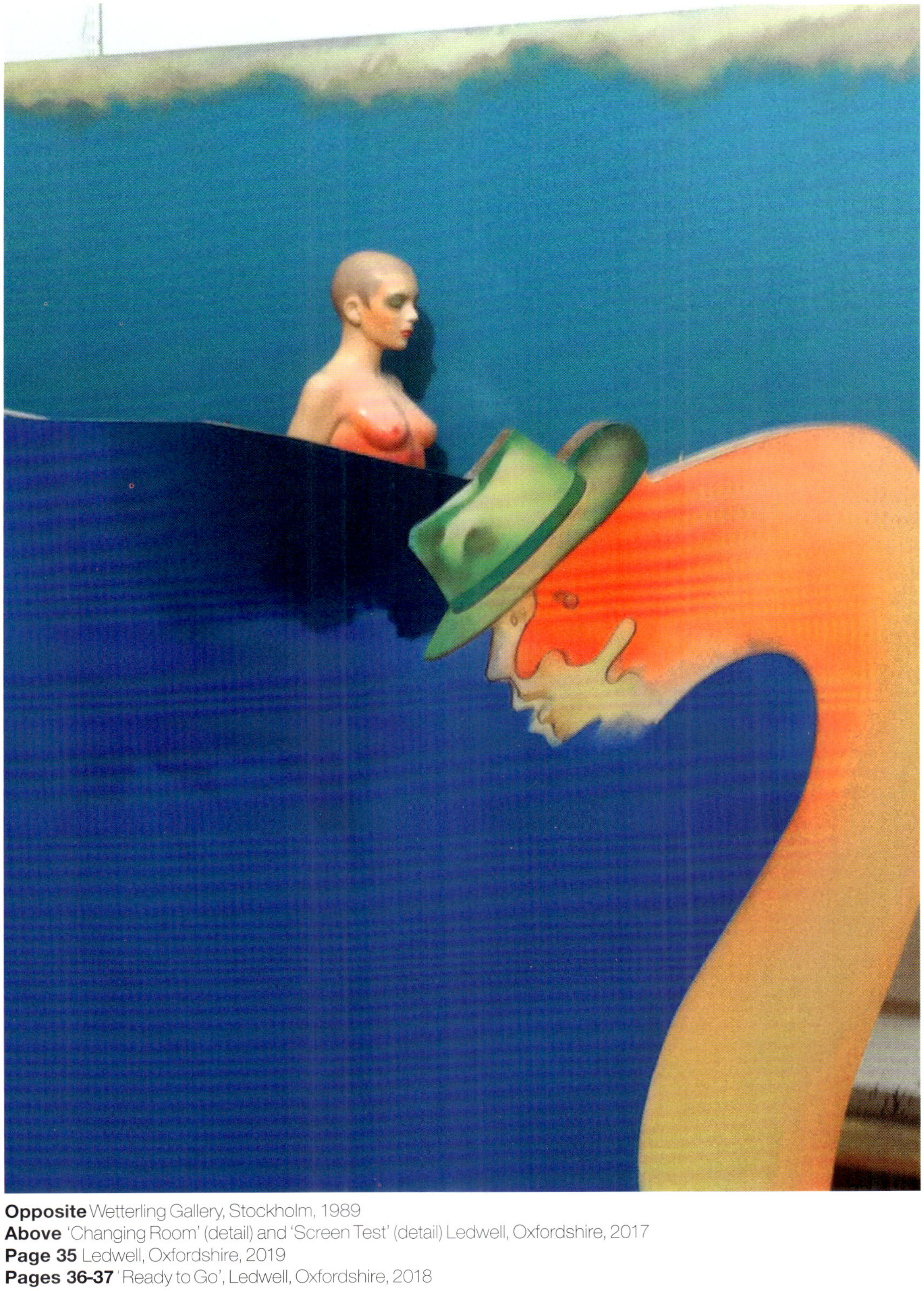

Opposite Wetterling Gallery, Stockholm, 1989
Above 'Changing Room' (detail) and 'Screen Test' (detail) Ledwell, Oxfordshire, 2017
Page 35 Ledwell, Oxfordshire, 2019
Pages 36-37 'Ready to Go', Ledwell, Oxfordshire, 2018

I often photograph my works in progress, fixing a detail or visual effect that might well become lost in the finished artwork. Taking pictures has become a way of exploring the relationship between my sculptures and paintings.

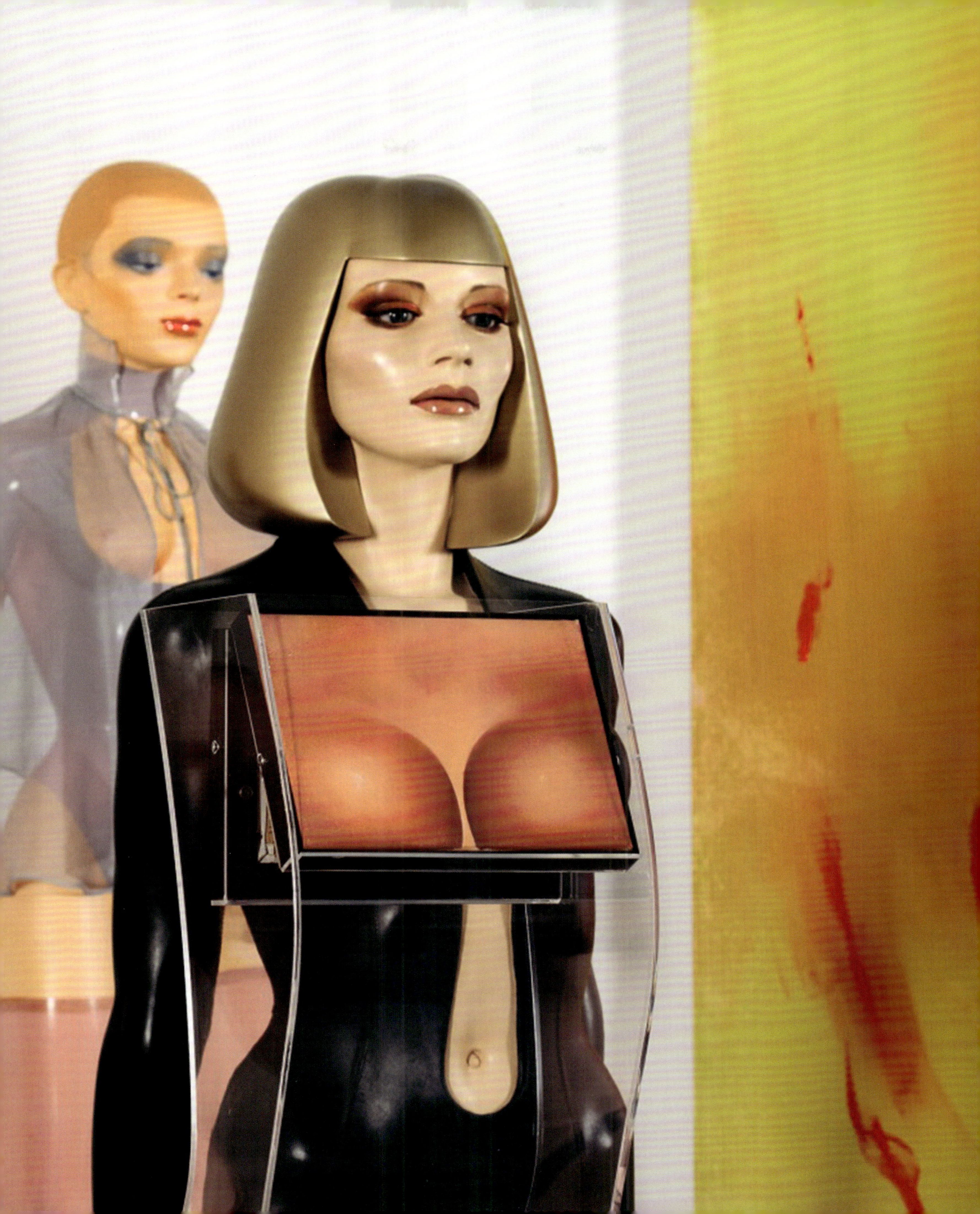

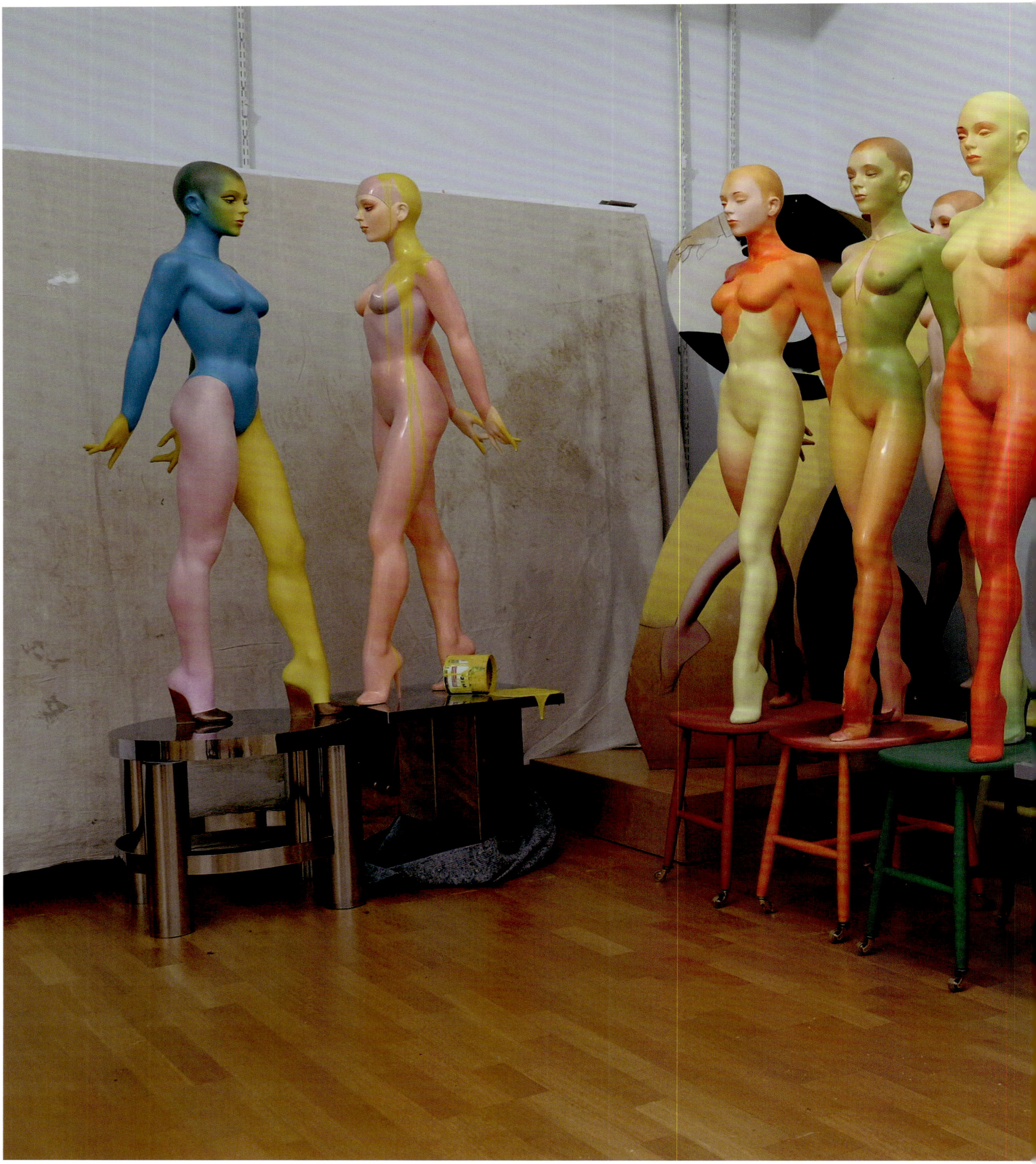

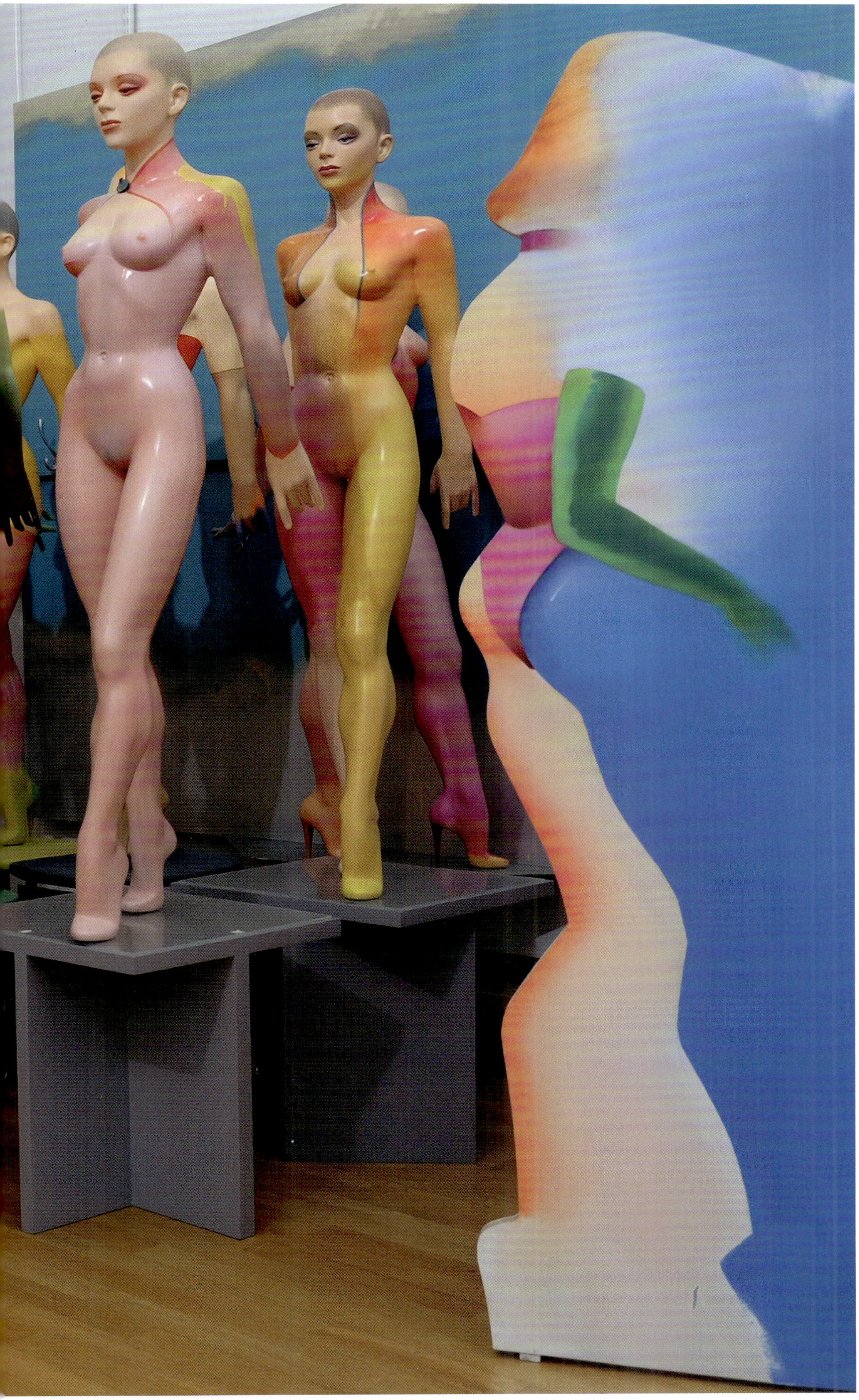

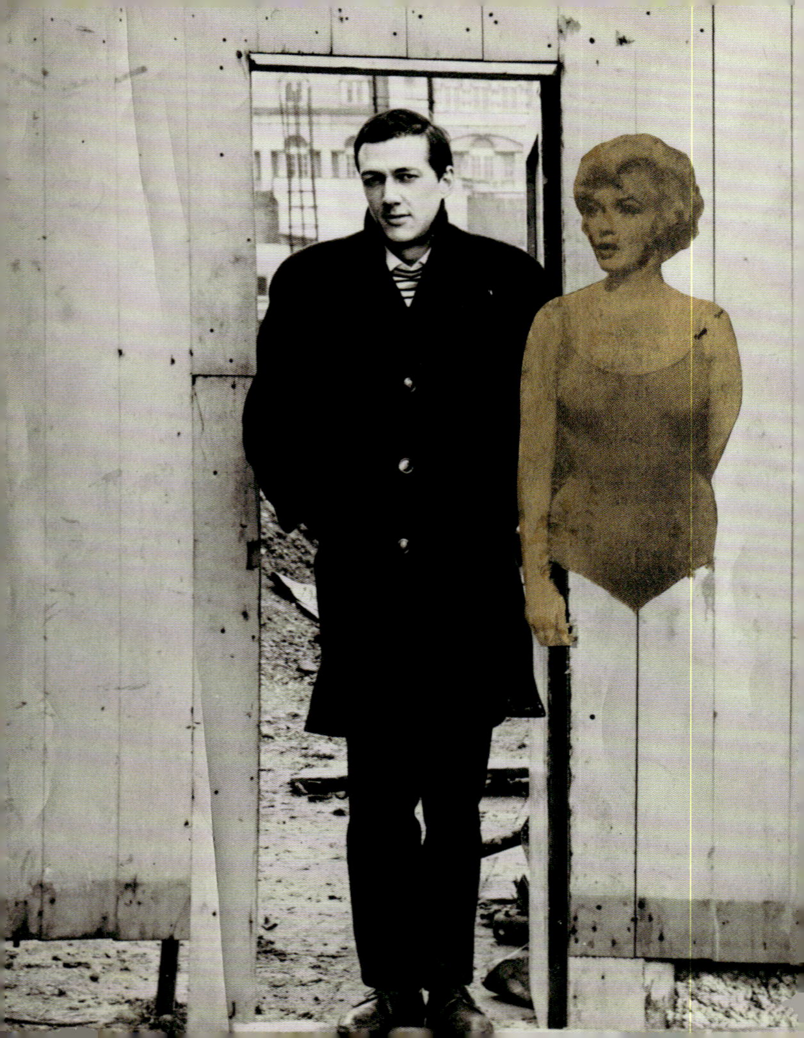

Piecing things together

Opposite ' At the Royal College of Art', collage, 1959

At the end of five years at Hornsey, when you had finished your exams and sat the entrance exam to the RCA, there was a sort of lull of almost a term. A lot of students just slipped off and started their holidays early and that was the end of that. But I realised that it would be good to use the time to take advantage of facilities available in the school. So I did a course on photography. I was given the camera and went out and took photographs. The first were taken when it was snowing at a derelict railway station on the top of Crouch Hill in Hornsey.

I used to commute to the school from the other side of London and would exit from Finsbury Park. As you were walking up the subway from the station platform to the pavement, there was a kaleidoscope of light as you approached the end, which suddenly struck me as looking like the new Abstract Expressionist paintings coming from America. My use of the camera wasn't to gather subject matter or as an aid for a painting. I thought that the visual phenomena were significant enough on their own. The photograph has always existed for me as a photograph.

I was conscious of the power of the photograph, its weight as an omnipresent way of seeing the world, of dealing with news and so much else, let alone movies and film stars and all the rest of it. Many students would take photographs as a means of building their compositions or to help them with a life pose, but that never much mattered to me, though I did like the inevitable thing of making collages. This seemed to me a distinct and legitimate artistic activity, and sometimes a way of adding a frisson, another dimension to one's abilities with the pencil. There were games to be played, including with gender. I liked the idea that you could carefully cut out the heads of two models and swap them over if the pose and the situation was right. I think of the cutting of a male and a female model in wide-shouldered suits on which I switched their heads. You could play games with people's expectations from the medium. This is different from the classic use of collage, such as my dropping a cutting of Bardot into a reproduction of a Paris street scene by Utrillo.

In another instance, I gave a new dimension to something I had painted by making a print that laid this work on a photograph of Liz Taylor's cleavage. In conjunction with the photograph I could greatly extend the implications of the original image.

That initiation at Hornsey gave me the impetus to make photographs as an end in themselves and also to use my own or appropriated photographic images within various mixed-media experimentations.

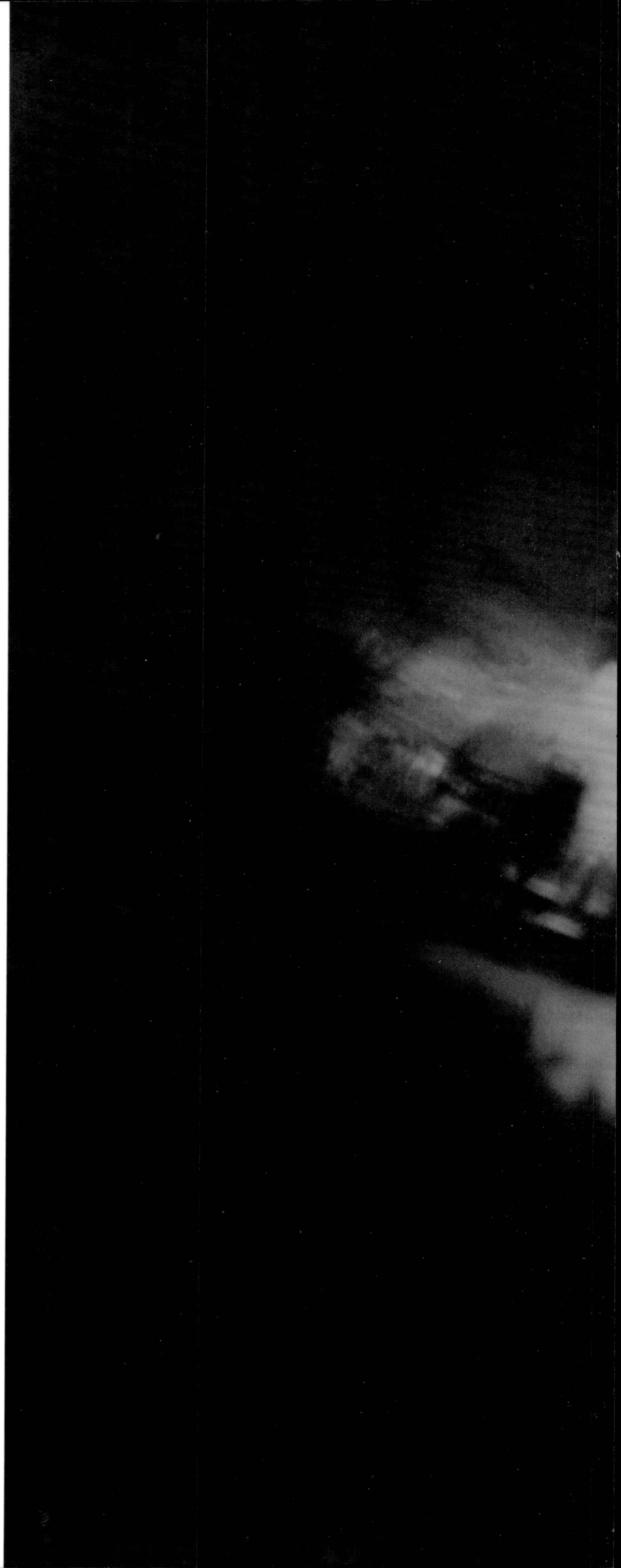

Finsbury Park underground station, London, 1959

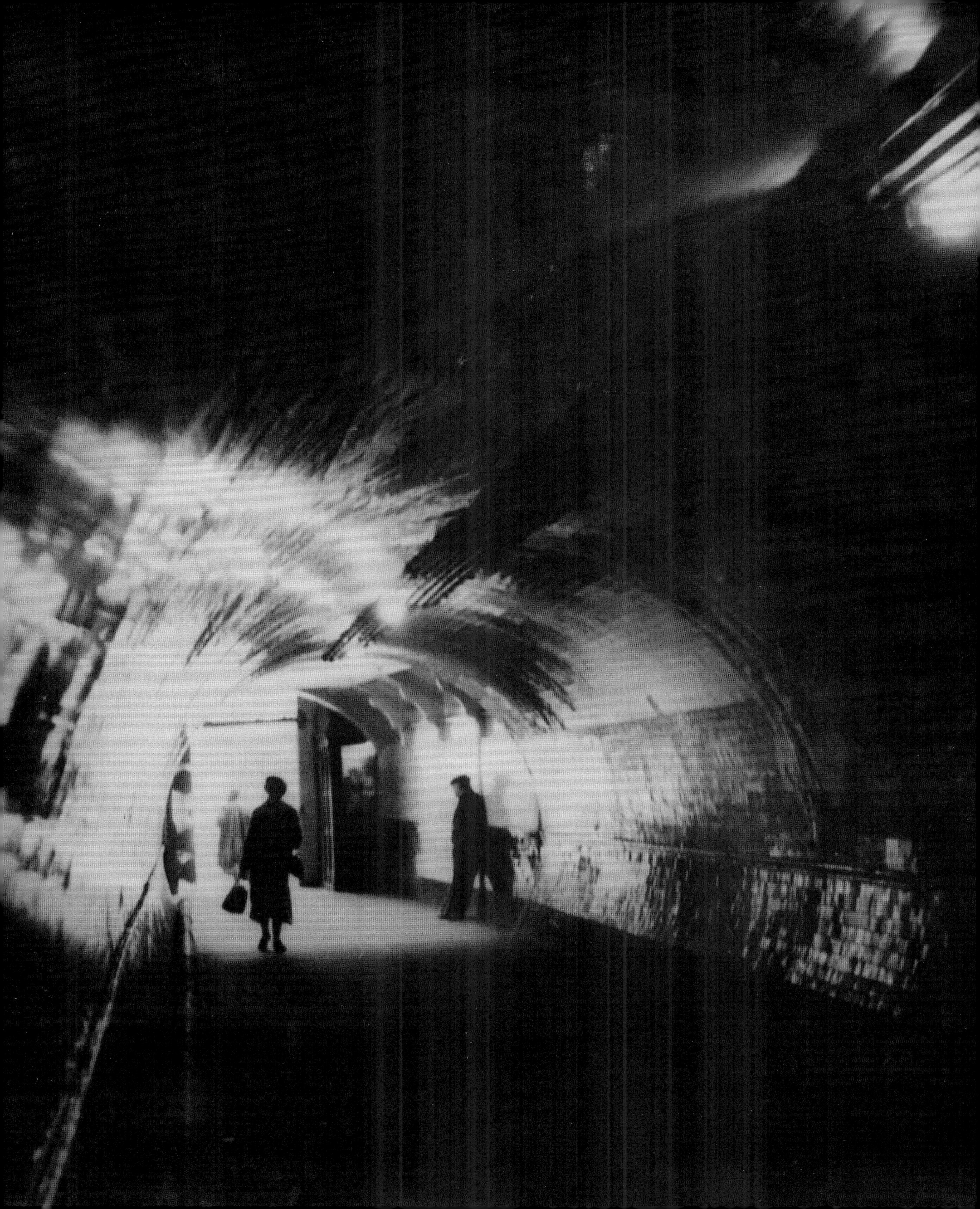

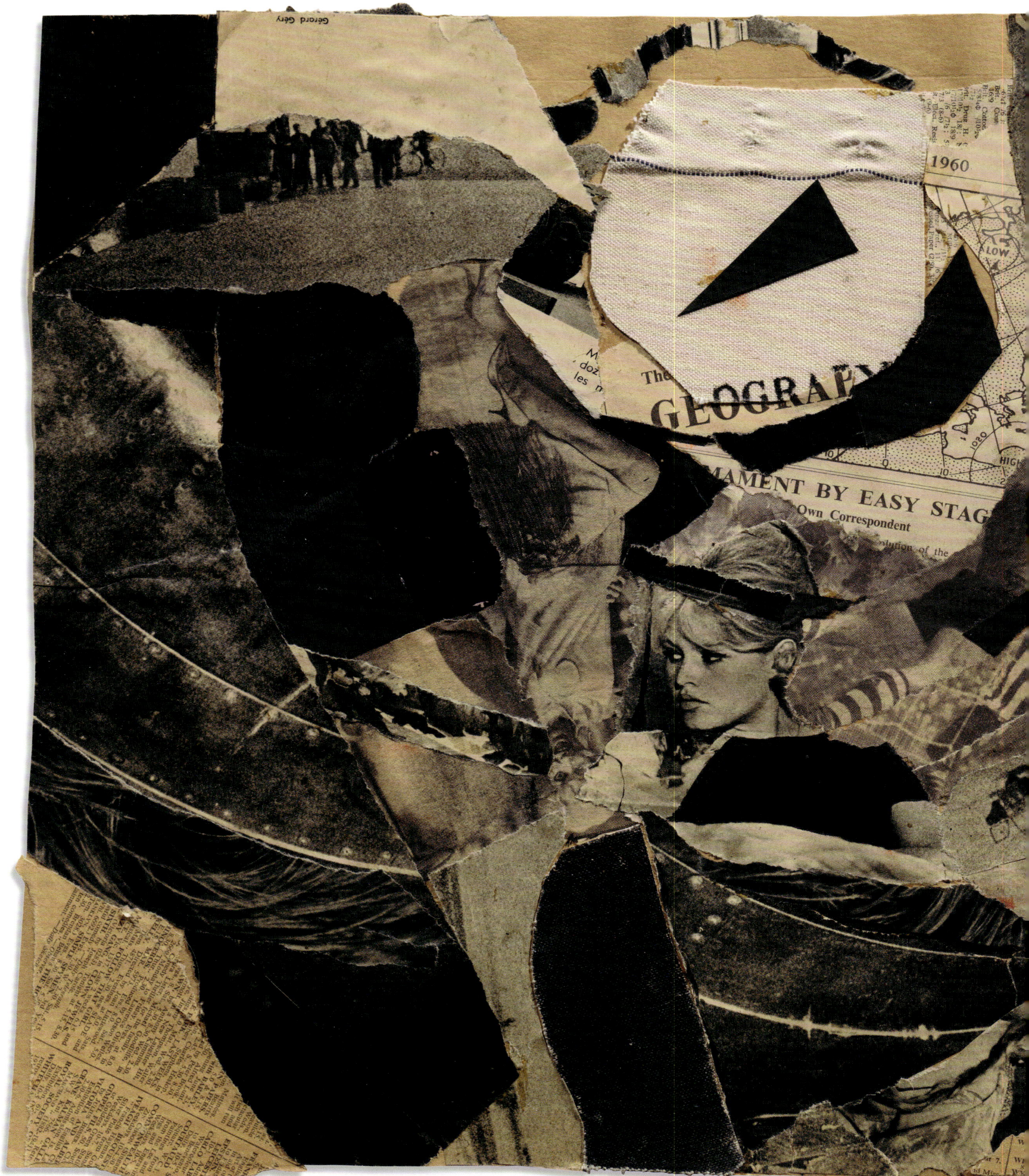
1960
GEOGRAF
MAMENT BY EASY STAG
Own Correspondent

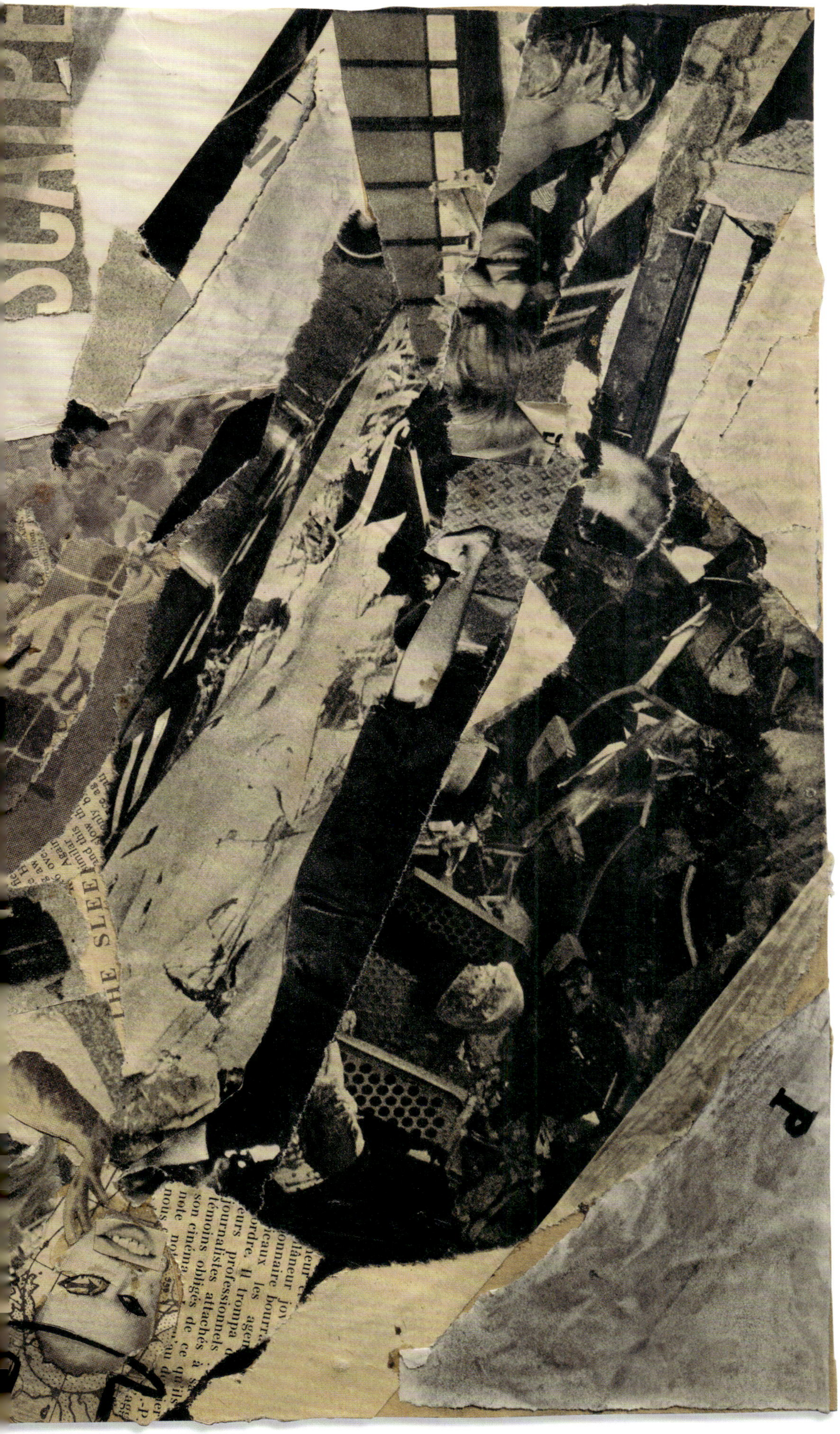

Collage, circa 1960–61

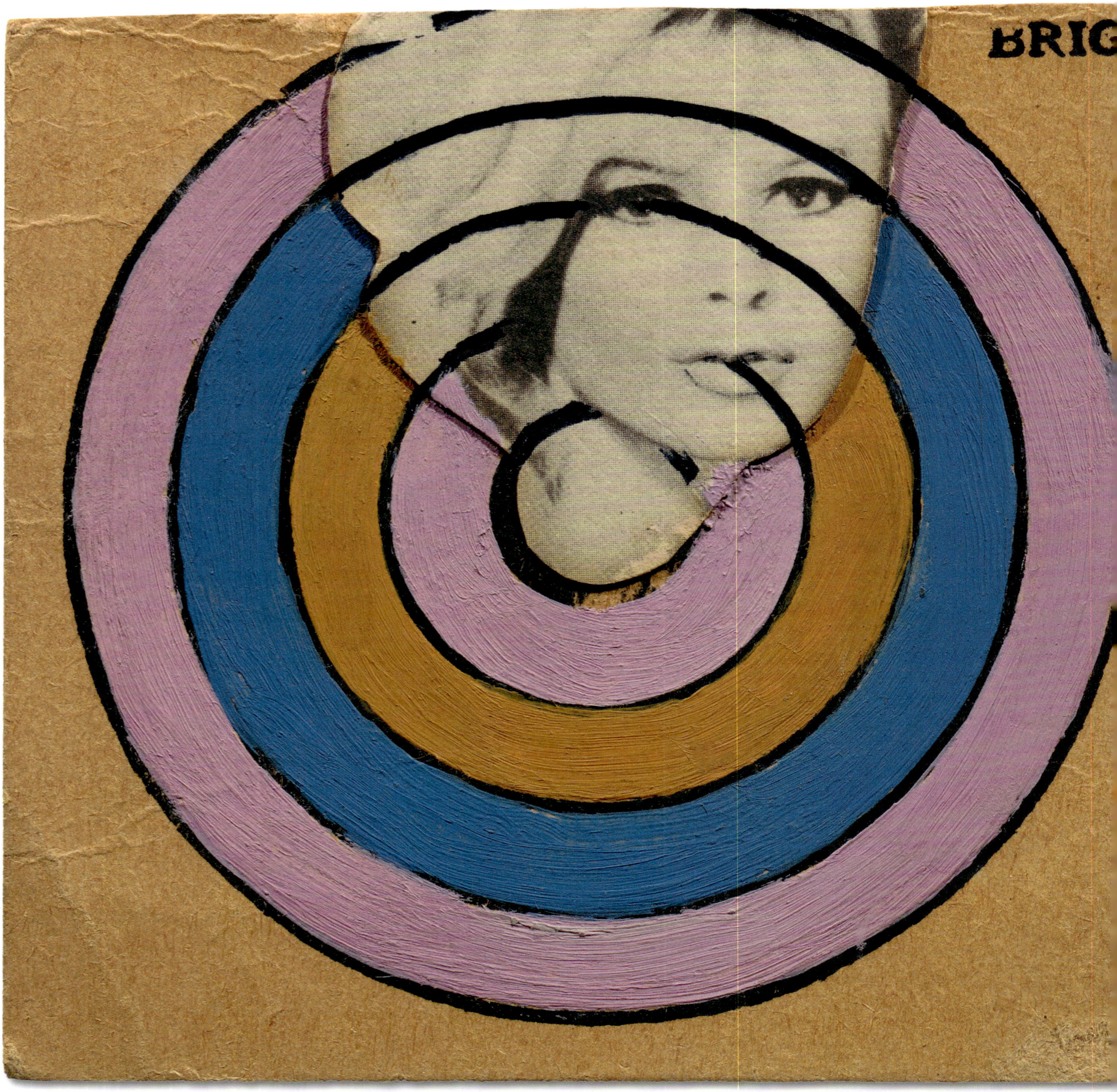

'Brighton', gouache and collage, 1958

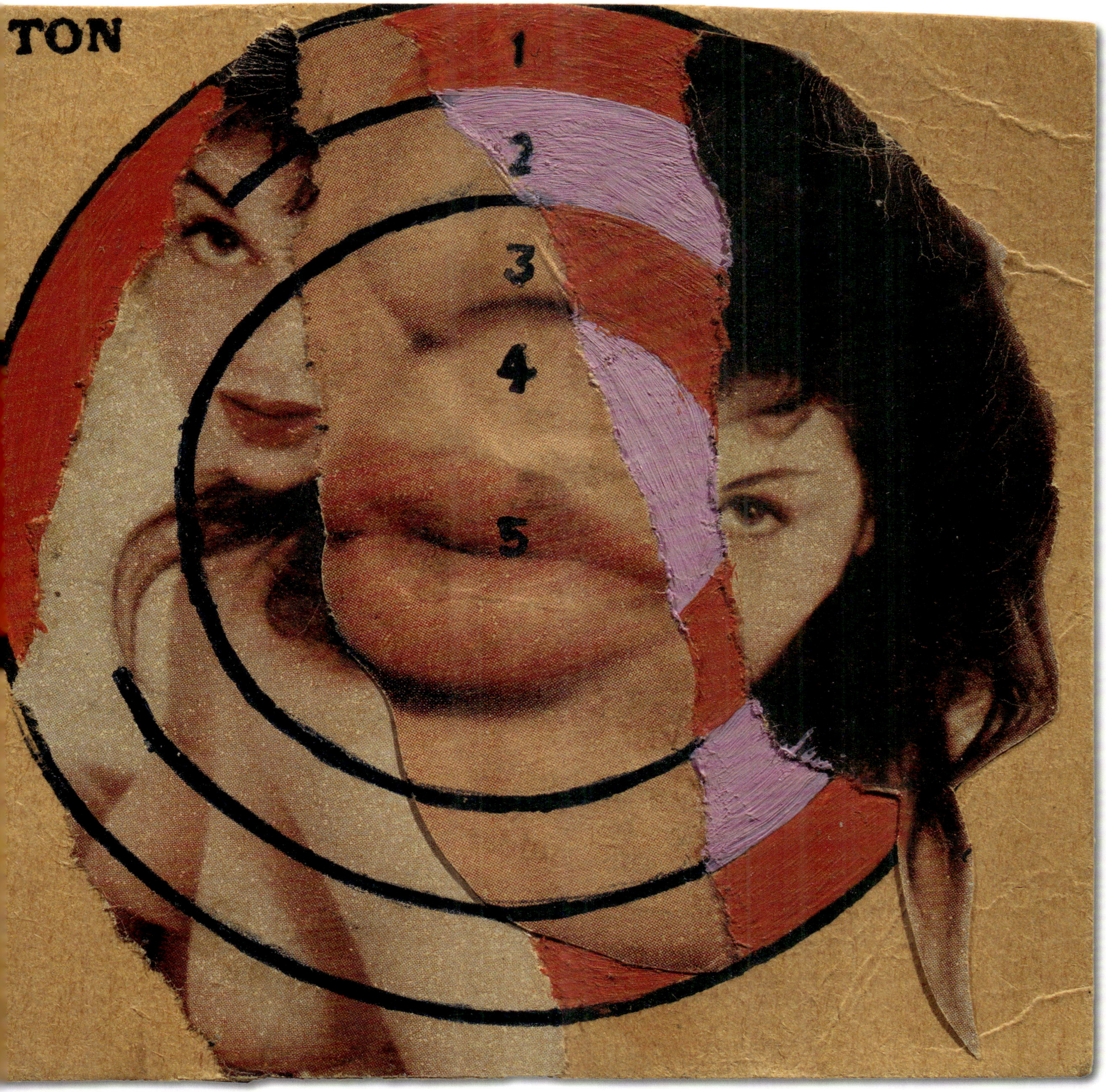
TON
1
2
3
4
5

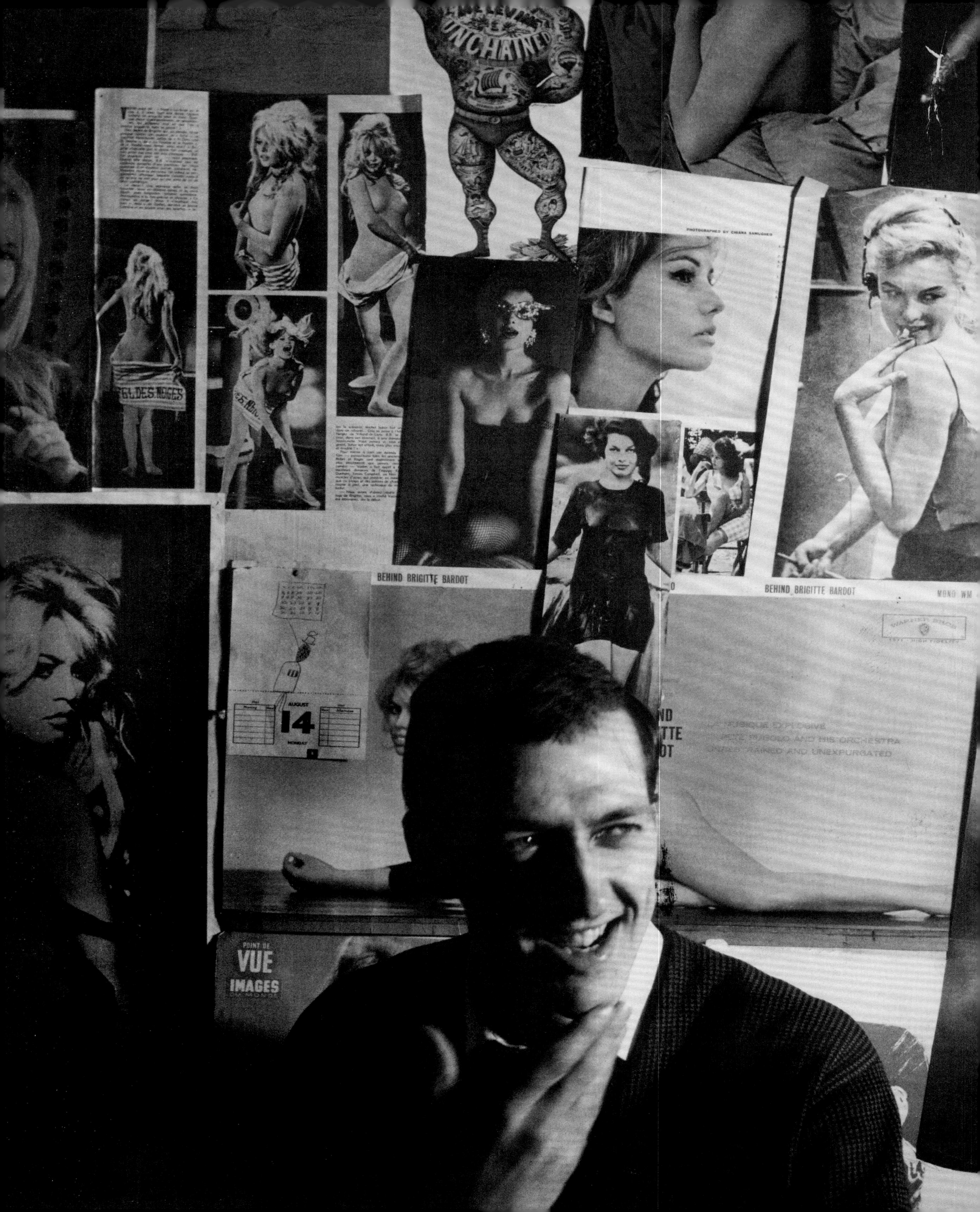
UNCHAINED
BEHIND BRIGITTE BARDOT
BEHIND BRIGITTE BARDOT
AUGUST
14
POINT DE
VUE
IMAGES

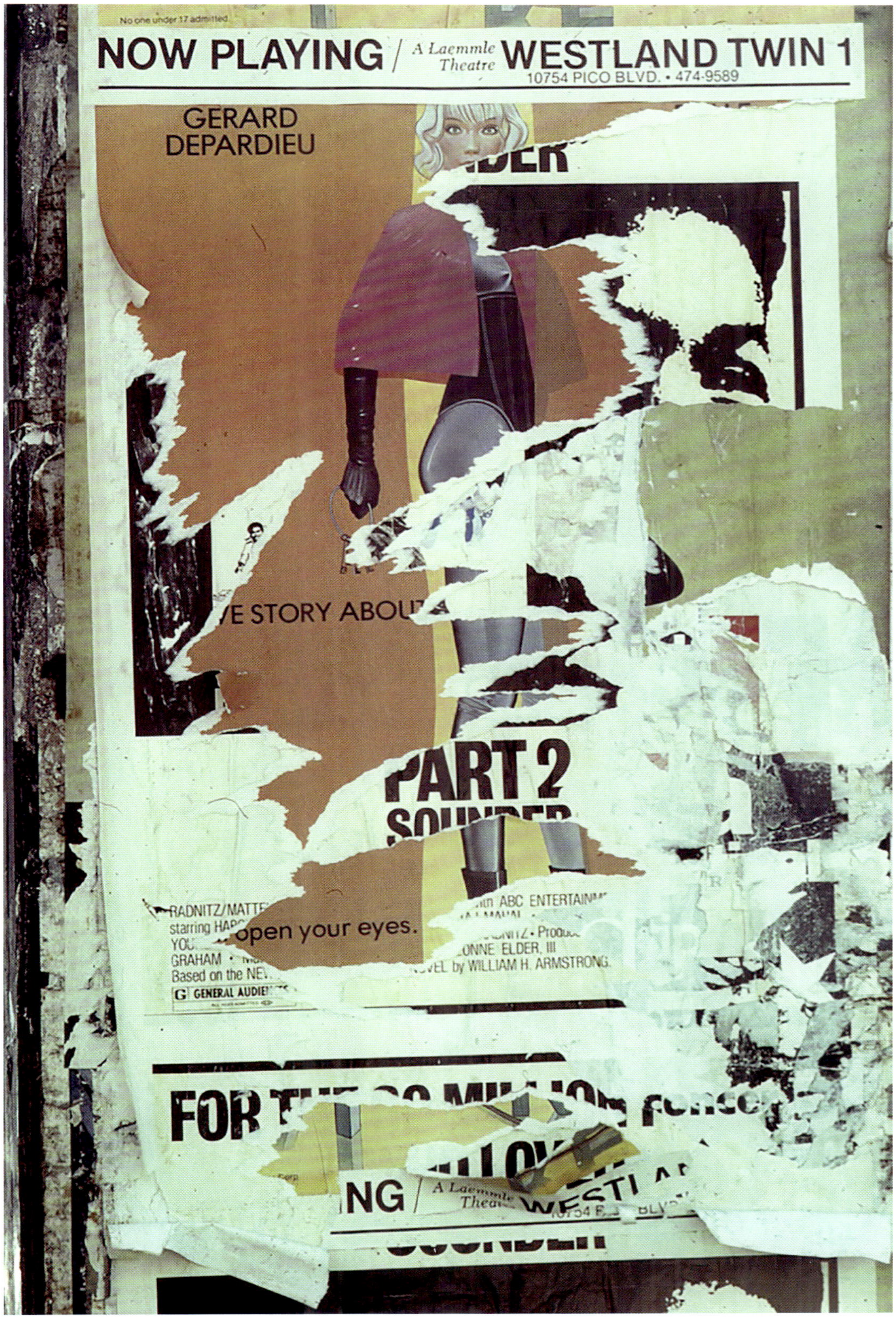

Opposite Allen Jones, photograph by Michael Cooper, 13 Paultons Square, London, circa 1963–64
Above 'Maîtresse' poster, Los Angeles, 1977

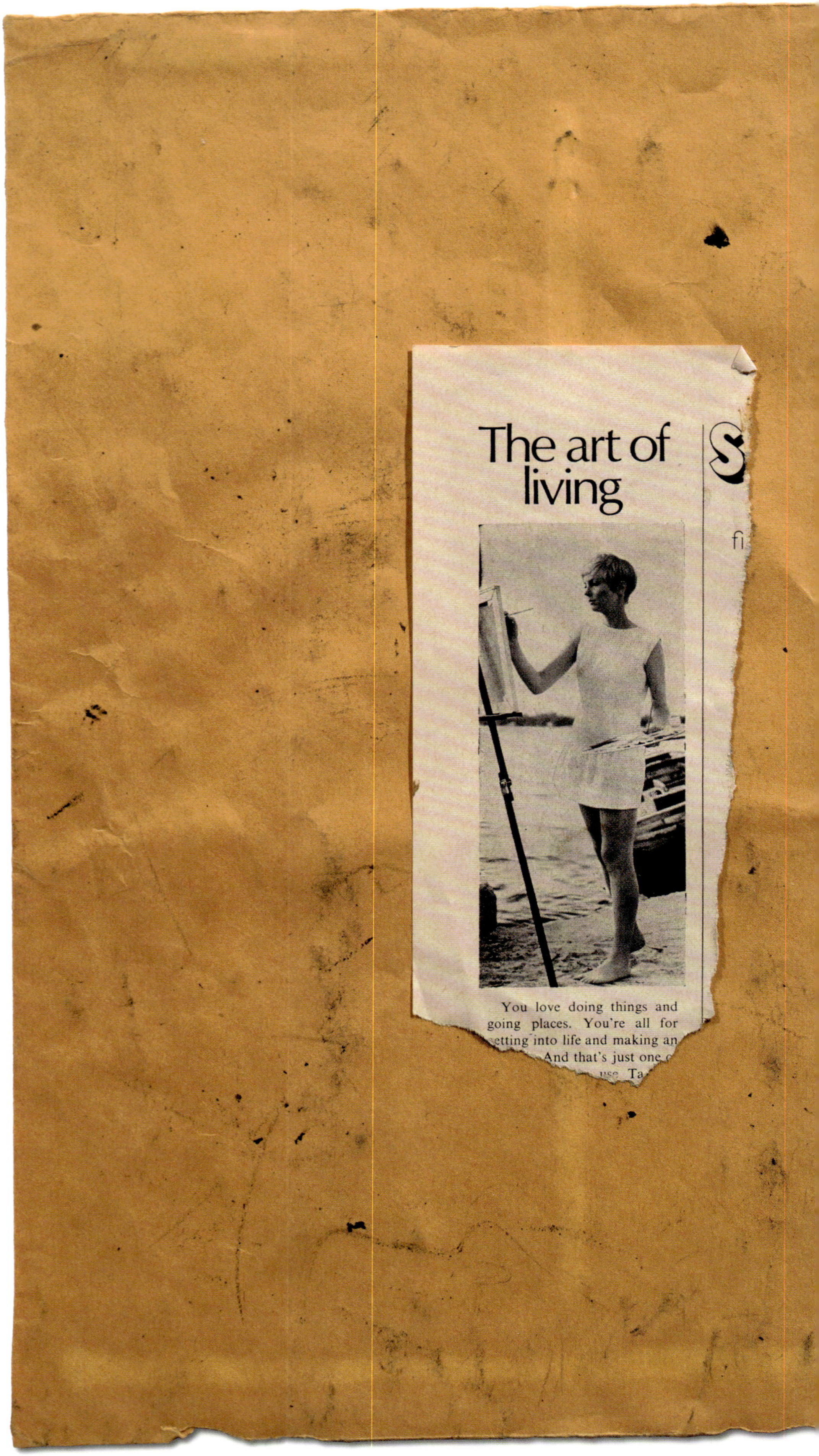

Artwork for Waddington catalogue cover, 1980

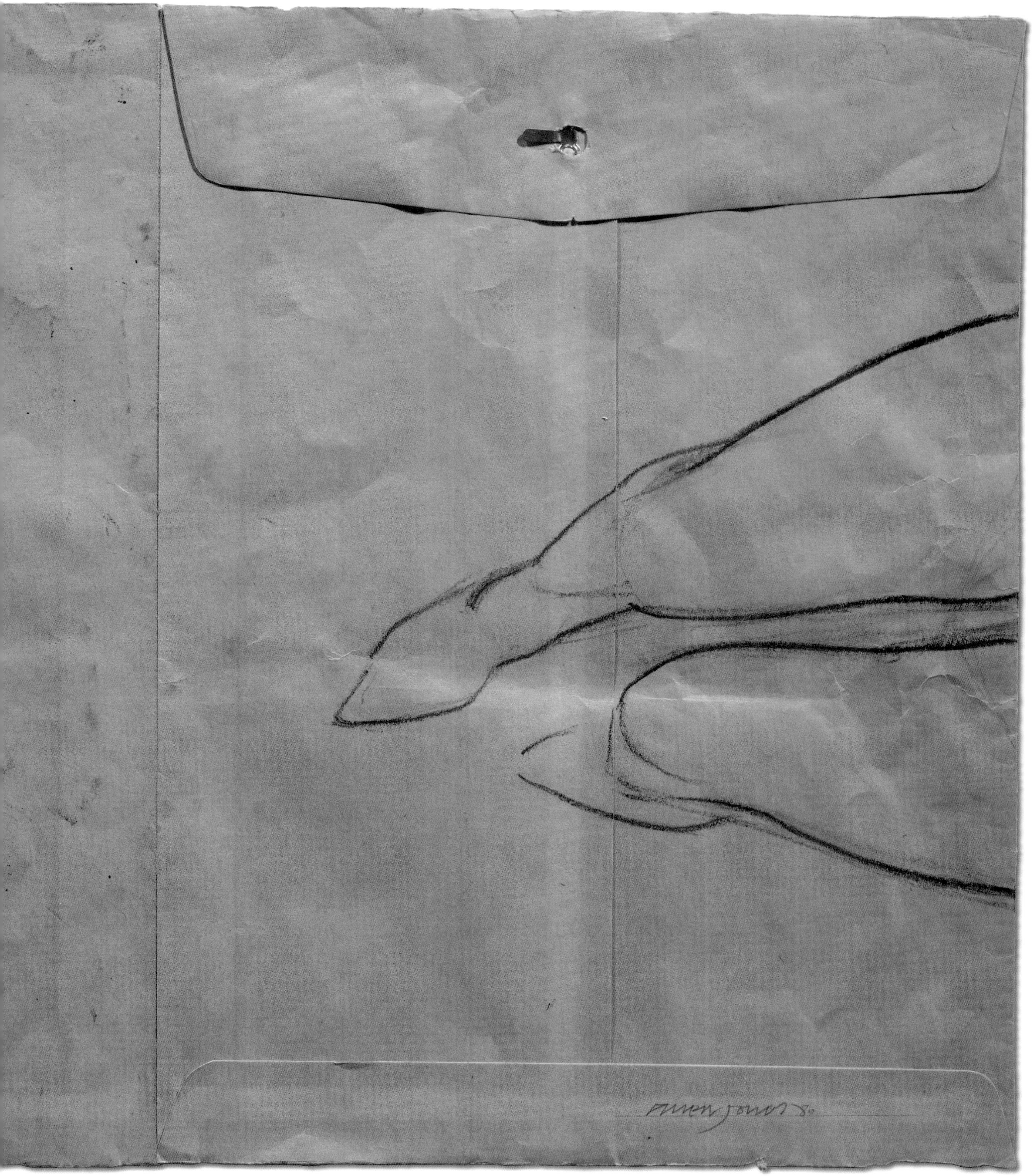

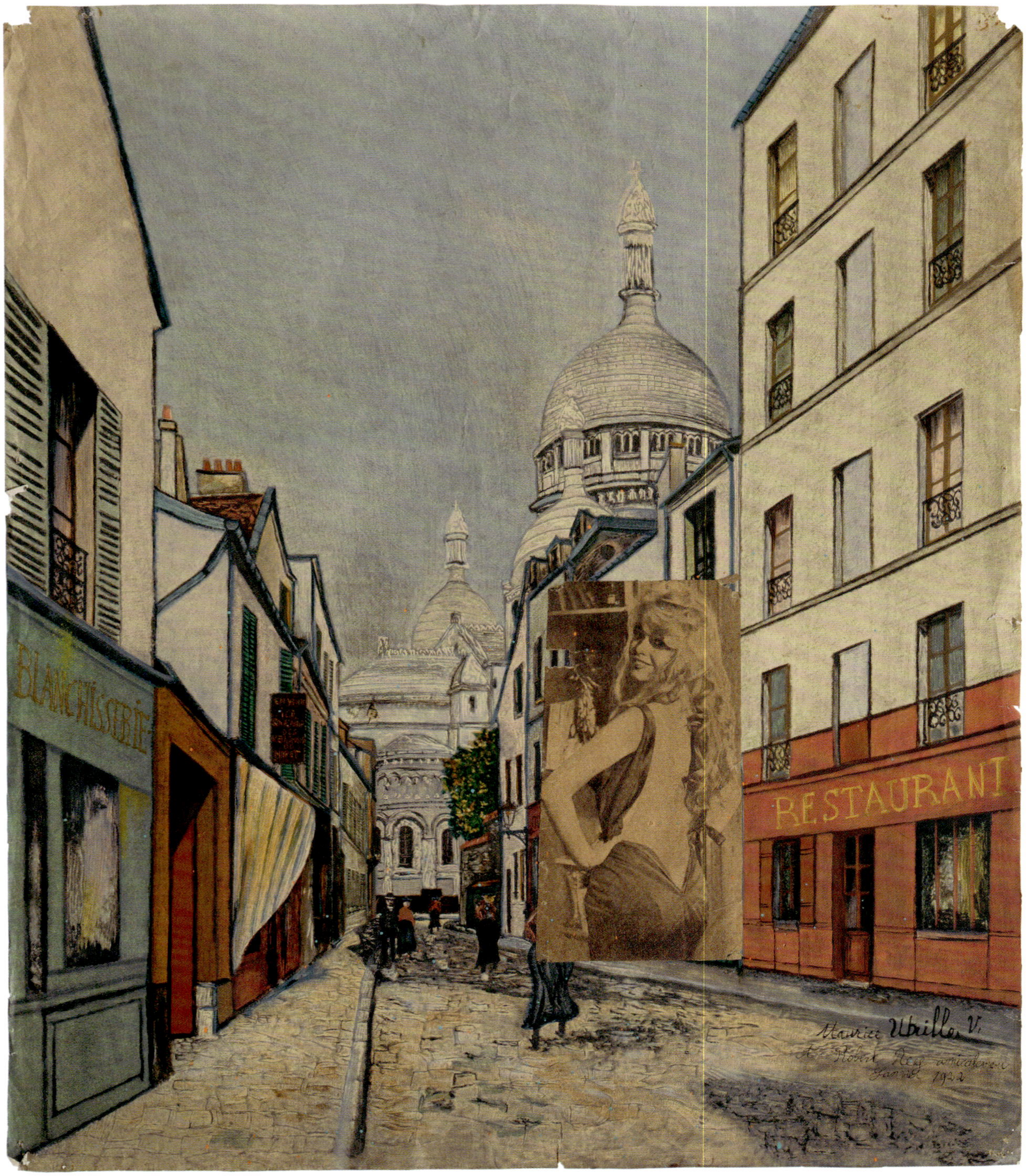
BLANCHISSERIE
RESTAURANT

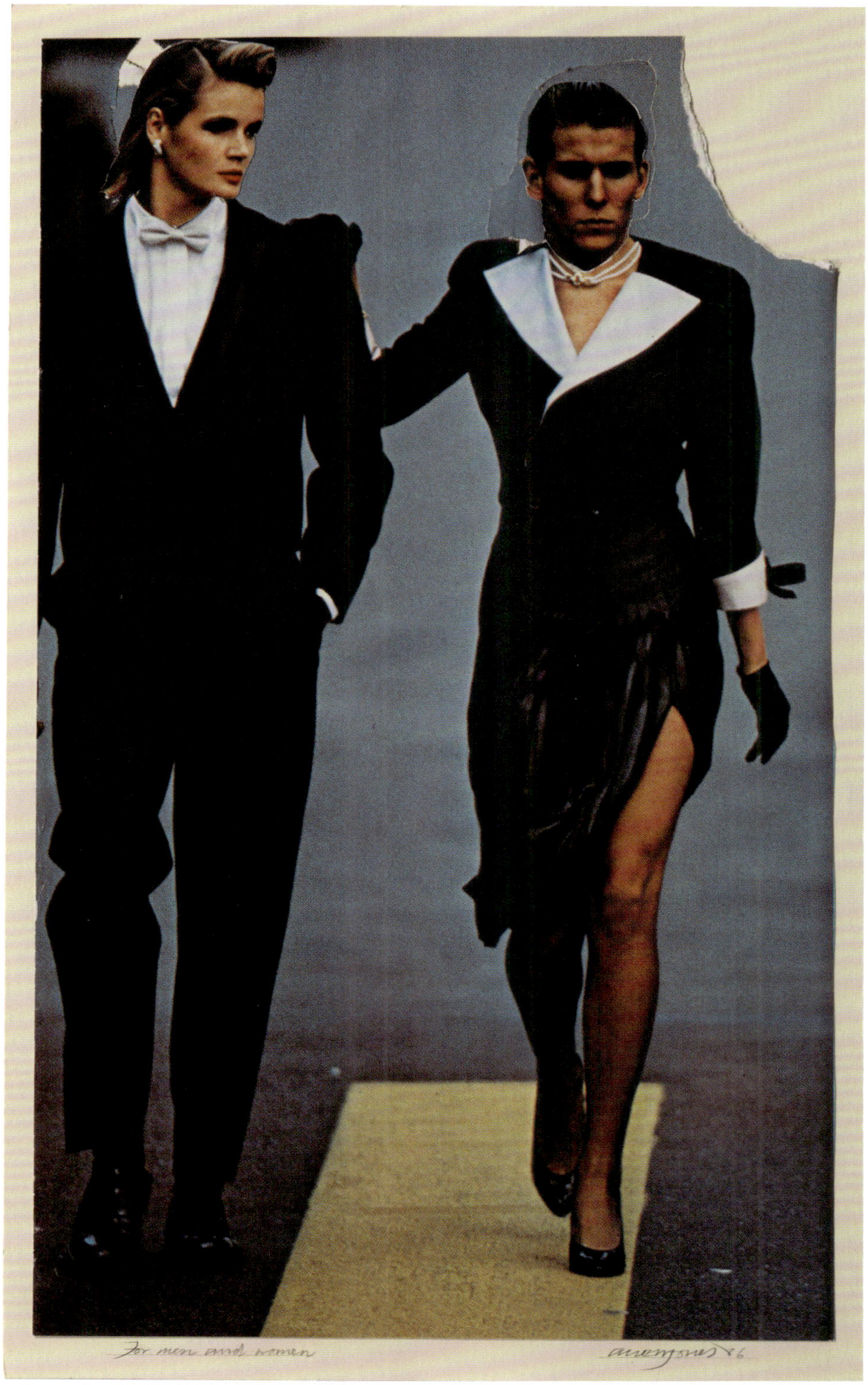

Opposite Bardot / Utrillo collage, 1960
Above Collage, 1986
Overleaf Two pages from 'Ways and Means', silkscreen book, printed by Chris Prater at Kelpra Press, London, 1976–77
Page 55 'Woman', lithograph, printed by Irwin Hollander, New York, 1965
Pages 56-57 'Secret Valentines', lithograph, printed at Croydon School of Art, 1962

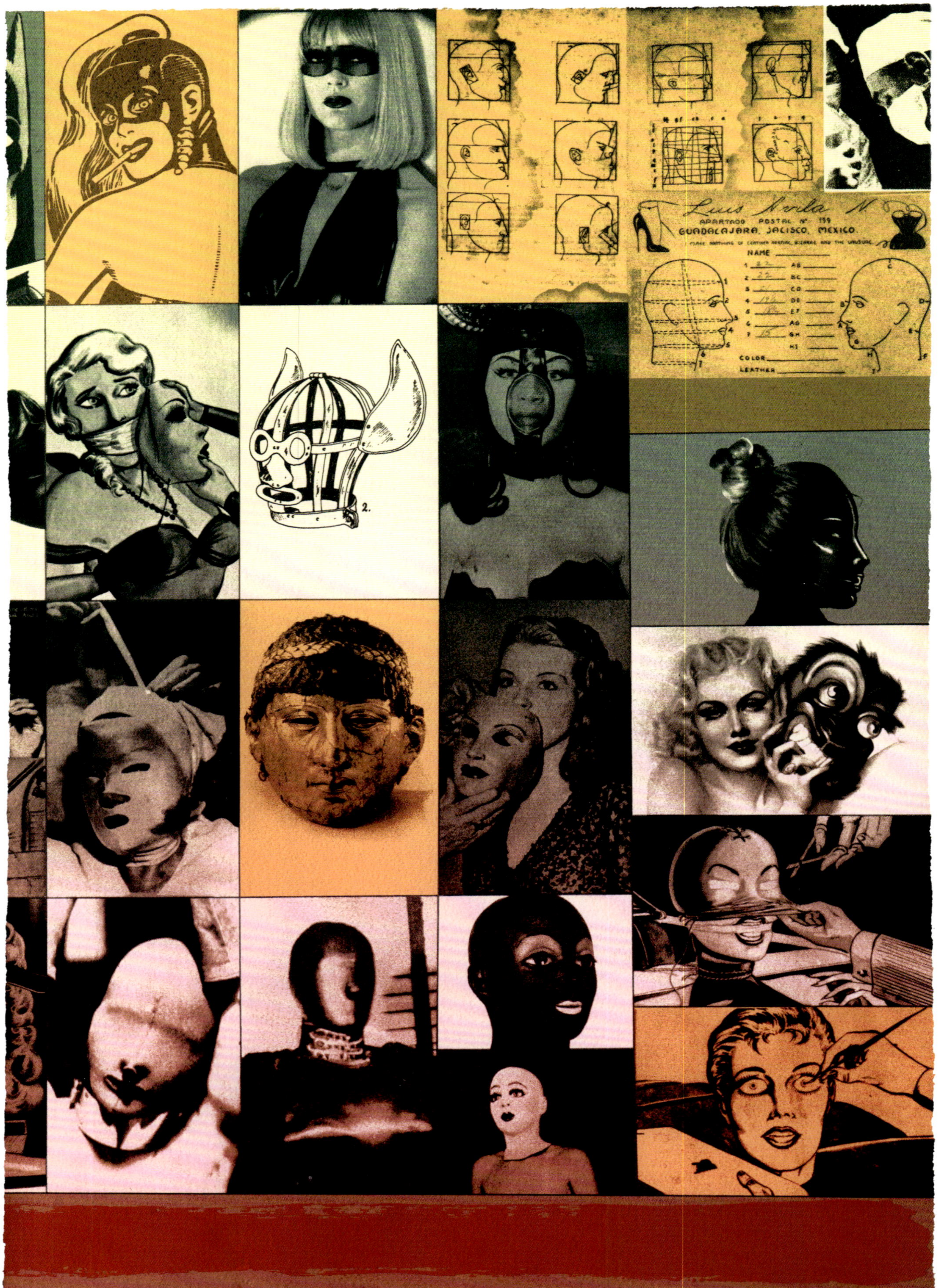
Luis Avila N.
APARTADO POSTAL Nº 199
GUADALAJARA, JALISCO, MEXICO.
NAME
COLOR
LEATHER

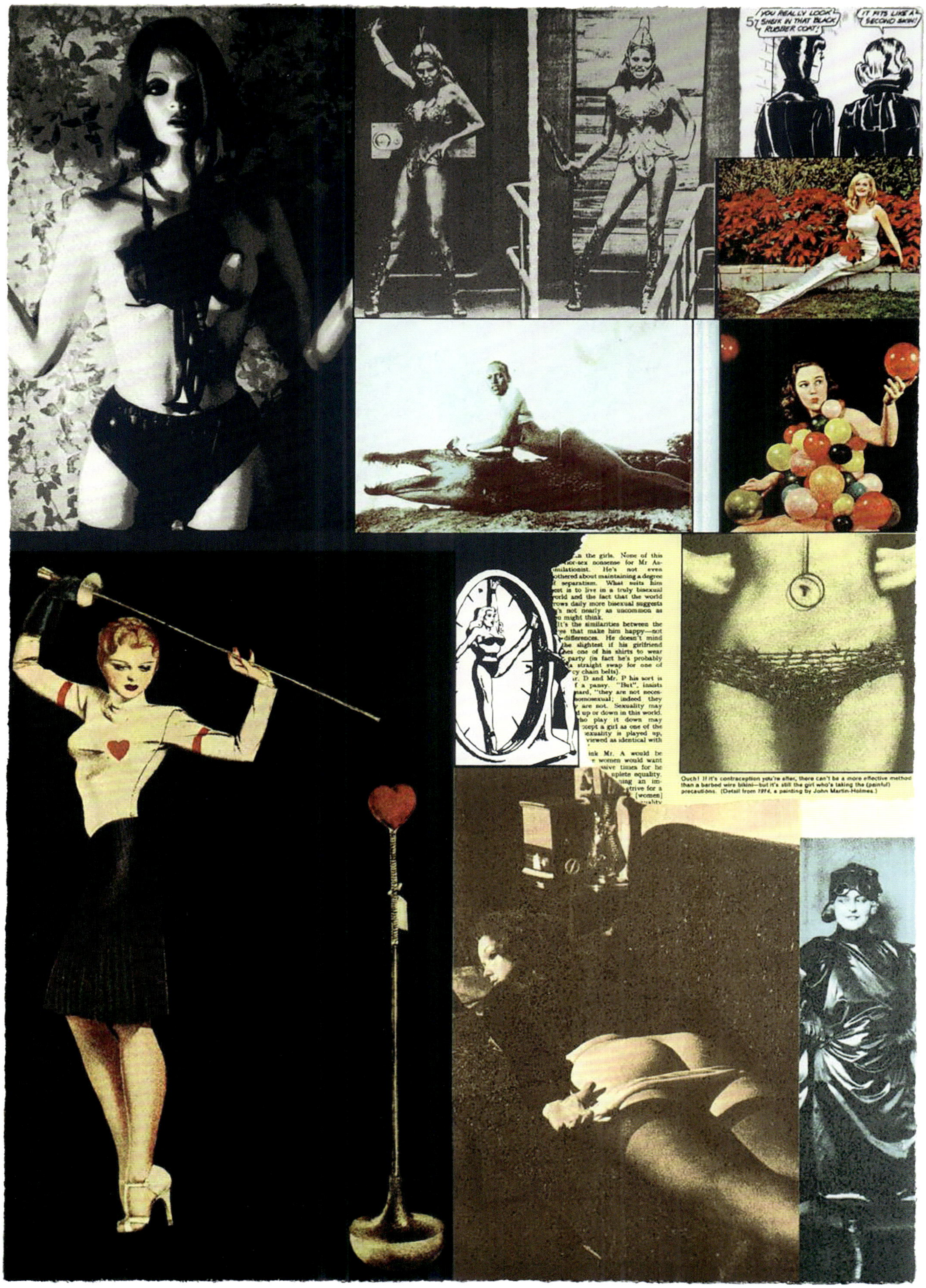

5
YOU REALLY LOOK SHEIK IN THAT BLACK RUBBER COAT!
IT FITS LIKE A SECOND SKIN!
the girls. None of this
or-sex nonsense for Mr As-
imilationist. He's not even
othered about maintaining a degree
separatism. What suits him
est is to live in a truly bisexual
world and the fact that the world
rows daily more bisexual suggests
's not nearly as uncommon as
might think.
It's the similarities between the
that make him happy—not
differences. He doesn't mind
the slightest if his girlfriend
es one of his shirts to wear
party (in fact he's probably
a straight swap for one of
cy chain belts).
r. D and Mr. P his sort is
f a pansy. "But", insists
nard, "they are not neces-
homosexual; indeed they
are not. Sexuality may
up or down in this world.
who play it down may
ccept a girl as one of the
exuality is played up,
viewed as identical with
ink Mr. A would be
women would want
sive times for he
plete equality.
ing an im-
strive for a
[women]
Ouch! If it's contraception you're after, there can't be a more effective method than a barbed wire bikini—but it's still the girl who's taking the (painful) precautions. (Detail from *1974*, a painting by John Martin-Holmes.)

A conceptual game is being played here, the apparently collaged photograph of Liz Taylor's cleavage is actually an integral part of the printed surface, whereas the interplay of complementary colour between red and green was achieved through collage for maximum effect.

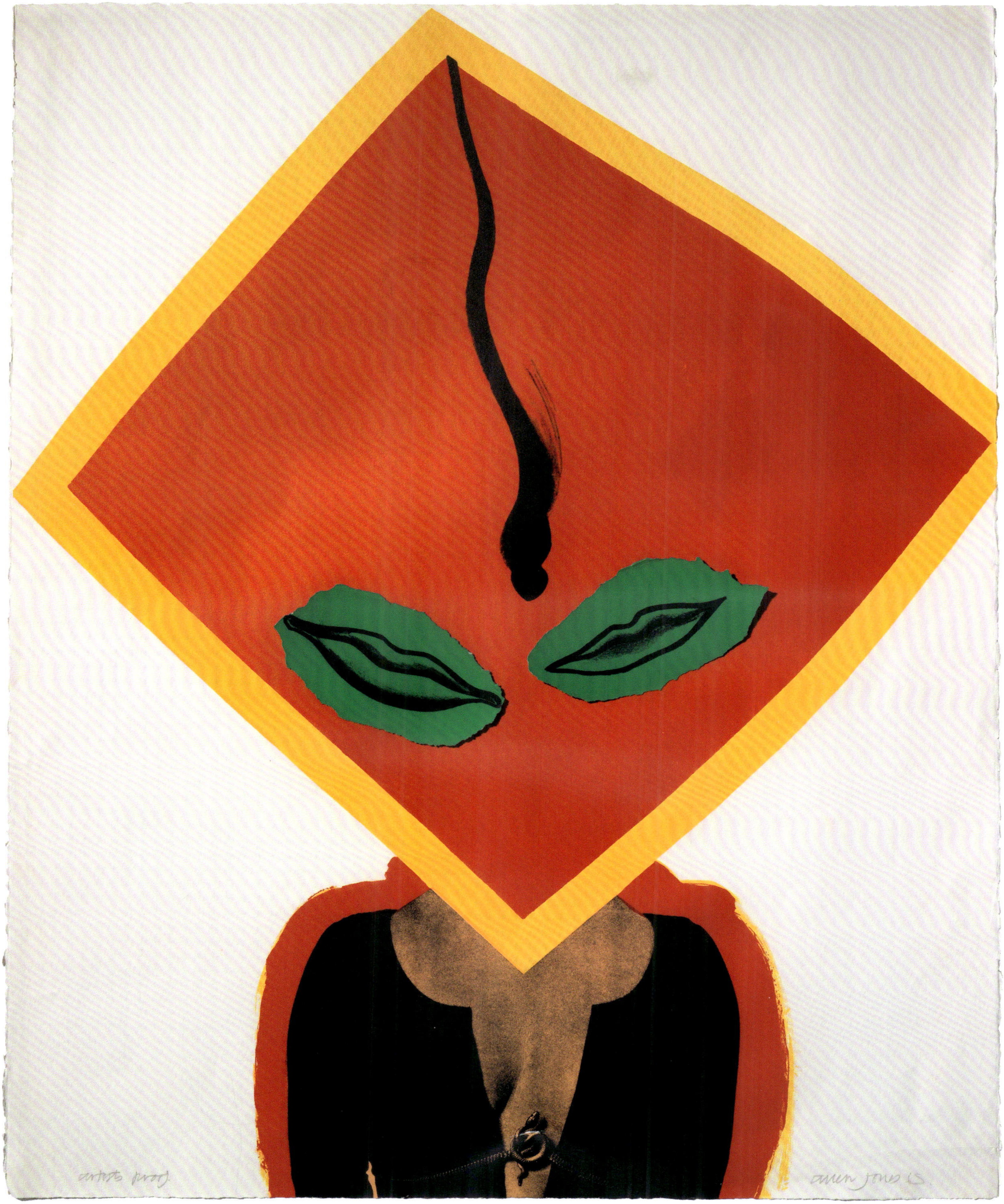

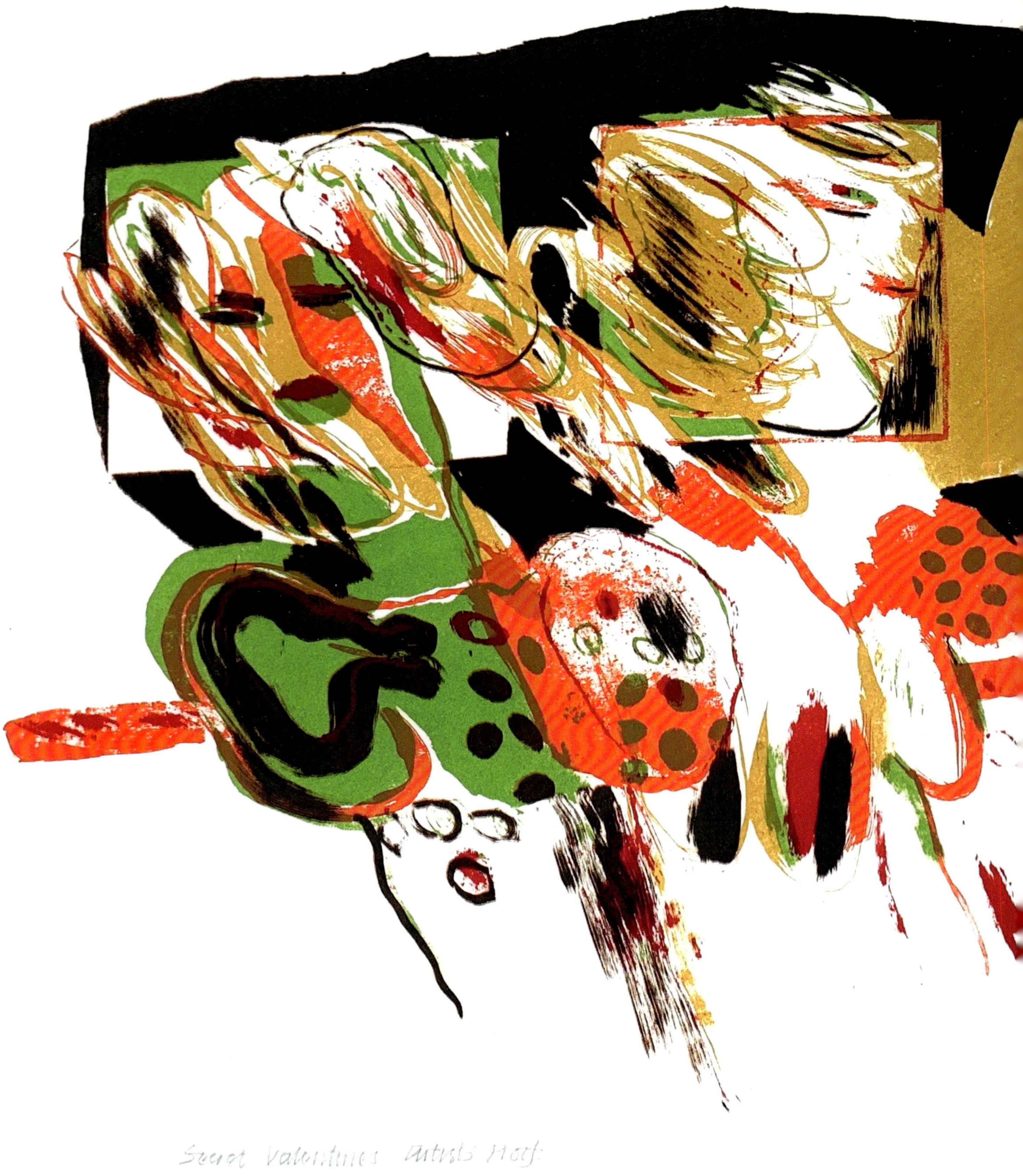
Secret Valentines Artists Proof

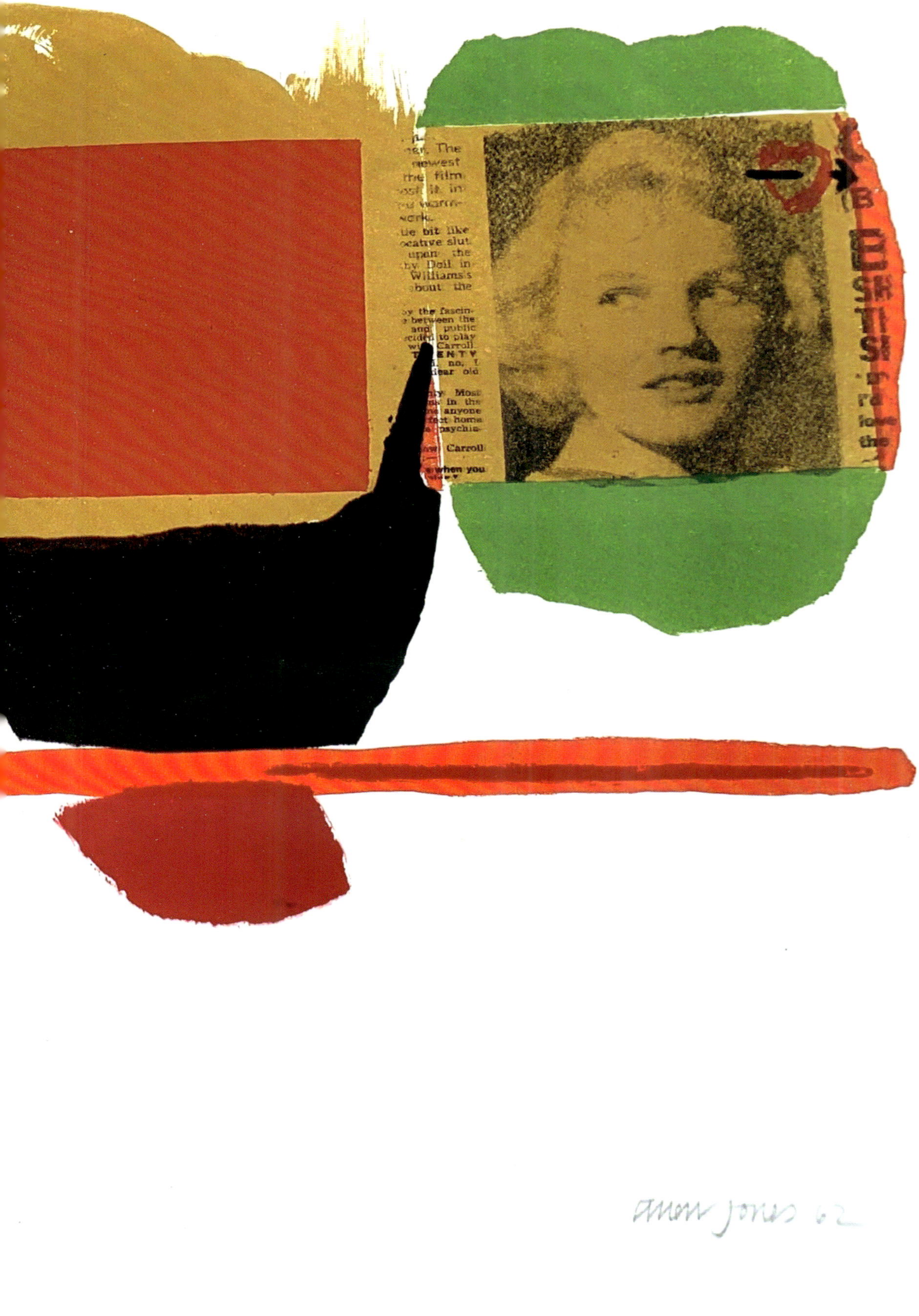

Paintings take a lot of time; a photograph can be made in an instant. They are very different disciplines, each allowing me its own distinct range of possibilities.

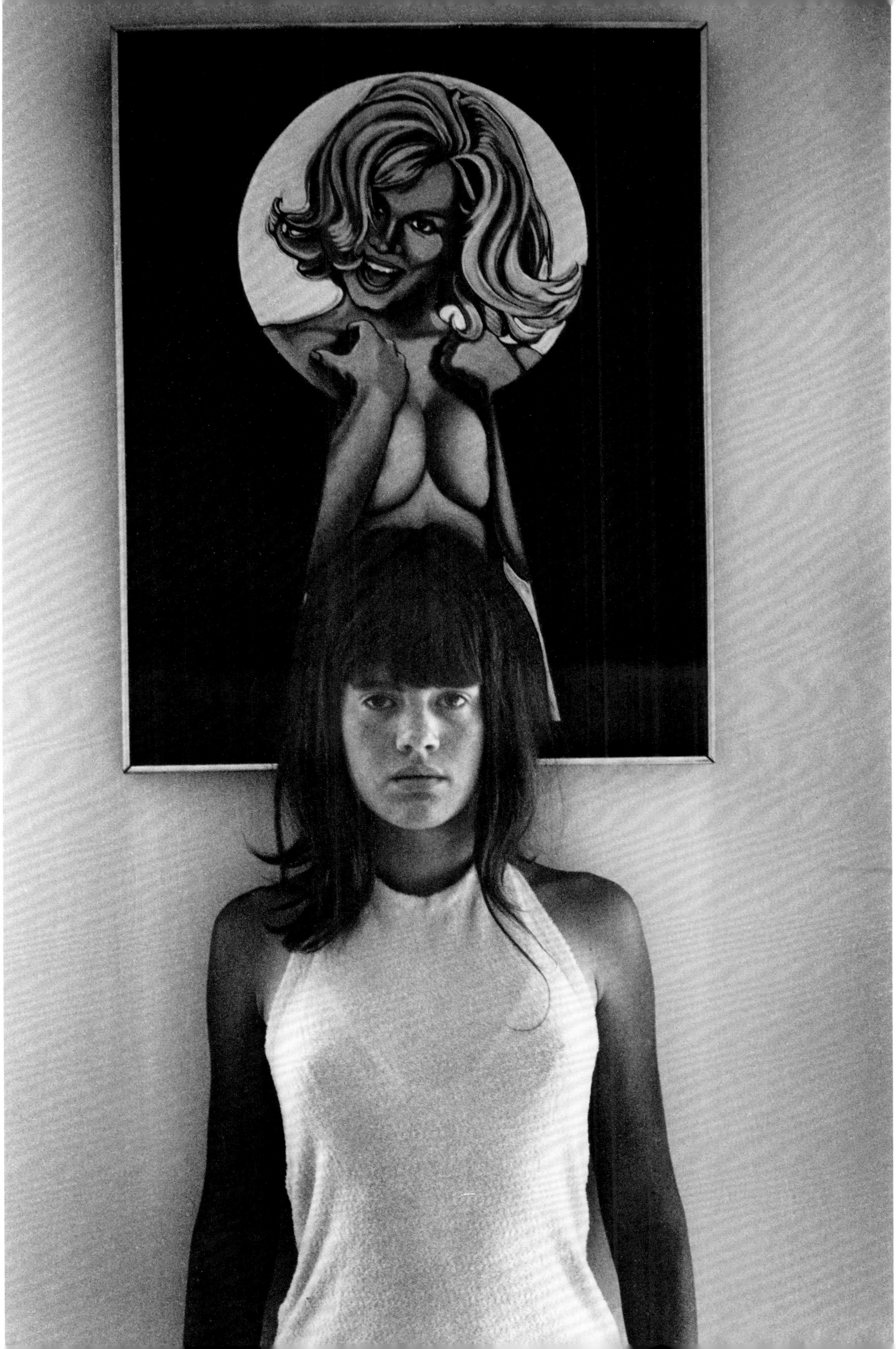

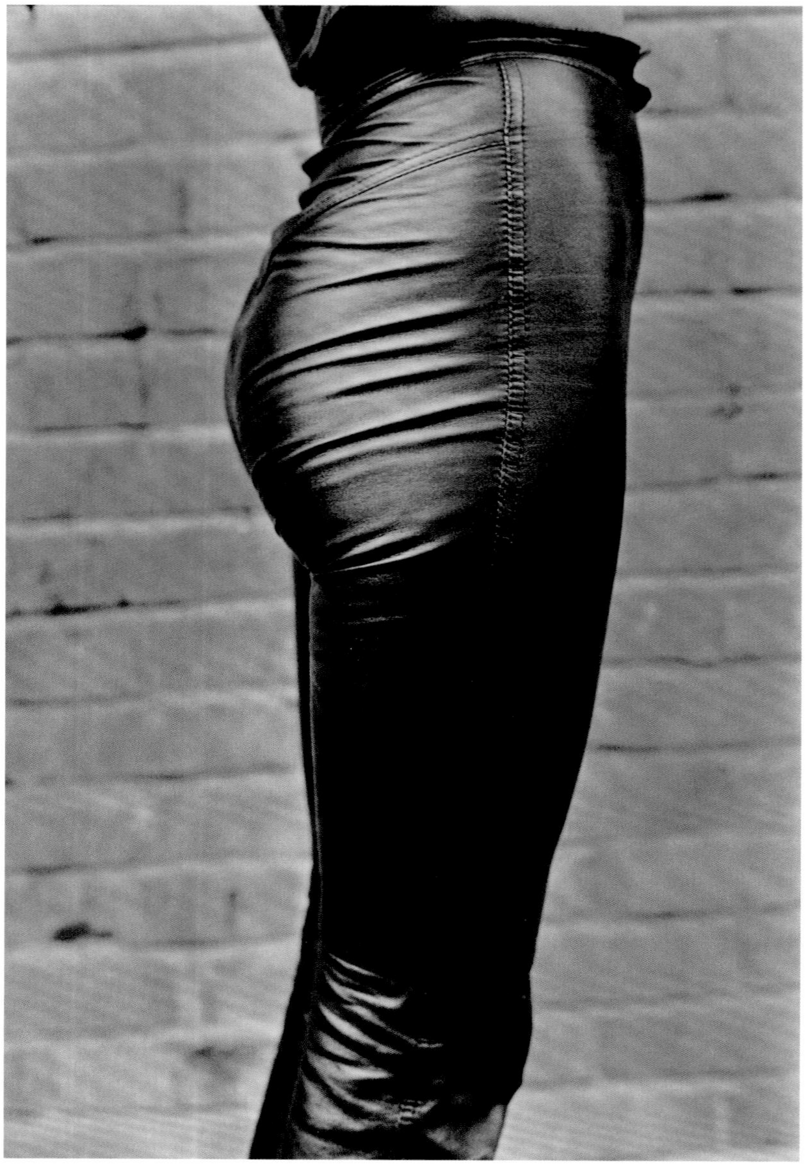

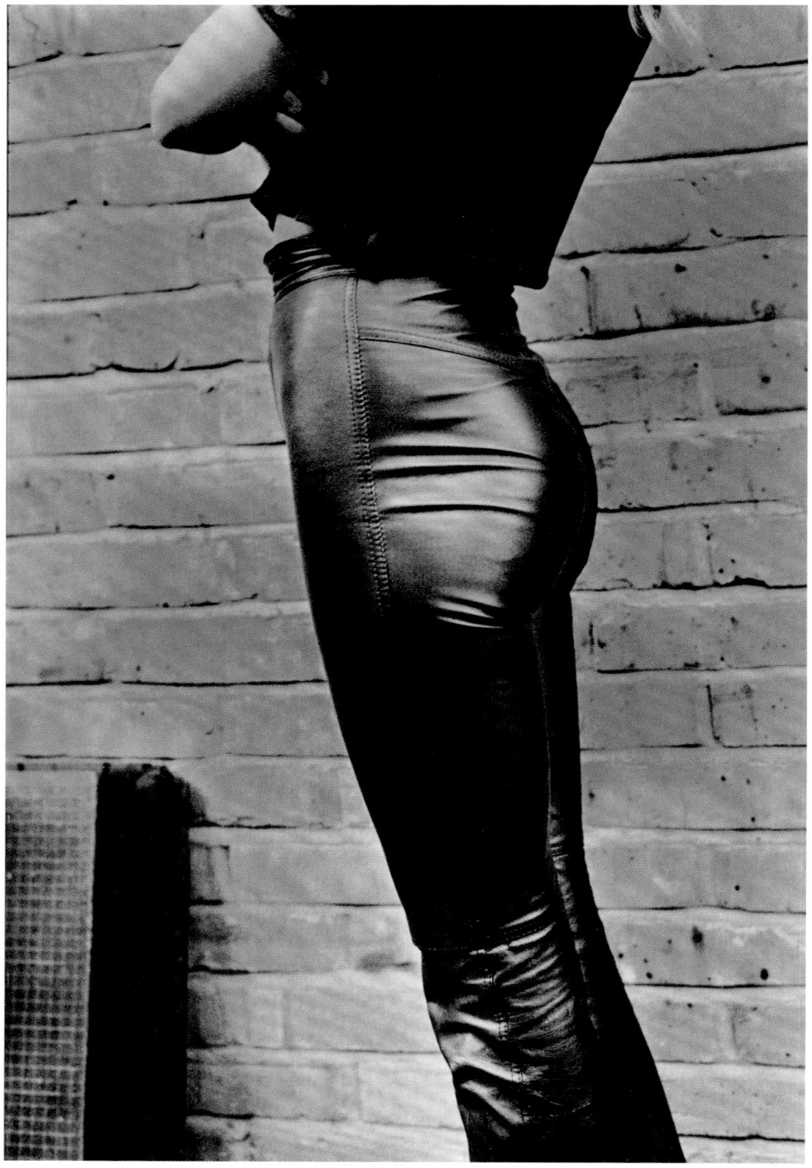

Previous page Susan Bowen, sister of Janet Jones, Edith Grove, London, 1968
Above and opposite Claude Phillips, wife of Peter Phillips, Edith Grove, London, 1968

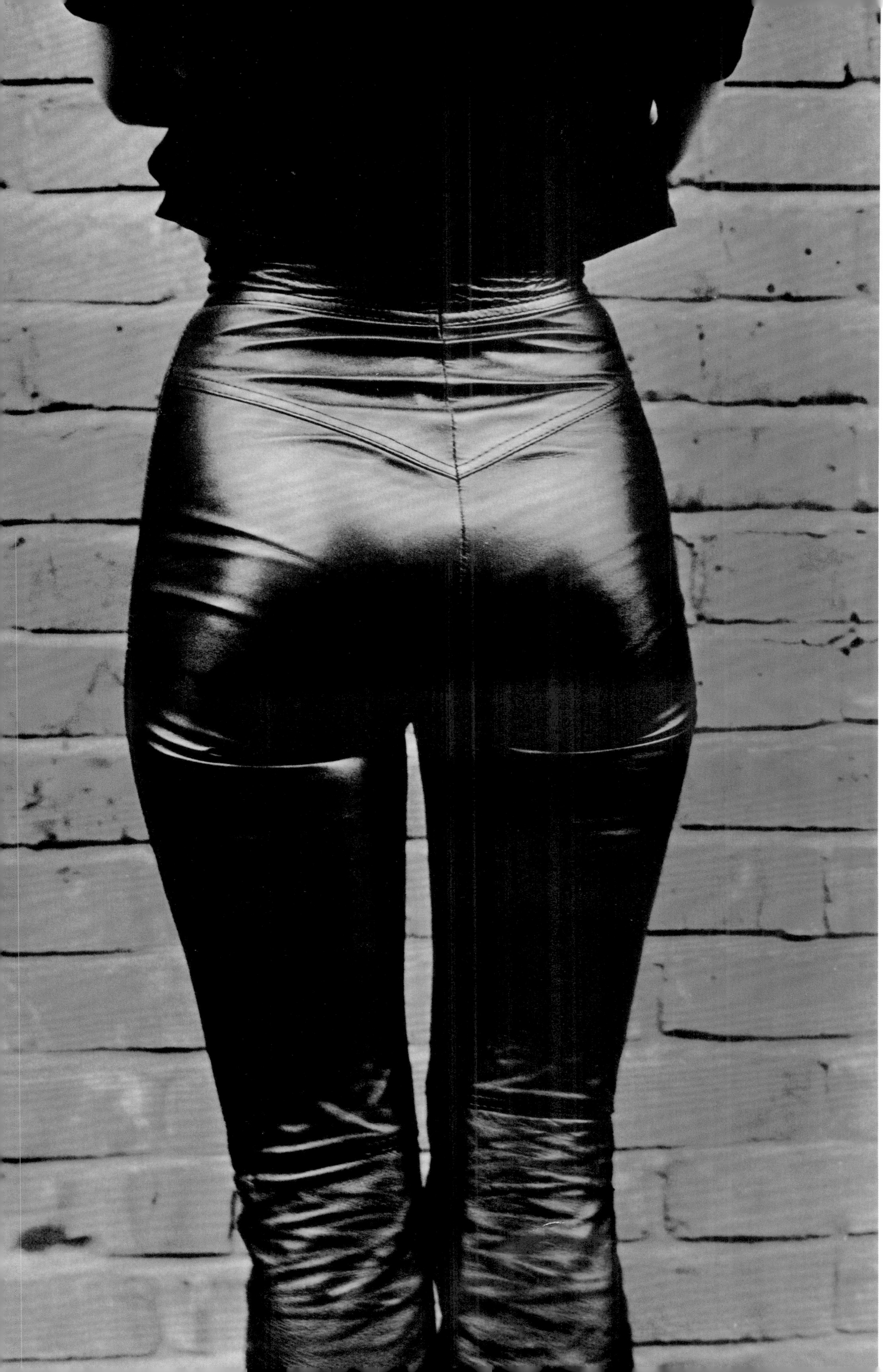

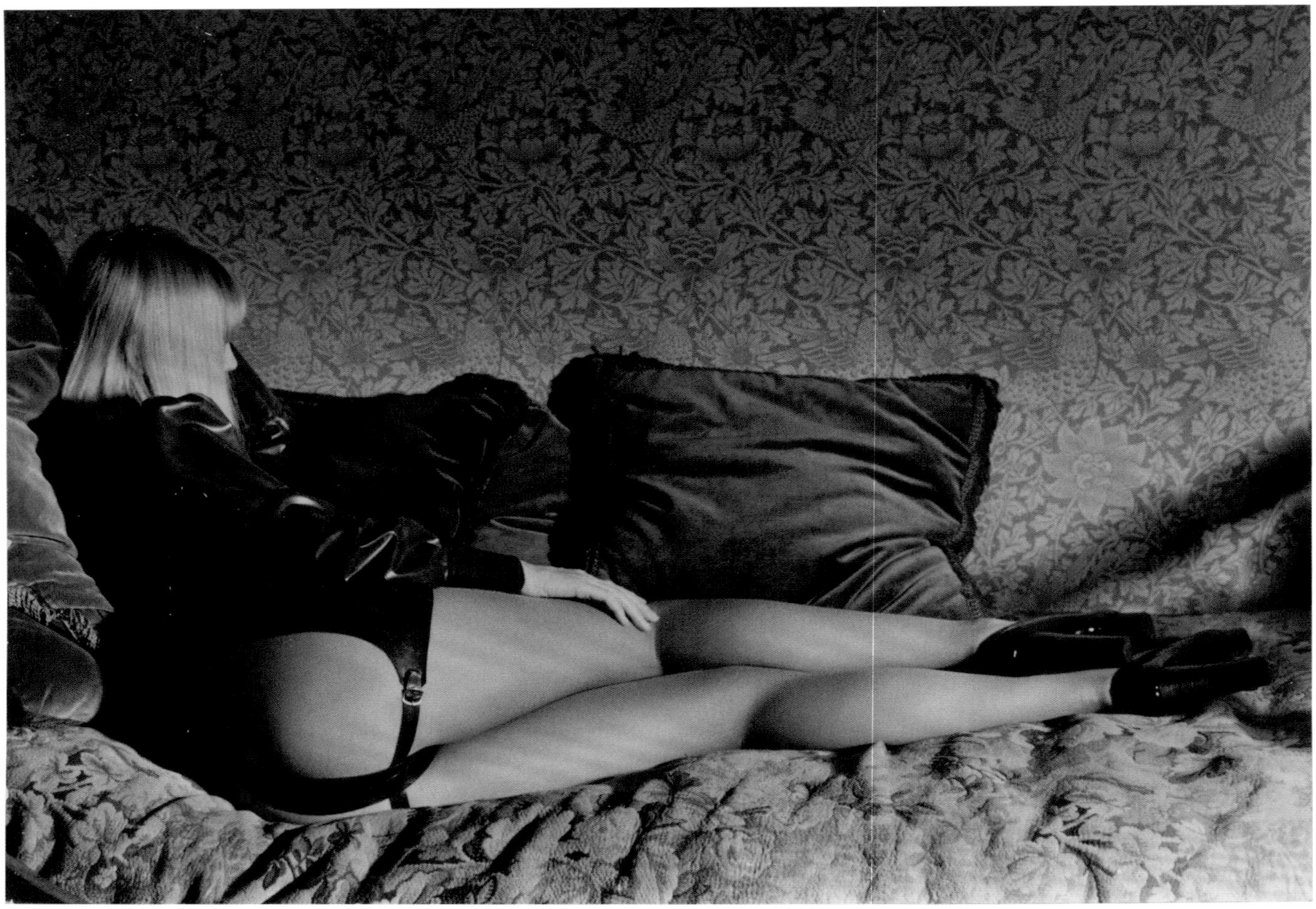

Above, opposite, and page 65 Janet Jones, Edith Grove, London, 1968–70

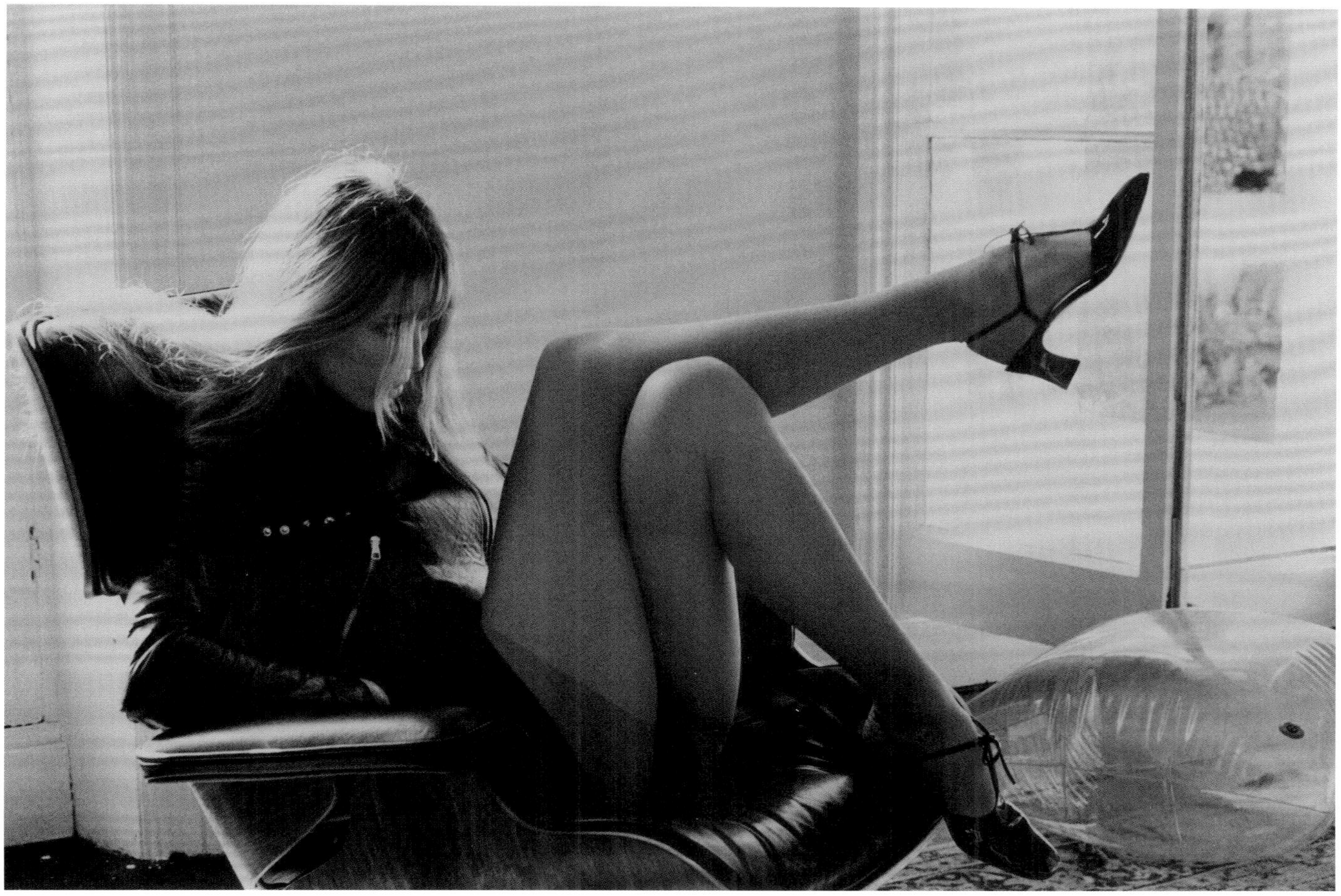

> The immediacy of photography was the most direct way to record the excitement of seeing a body hermetically sealed in a second skin. The latex or leather concealed all, yet at the same time revealed so much.

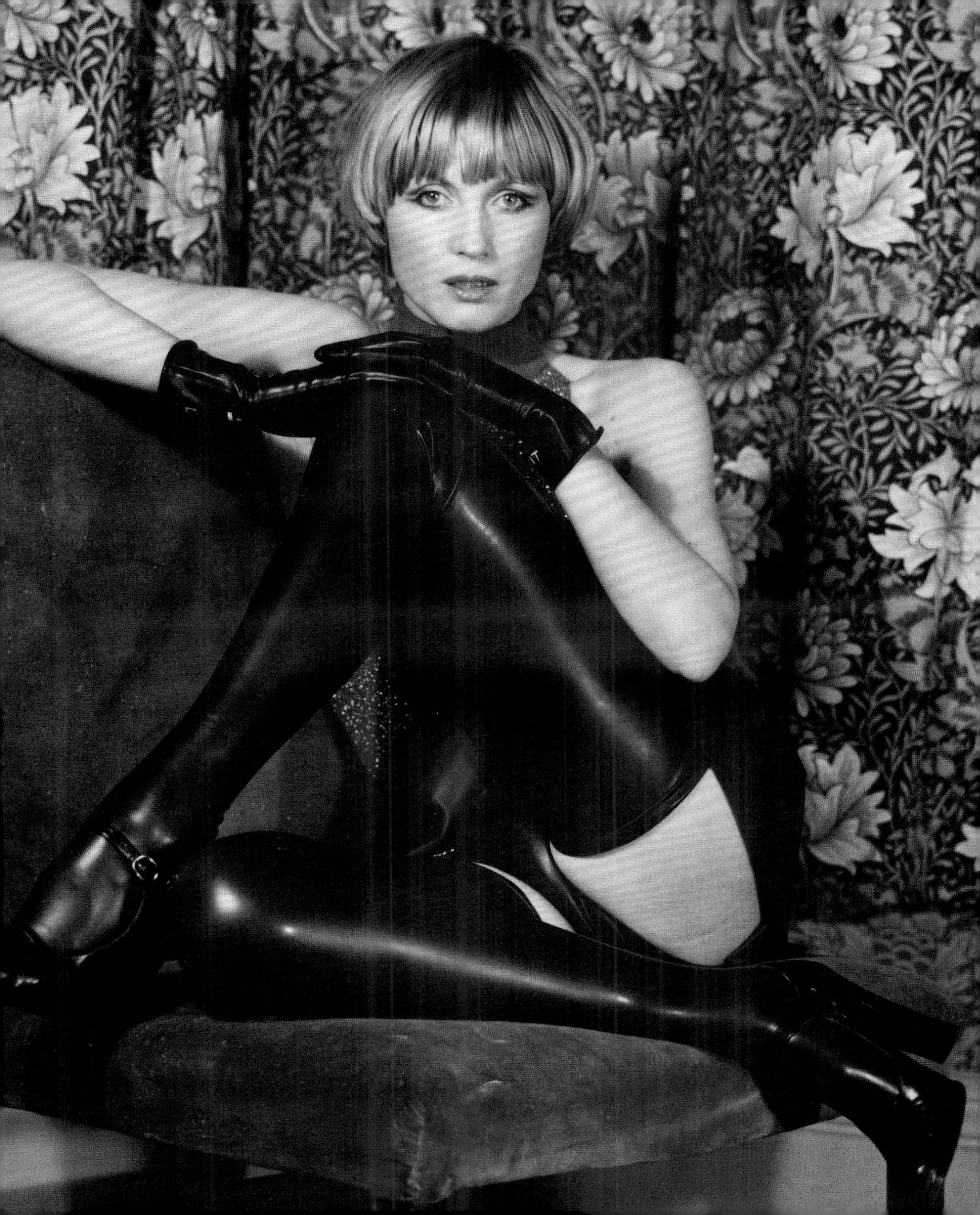

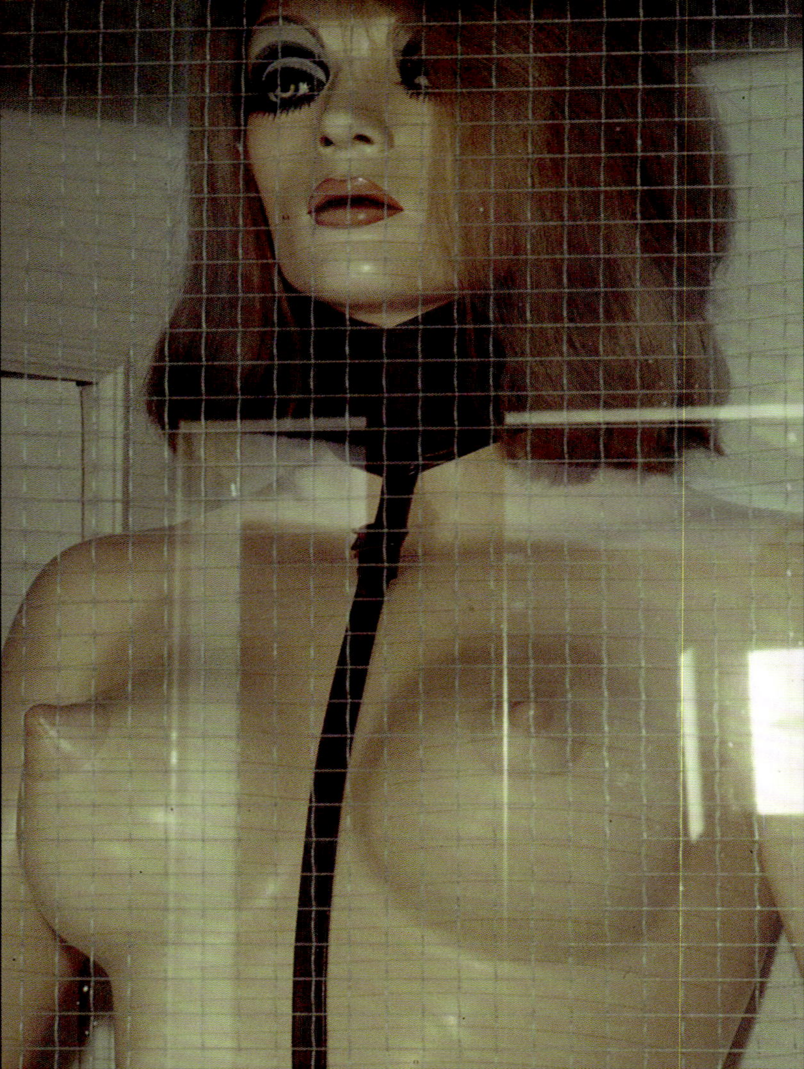

In the studio

In spite of popular perceptions regarding artists' lives, it is a rather monastic existence. One spends, I suppose, three-quarters of one's life in the studio; and I am acquisitive; I like collecting things, particularly if they relate to the figure in some way or if they are transgressive, which appeals to me. And what I have done over the years is make little displays. I have found that if you juxtapose objects which are totally out of scale, taking for example a little bust or just the head of a figure, something I have made or something I have acquired, and standing it next to a model motor car or a figure on a totally different scale, it is self-evidently amusing. And through the lens, you can frame and fix that scale differential, just as you can formalise in a photograph random oddities or the chance overlap of striking things in the studio which only become apparent if you are looking through the lens. The camera has a graphic effect and makes an interesting proposition out of something that just happens to be an arrangement in the room.

Opposite 'Hatstand', Charterhouse Square', London, 1980
Overleaf Charterhouse Square, London, 2015

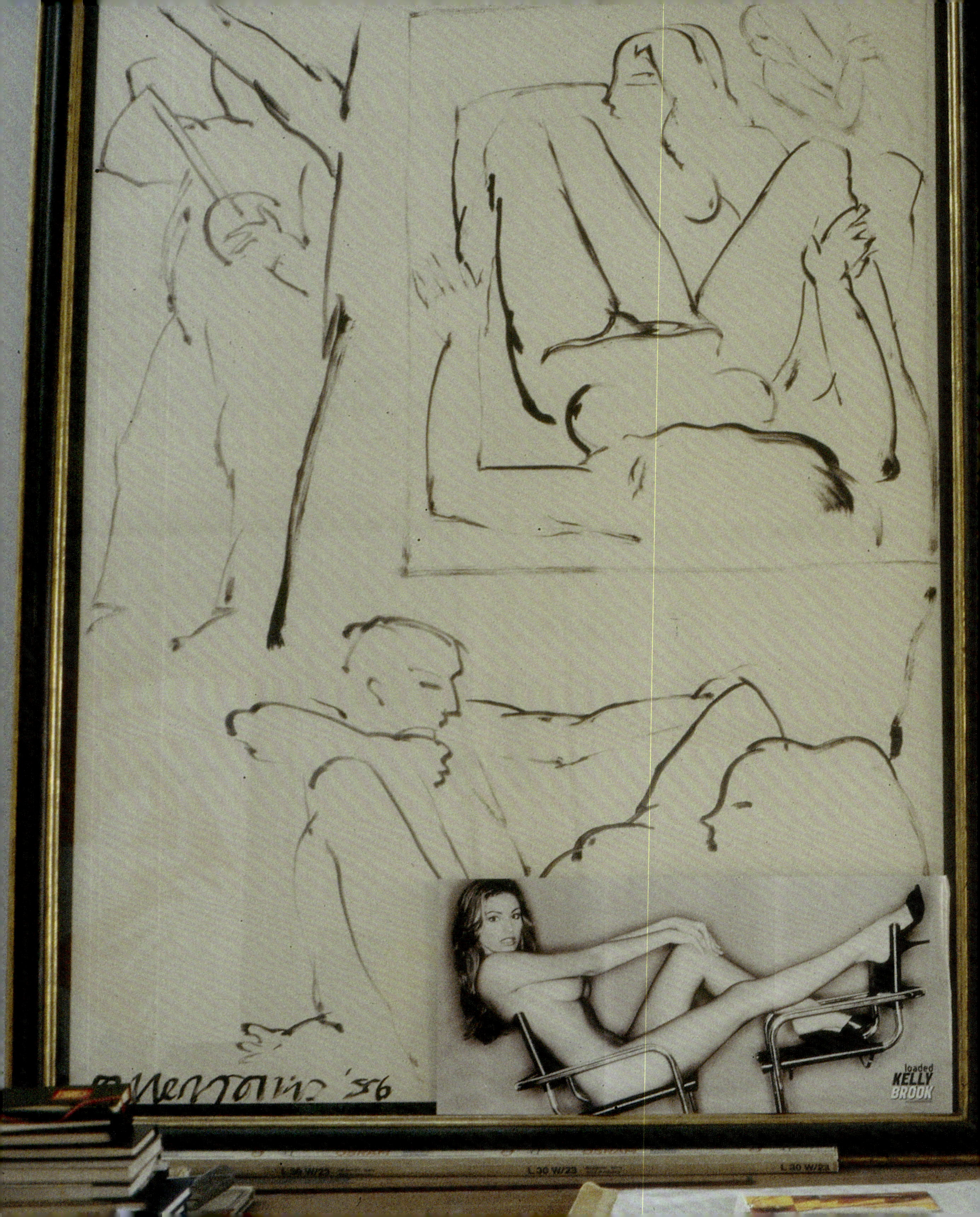
loaded
KELLY
BROOK
L 30 W/23

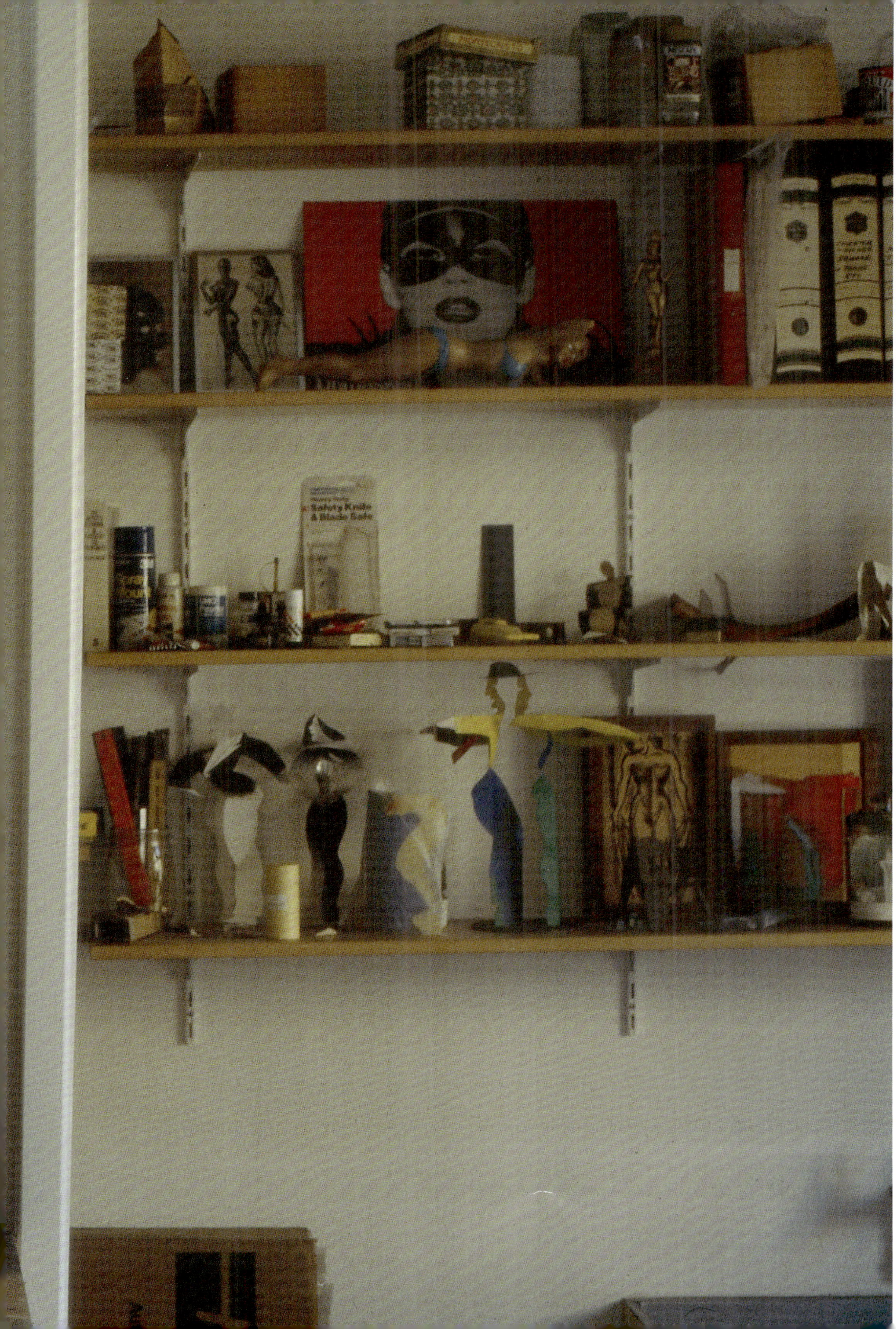
Safety Knife
& Blade Safe

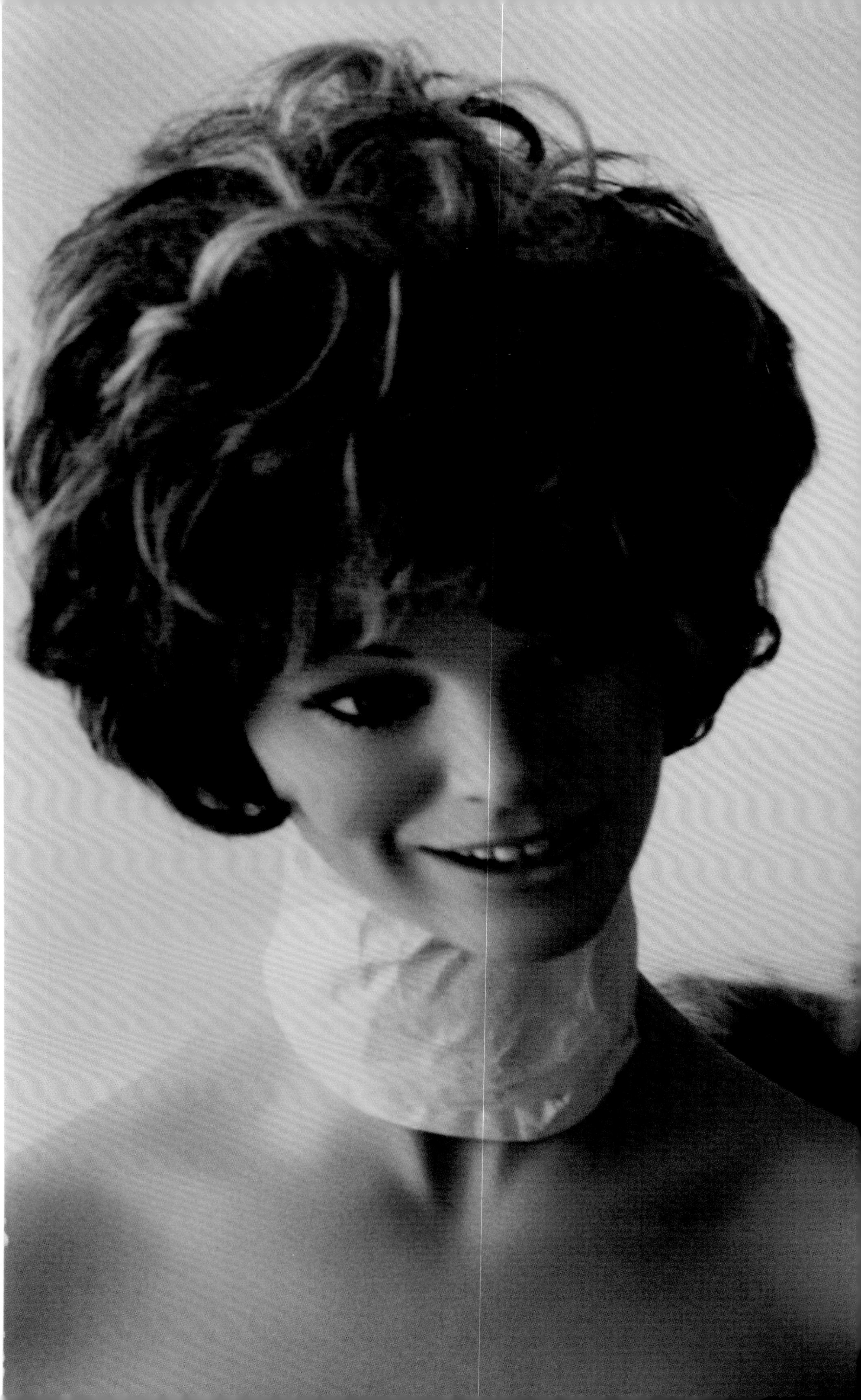

Los Angeles mannequin heads, acquired in 1978, Charterhouse Square, London, 1985

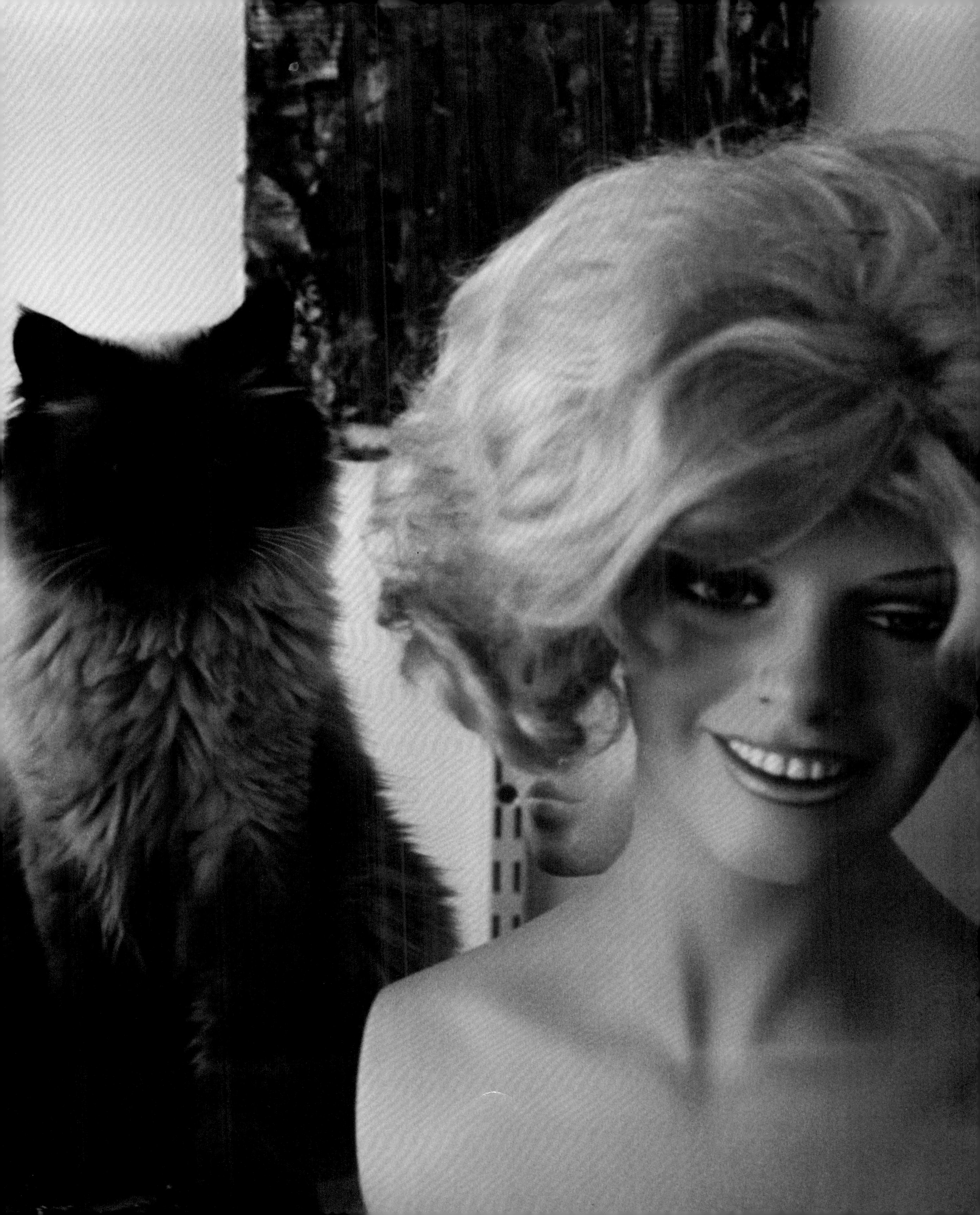

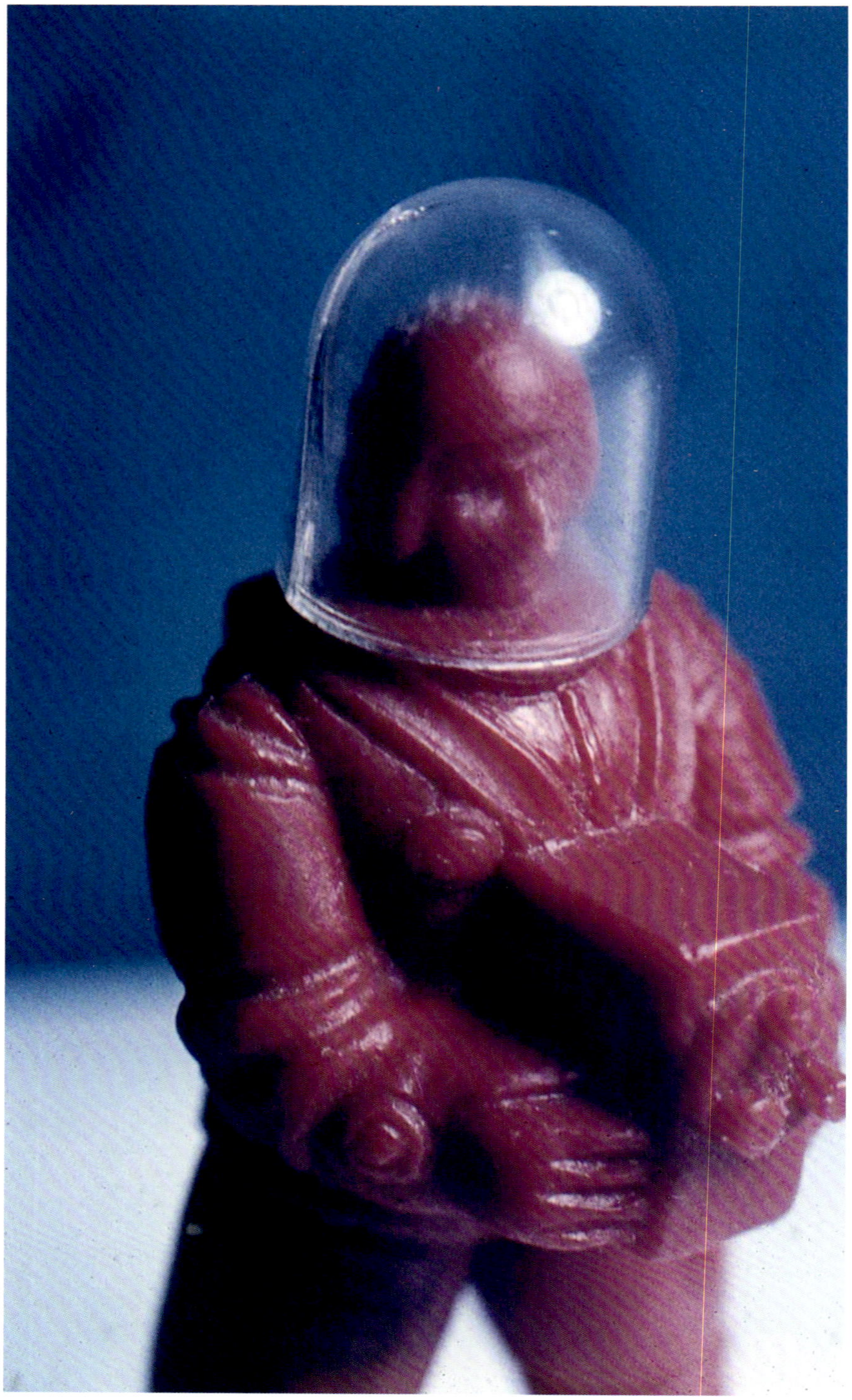

Above Corn Flakes spaceman, circa 1960, Charterhouse Square, London
Opposite 'Barbie and Friend', Charterhouse Square, London, 2015
Overleaf Charterhouse Square, London, 2015
Page 77 Charterhouse Square, London, 2018
Pages 78-79 Charterhouse Square, London, 2015
Page 80 'Hatstand' and collage, Charterhouse Square, London, 1980
Page 81 'Artist and model', Charterhouse Square, London, 1980

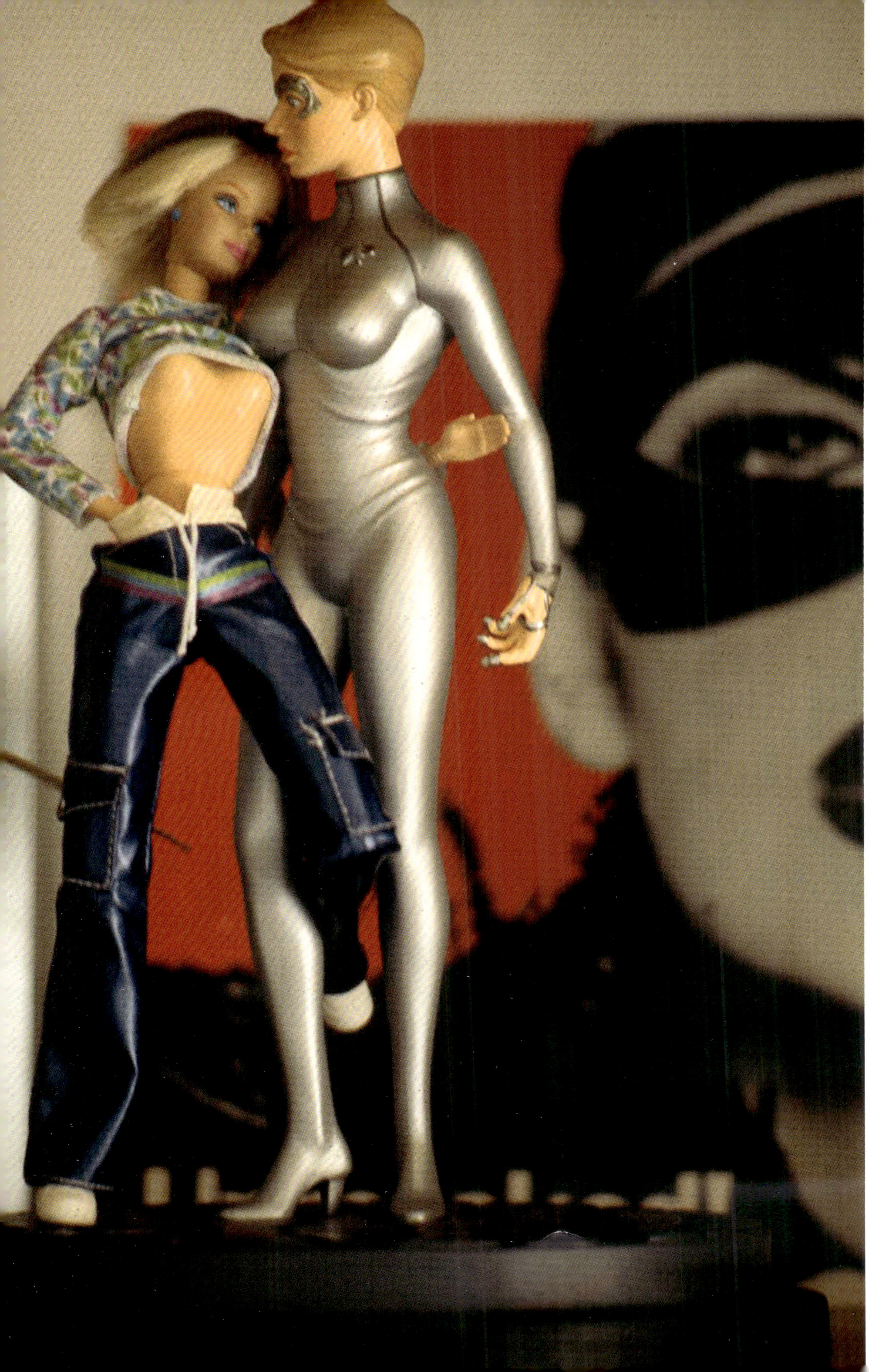

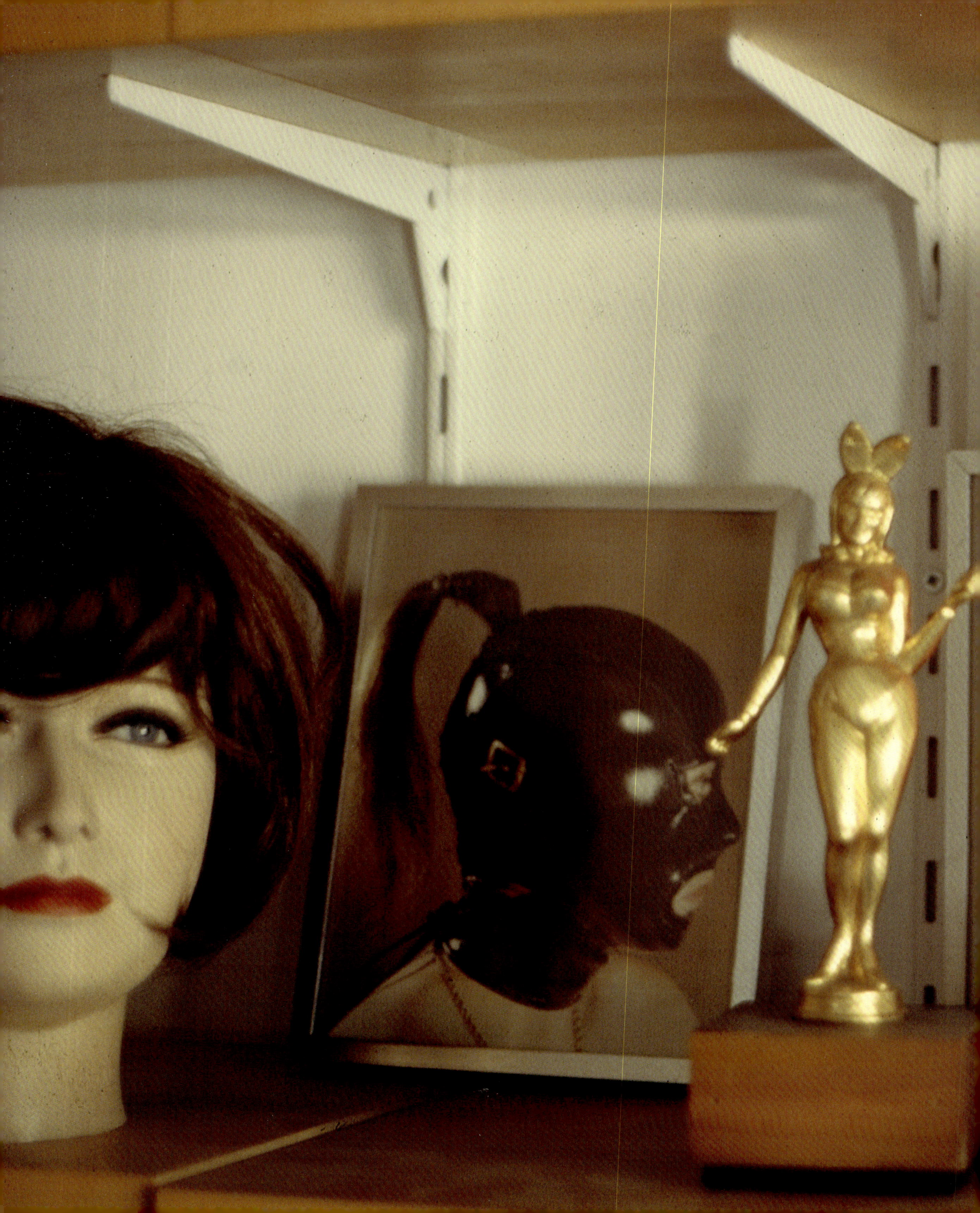

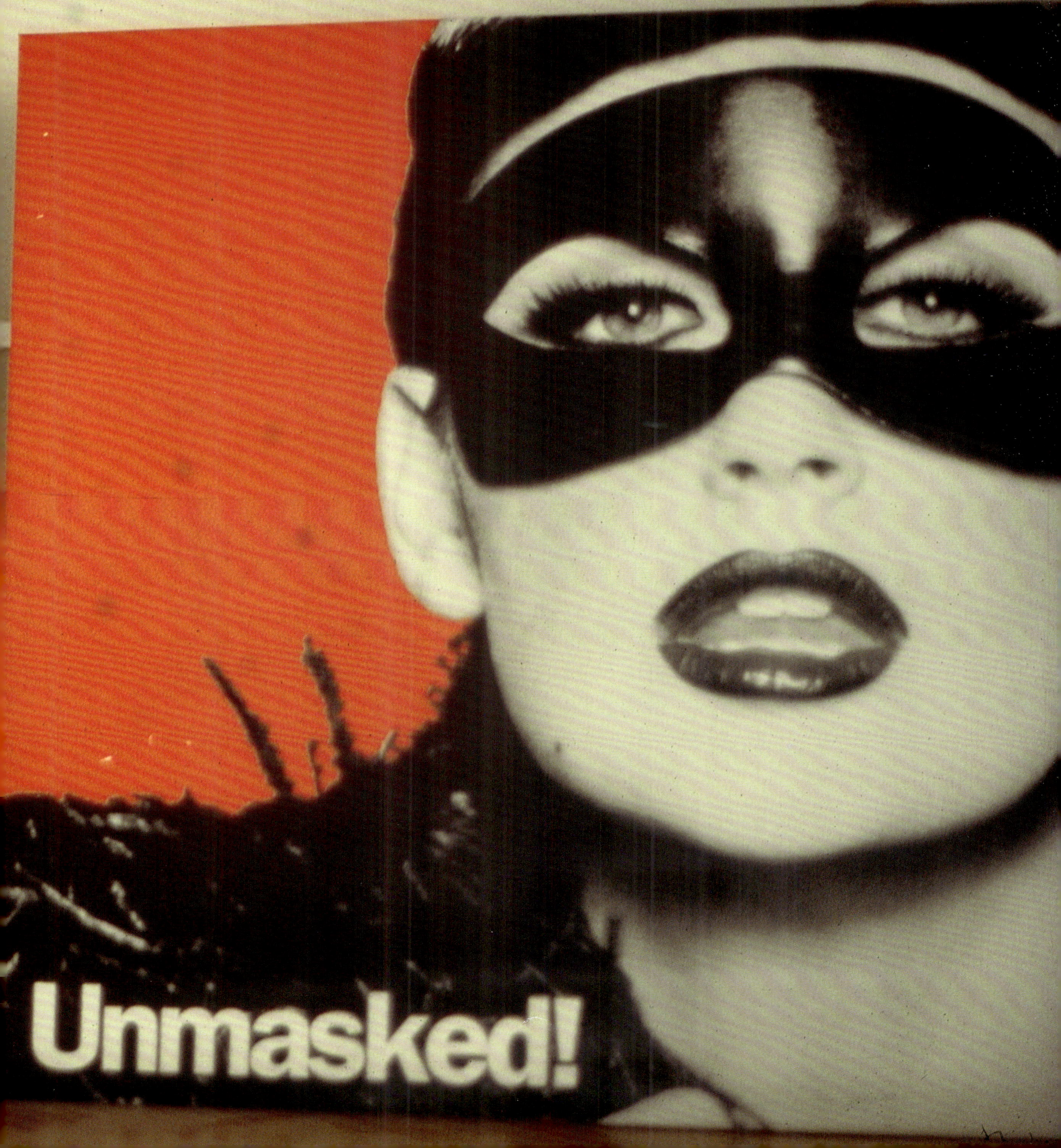
Unmasked!

‘My work as a painter is a solitary, studio-based activity. But I love collecting things. In a playful way, rows of shelves juxtapose my paper models and maquettes with other objects and ephemera acquired over time.’

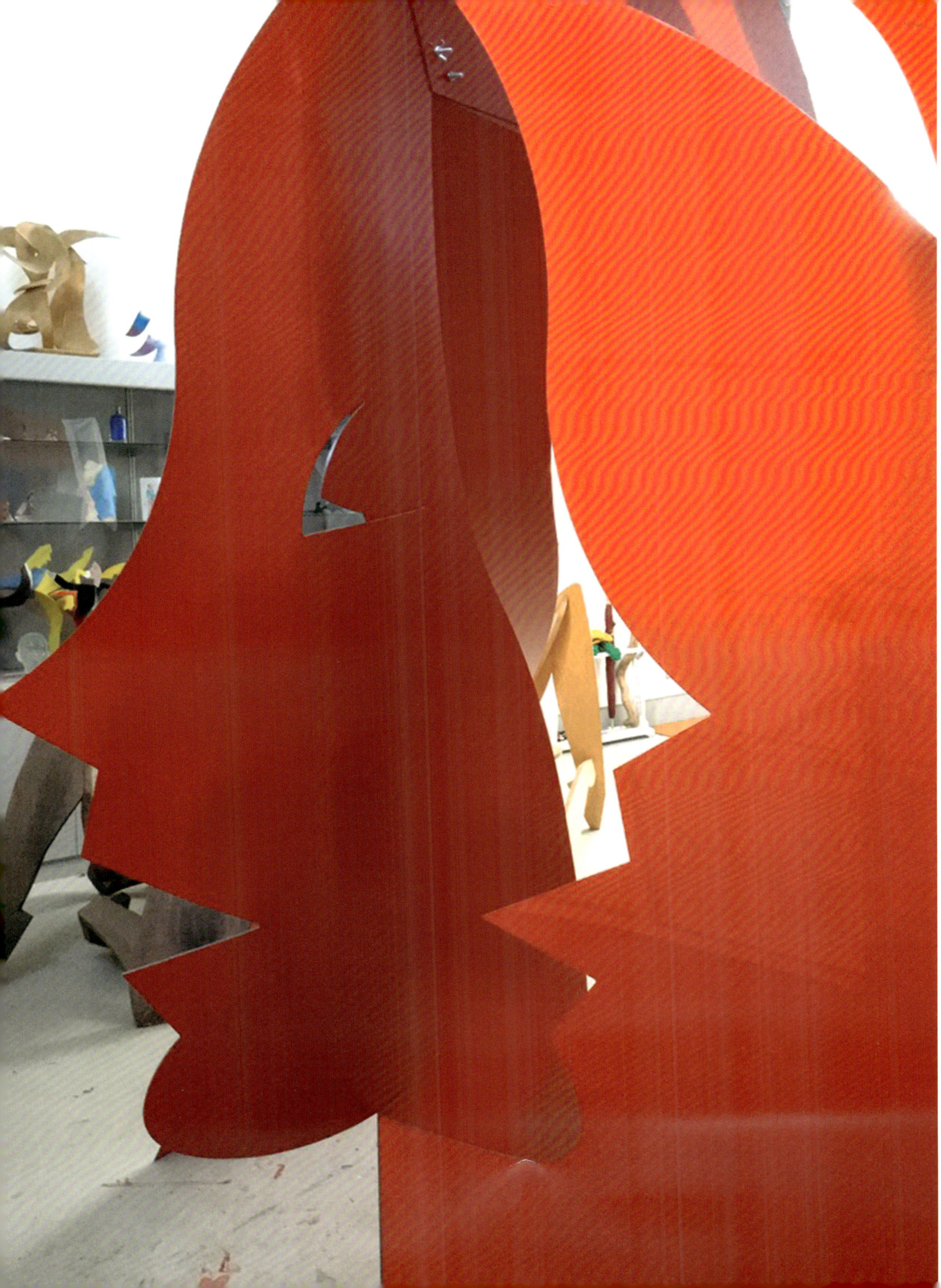

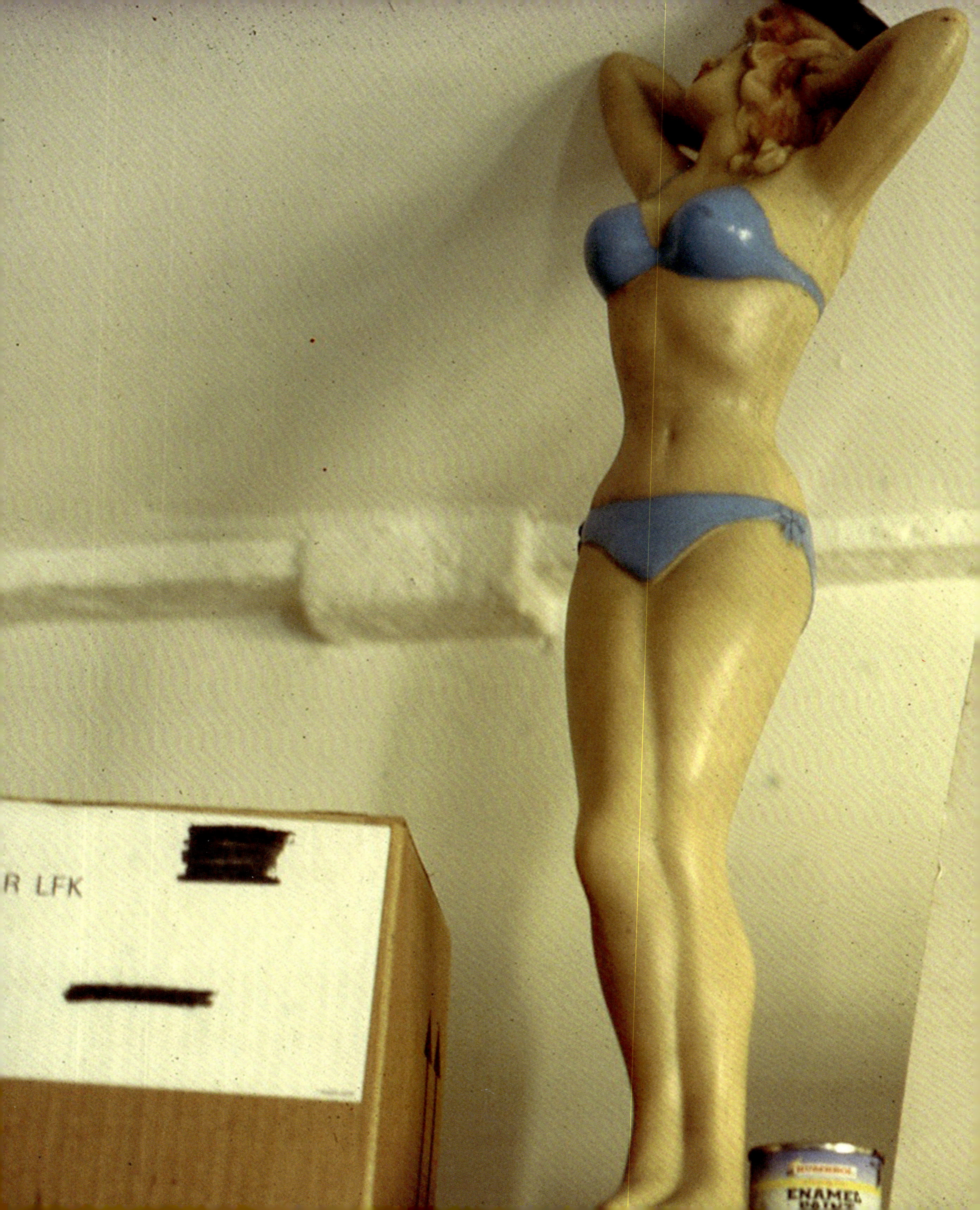
R LFK
ENAMEL

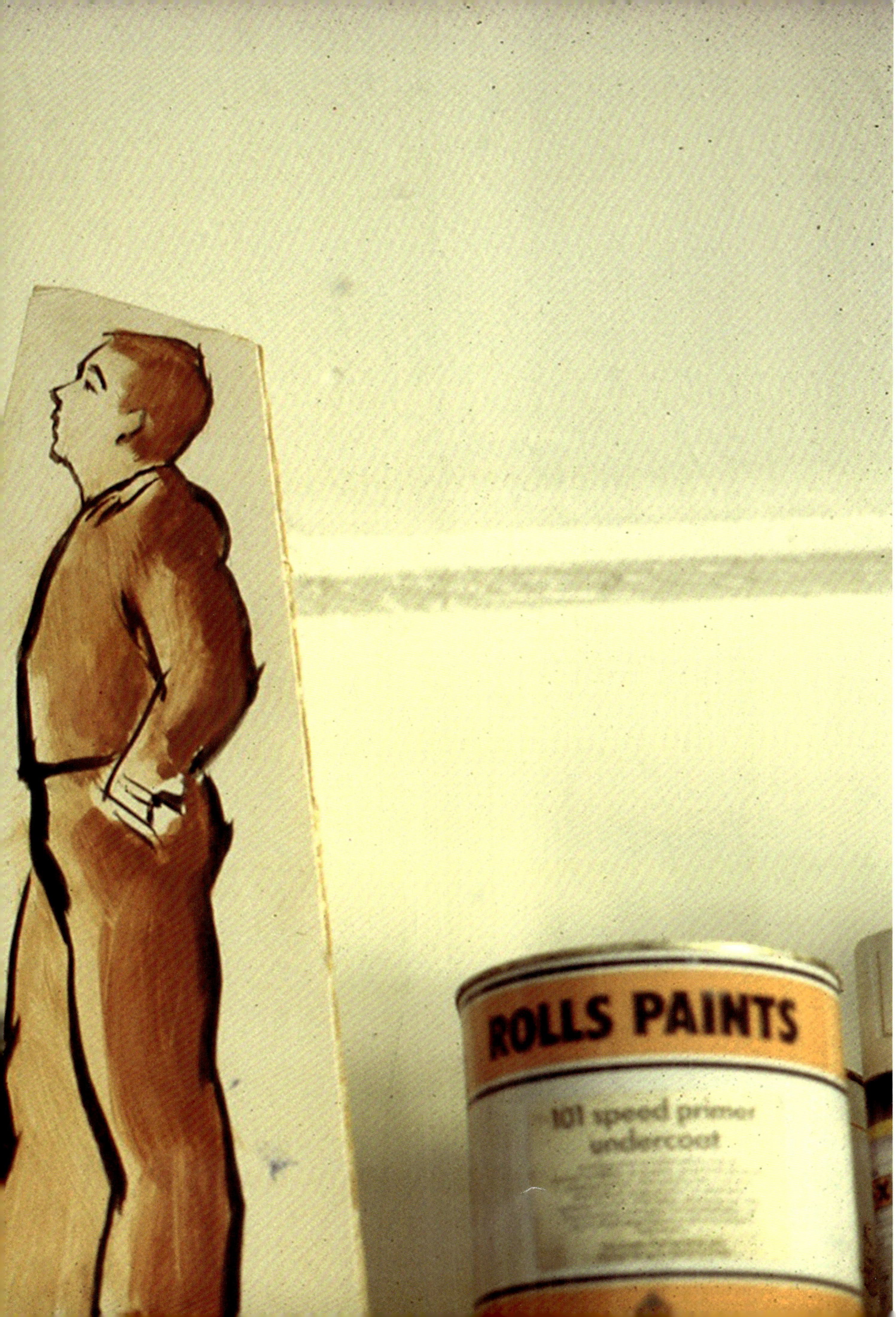
ROLLS PAINTS
101 speed primer
undercoat

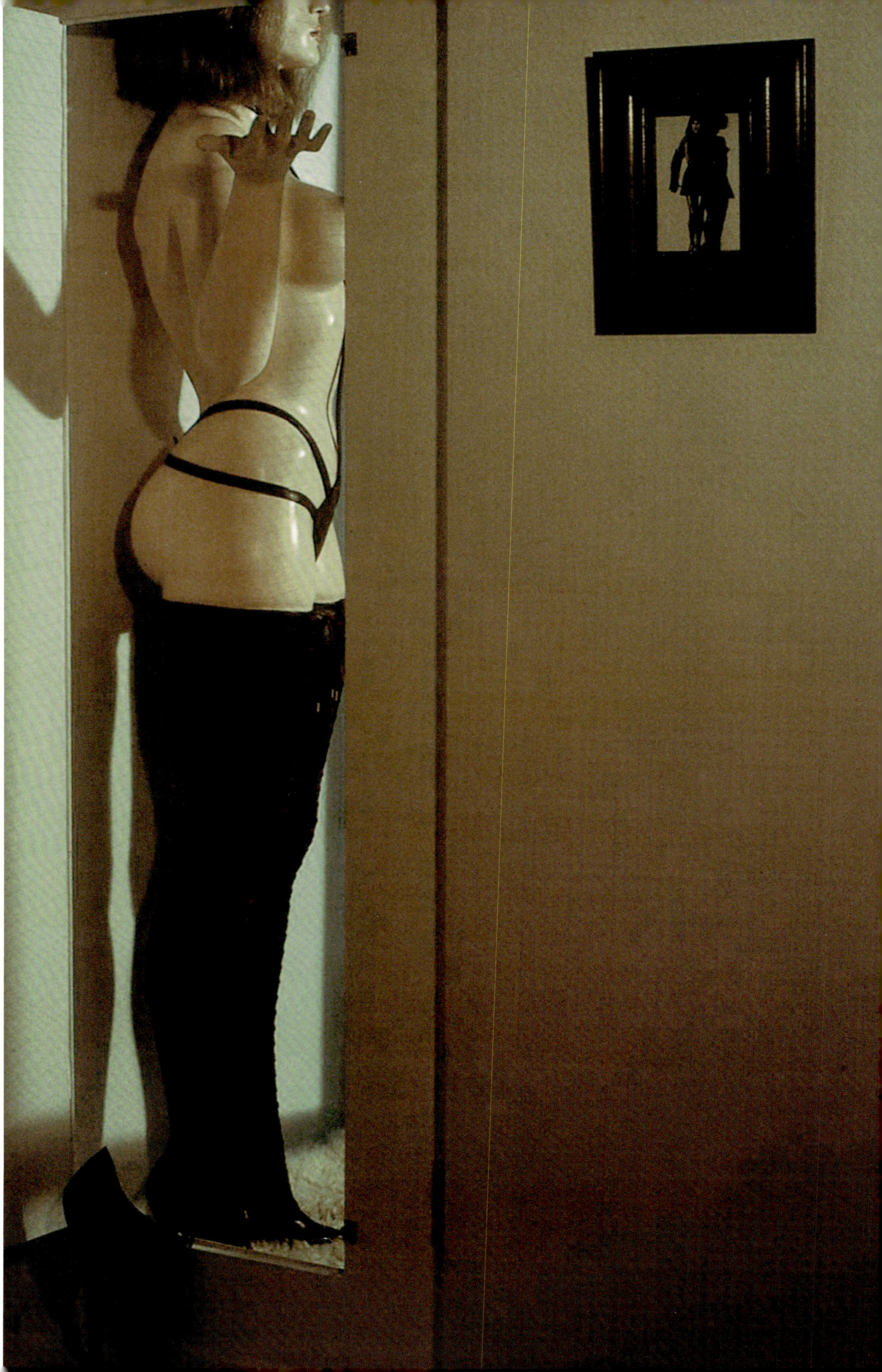

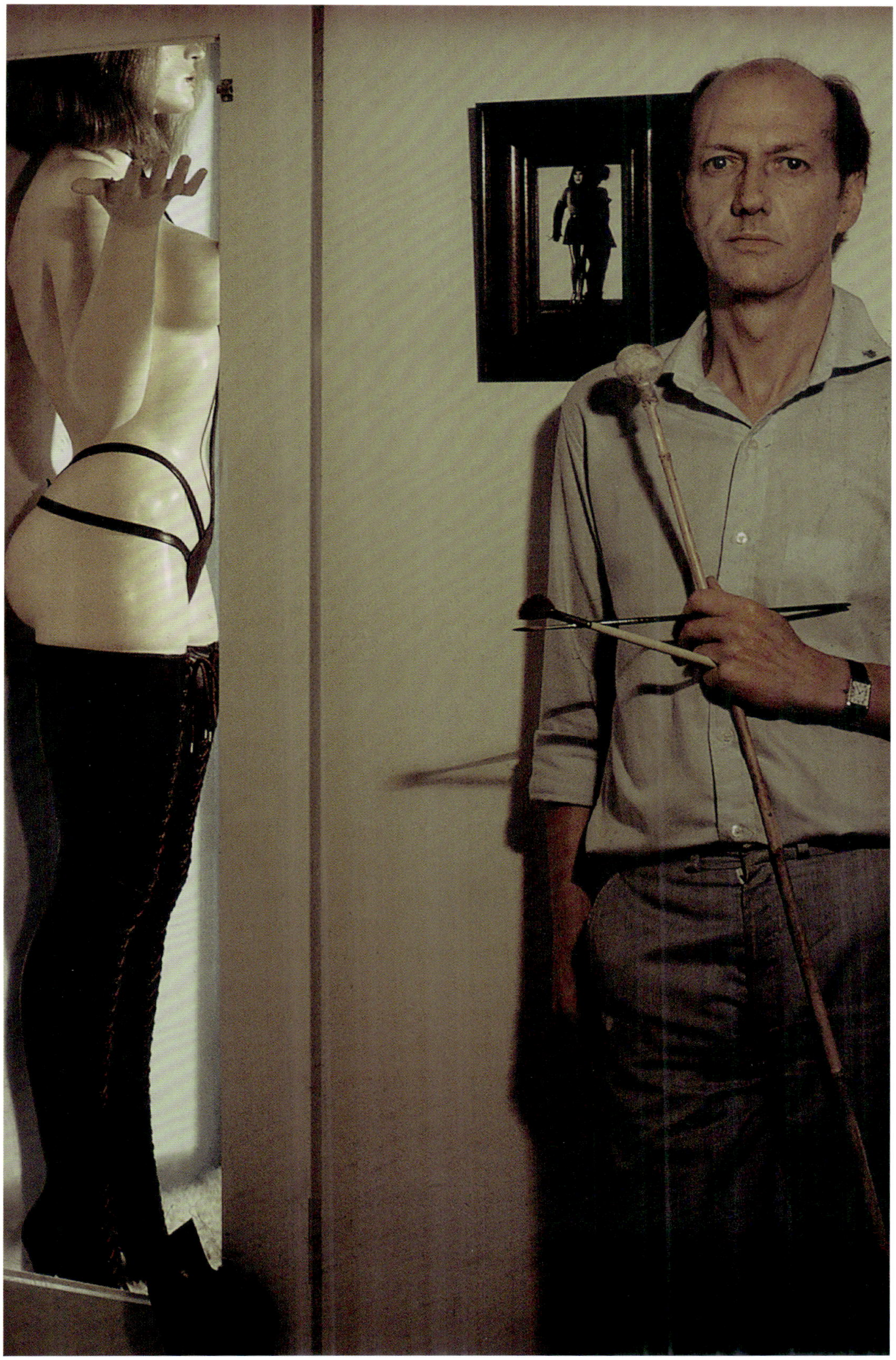

Waitress

I had been obsessed with photographing my wife Janet in latex clothing, which then was very new and exotic and coincided with that whole King's Road explosion of the miniskirt and the body being displayed as never before. Now, with this second-skin material, the body could be revealed but not exposed, and also what I liked about the latex thing was that it was not fashionable and was below the radar. With the figure tightly encased, your eye was immediately drawn to the surface. It was very tactile and it was a physical manifestation of something which was beginning to happen in my paintings.

The waitress theme was in my mind from *A Clockwork Orange*. Kubrick had sent me the book to read, because he had seen my furniture sculptures and he wanted me to contribute to the film. The Korova Milk Bar scene gave me the idea of designing a waitress costume, but it was never used. My thought was that in the Korova Milk Bar, in the age of automation, you didn't need waitresses or waiters. The point of the waitress was that the milk bar was the only place of social interaction left in the city. So I could imagine someone with great allure coming to you; but they were only delivering food, and once they put the food down, they were no longer functional; they became decorative. The idea was that, as they walked away, the bottomless costume would give you an aesthetic eyeball hit.

The outfit was made especially for me by a company in Covent Garden called AtomAge, founded by a certain John Sutcliffe. They worked principally in leather, and I had worked with them on the stylised accoutrements for my furniture sculptures.

I had photographed Janet in the costume, but I wanted my visual concept executed to a high professional level. I had among my close friends at one time a number of photographers who shared a general interest in the figure and glamour. I enlisted the skills of one, Tim Street-Porter, to fulfil this series of images. I also had the notion that it might be interesting to locate this mythical waitress within a range of eating possibilities – from Fortnum's to a truck drivers' diner. Tim took photographs of the chosen locations and then we used a Fleet Street retoucher he knew to put the images together. In the end, I was happier with the figure against a neutral background.

Opposite Fitting the 'Waitress' costume, London, 1971

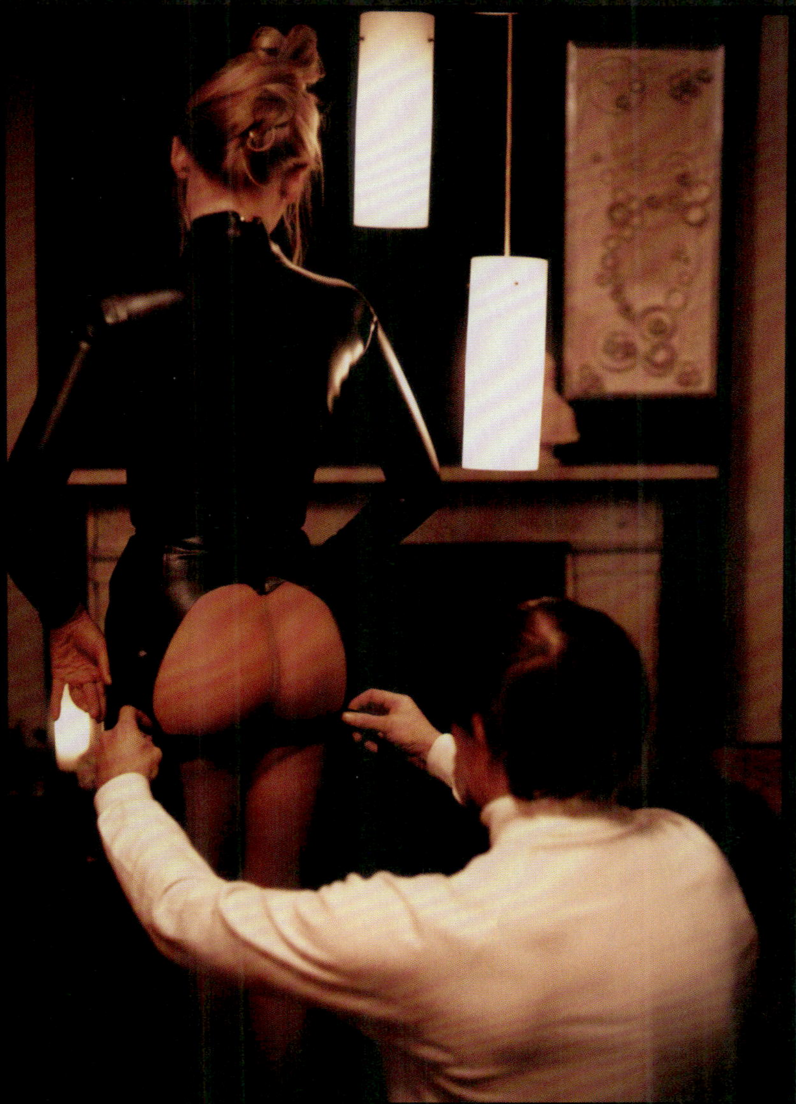

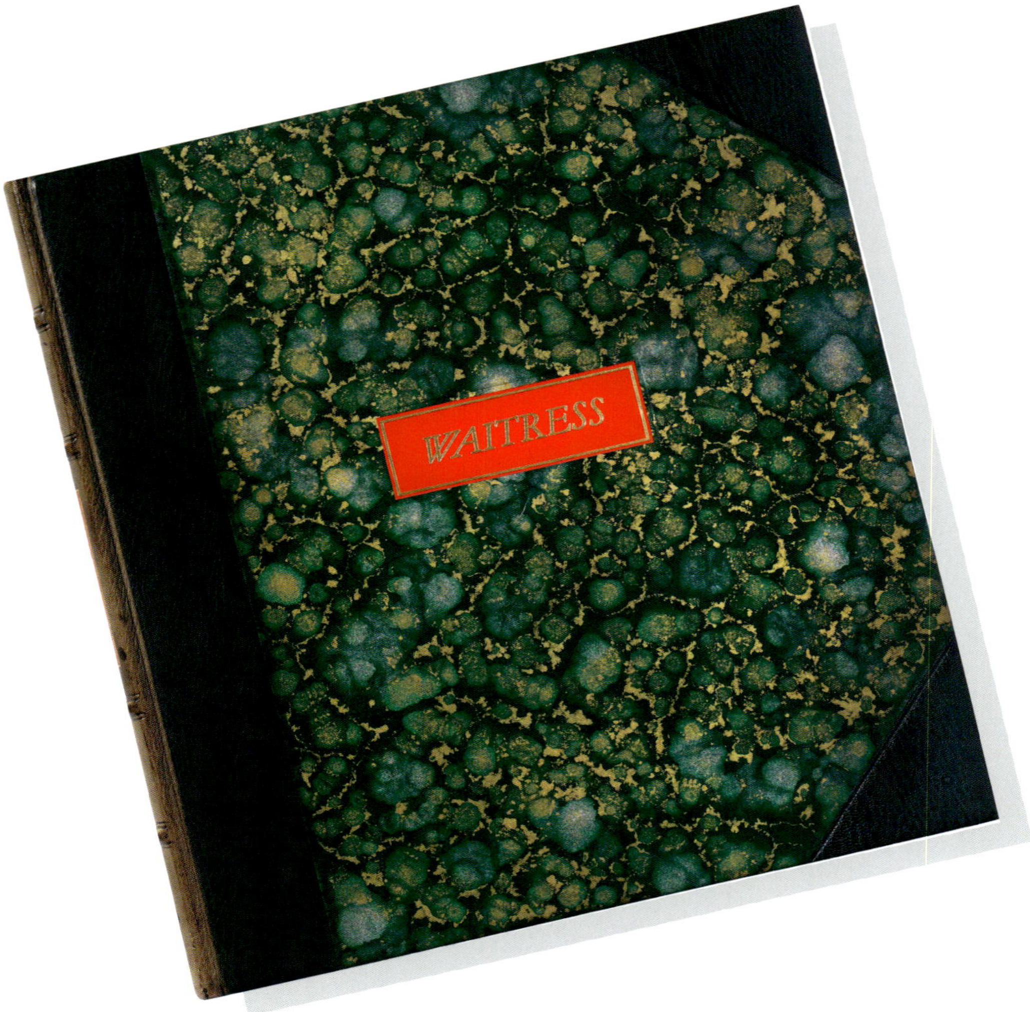

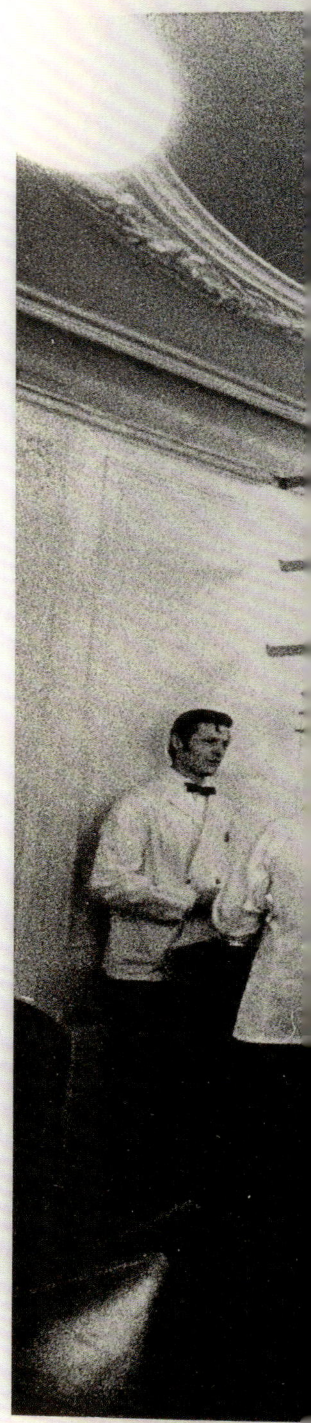

Above 'Waitress' cover, 1971
Opposite Montage plate from 'Waitress', situating her in Manzi's, 1971
Pages 86–89 Images from the 'Waitress' studio suite, 1971

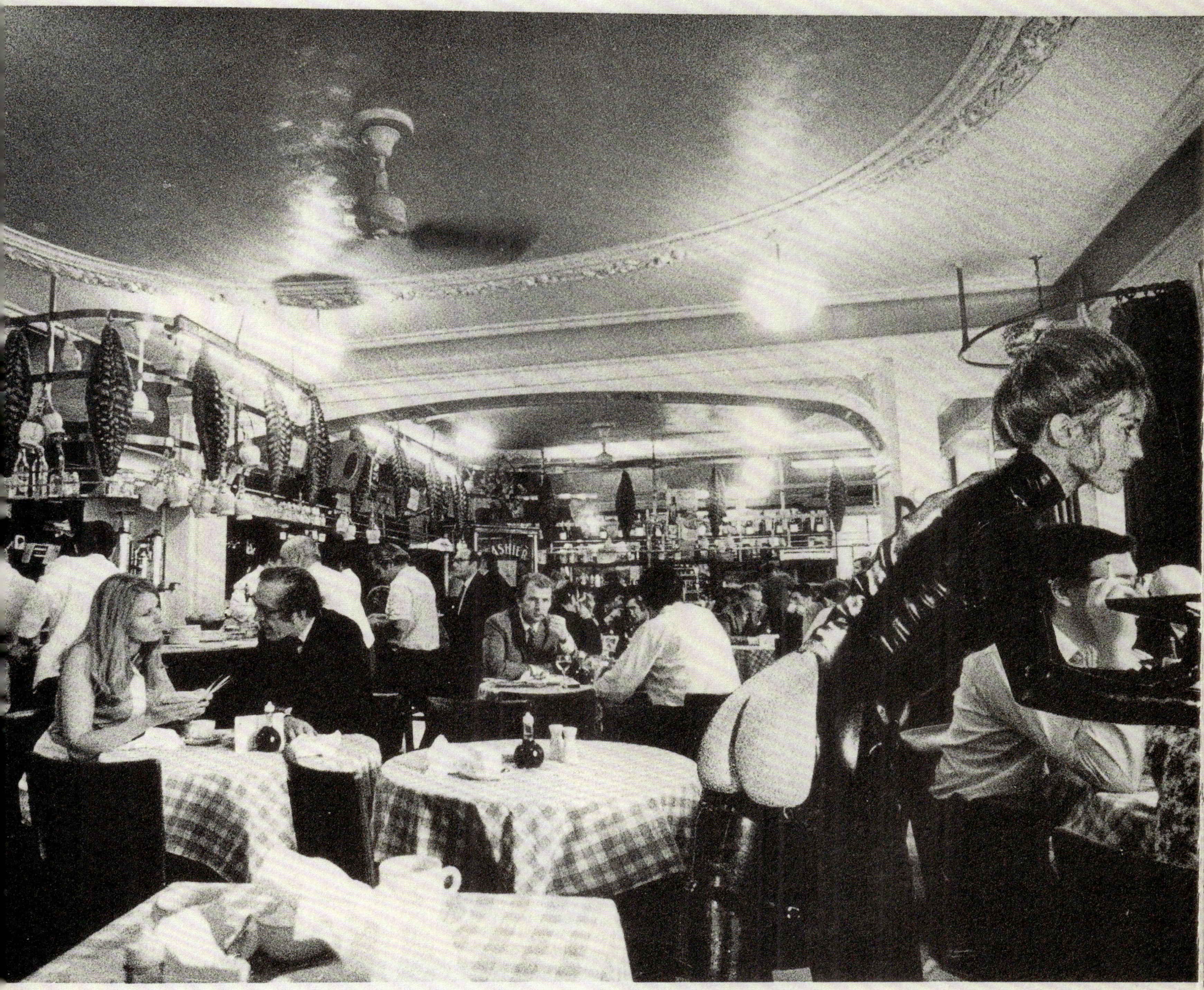

V

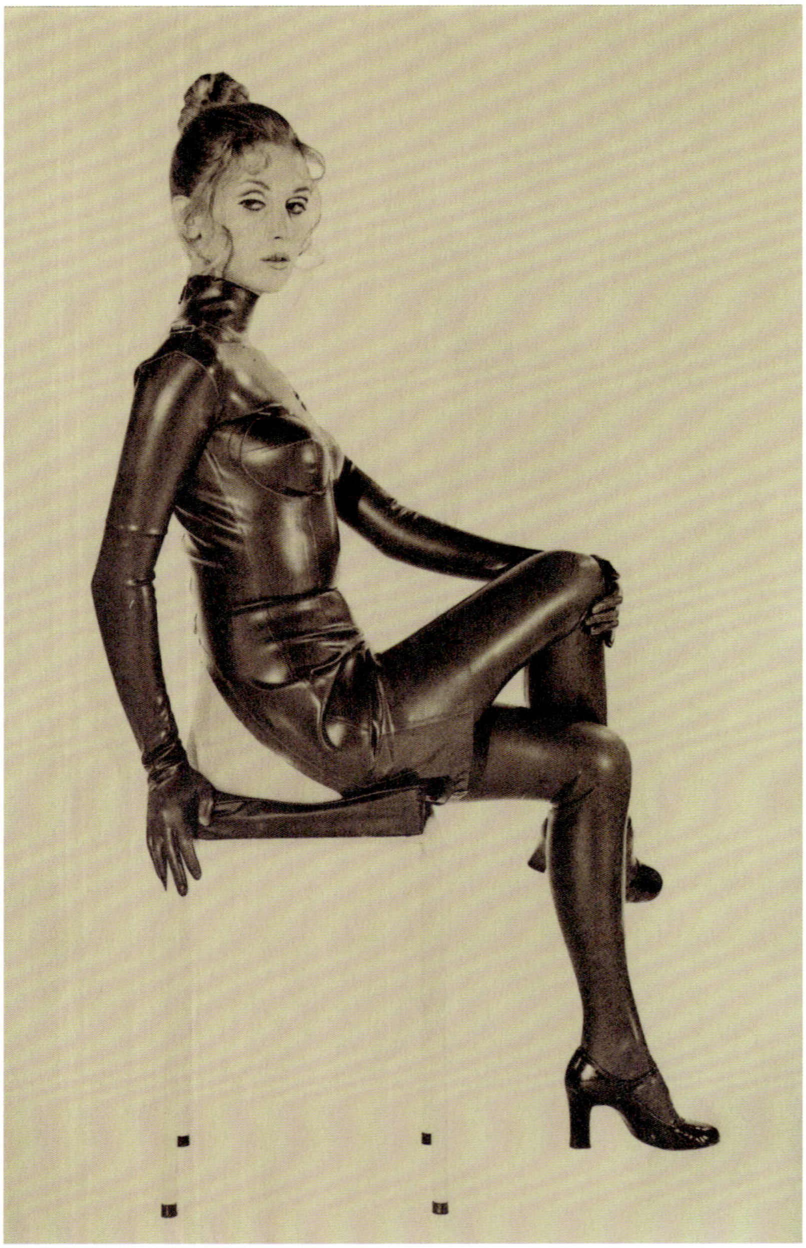

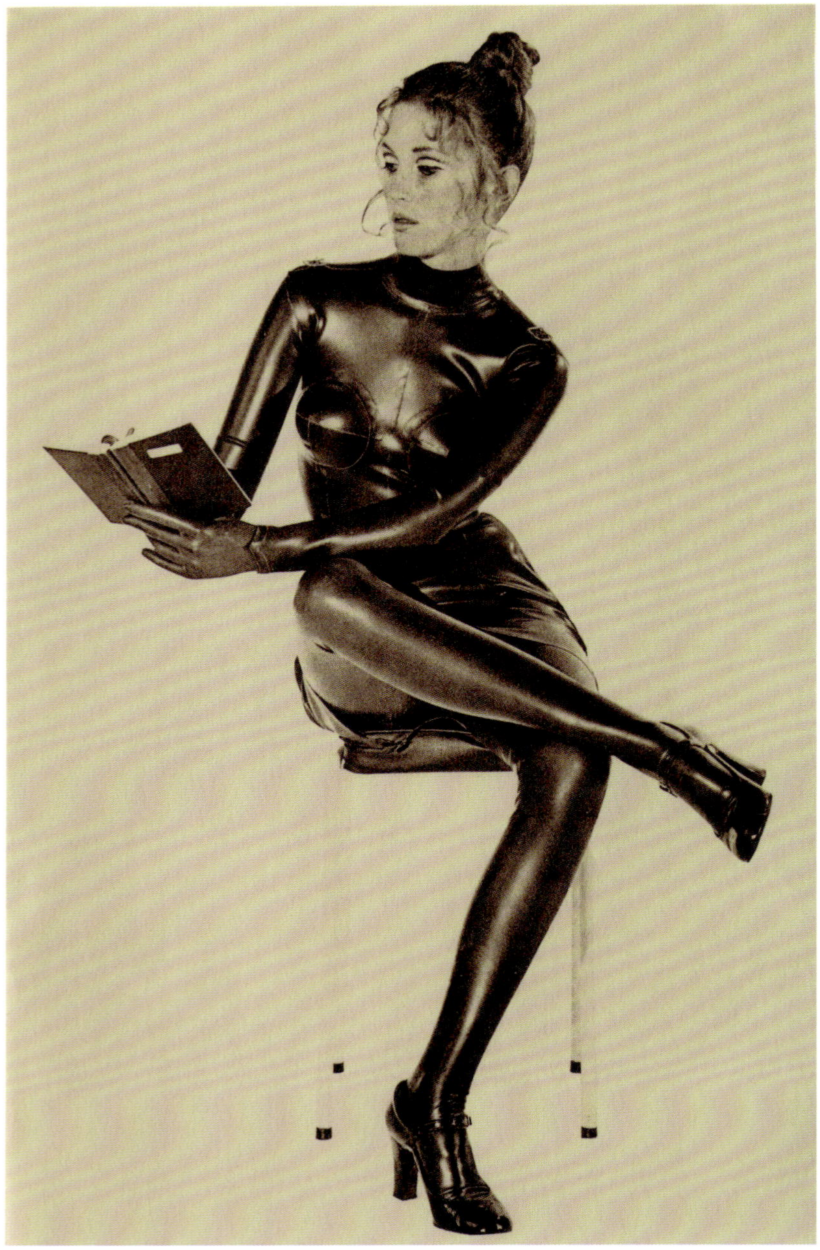

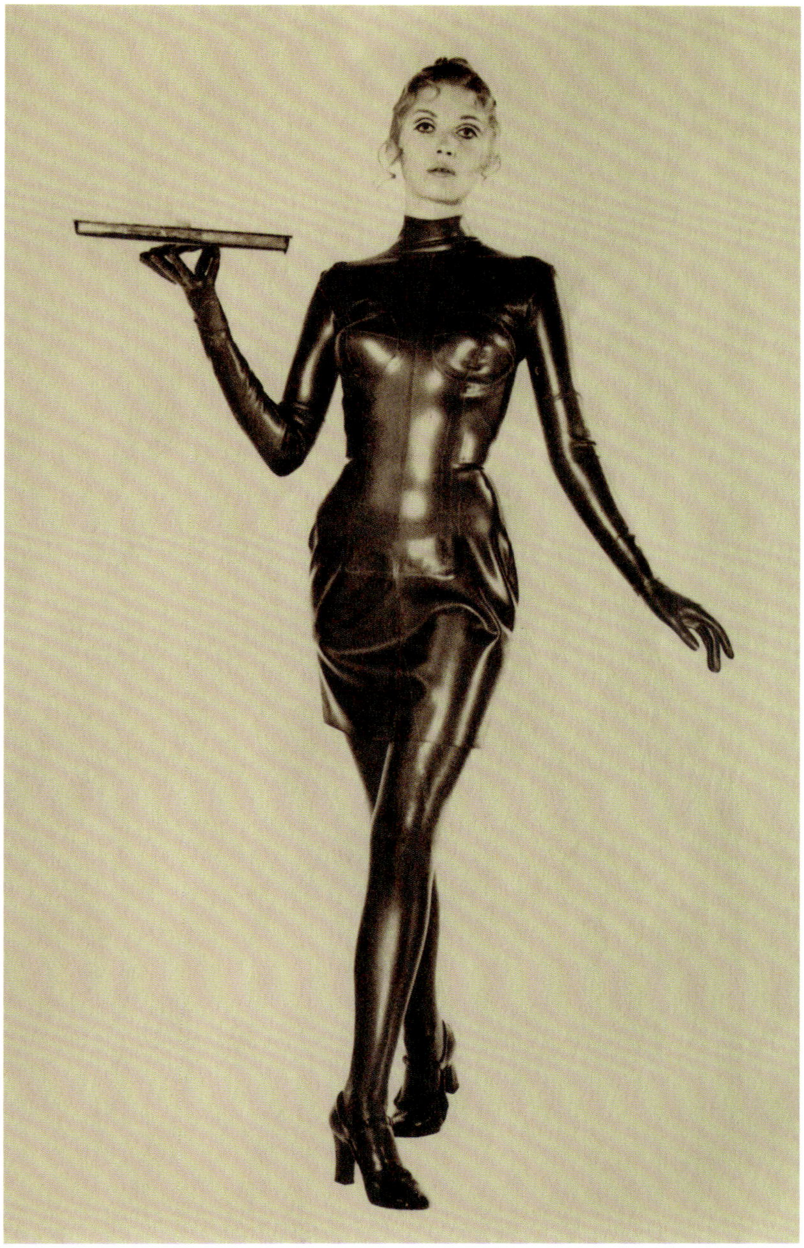 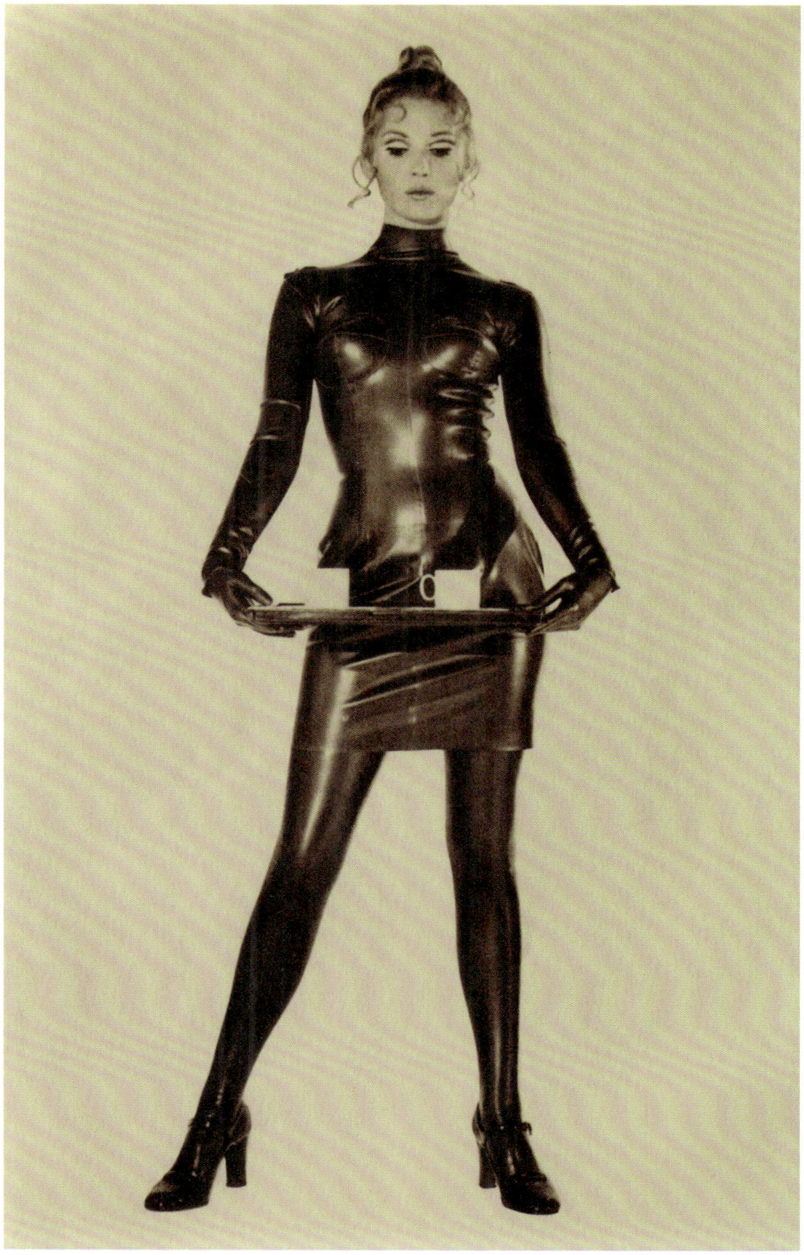

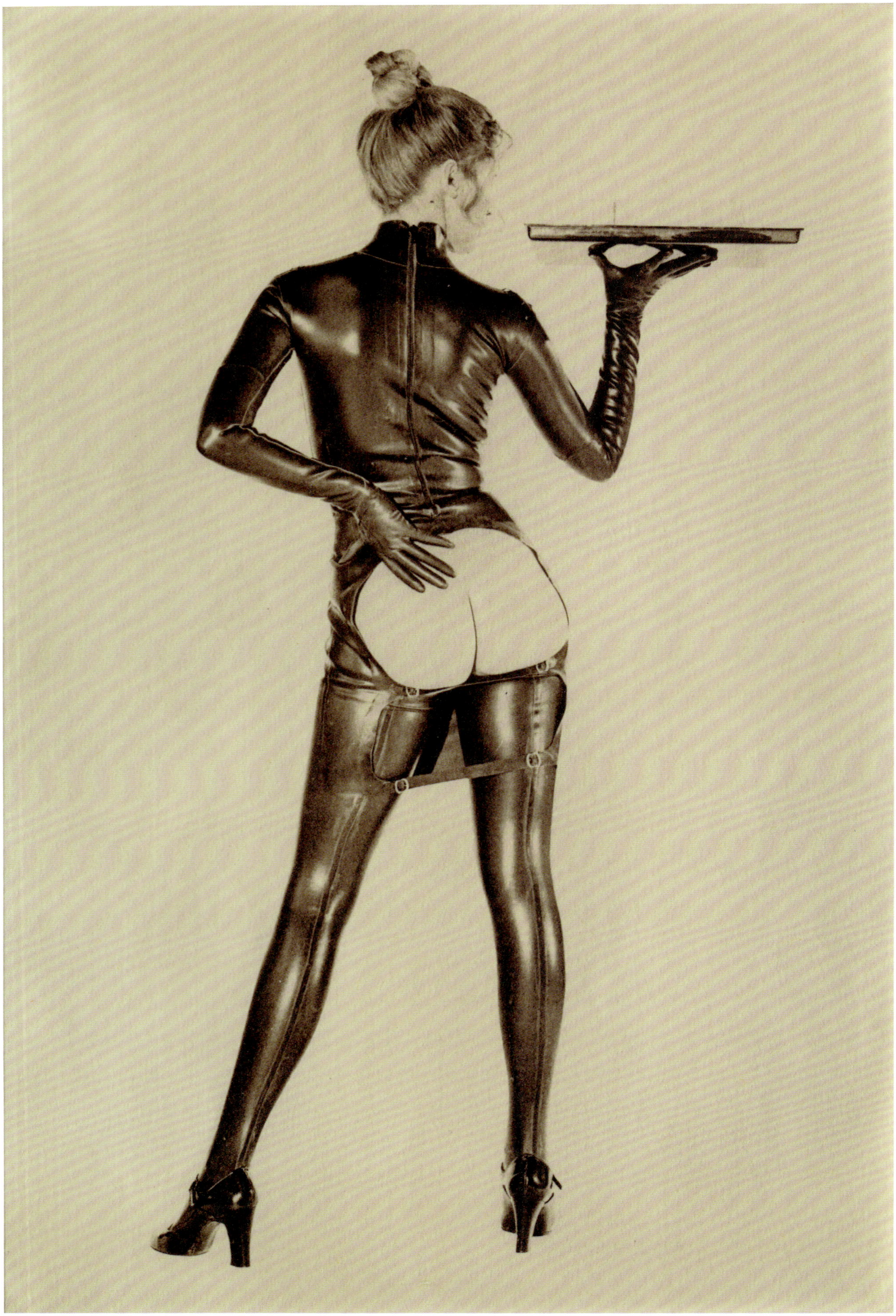

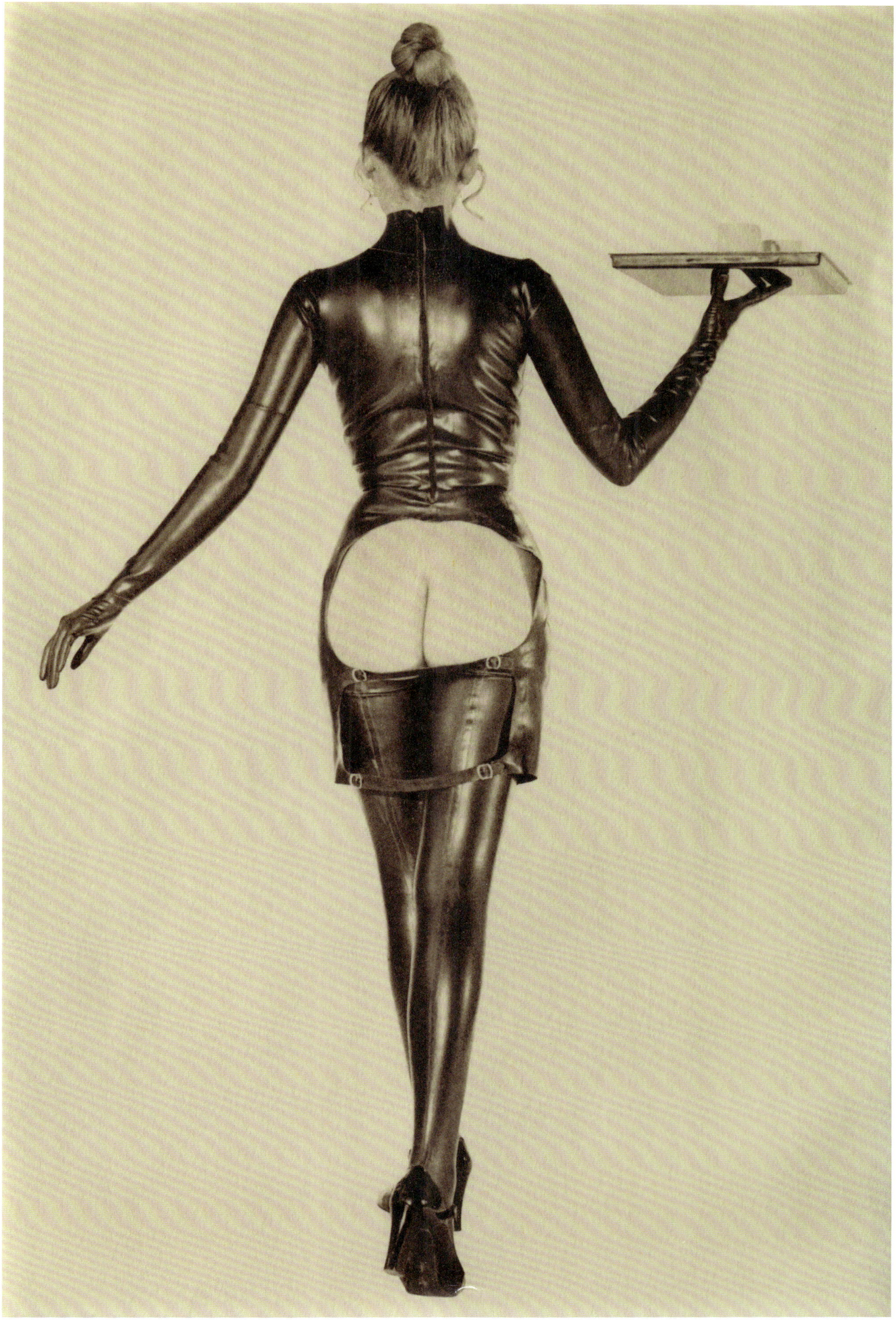

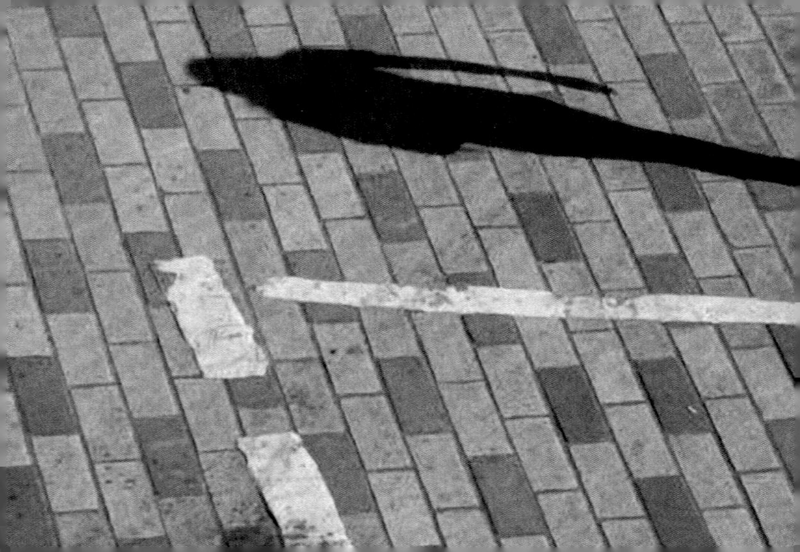

Road markings

When I was finishing at art school, I was making a bit of pin money with a friend by giving lectures at art schools around Greater London and I conceived a lecture without words. The thrust was that students wanting to be artists should not be limited by a notion of what was fitting subject matter and that it wasn't necessarily nature, the landscape, and the figure, but actually the reality of their everyday surroundings that could be the source of inspiration.

I went round Soho and the West End, photographing, among other things, the parking markings that had just been introduced. I realised when I looked through the lens that the white marks against the tarmac looked like American Abstract Expressionist paintings – no-one's in particular, but they just reminded me of paintings and you could see the gesture even though they were made with stencils. And so I photographed a sequence of these road markings and they varied according to whether they were just indicating the bay or ending the zone and so on. These became part of the lecture, to show that even if you were just standing looking down at the pavement, there might be something in it for you. It was implicit in the slide show.

Many years later, living in the Smithfield area, I became interested in the proliferation of road markings and conceived the idea that within this limited subject there was an equivalence of a historic development from primitive to Classic to Baroque. First we had white lines, then yellow. More recently they introduced red. It's as though at first we are being asked, then told, and then shouted at, and it makes an interesting little narrative.

Opposite Charterhouse Square, London, 2017

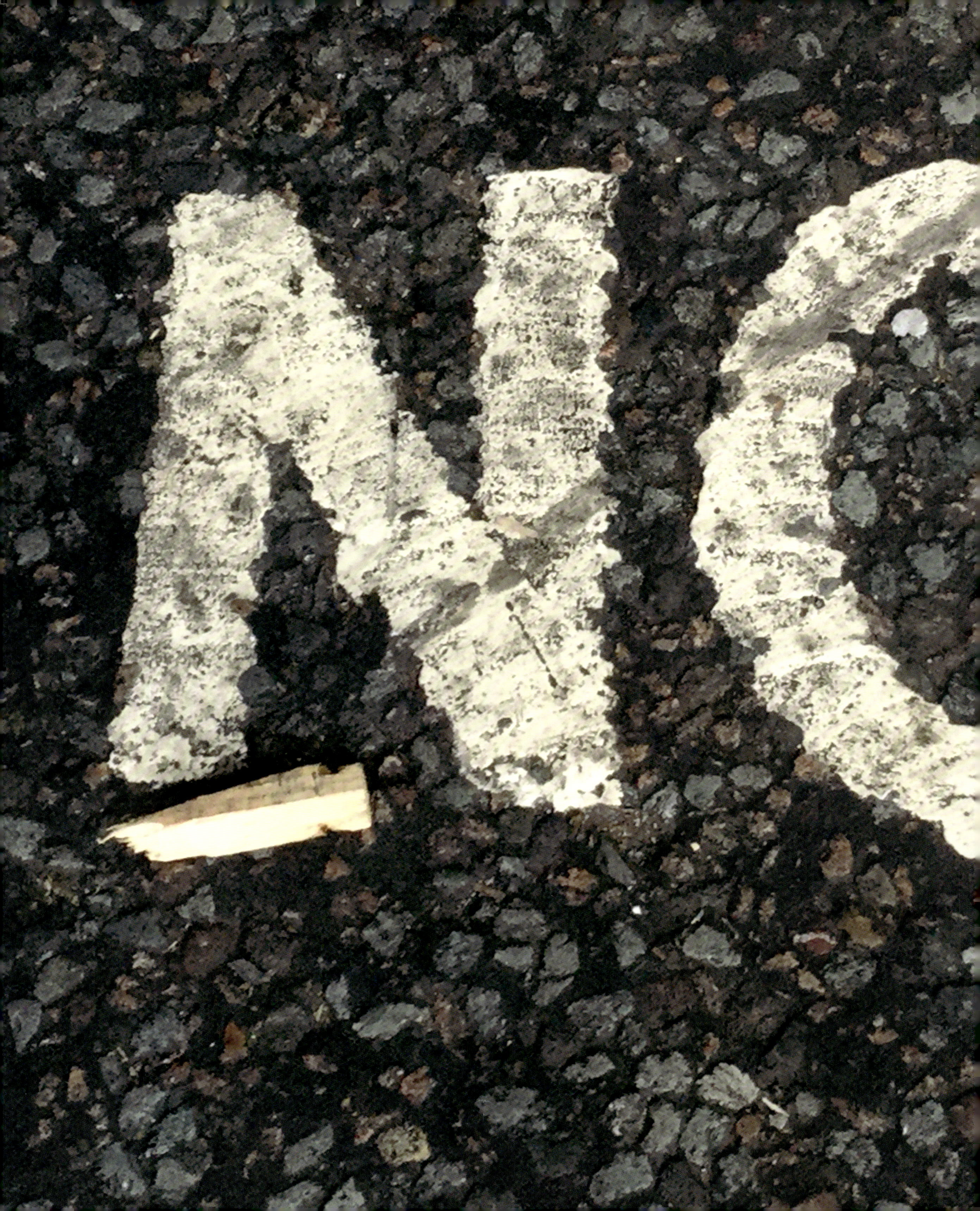

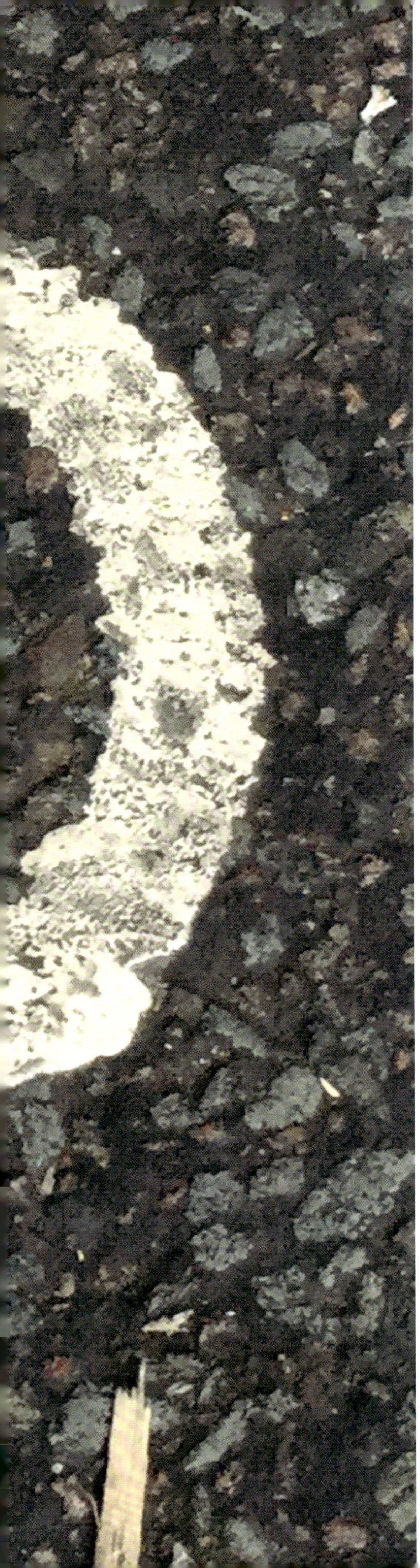

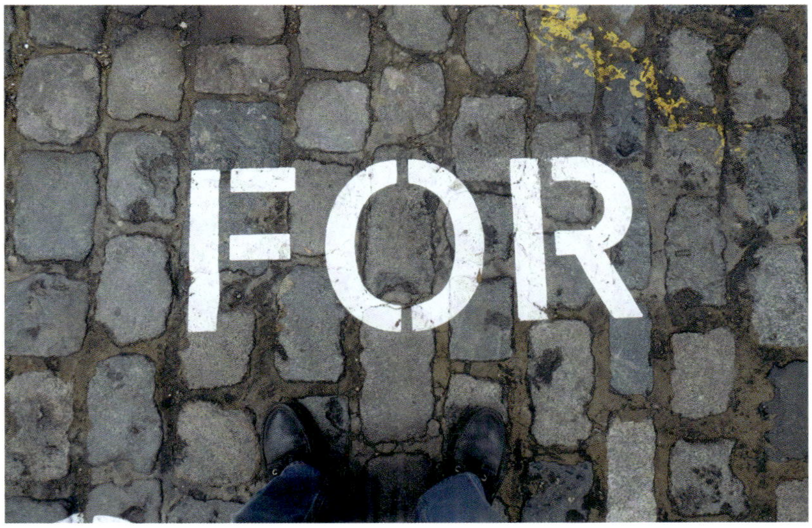

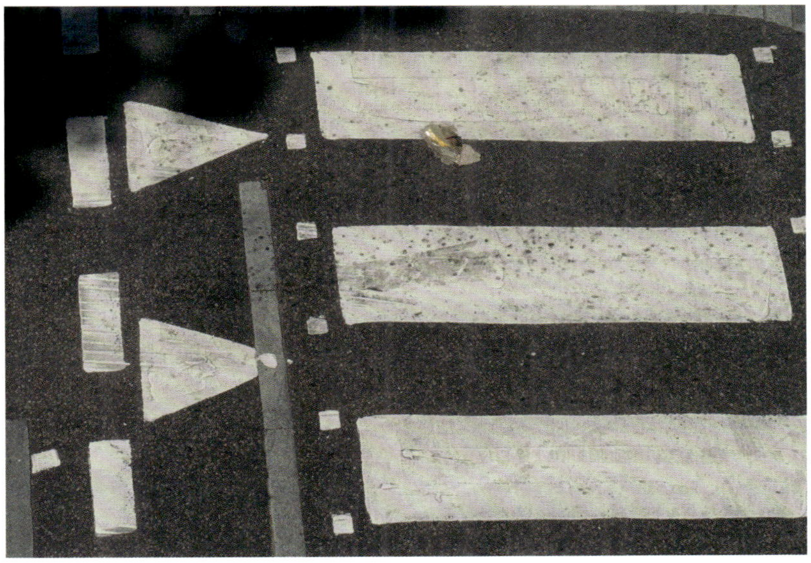

Left Smithfield, London, 2014
Top Smithfield, London, 2014
Above Charterhouse Square, London, 2017

Above Smithfield, London, 2017
Opposite London, 2017

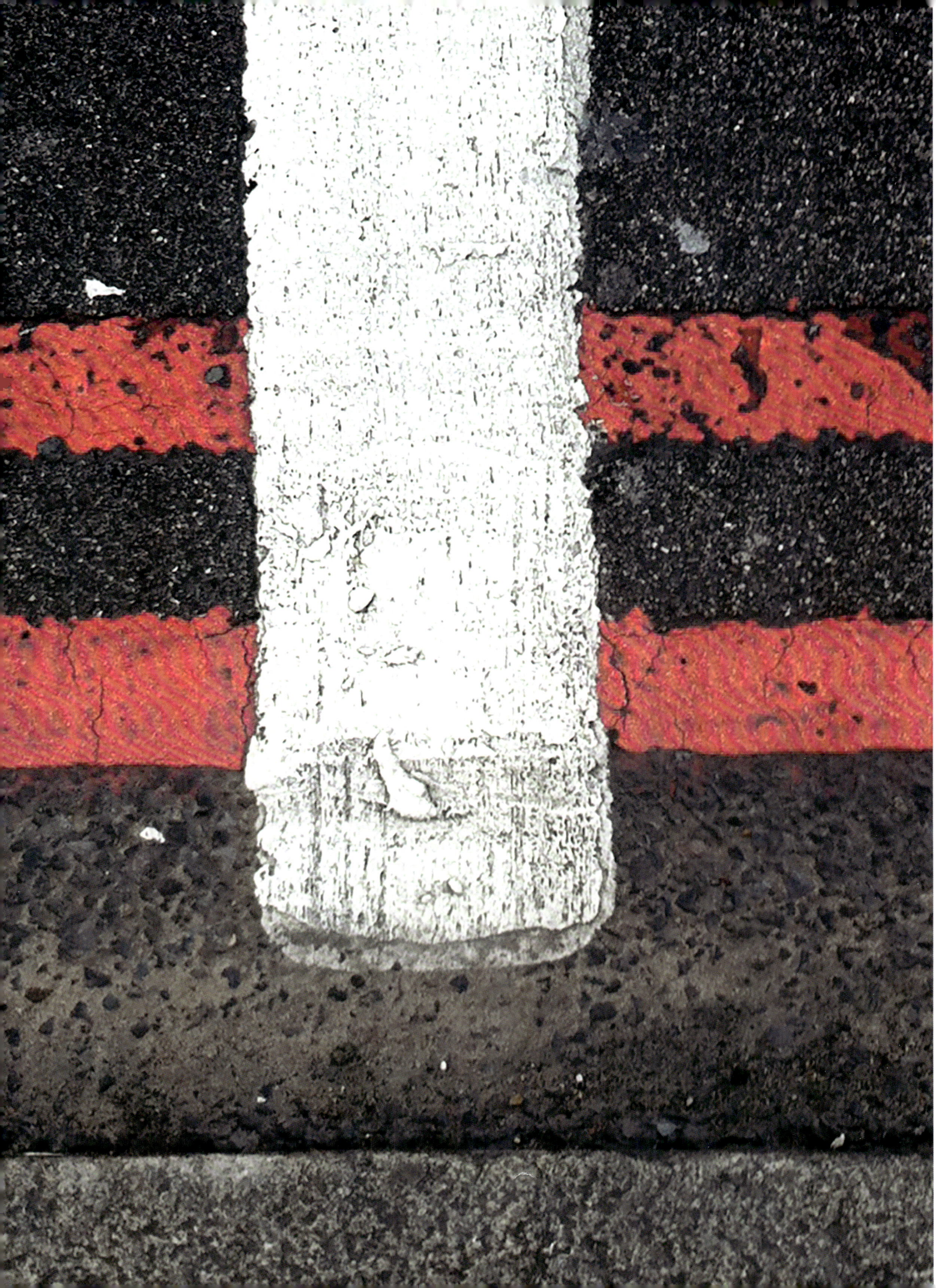

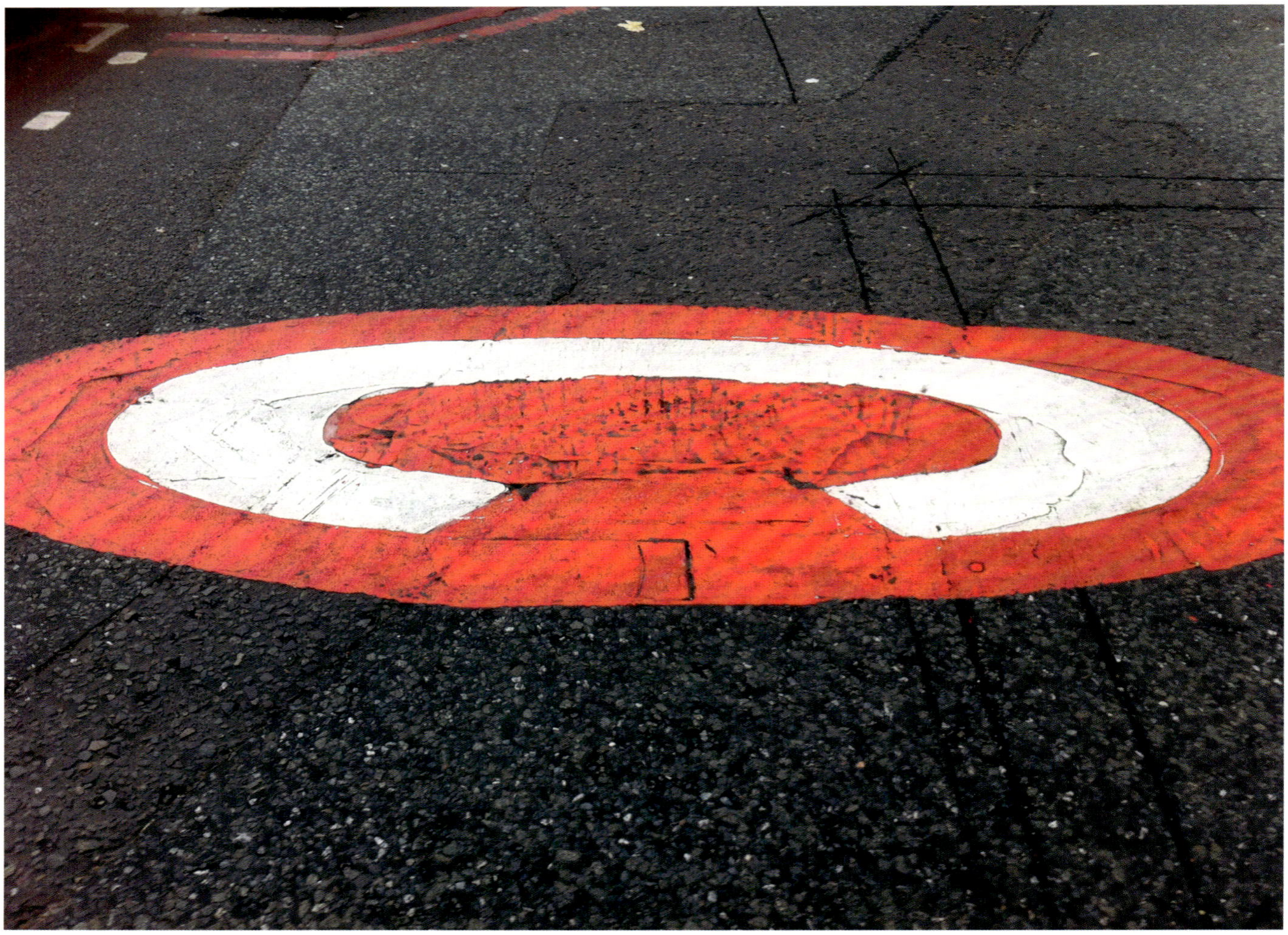

Marylebone, London, 2017

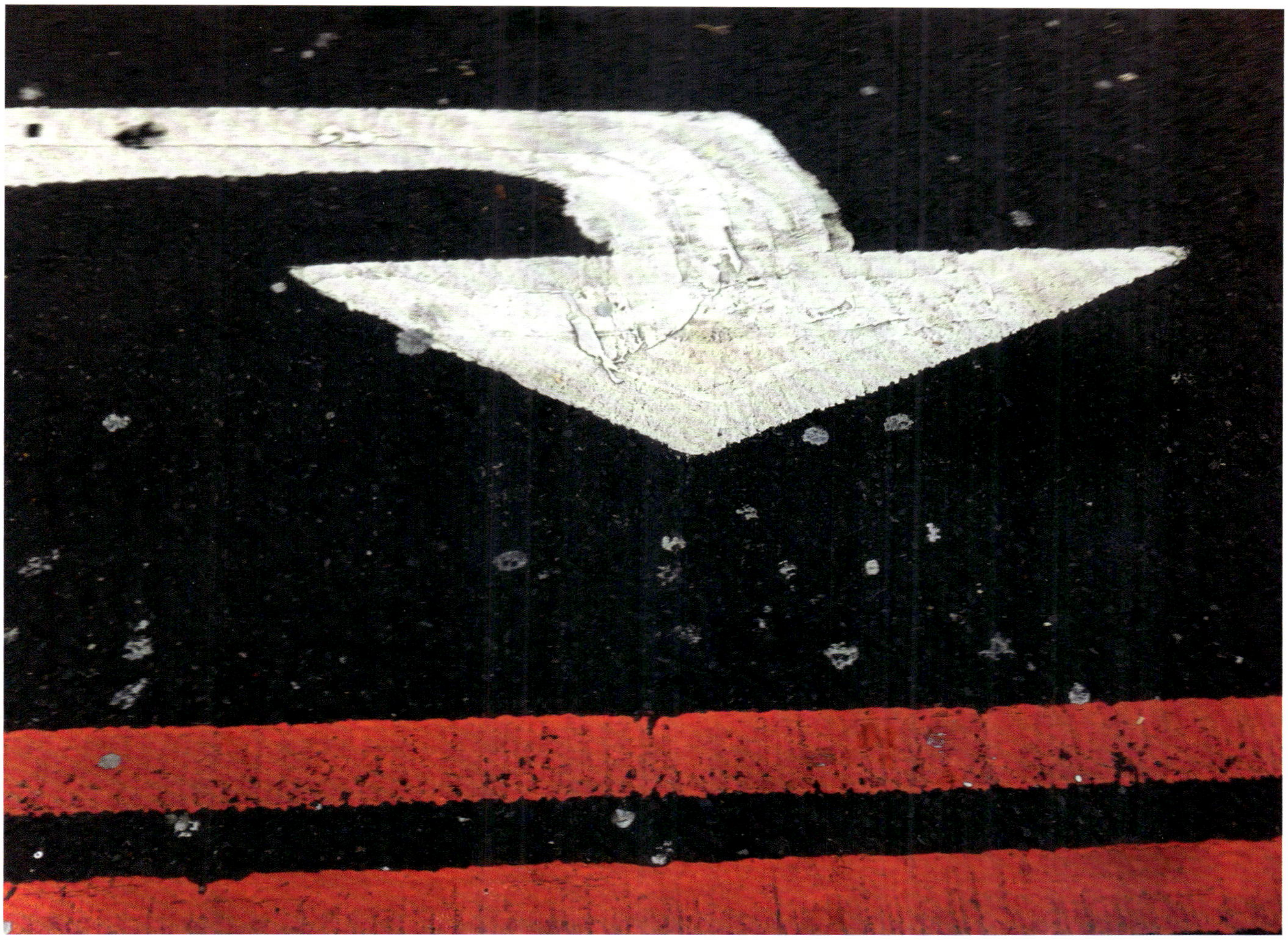

London, 2017

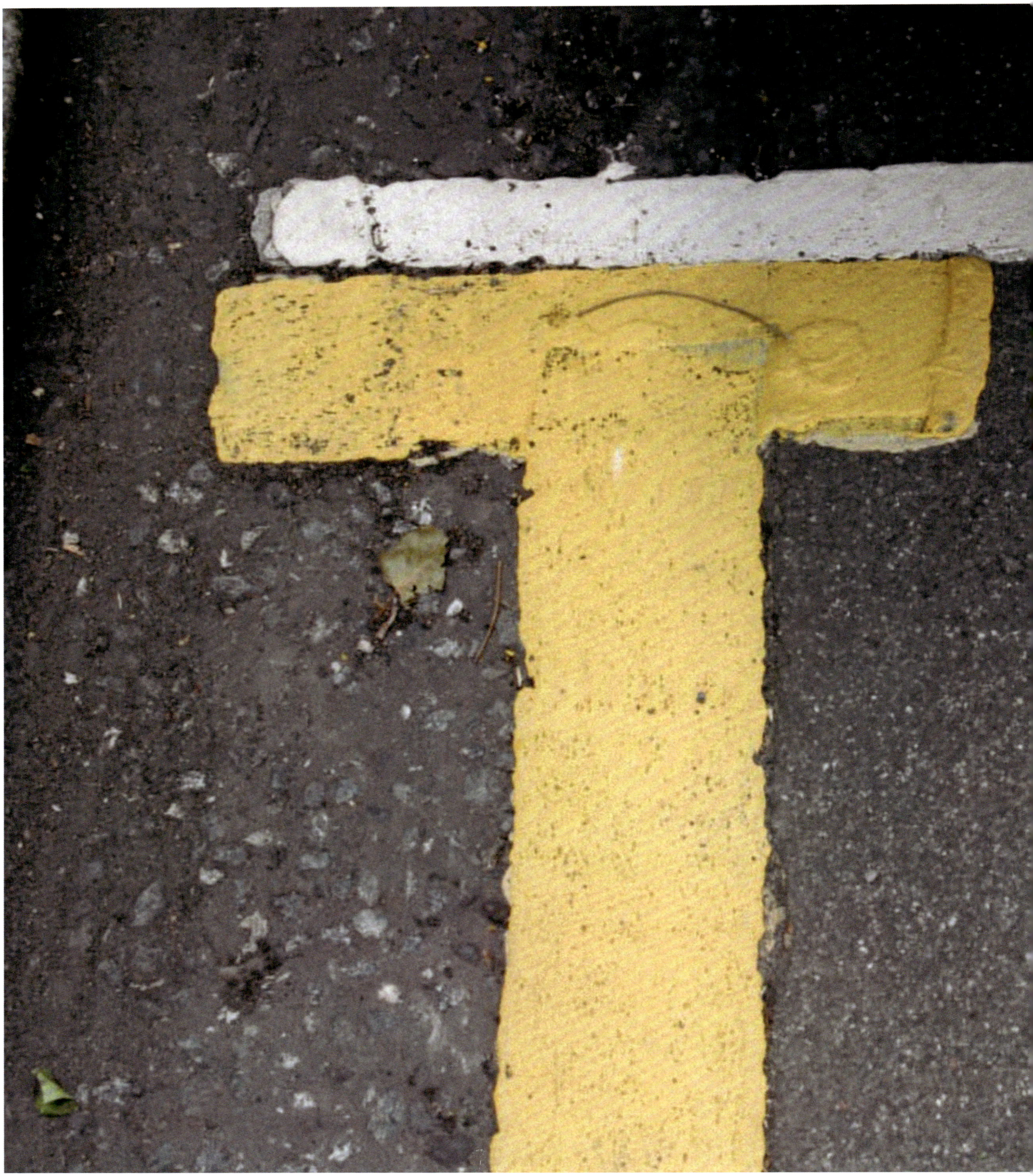

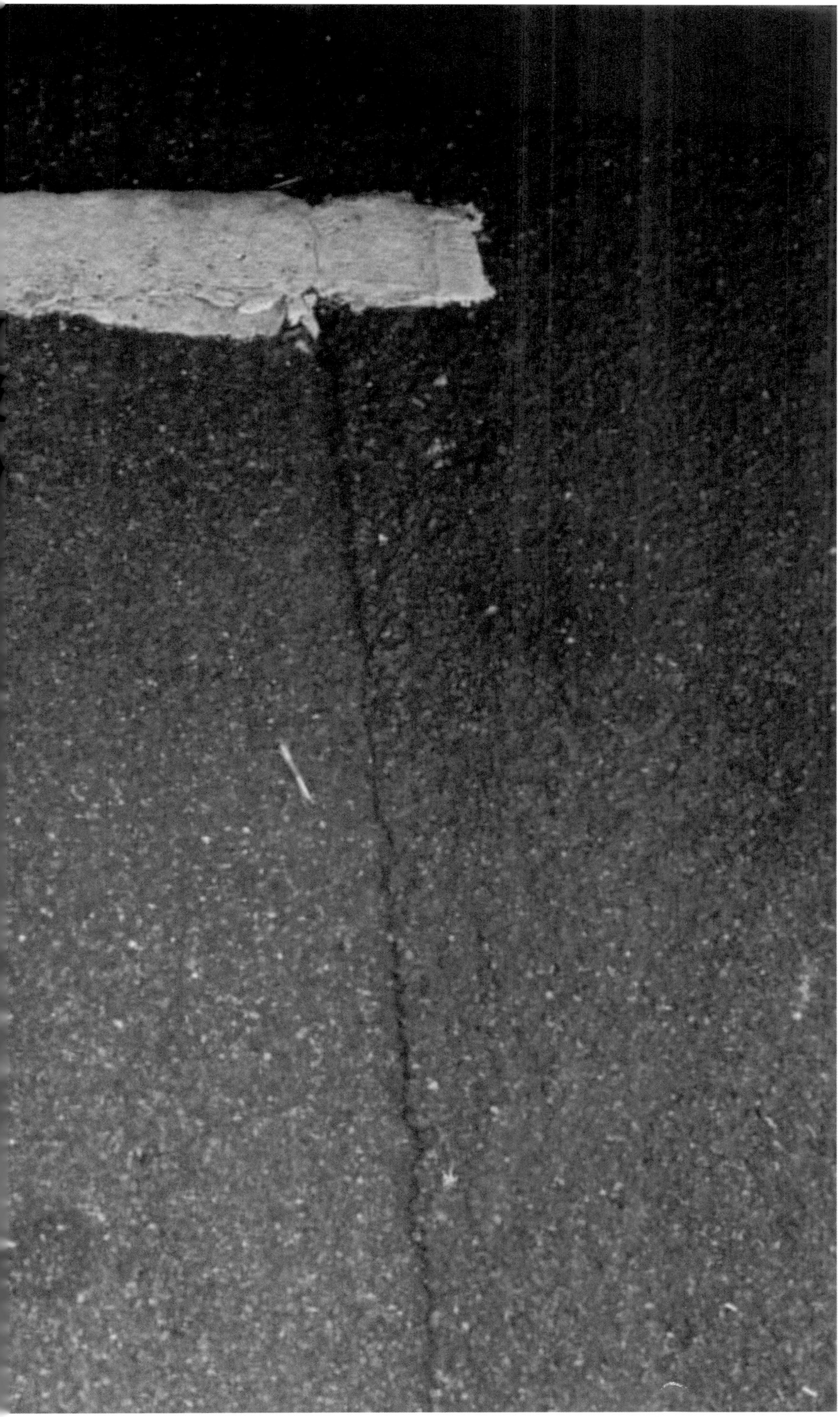

Smithfield, London, 2017

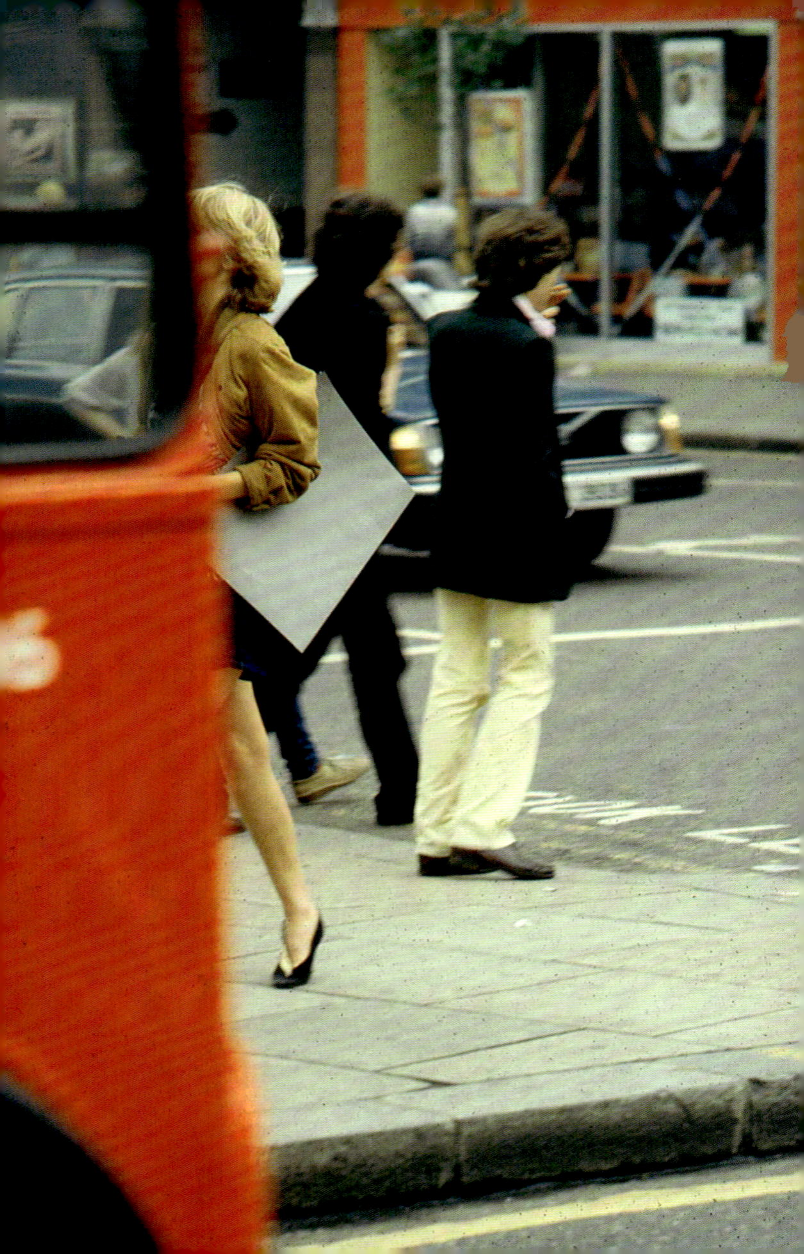

Out and about

When I was an art student, one of the things we learned about was architecture and you would learn to differentiate between the 17th century and the Gothic, or whatever it might be, and I really got into that. I discovered that being interested in your environment animates a lot of your time on the street or on the road, which otherwise is spent just getting from A to B. I have done a fair amount of travelling at one time or another. My first big trip was the opportunity I had to drive around America when I first went there. That was in the mid-Sixties. I was there for about eighteen months, living in New York, and I made a three-month road trip with Peter Phillips, an artist from the college, a Pop artist, who was in New York at the same time. He was there on a Harkness Fellowship, during which you were obliged to travel outside of your chosen place of residence for three months and for which they gave you a car – for free. We split the petrol and made the most of this opportunity.

Our route was partly determined by the prevalent politics. This was the time of Martin Luther King and the Civil Rights Movement. We thought we would cover the map: drive down the coast, Key West, up across New Orleans, Biloxi, across the desert, and up from San Diego was the idea and in fact we did that pretty well, but New York friends warned us: 'You're not going to go down through the South are you? They will torch the car, or vandalise it and give you a bad time.' I said, 'Oh no, we're British.' They collapsed in laughter at our naivety. So we stuck to the coast road and consequently the part of America I regretted not seeing was around Alabama. I was very interested in the American Civil War, even as a schoolboy.

I was busy with my camera recording something which I knew only through motion pictures. These were mythical places, and we were in them. I suppose in a way the camera was a substitute for sketching. As a youngster you'd have your sketchbook and you would be sitting drawing something but the camera gave the possibility to record things that you could not possibly have sat and drawn. I could capture these sights at the click of a button.

Looking back on all the photographs I have taken in different places, including London, I can see how I am mostly drawn to the light and colours and oddities and curious juxtapositions of urban subject matter. I was brought up in suburbia, in Ealing, and Marble Arch was the railhead. London's West End was my introduction to the big city lights.

Opposite London, undated

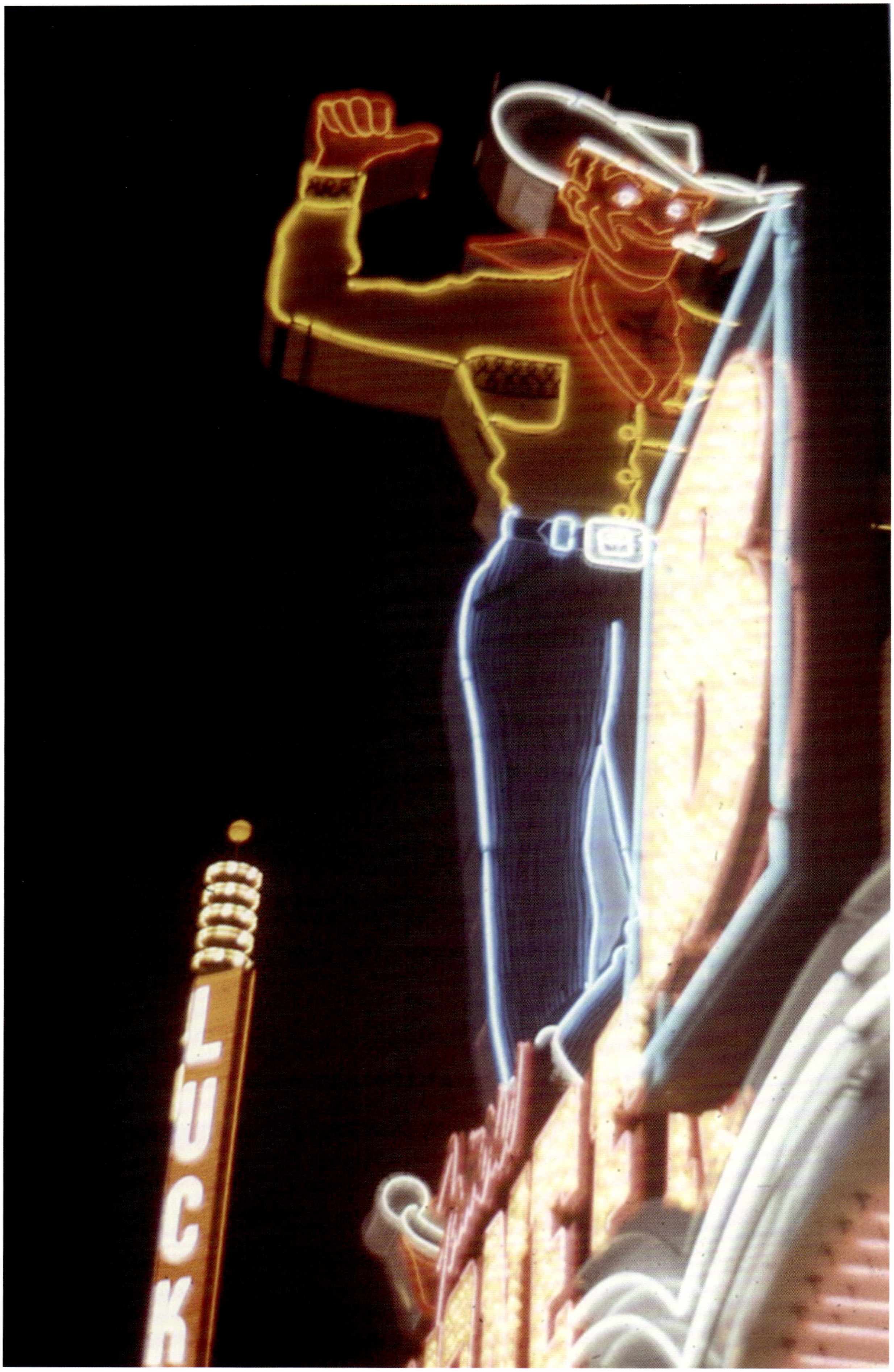
LUCK

The road trip made with artist friend Peter Phillips in the mid-Sixties provided us with an opportunity to experience the reality of America hitherto only known to us through magazines and the movies.

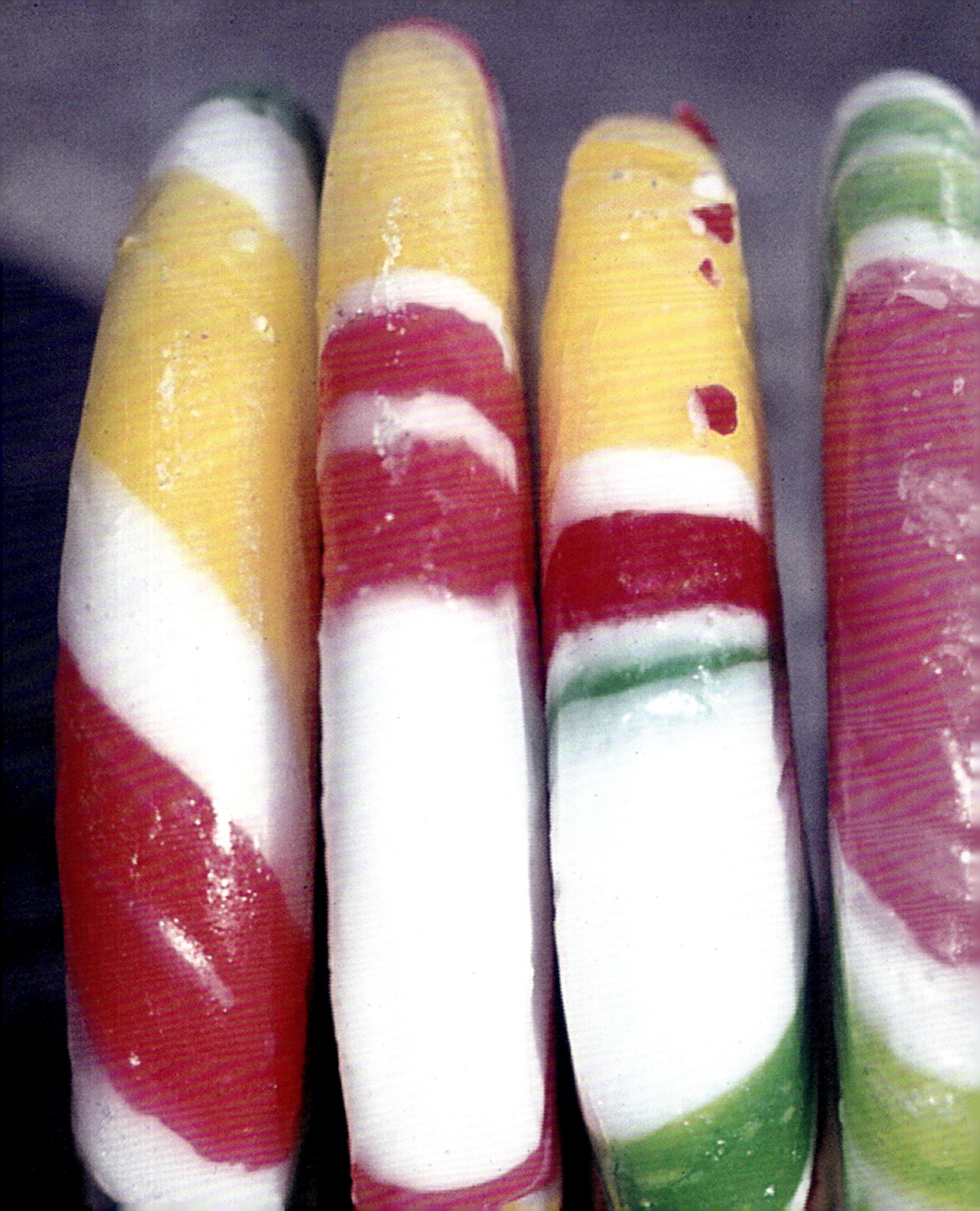

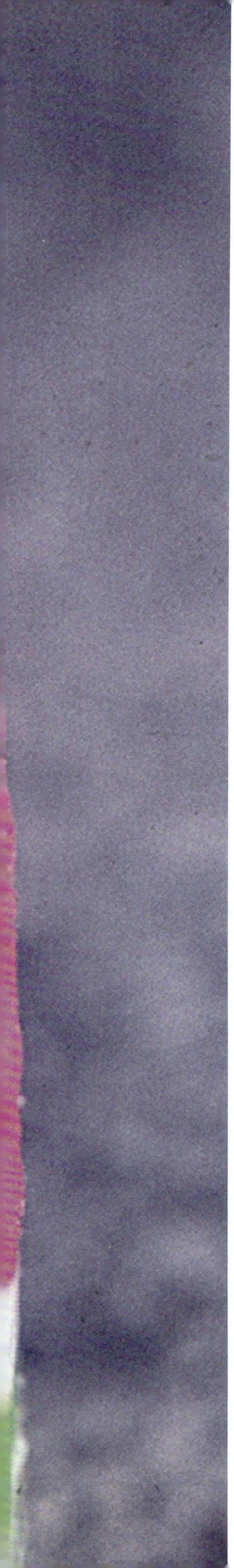

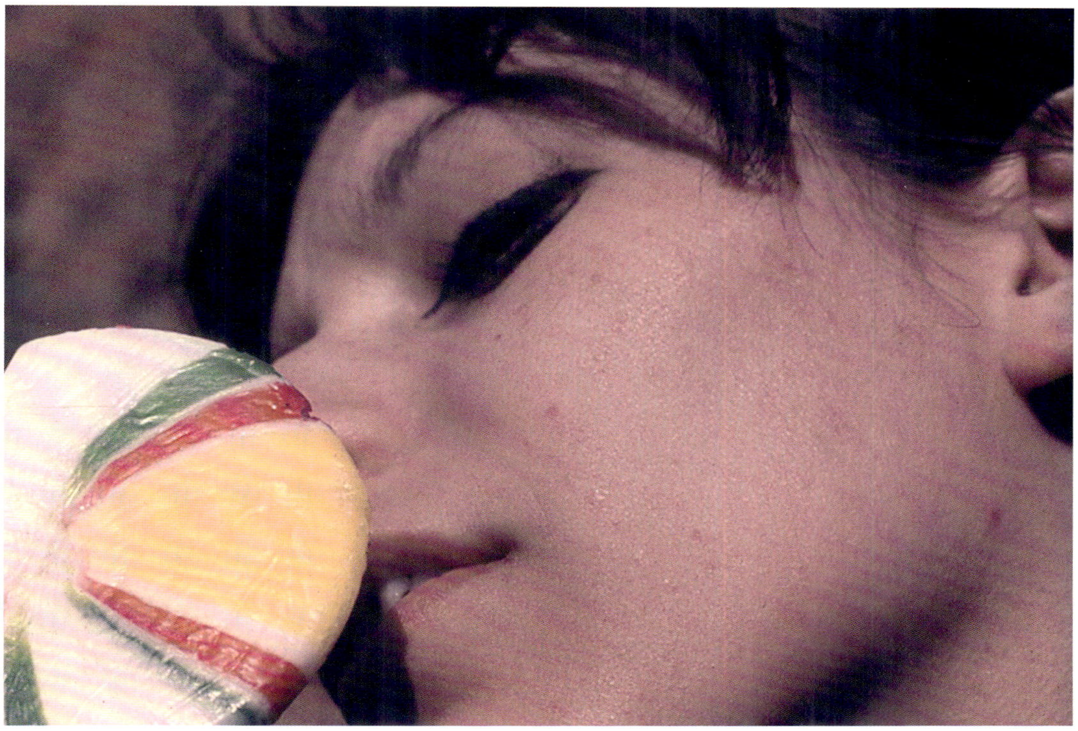

Previous pages Las Vegas, 1965
Left Lollipops, Hornsey, 1959–60
Above Devika Mehta, Hornsey, 1959–60
Overleaf Great Salt Lake, 1965

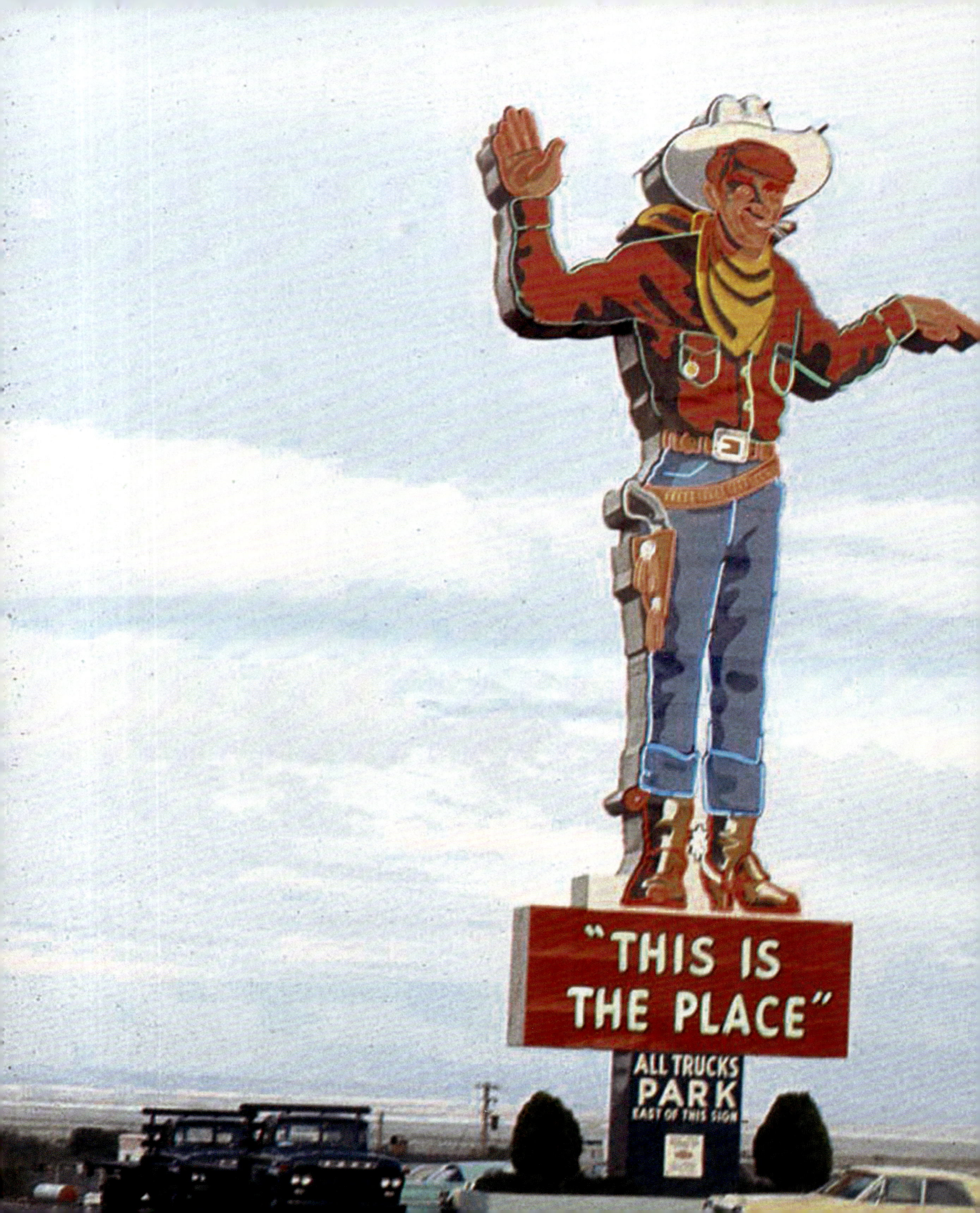
"THIS IS
THE PLACE"
ALL TRUCKS
PARK
EAST OF THIS SIGN

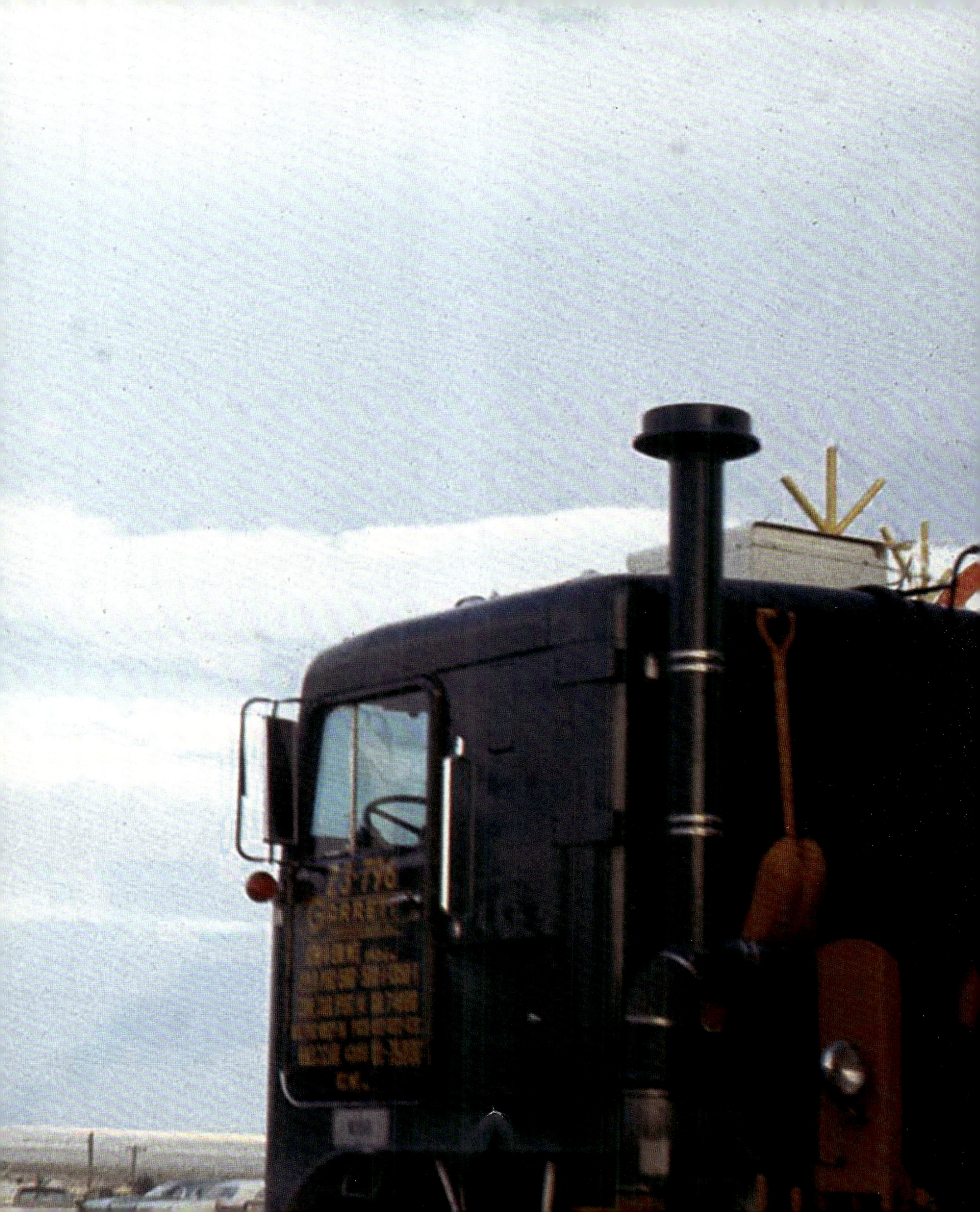

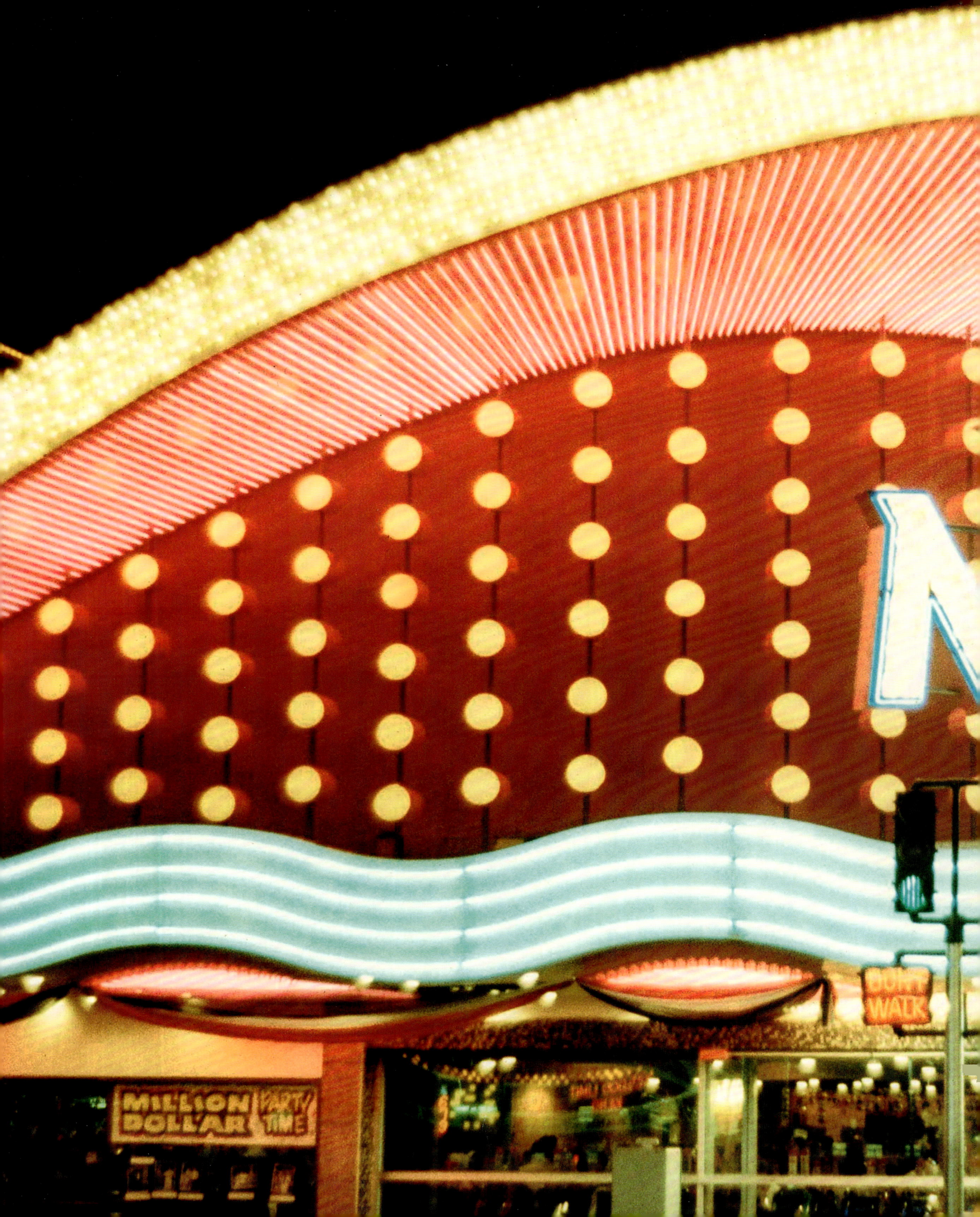
MILLION DOLLAR
PARTY TIME
WALK

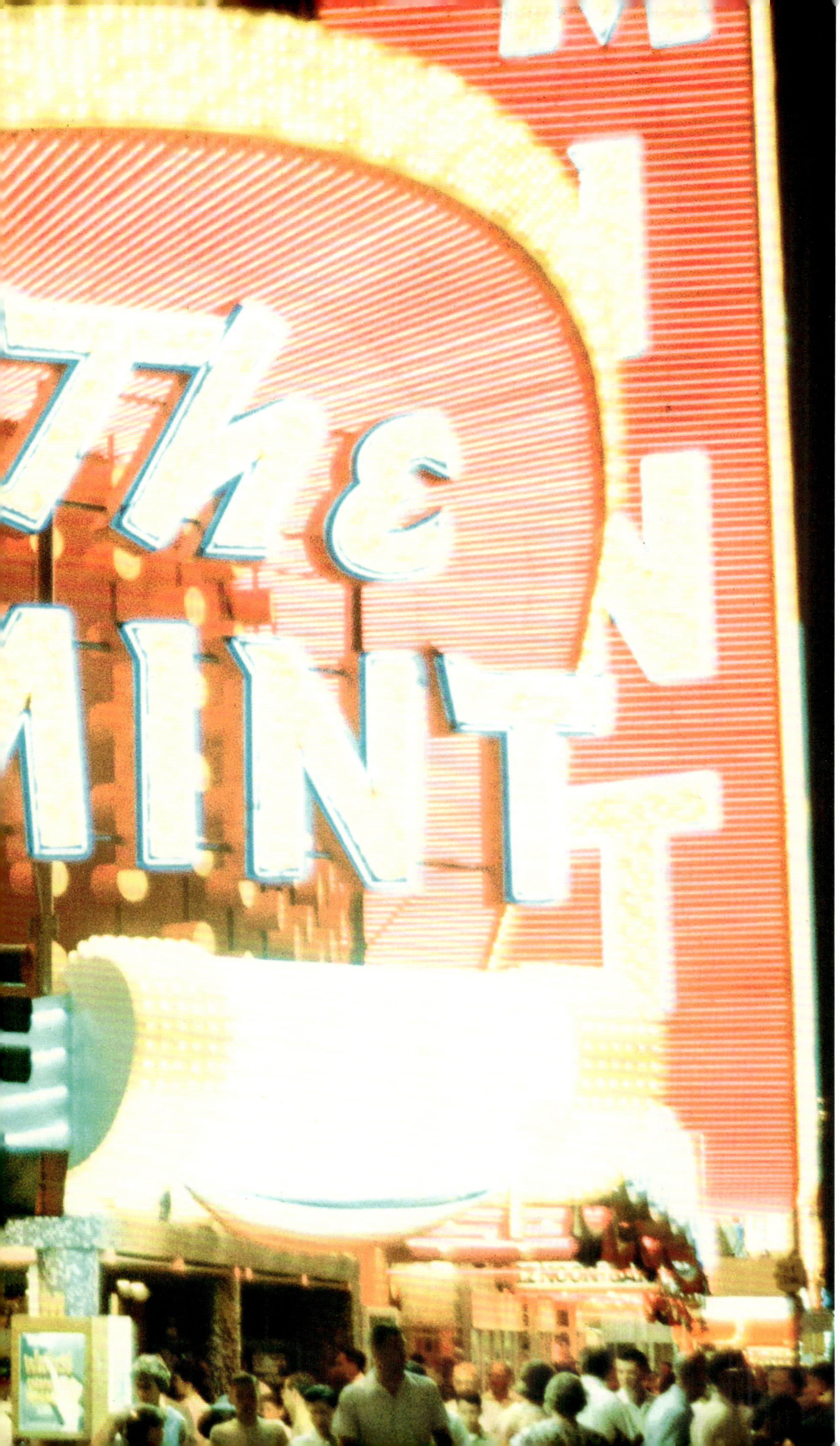

Las Vegas, 1965

> There seemed little room for personal comment in a place like Florida, known universally through films – fact and fantasy. I chose to photograph facts: the chair we sat on, the car we hired, the public park, and our motel became subjects for a suite of lithographs.

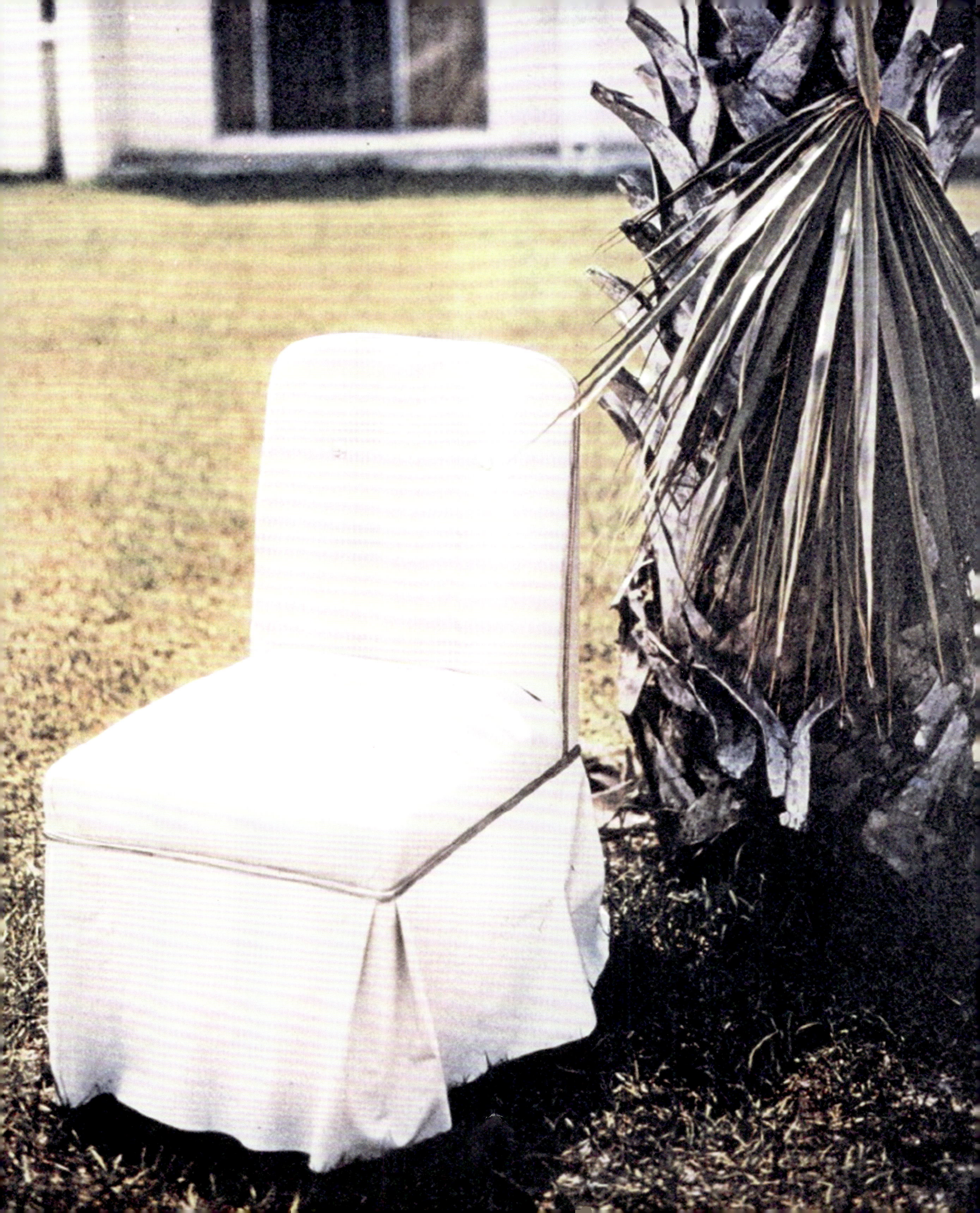

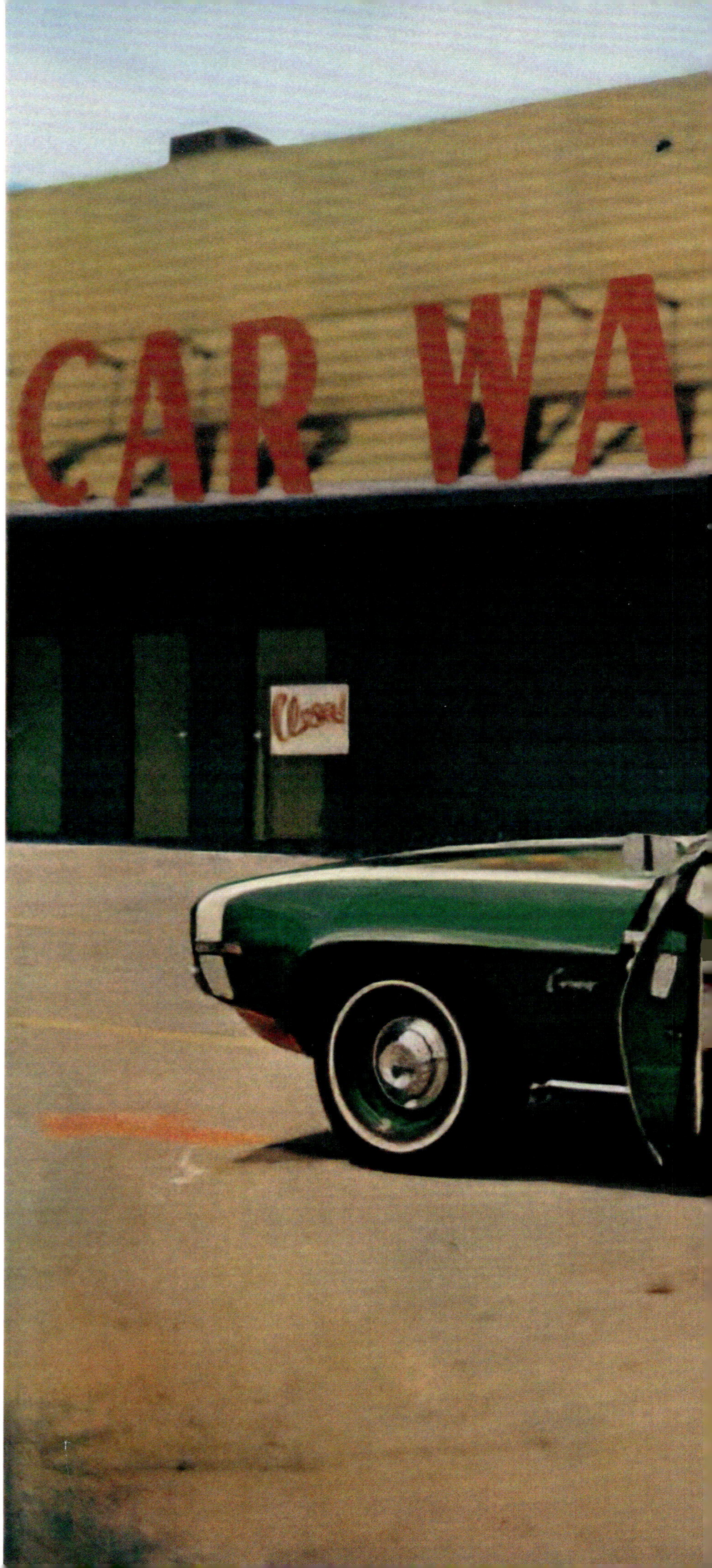

Previous page 'The Chair We Sat On', Florida Suite, 1969
Right 'The Car We Drove', Florida Suite, 1969

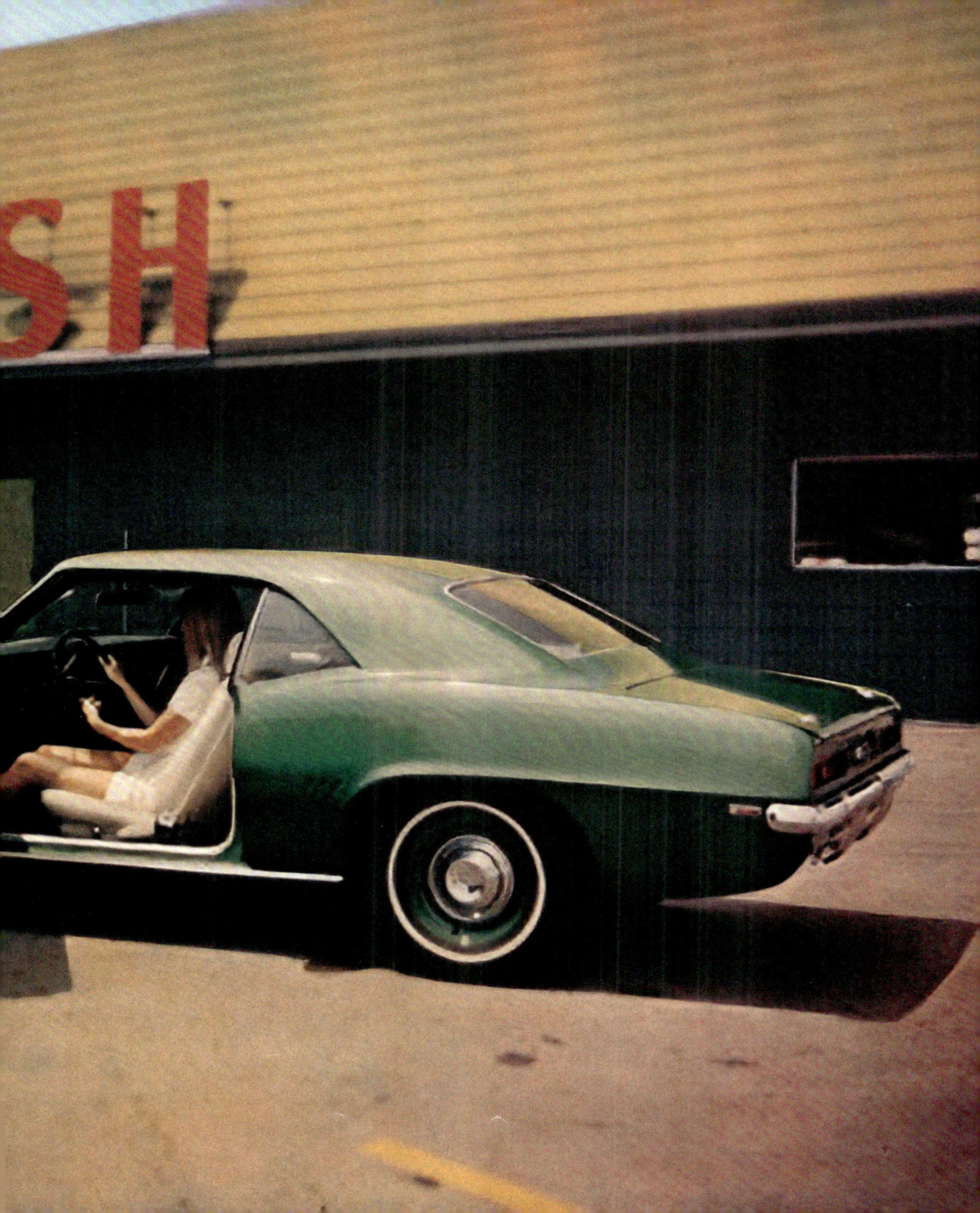

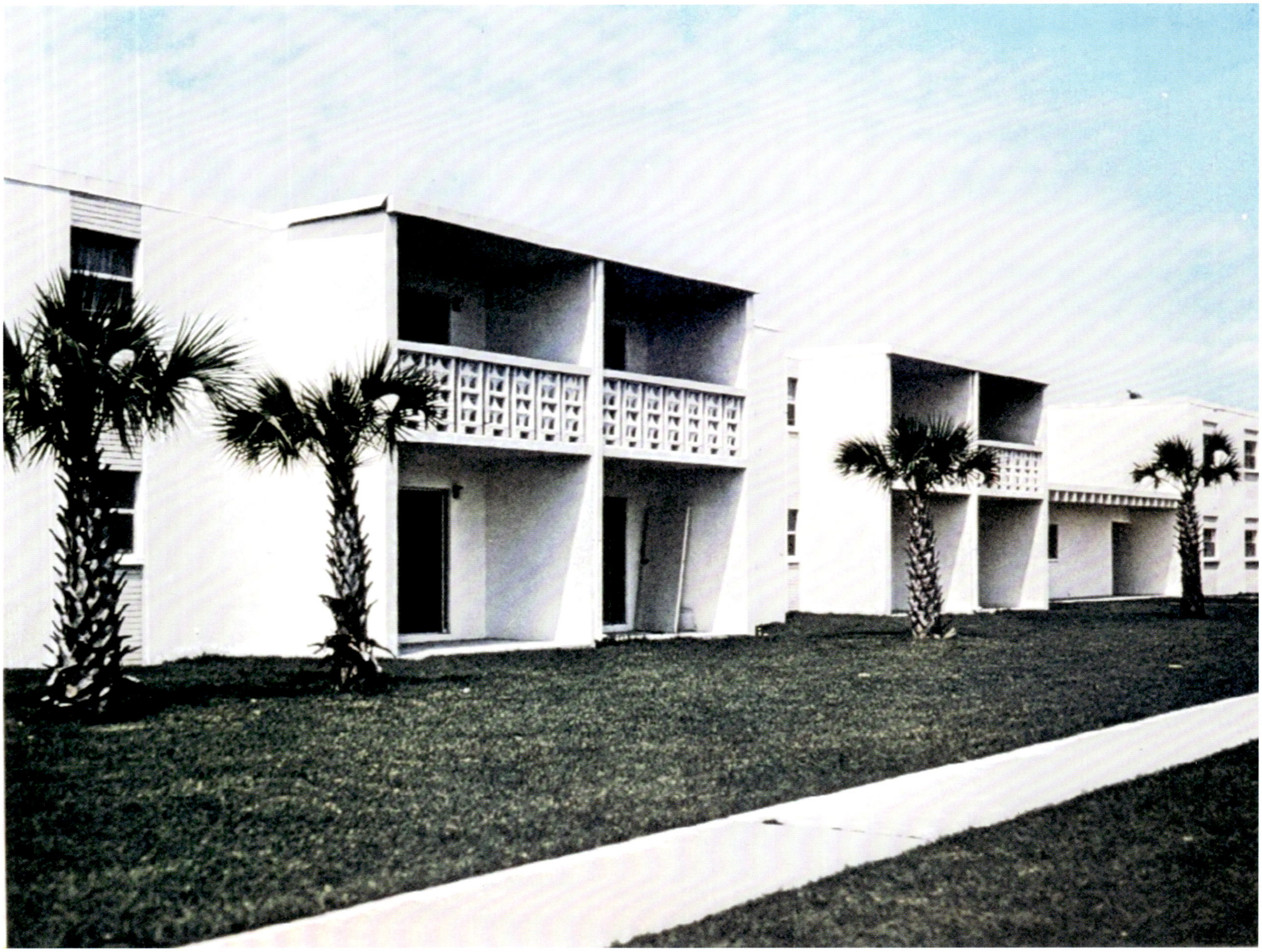

'The Flat We Lived In', Florida Suite, 1969

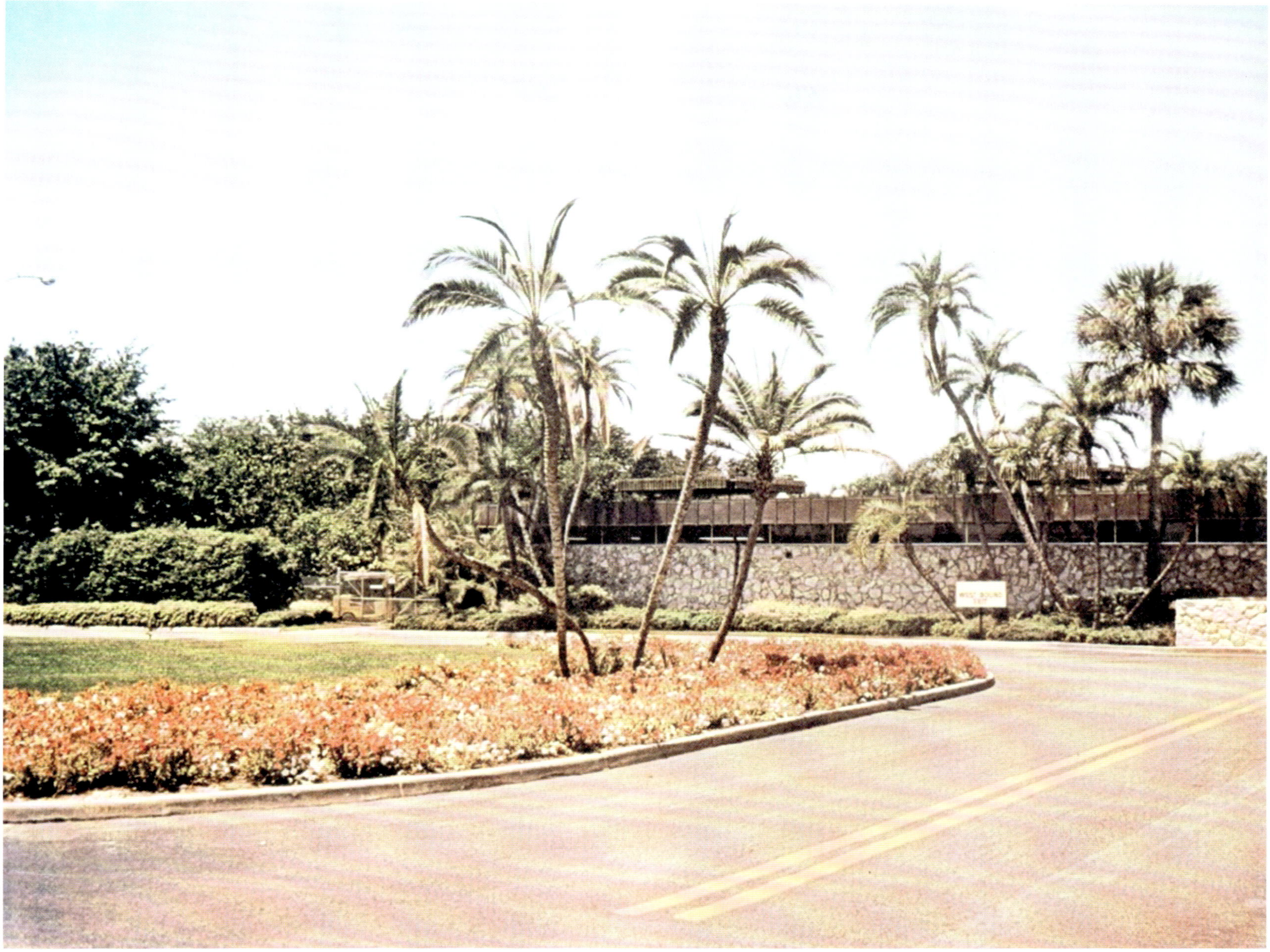

Above 'The Park We Went To', Florida Suite, 1969
Overleaf Florida architecture, 2015

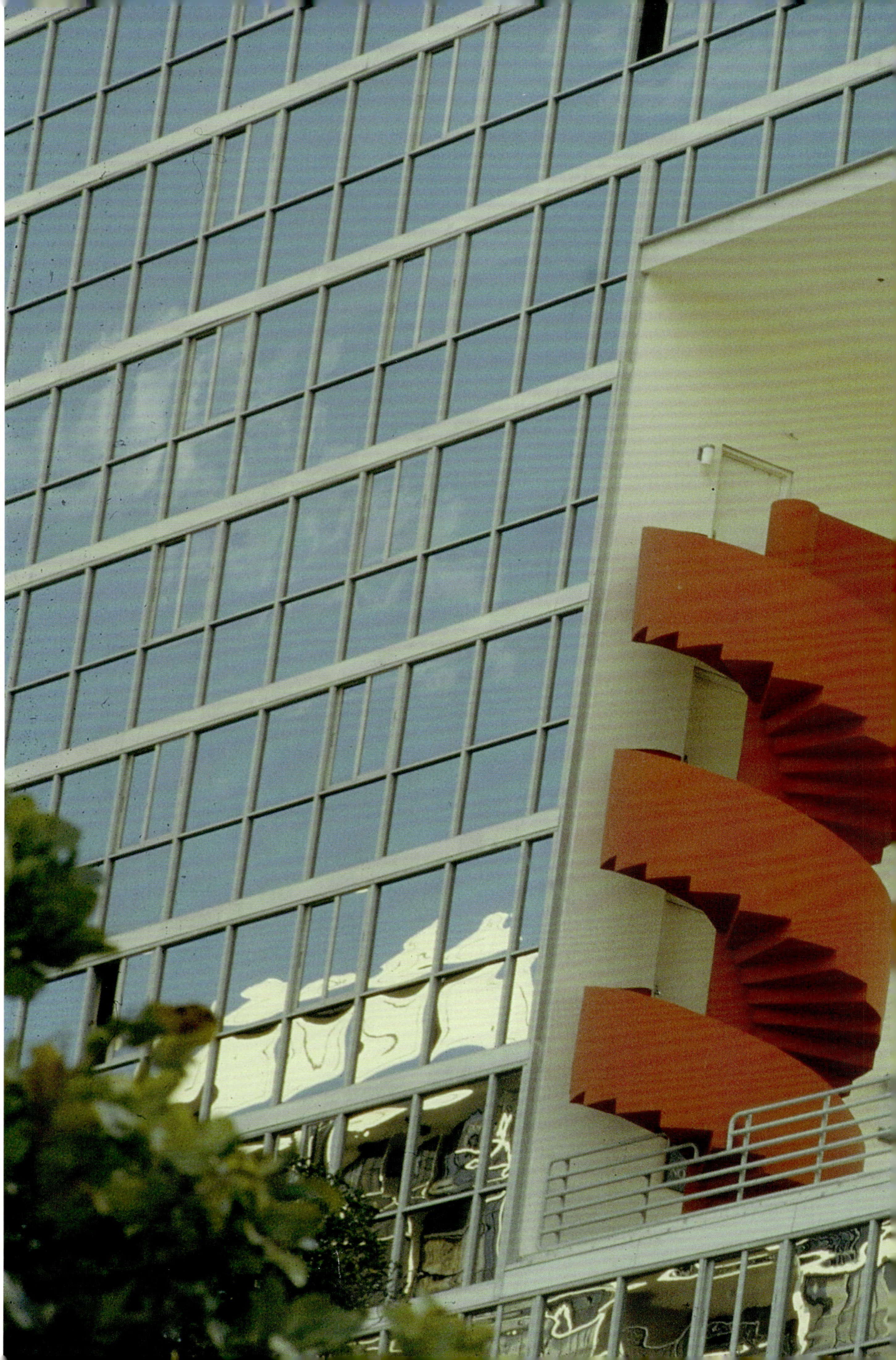

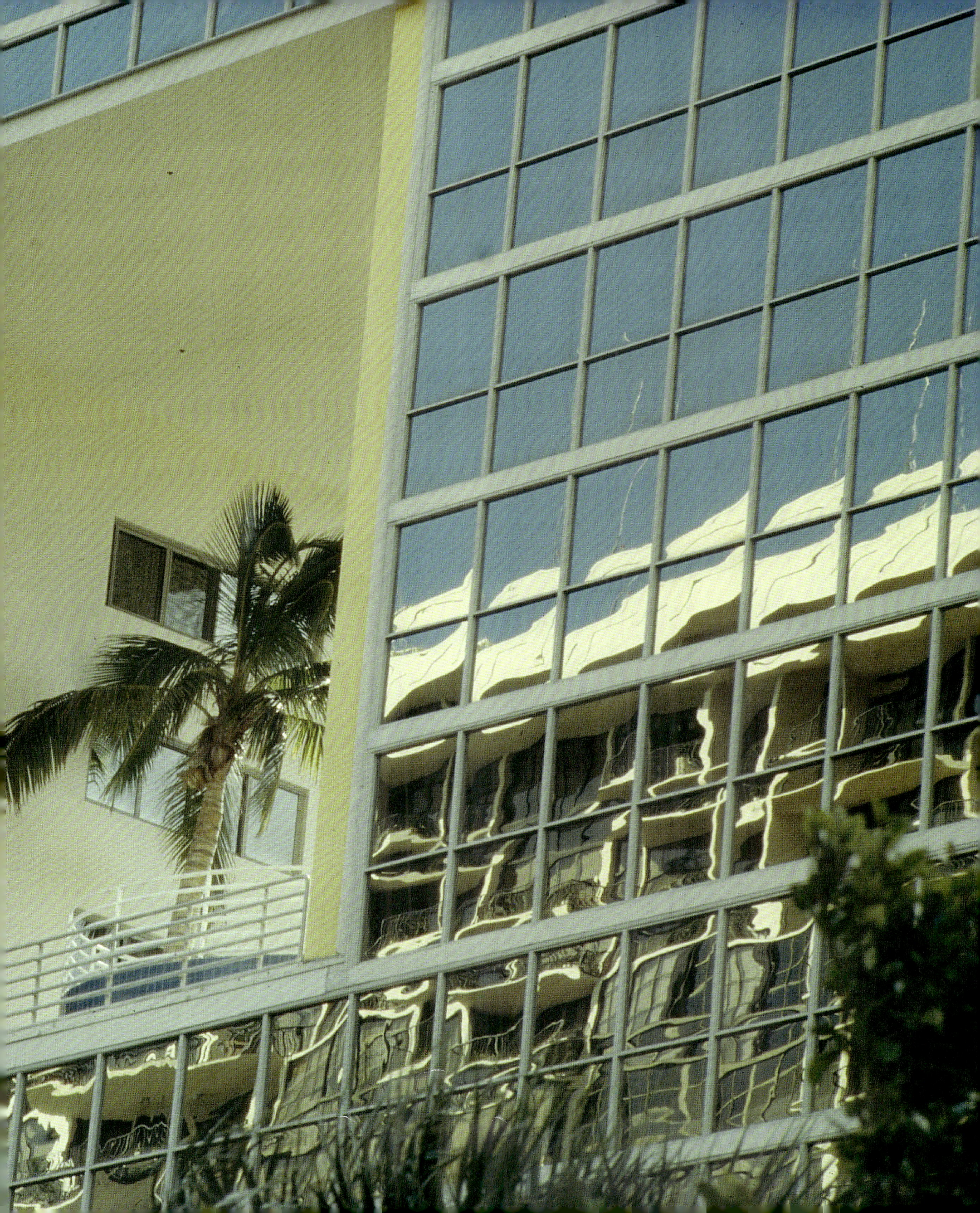

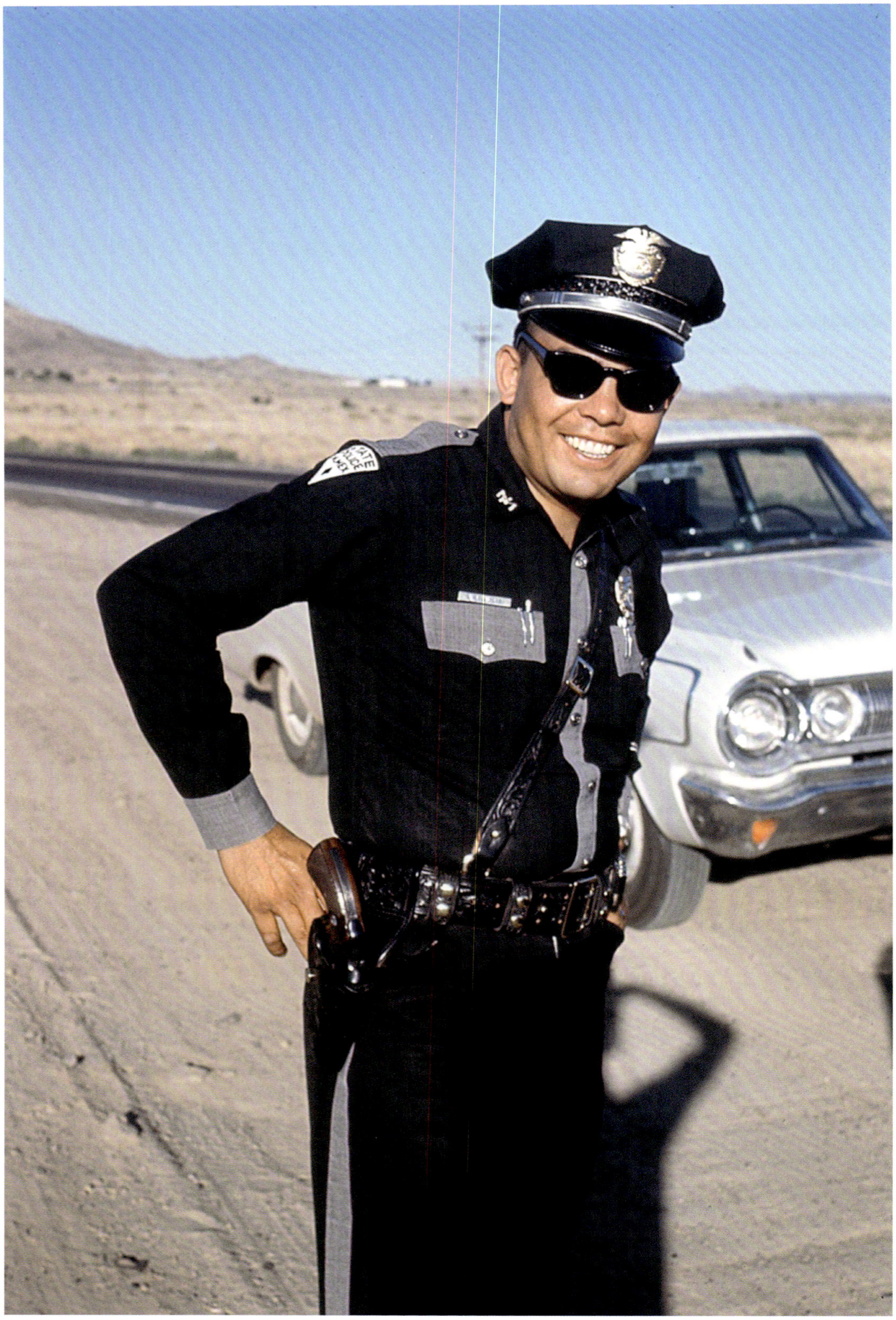

New Mexico, 1965

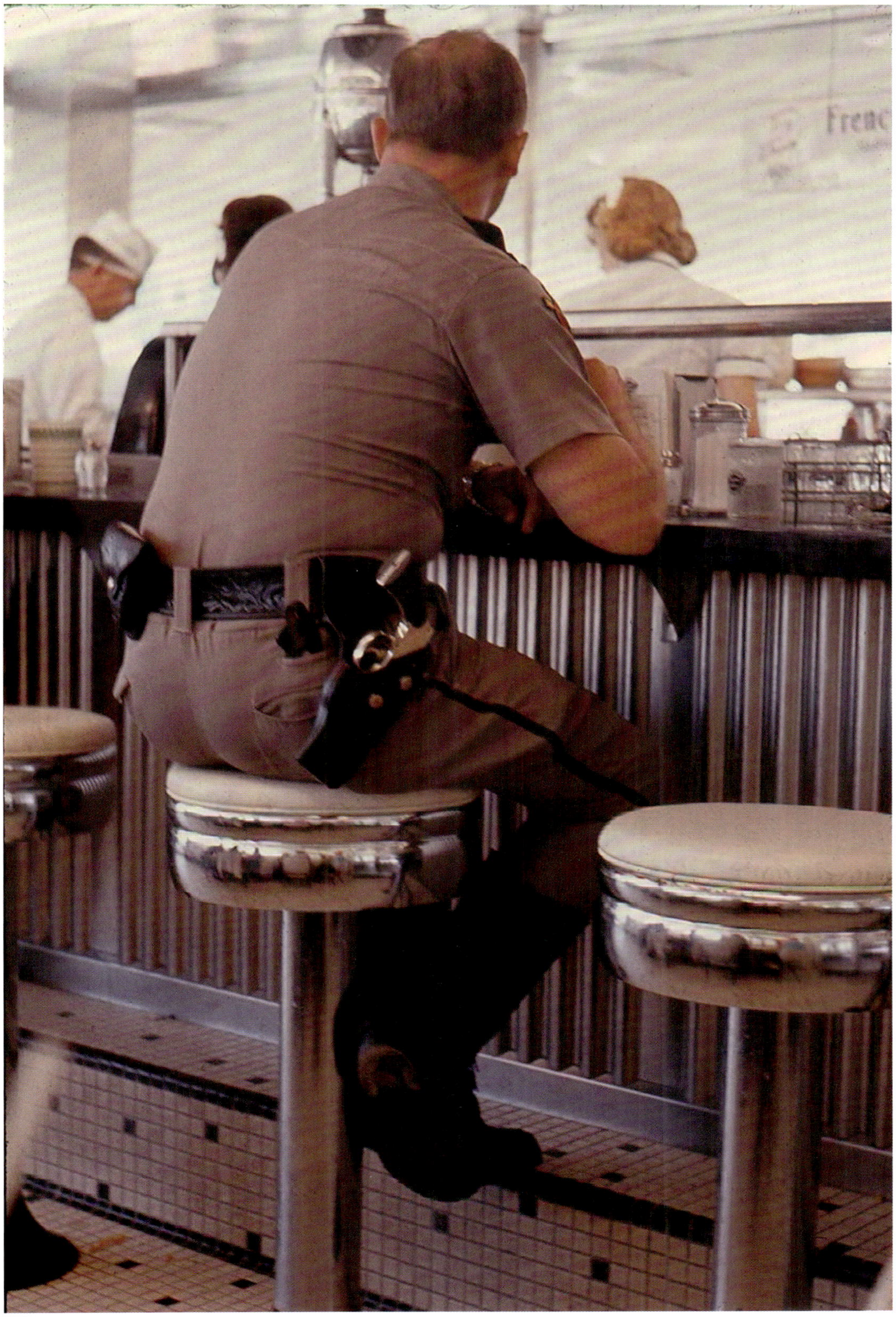

Daytona, 1965

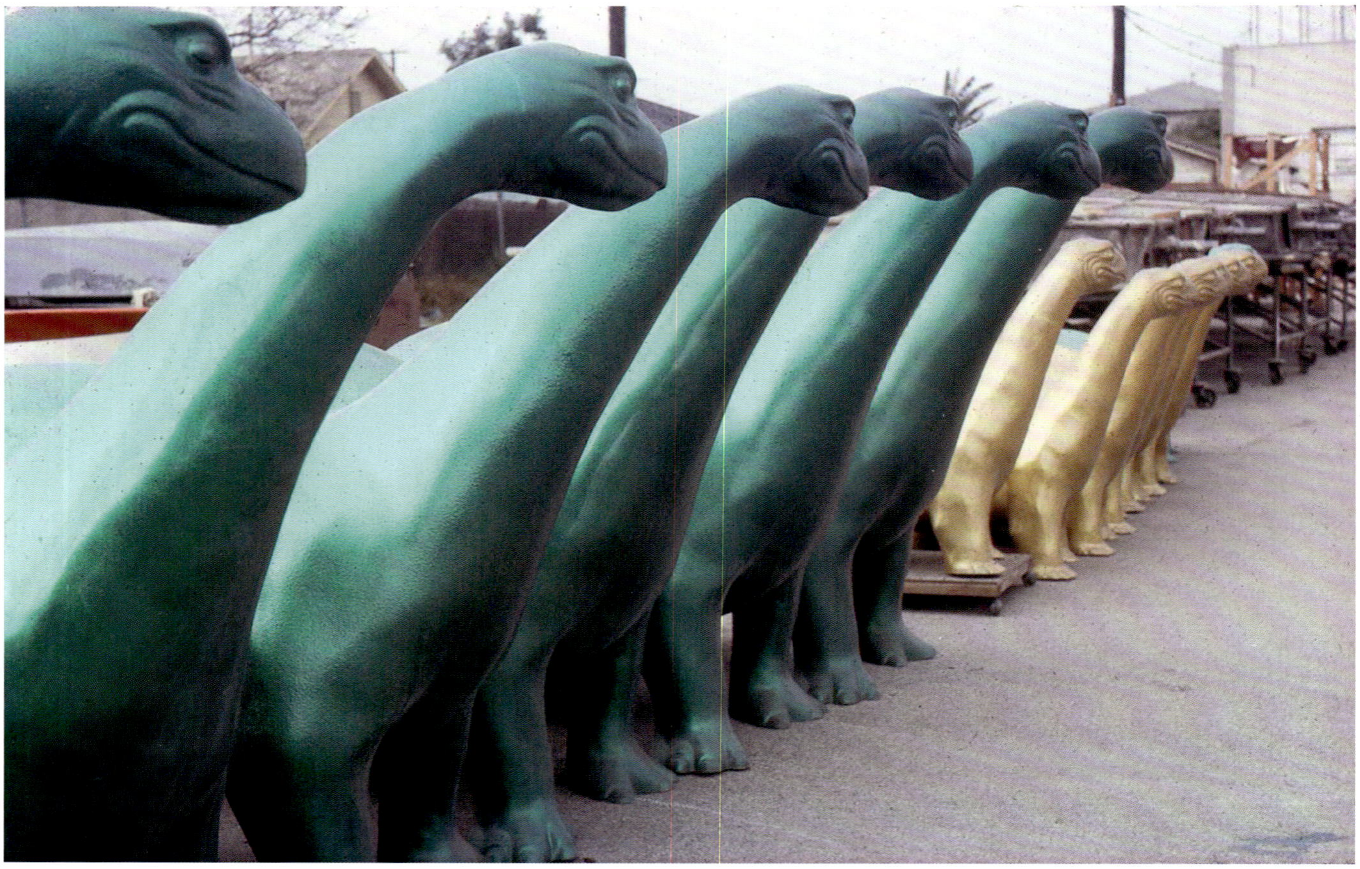

Above Sinclair Petrol dinosaur, Los Angeles Fabricators, 1965
Opposite Fort Lauderdale, en route to Miami, 1965
Overleaf Los Angeles, 1972; Florida 1965
Page 123 Los Angeles, 1965; Key Biscayne, 1981

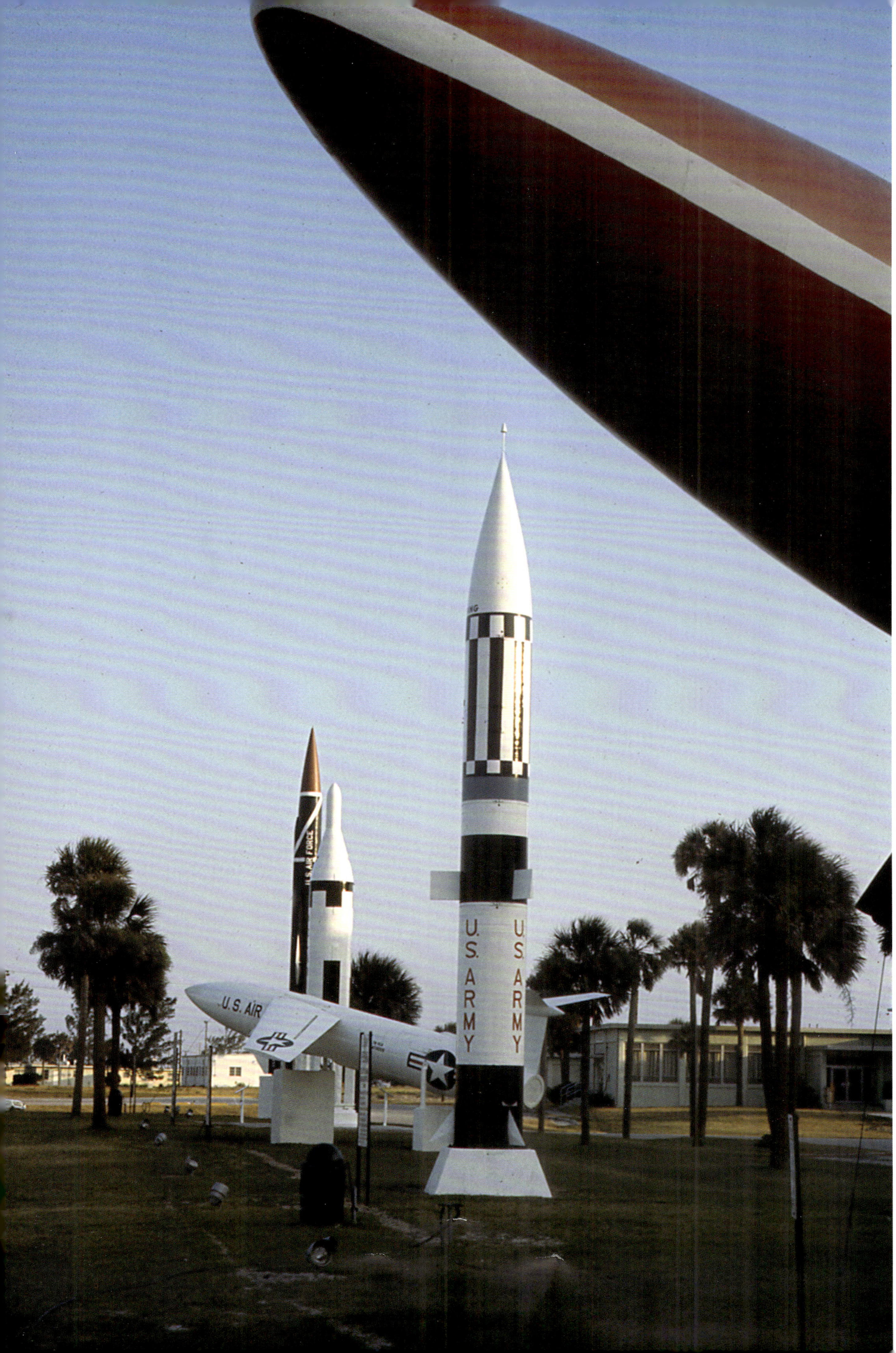
U.S. ARMY
U.S. ARMY
U.S. AIR

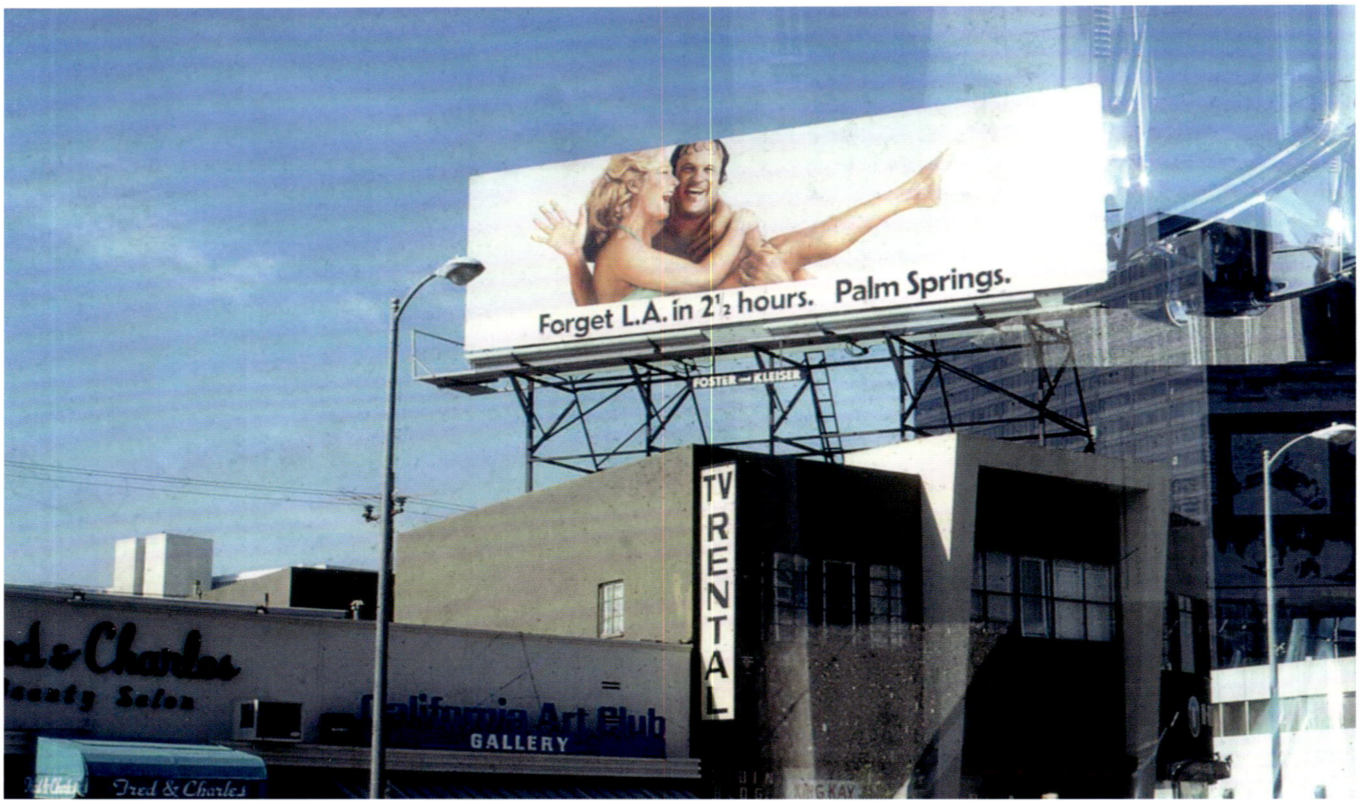
Forget L.A. in 2½ hours. Palm Springs.
TV RENTAL
California Art Club
GALLERY
Fred & Charles

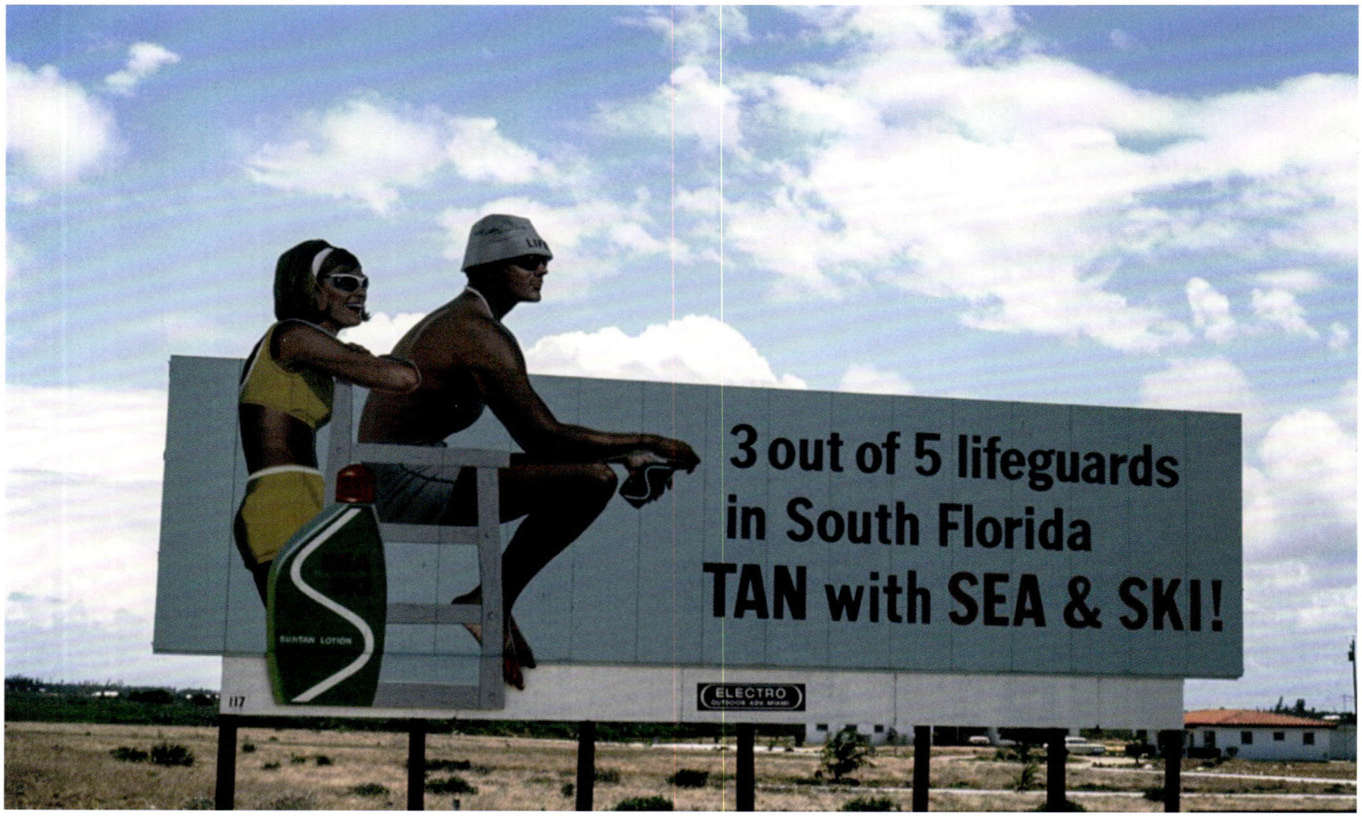
3 out of 5 lifeguards
in South Florida
TAN with SEA & SKI!
ELECTRO

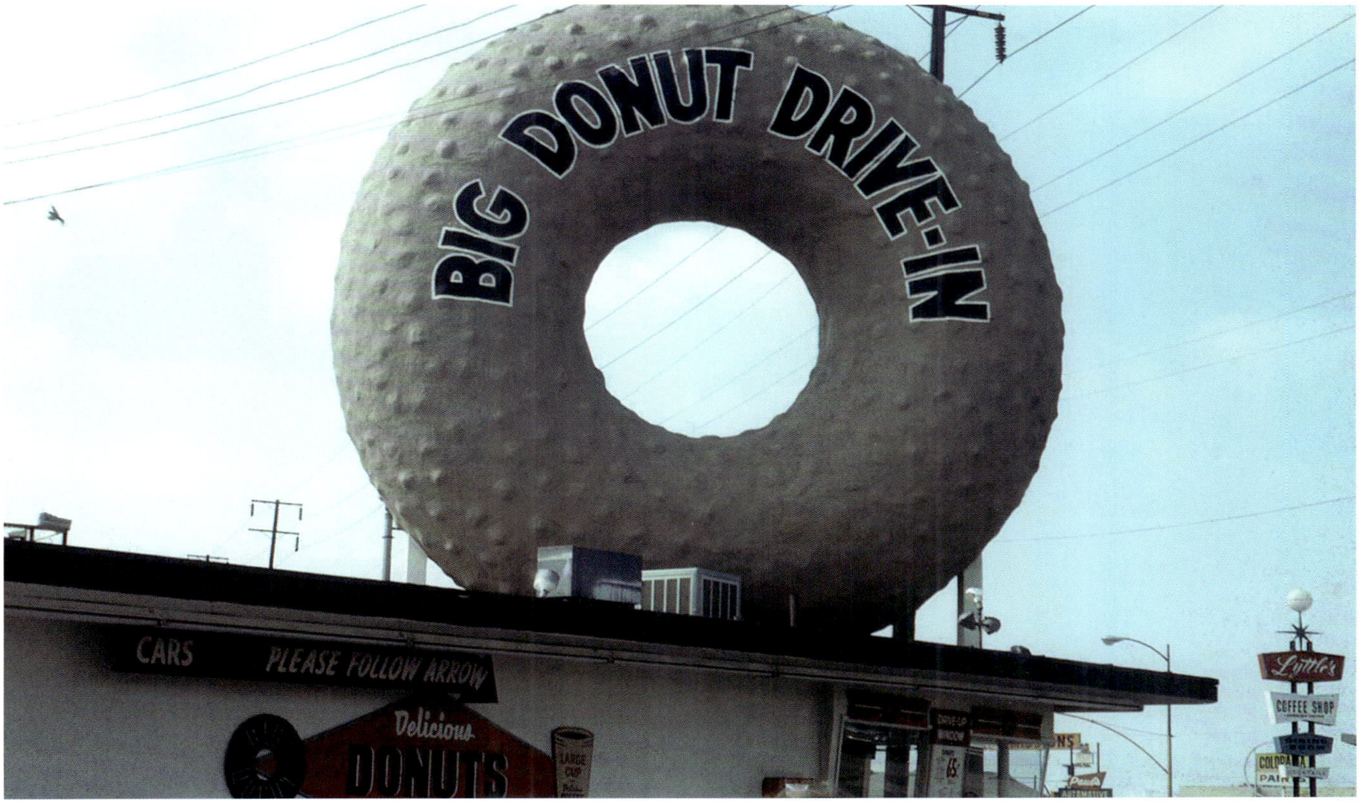
BIG DONUT DRIVE-IN
CARS
PLEASE FOLLOW ARROW
Delicious
DONUTS
COFFEE SHOP

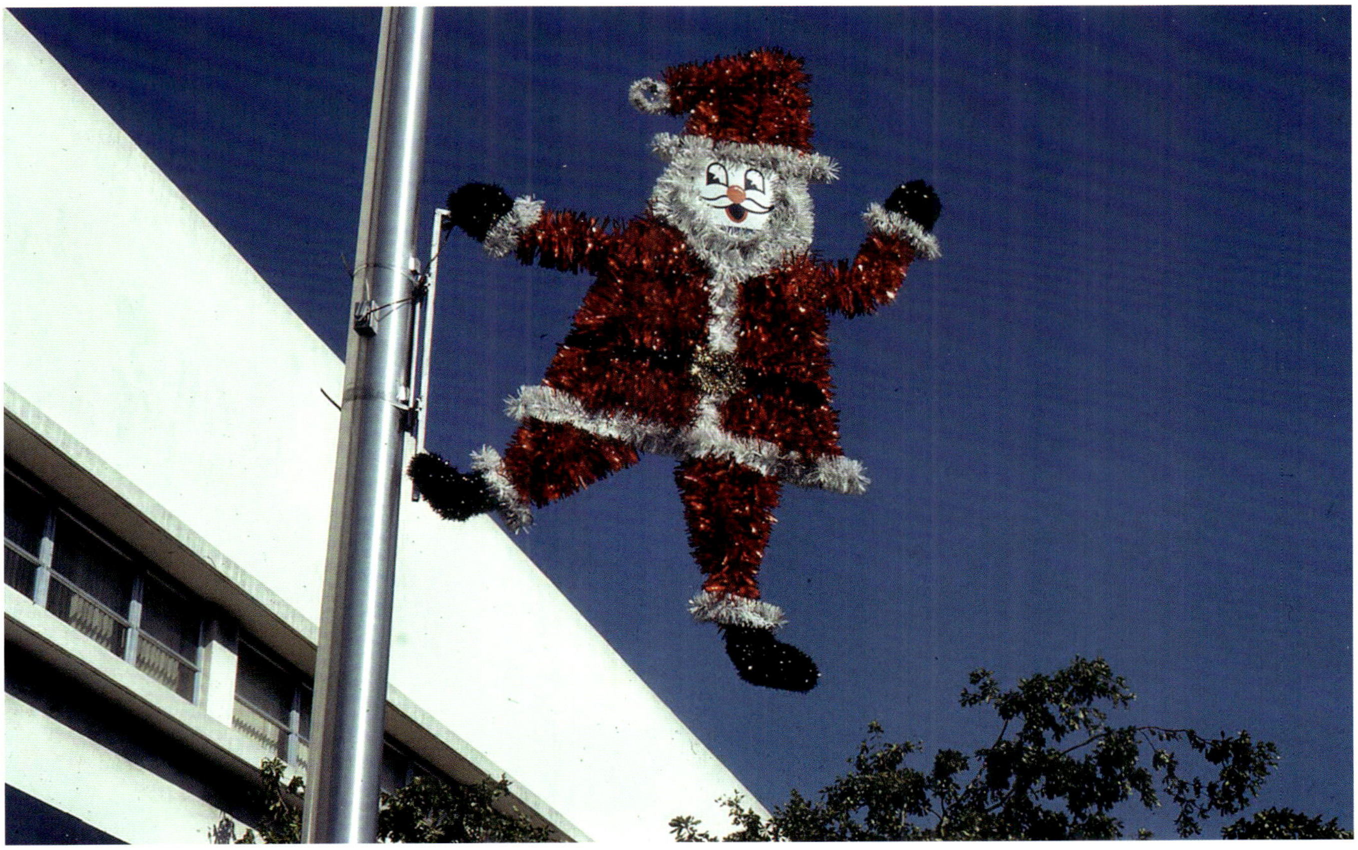

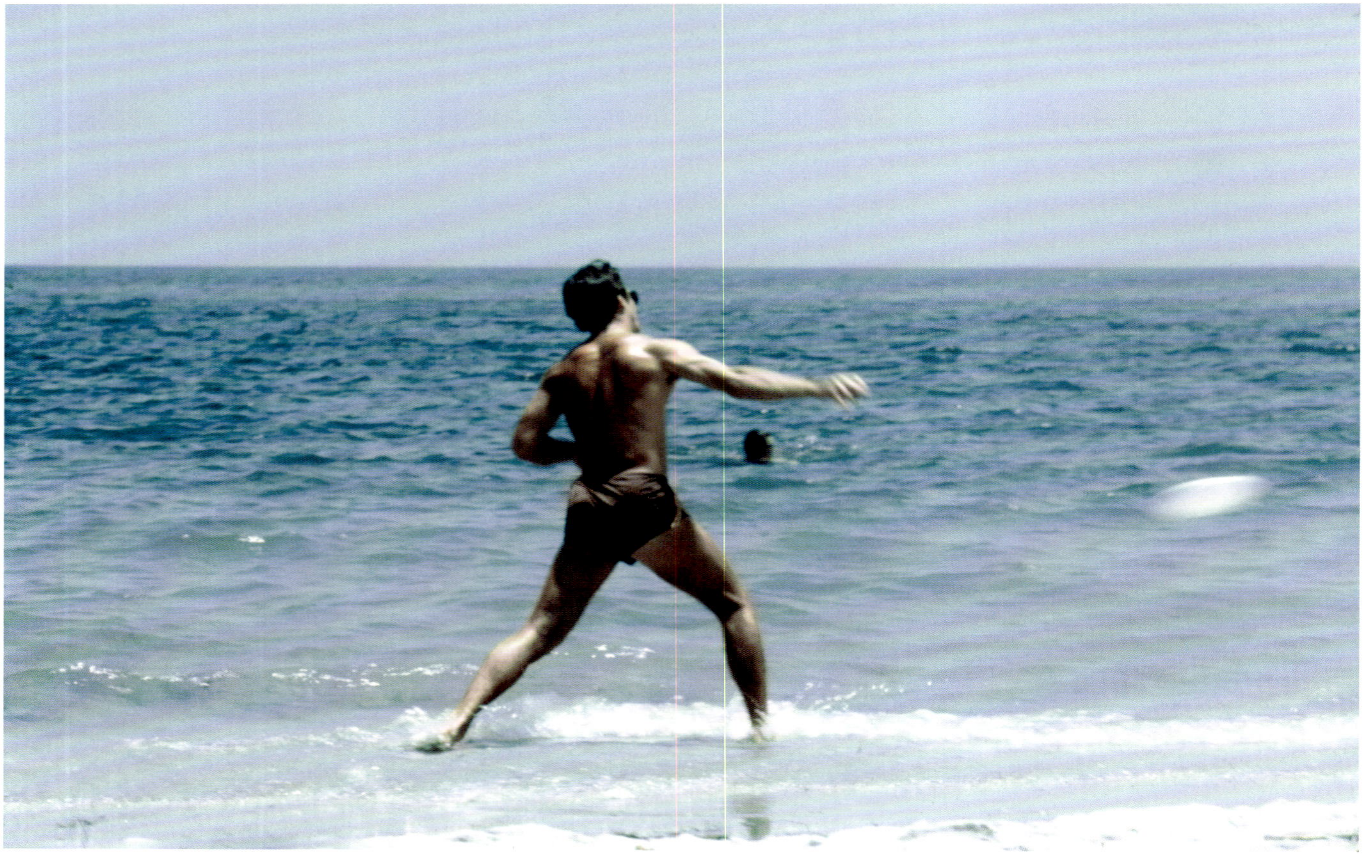

Key West, 1979

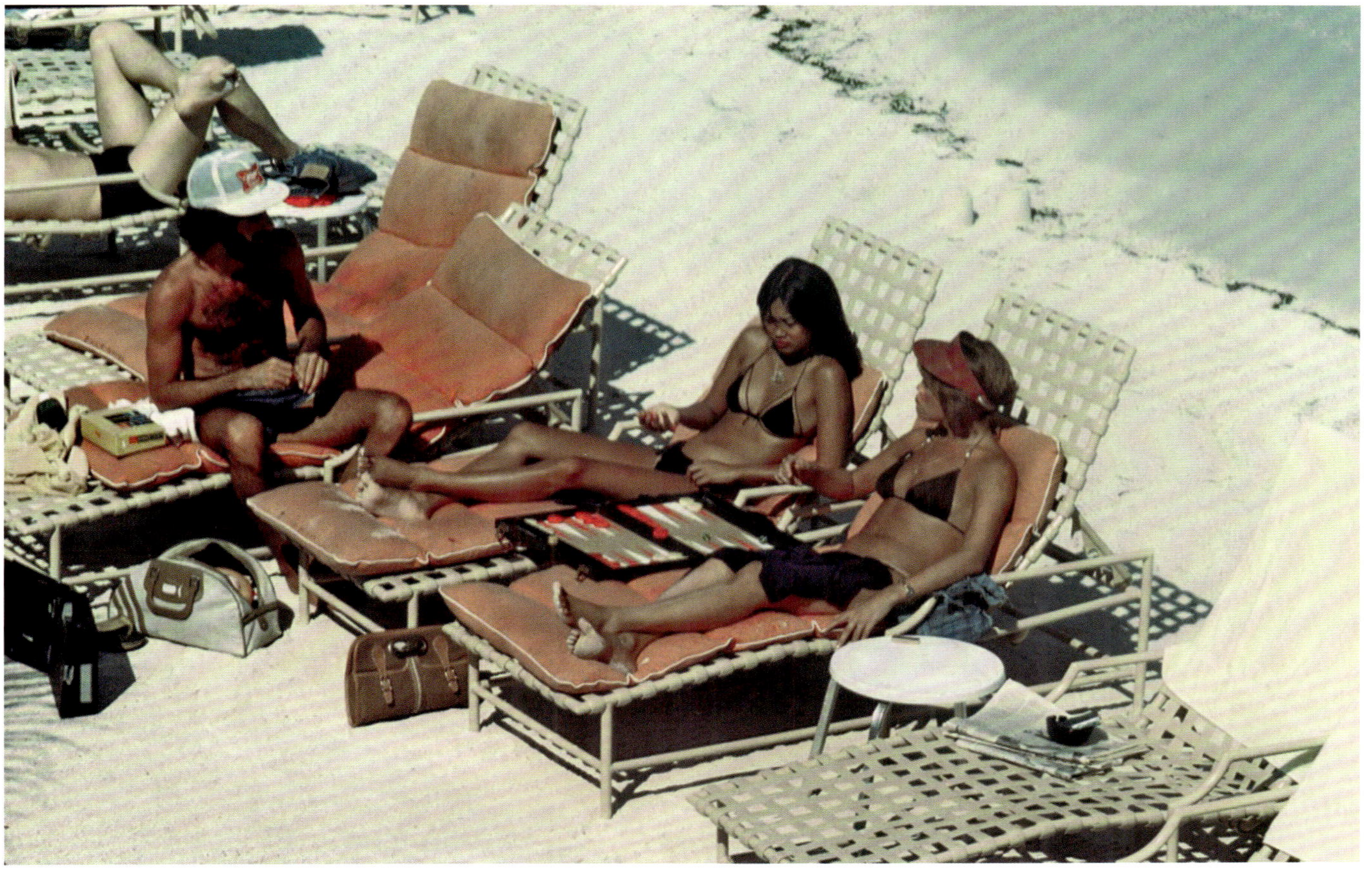

Key West, 1979

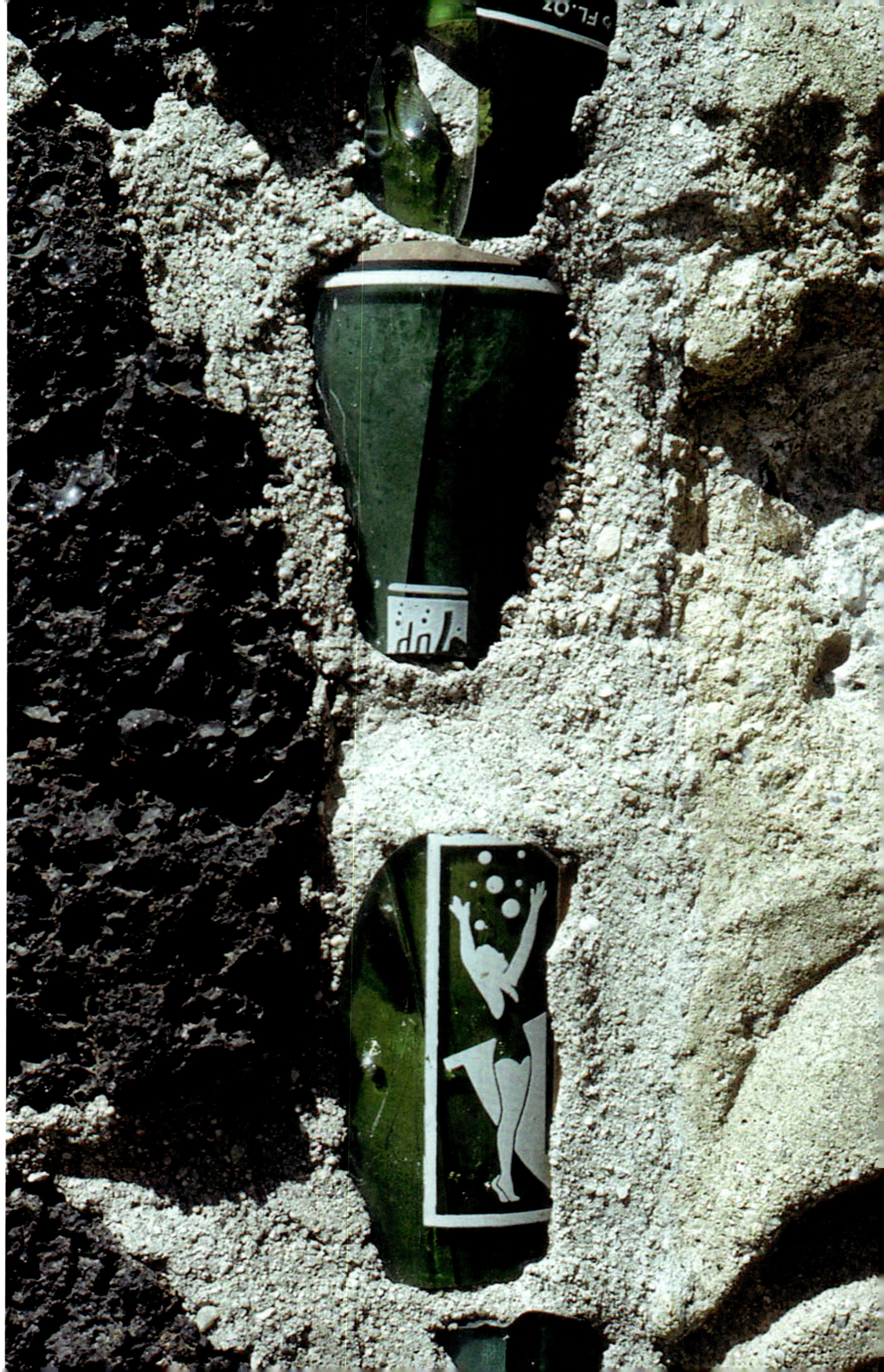

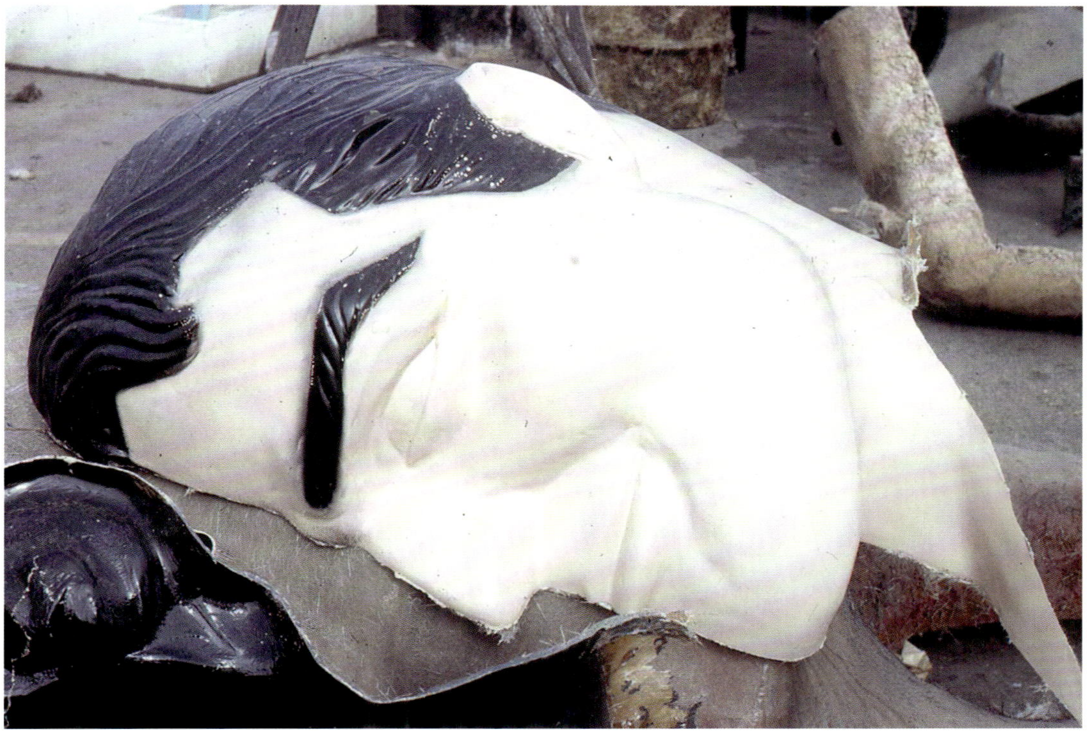

Opposite Watts Towers, Los Angeles, 1965
Above Los Angeles Fabricators, 1965
Overleaf Flagstaff, Arizona, 1965

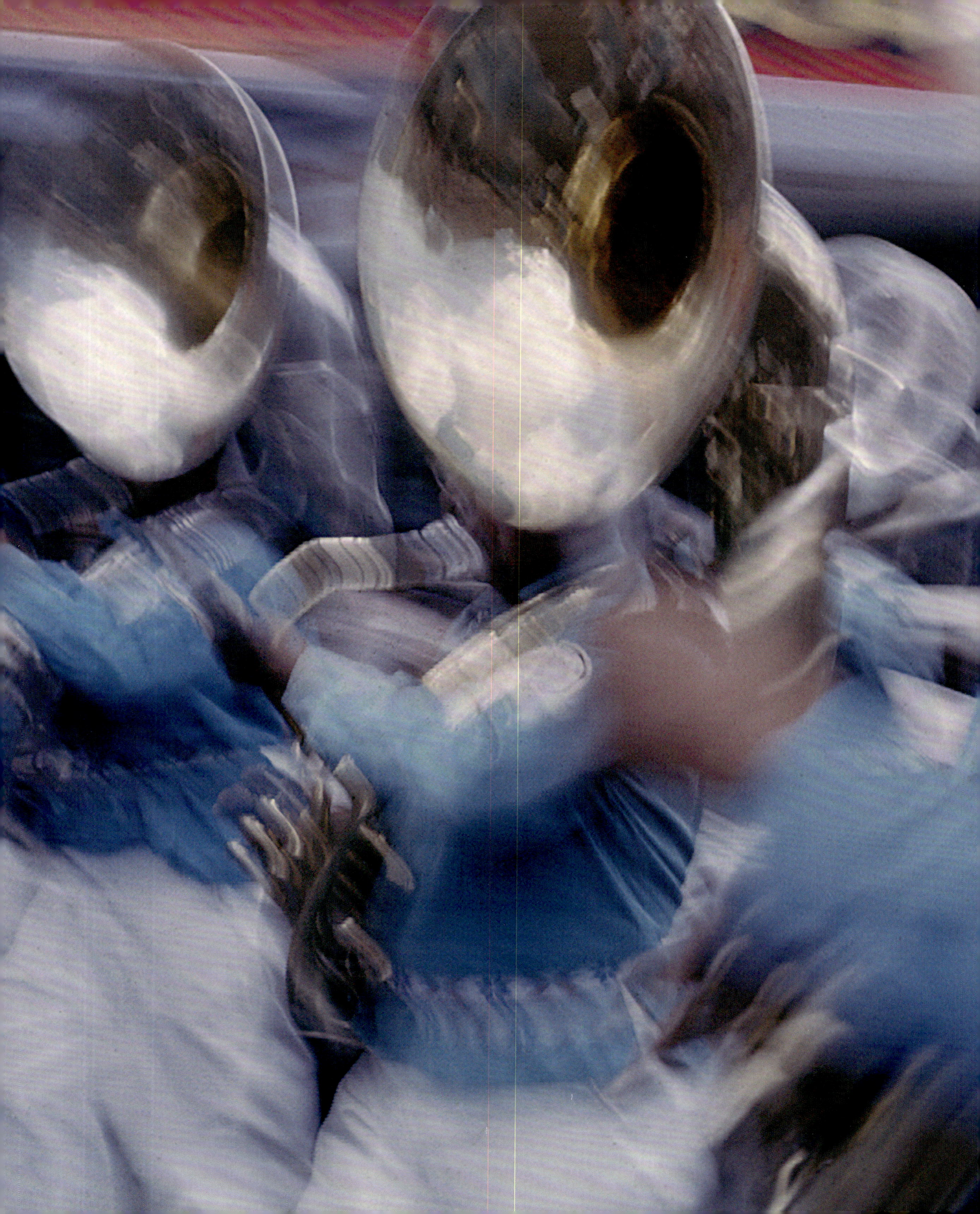

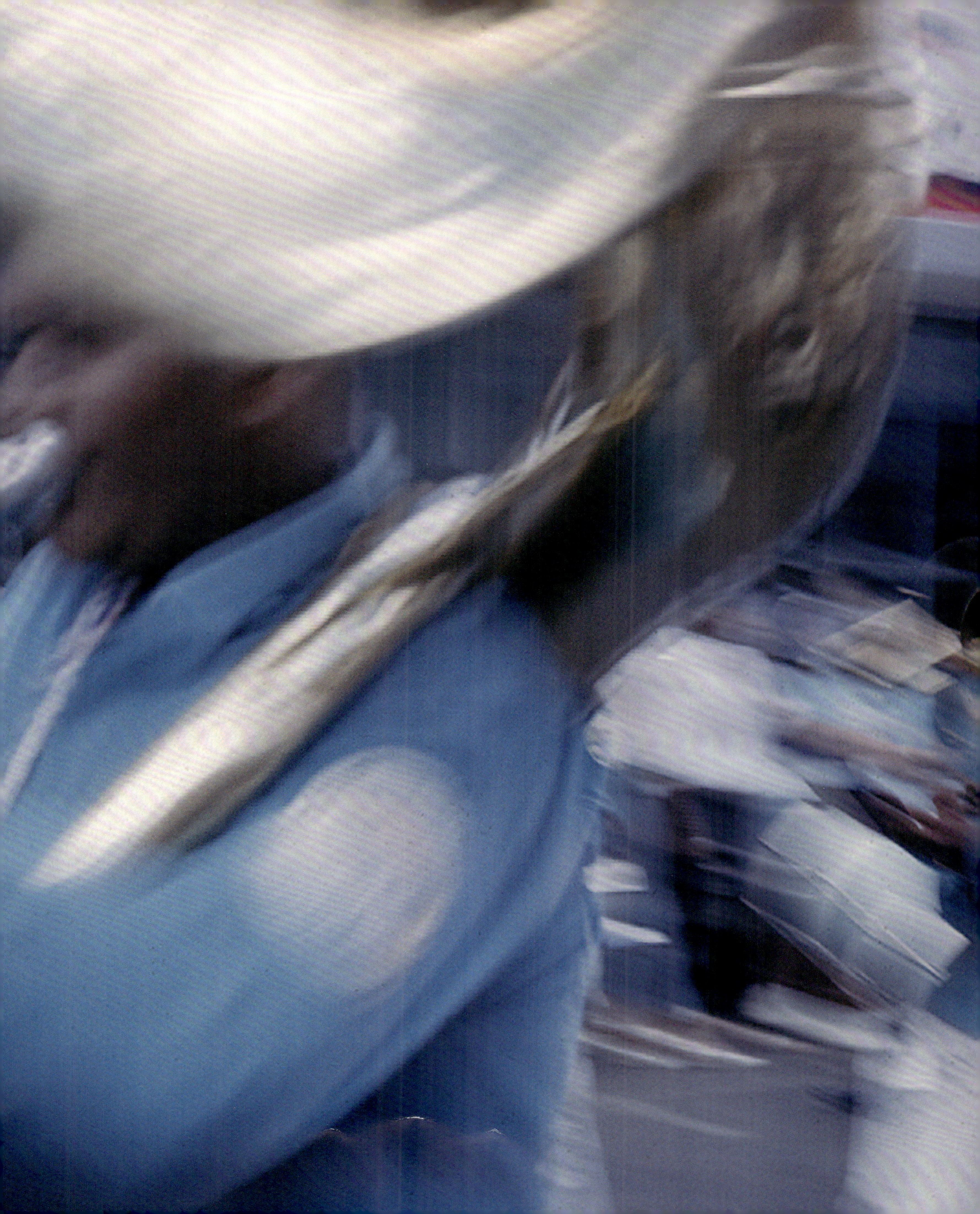

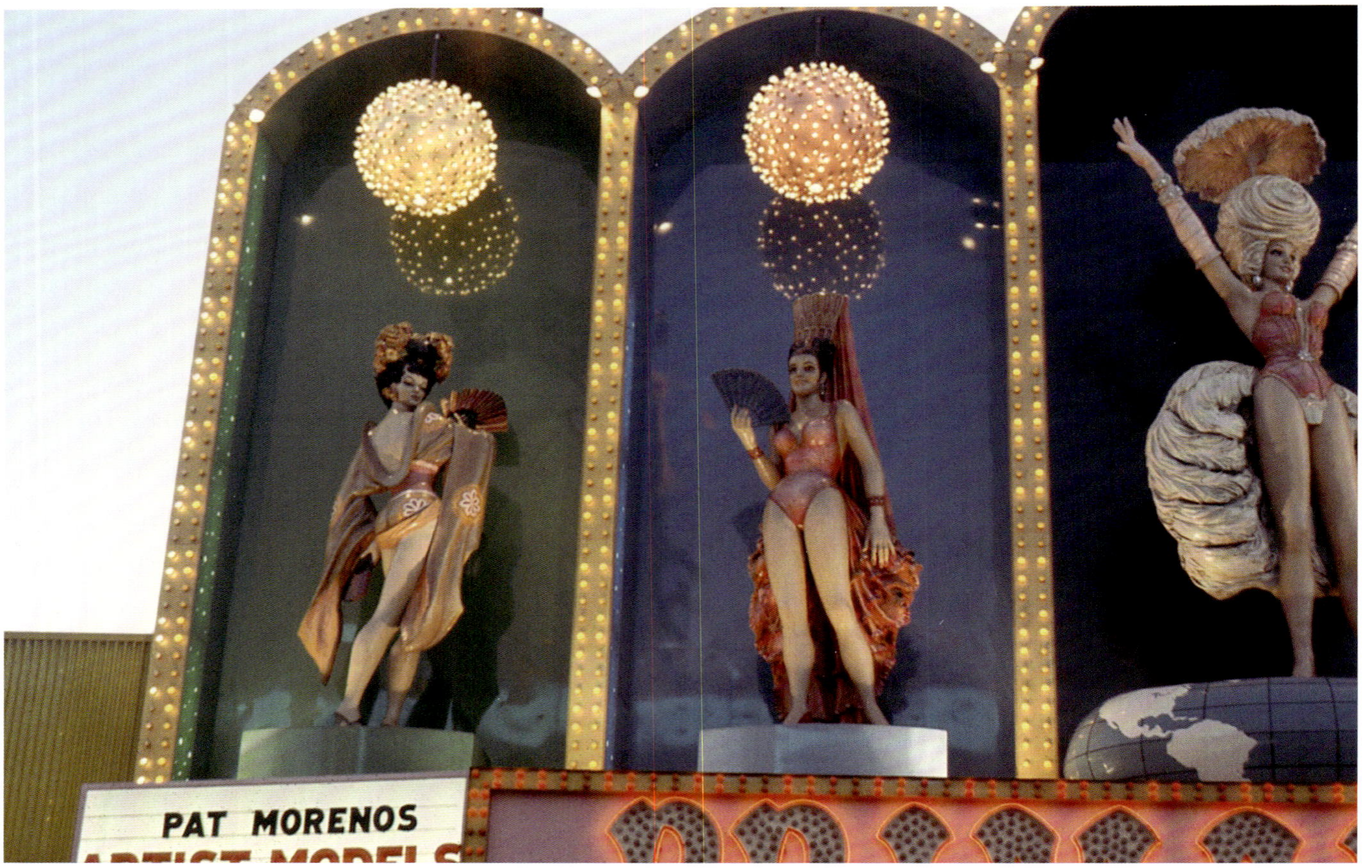

Reno, Nevada, 1965

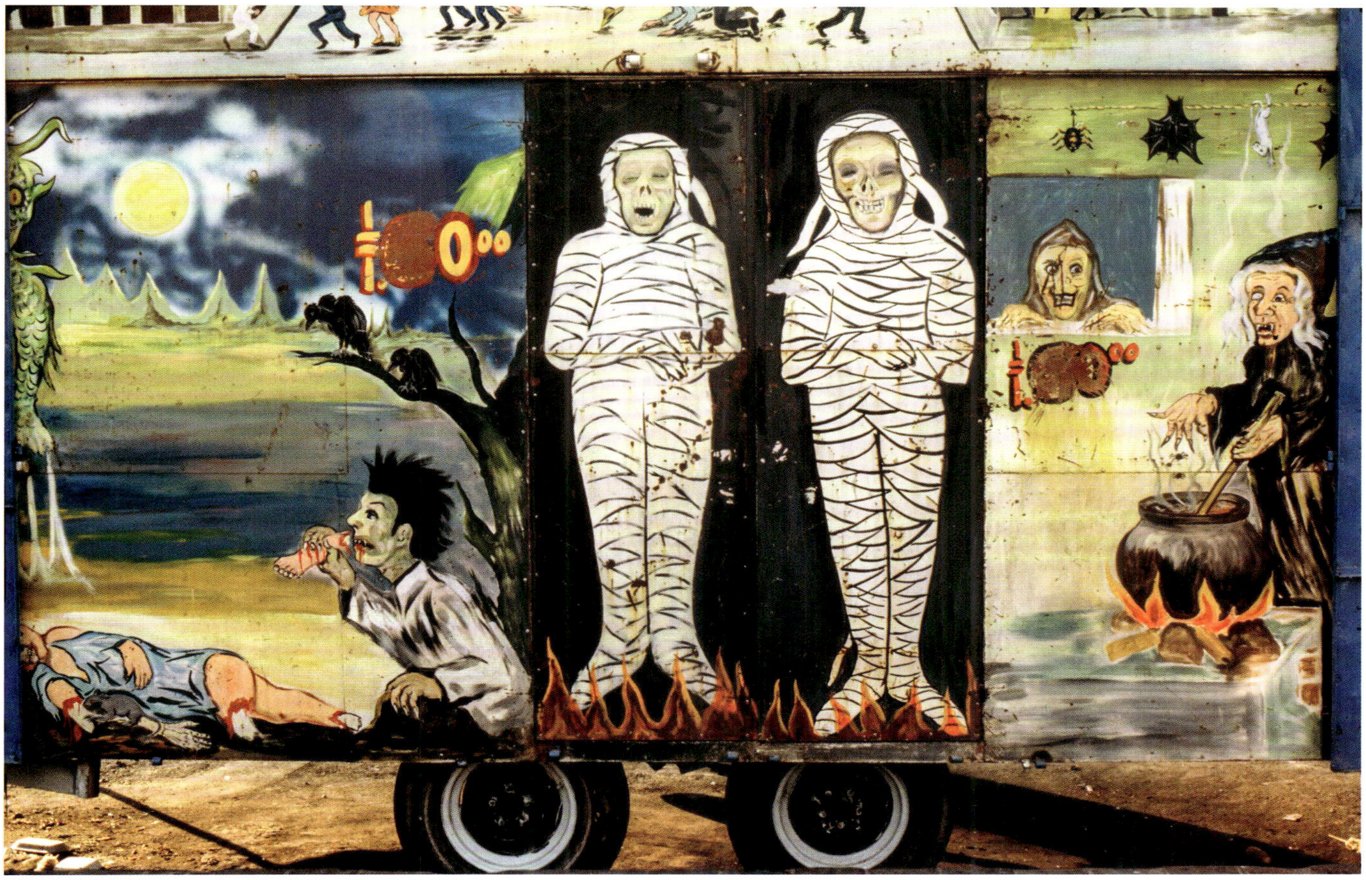

Above Mexico City, 1985
Overleaf Mexico City, 1985

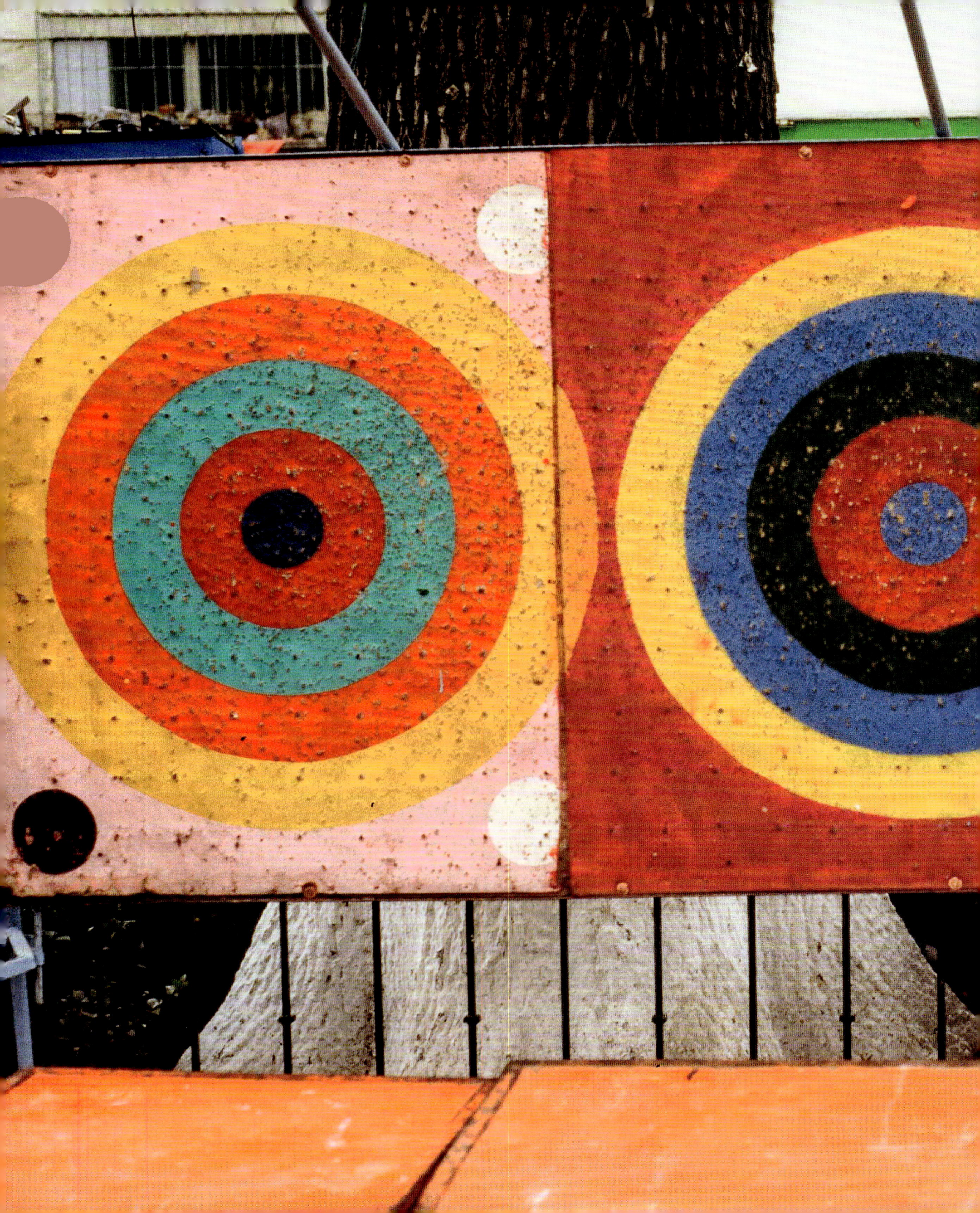

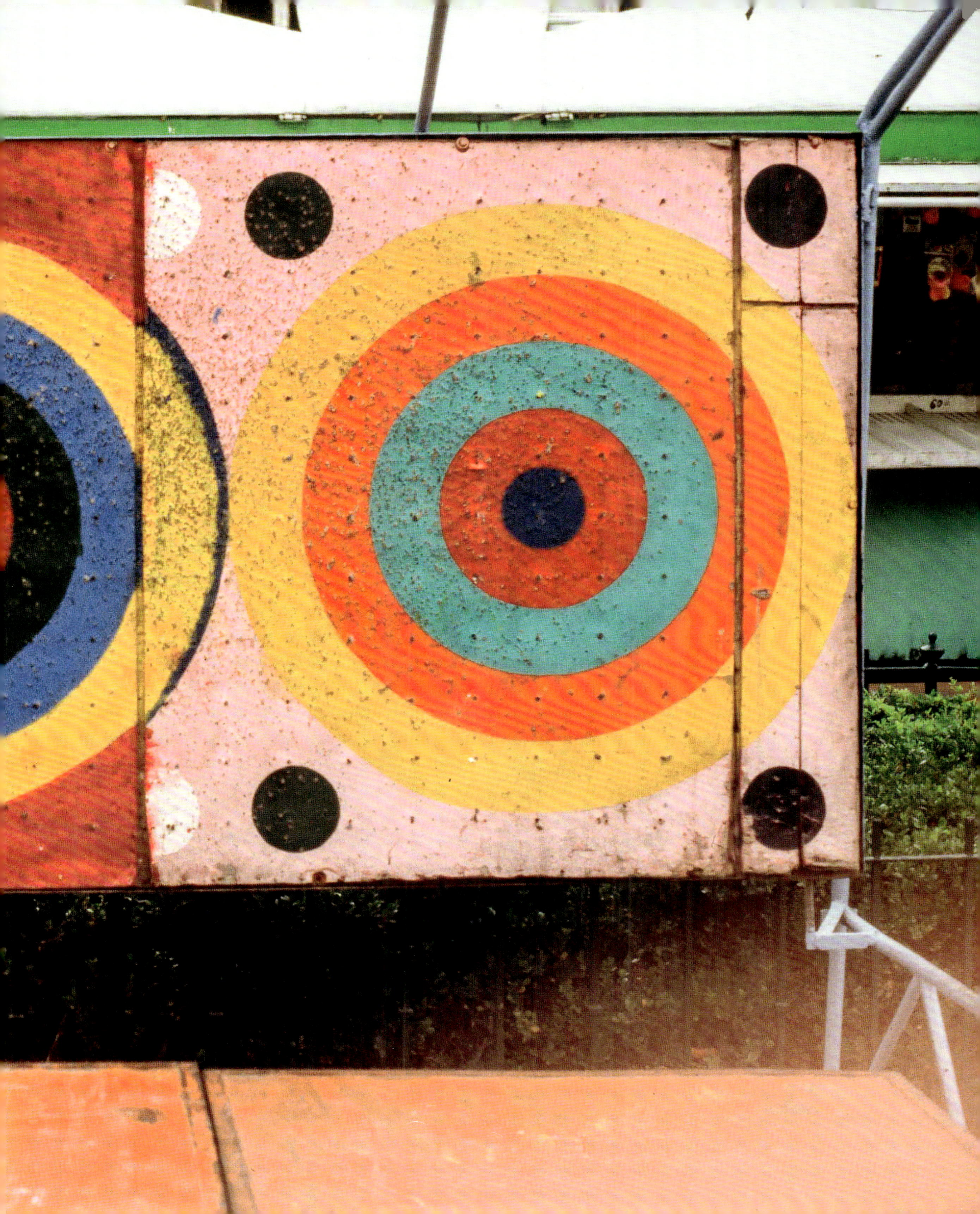

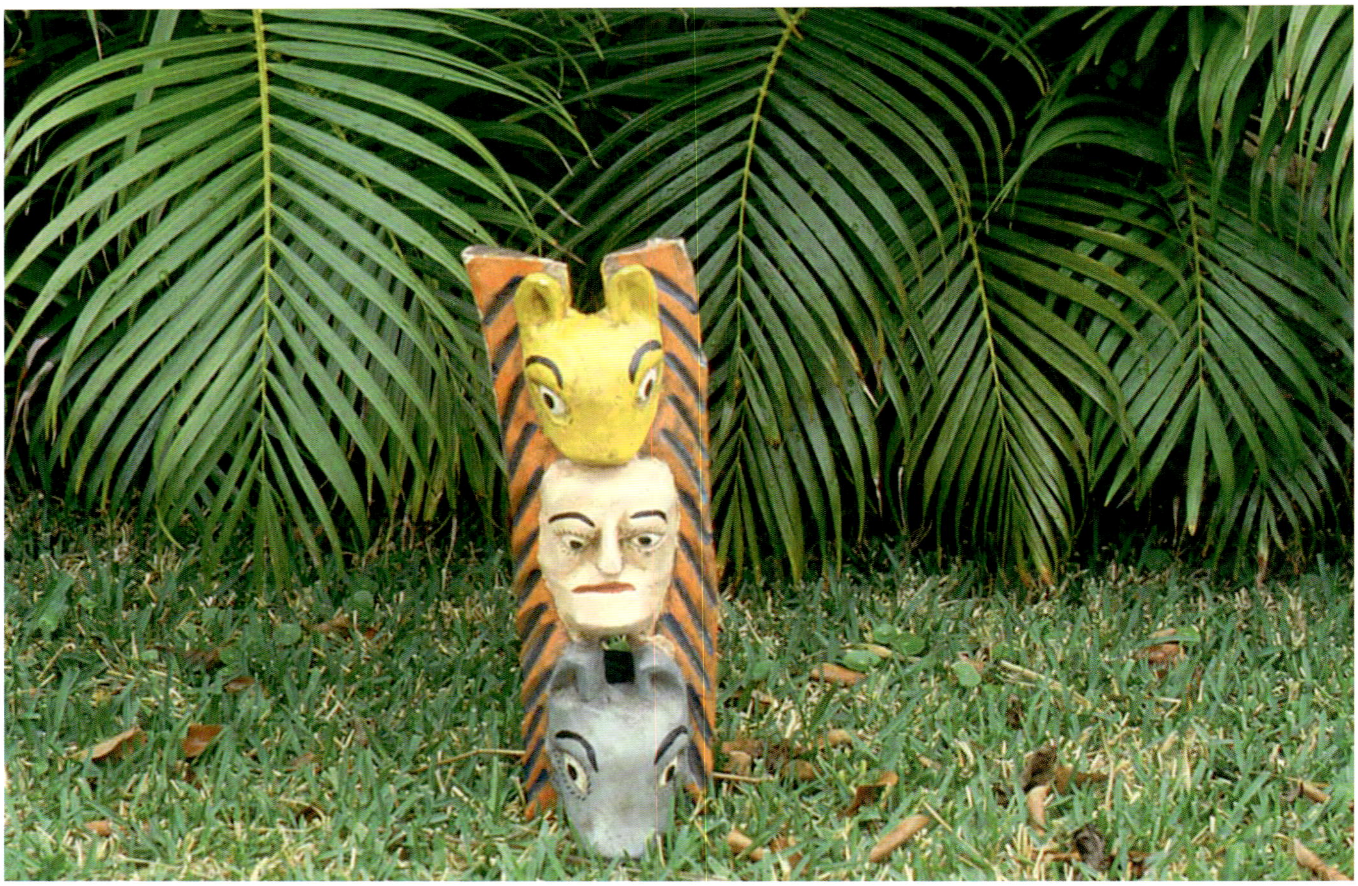

Yucatan, Mexico, 1978

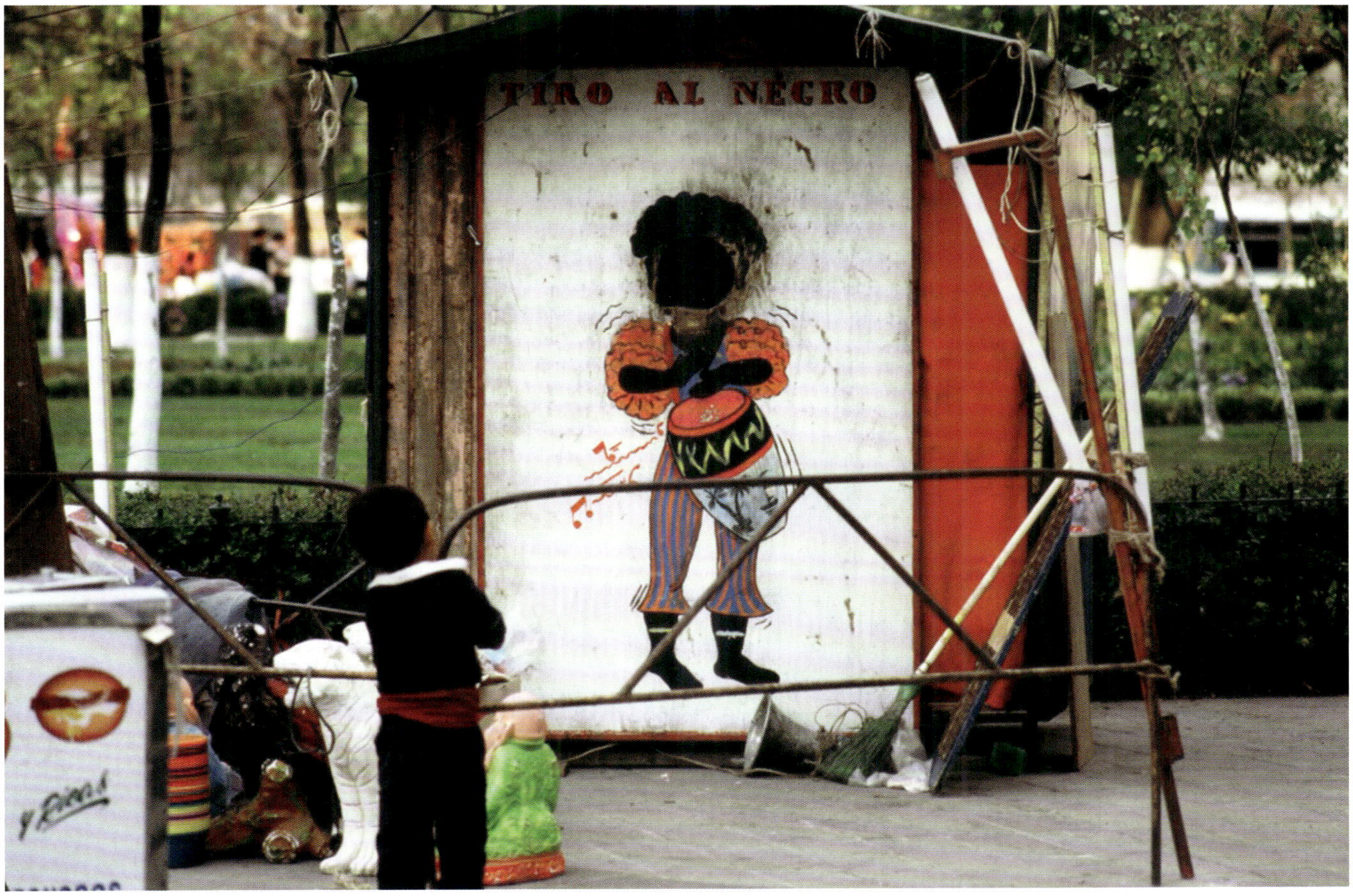

Above Mexico City, 1985
Overleaf Mexico City, 1985
Pages 138–139 Mexico City, 1985
Page 141 Athabasca Glacier, Jasper National Park, Canada, 1977

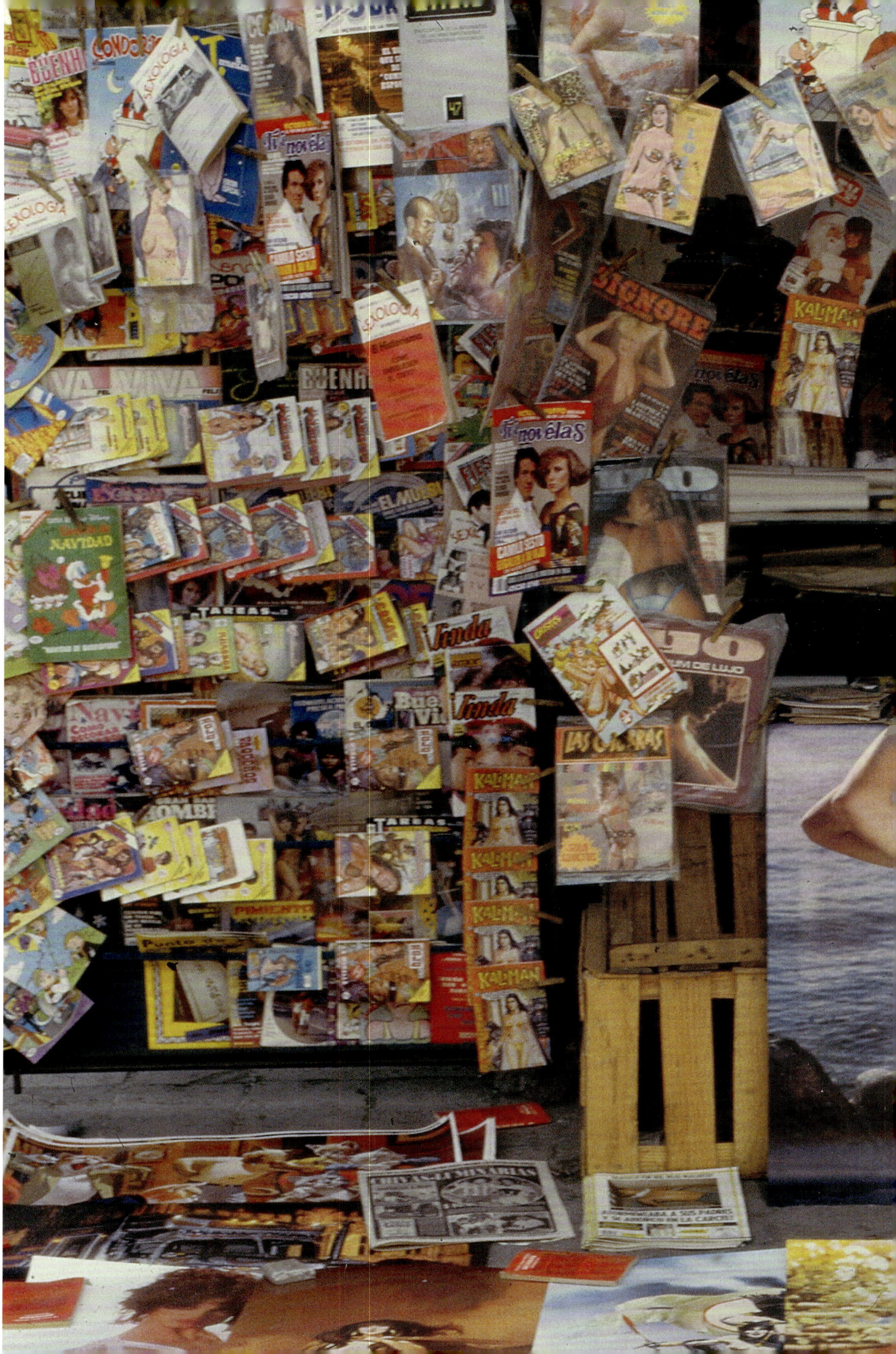
SEXOLOGIA
SIGNORE
KALIMAN
Linda
TAREAS
novelas

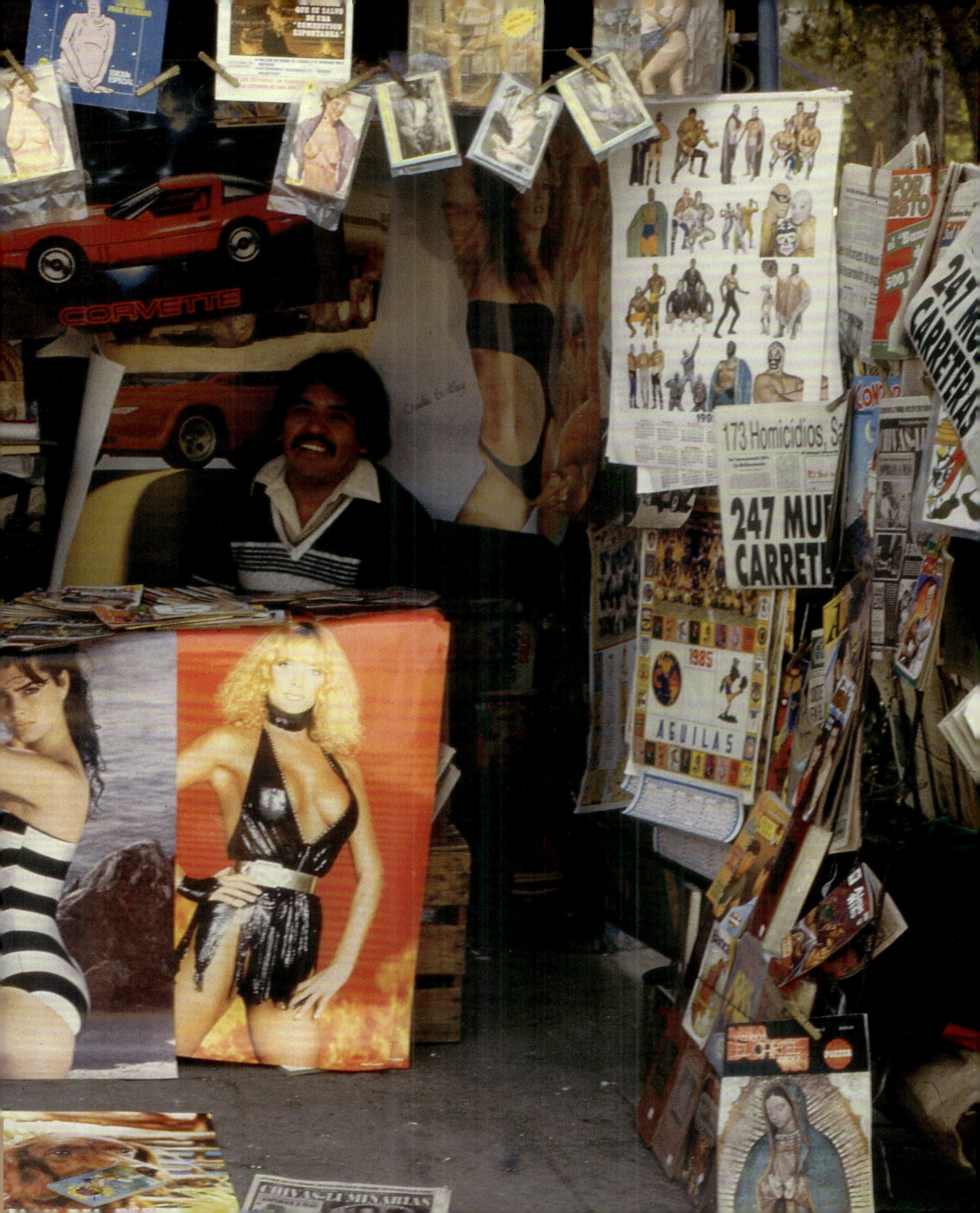
CORVETTE
173 Homicidios, Sa
247 MUE
CARRETE
247 M
CARRETERAS
1985
AGUILAS

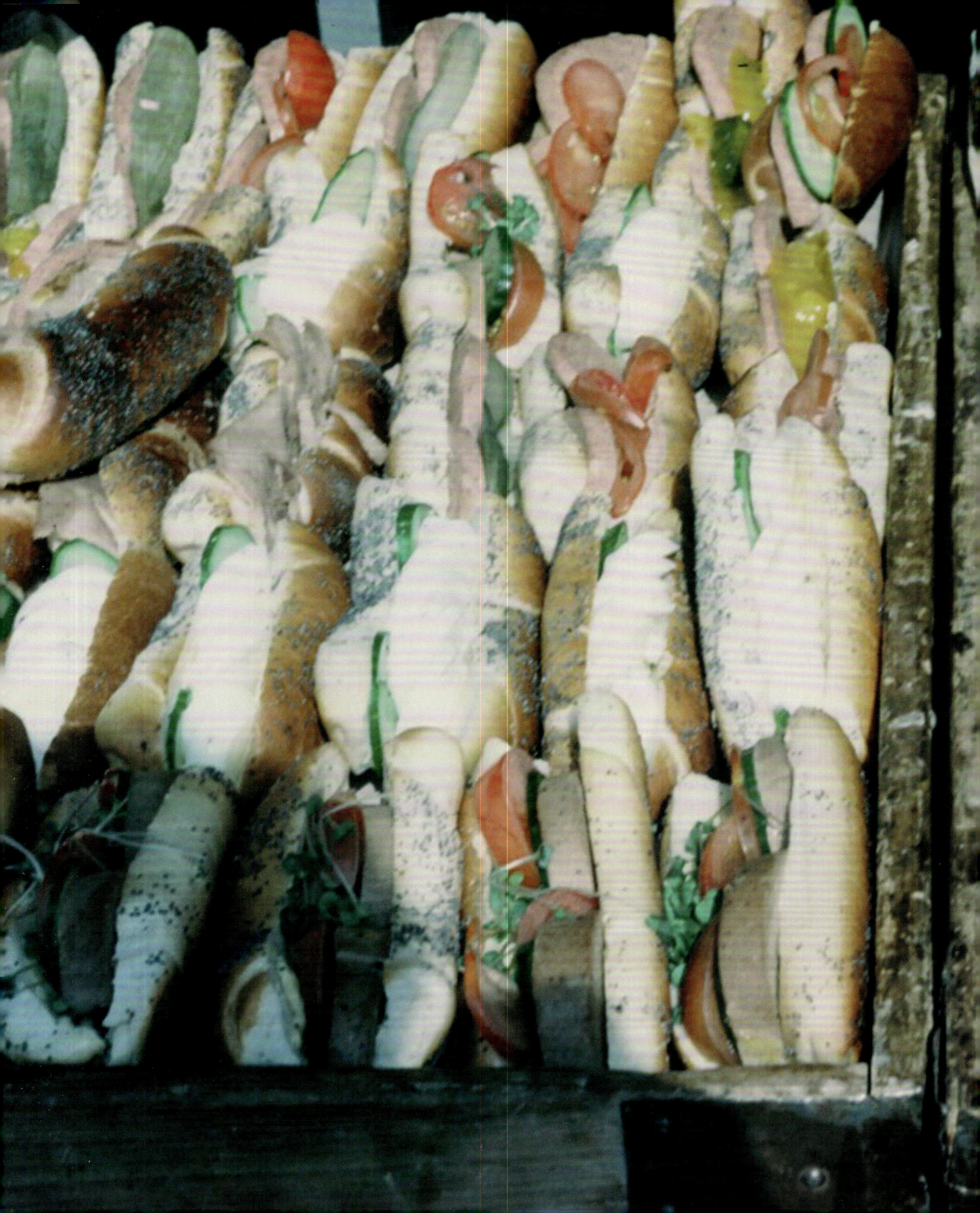

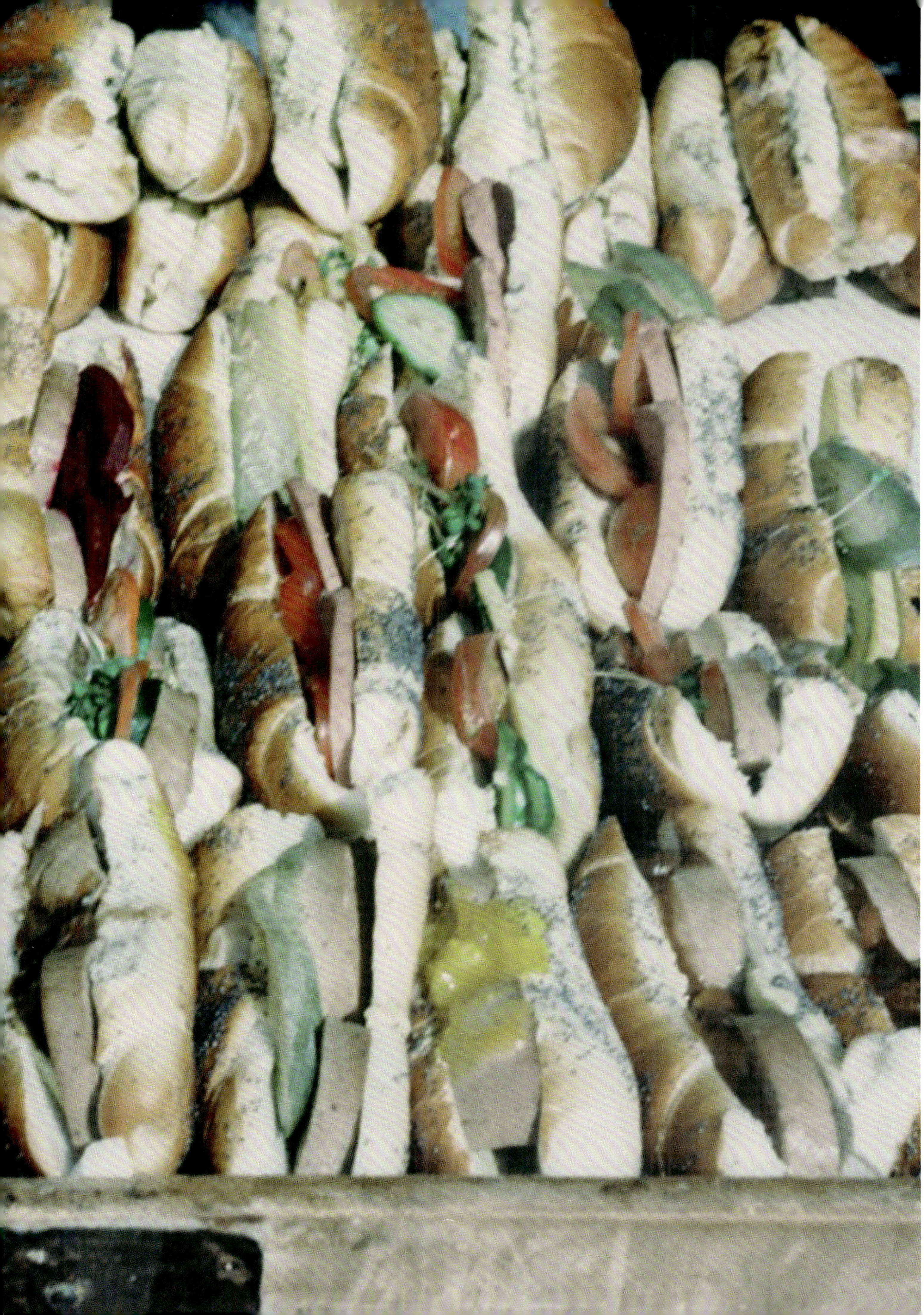

I am drawn to often unanticipated subjects for their pictorial and graphic possibilities. A potential hazard such as this crevasse can reveal its natural beauty and be transformed into a memorable image through photography.

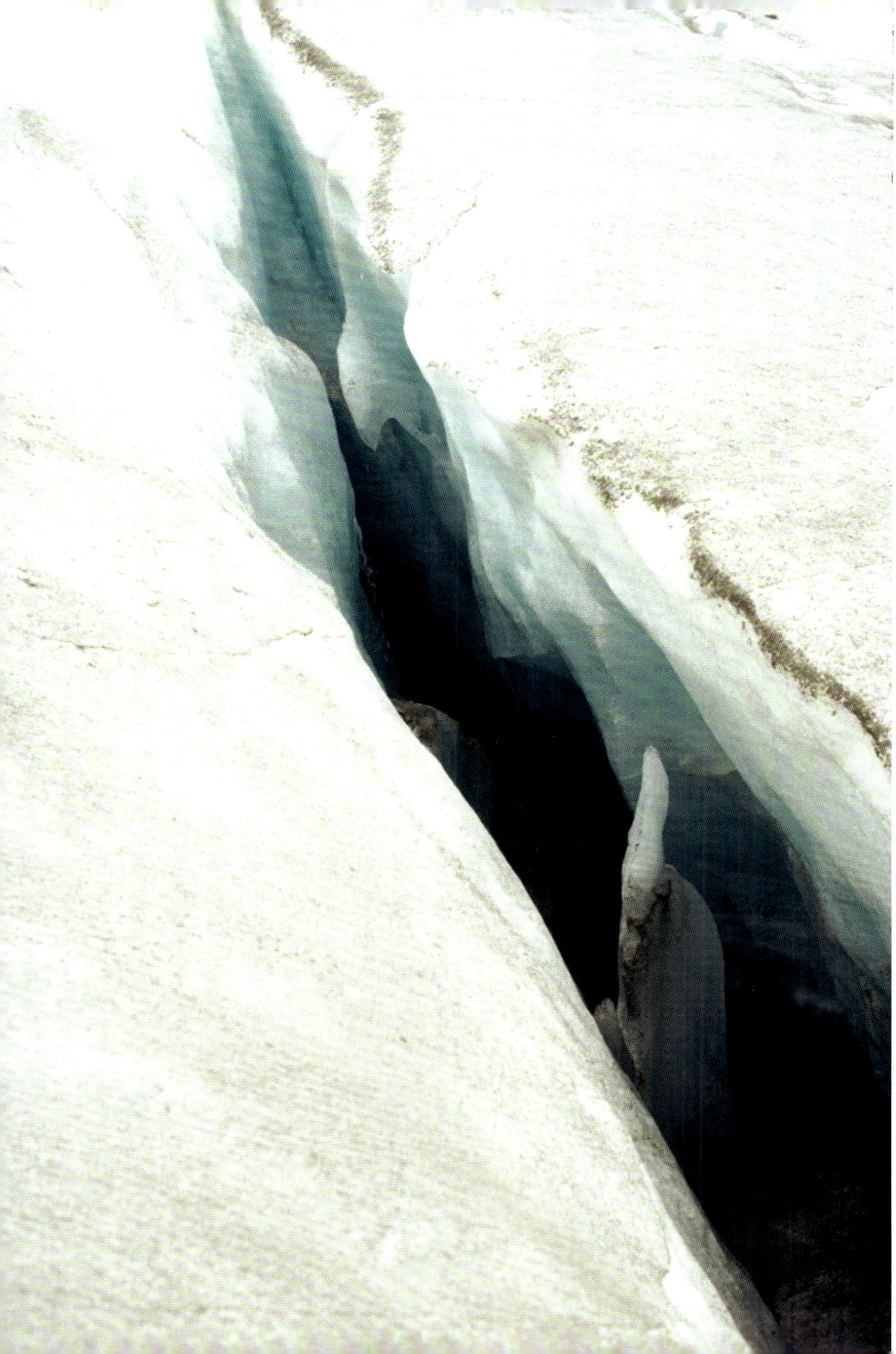

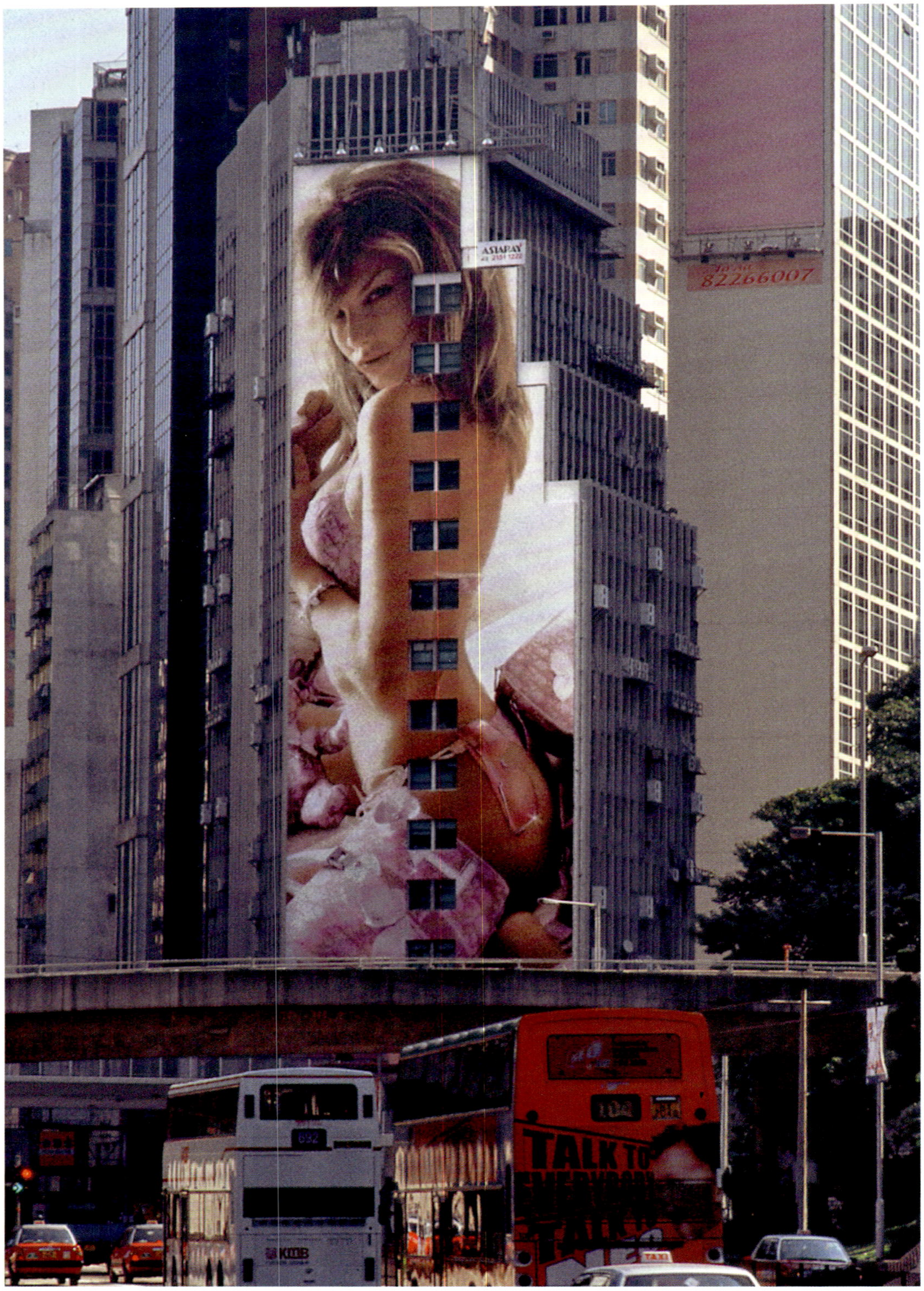

Happy Valley, Hong Kong, 2003

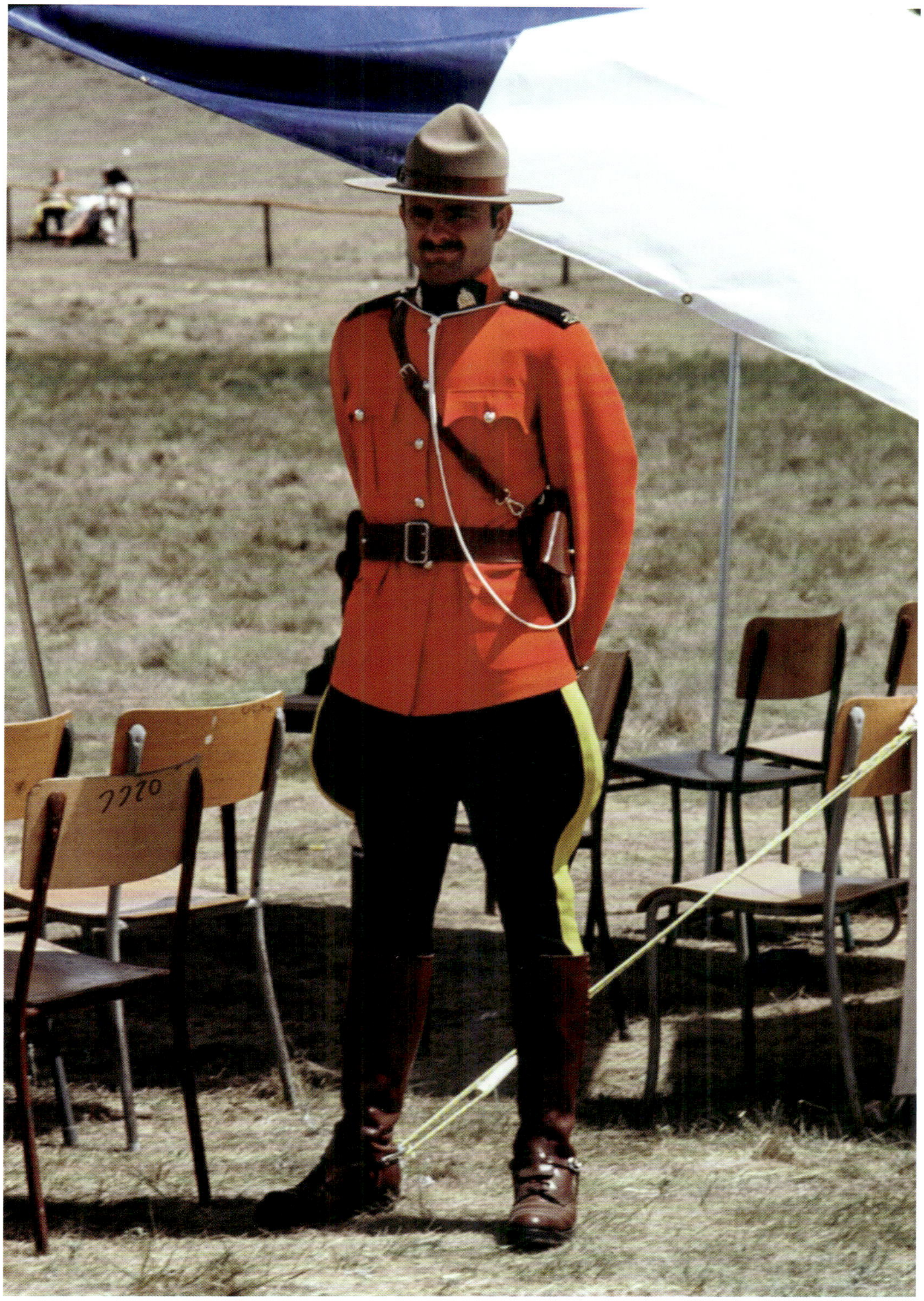

Above Calgary, Canada, 1977
Overleaf Calais, 1993

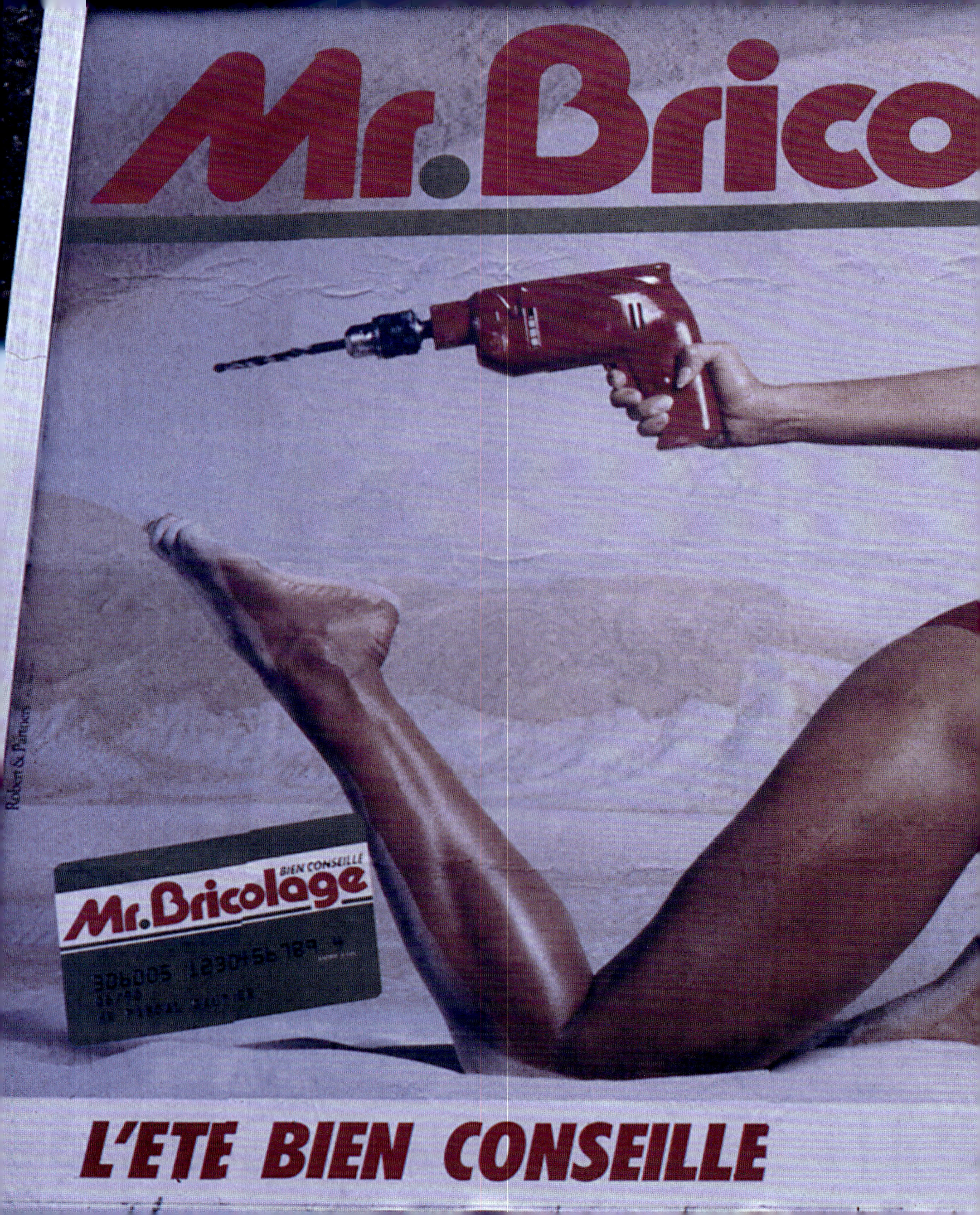
Mr.Brico
BIEN CONSEILLÉ
Mr.Bricolage
306005 1230456789 4
Robert & Partners
L'ETE BIEN CONSEILLE

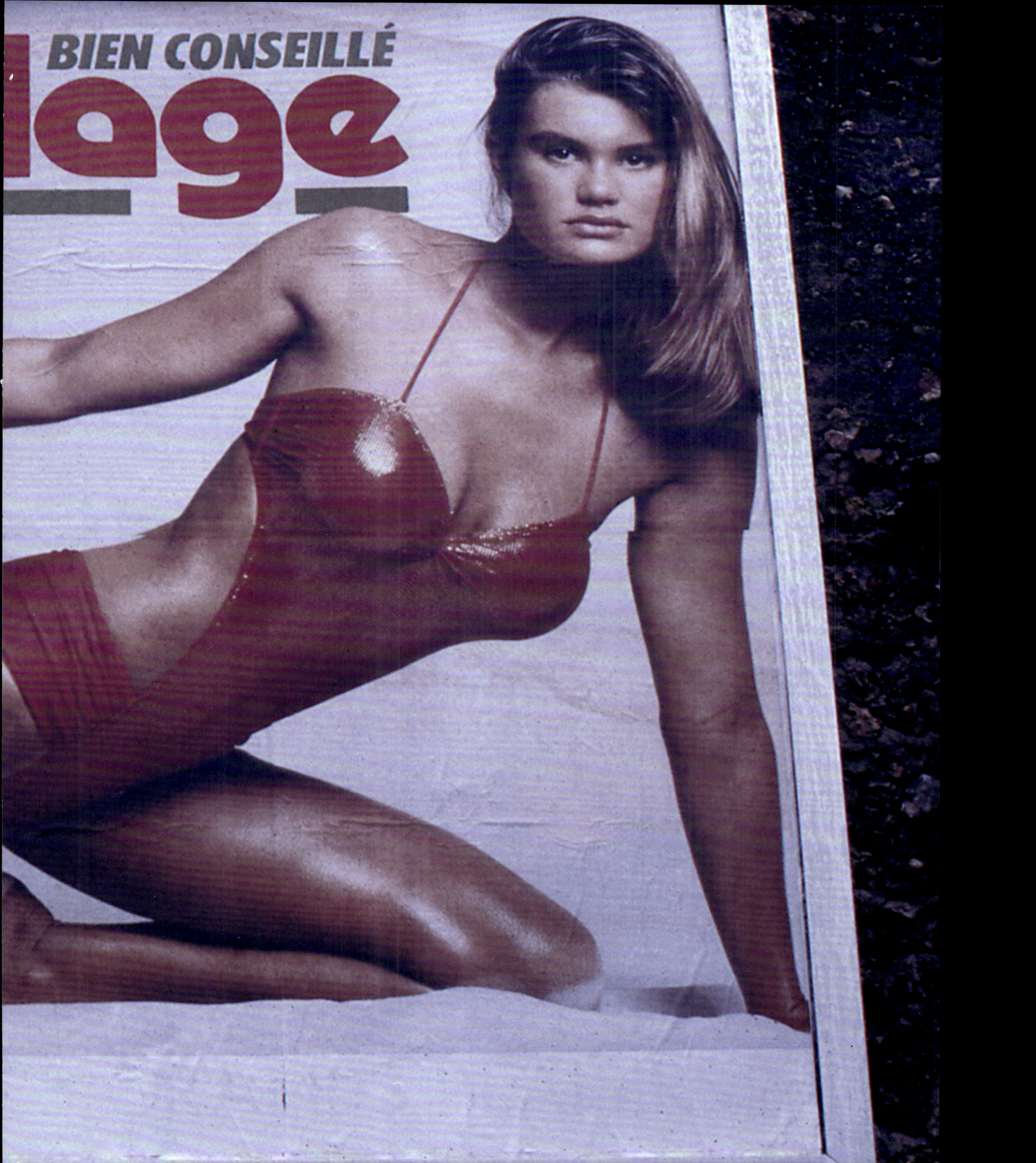
BIEN CONSEILLÉ
lage

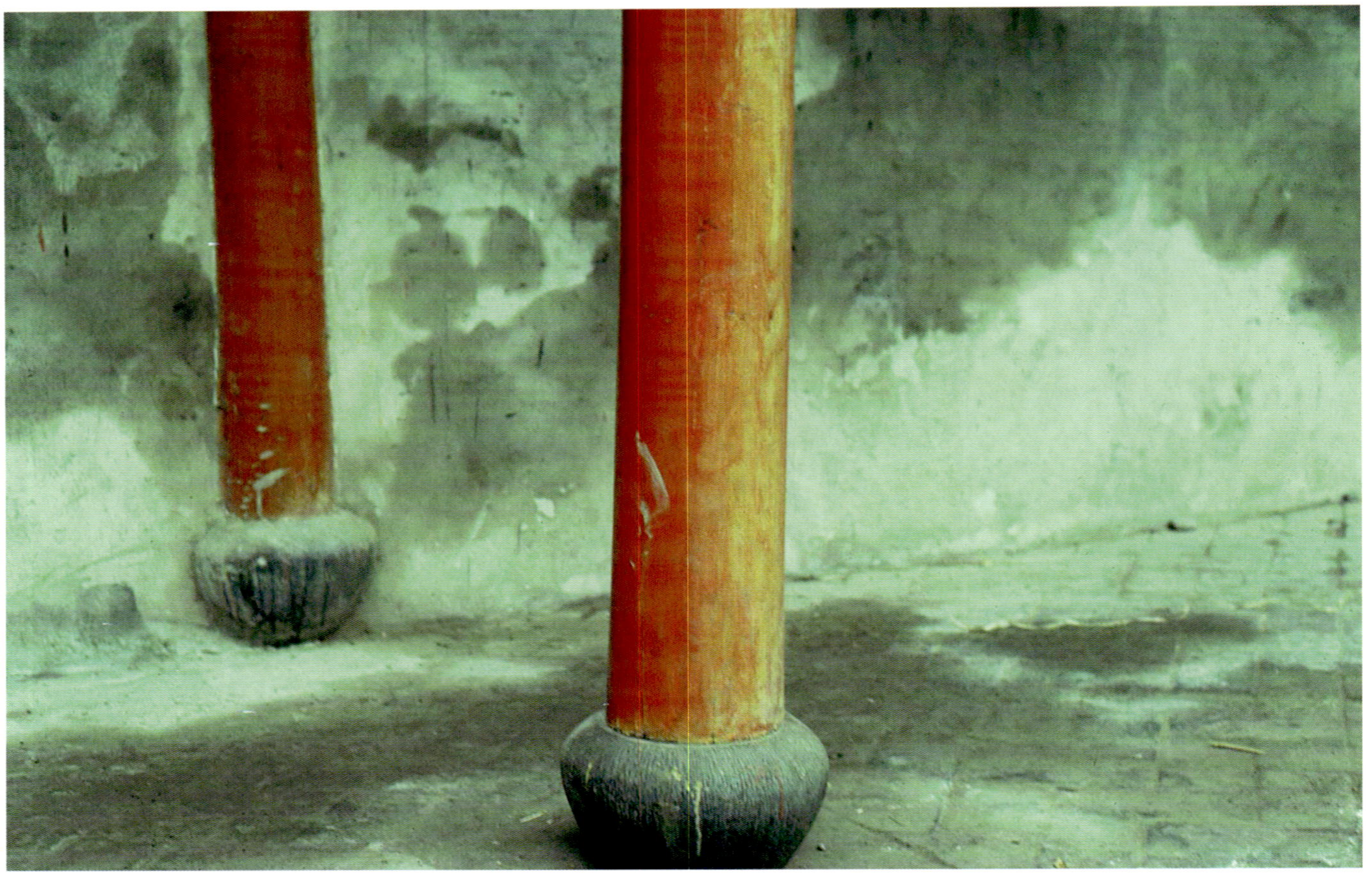
Ming tombs, China, 1979

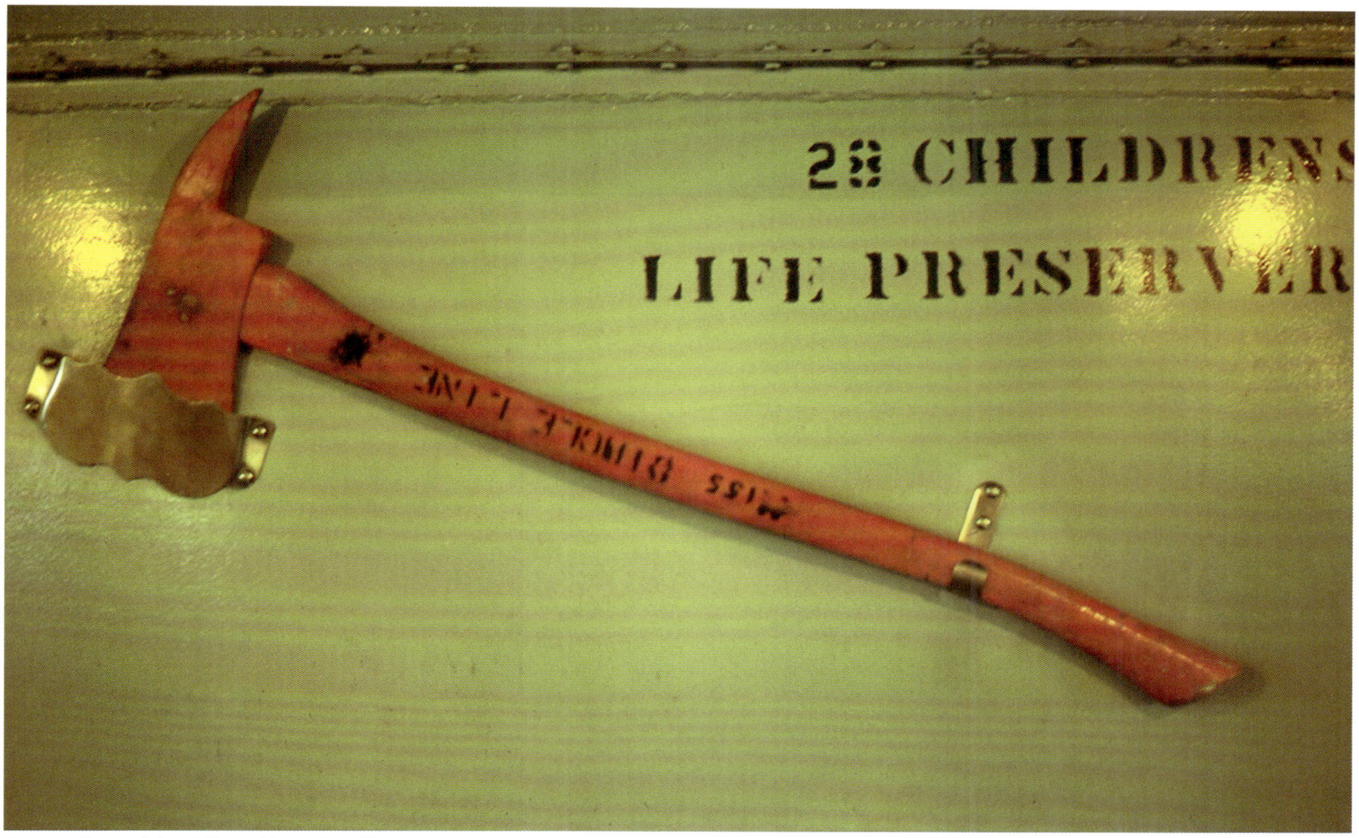

Above Staten Island Ferry, New York City, 1979
Overleaf Place de la Concorde, Paris, 1959
Pages 150–151 The Thames (East End), 1979

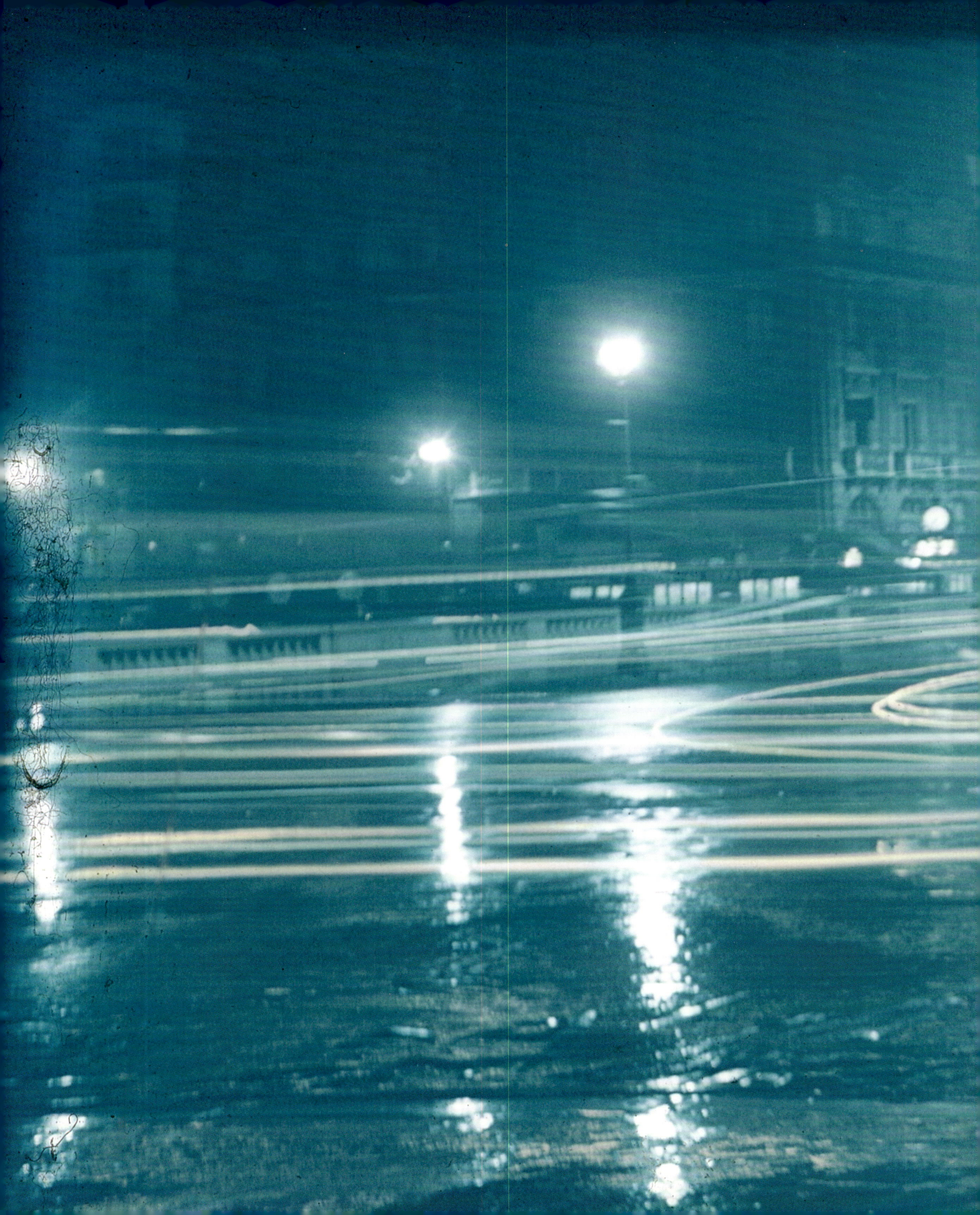

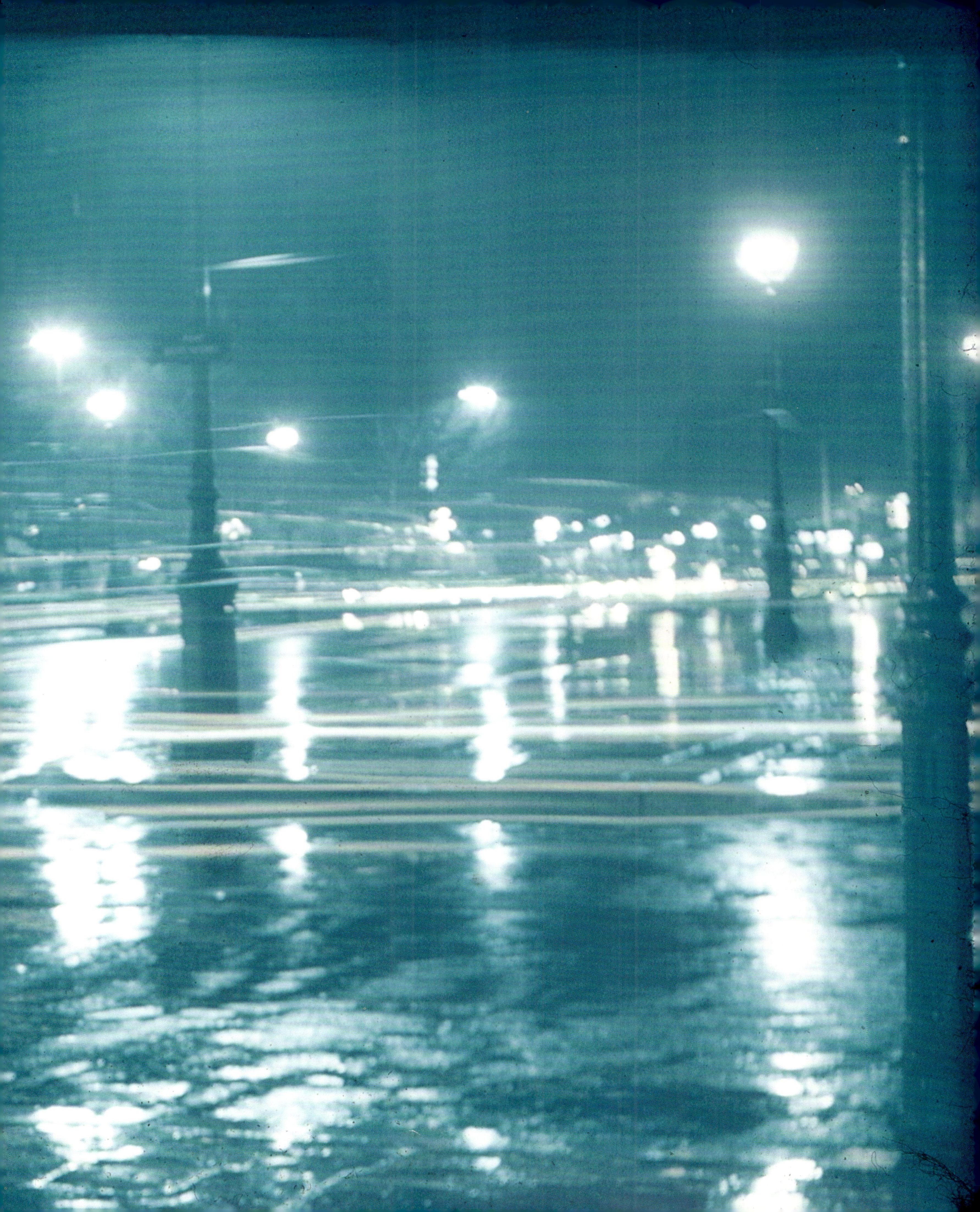

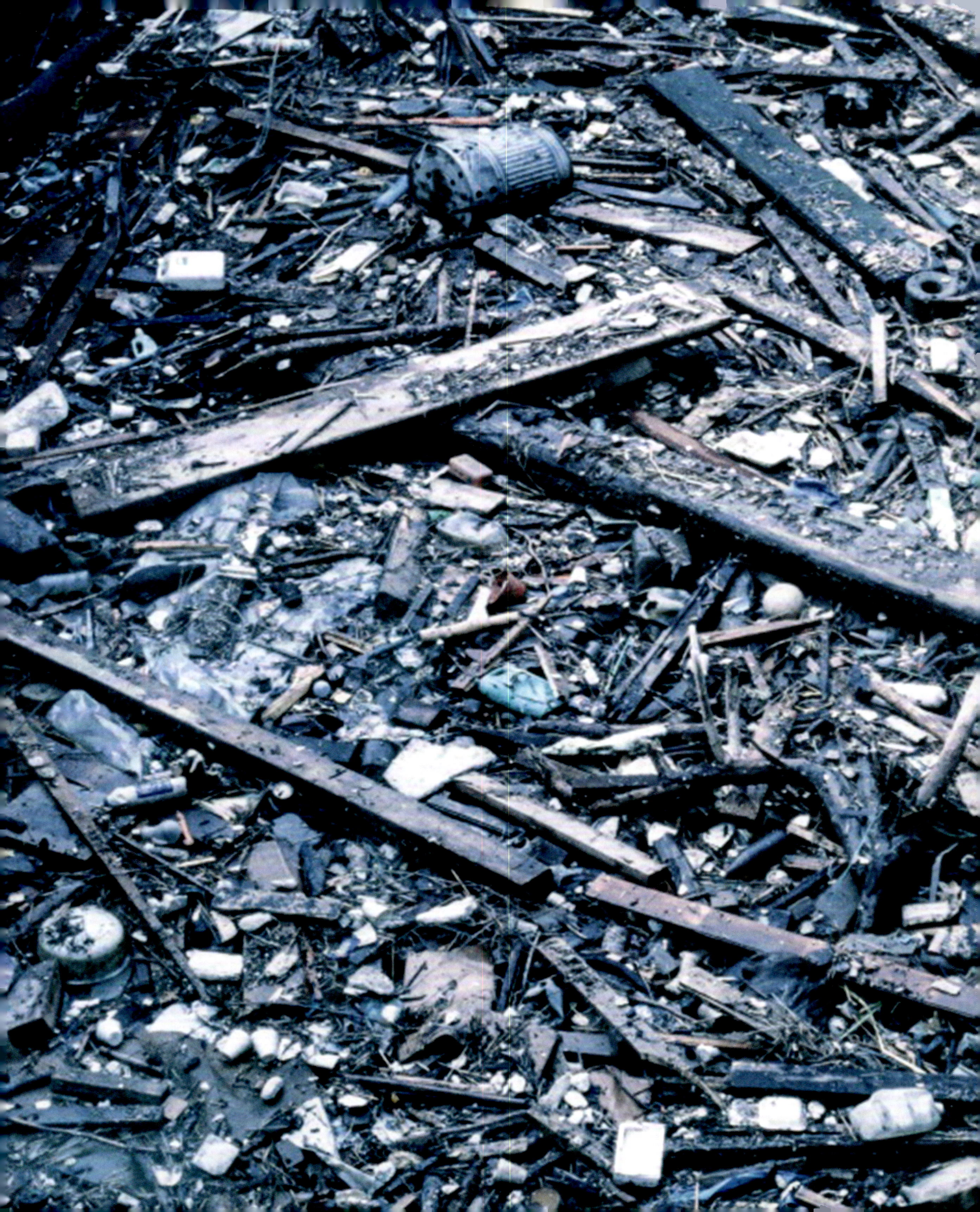

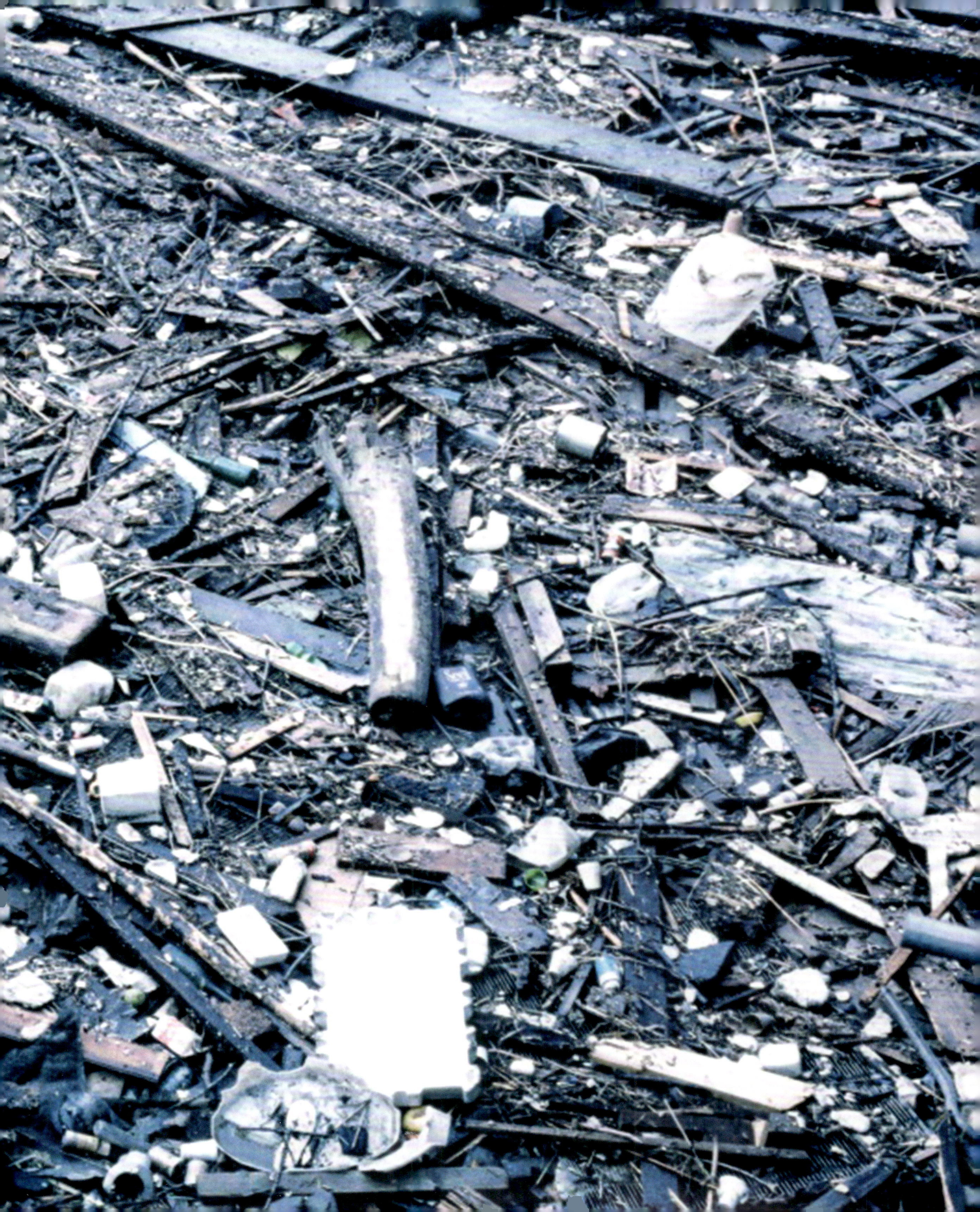

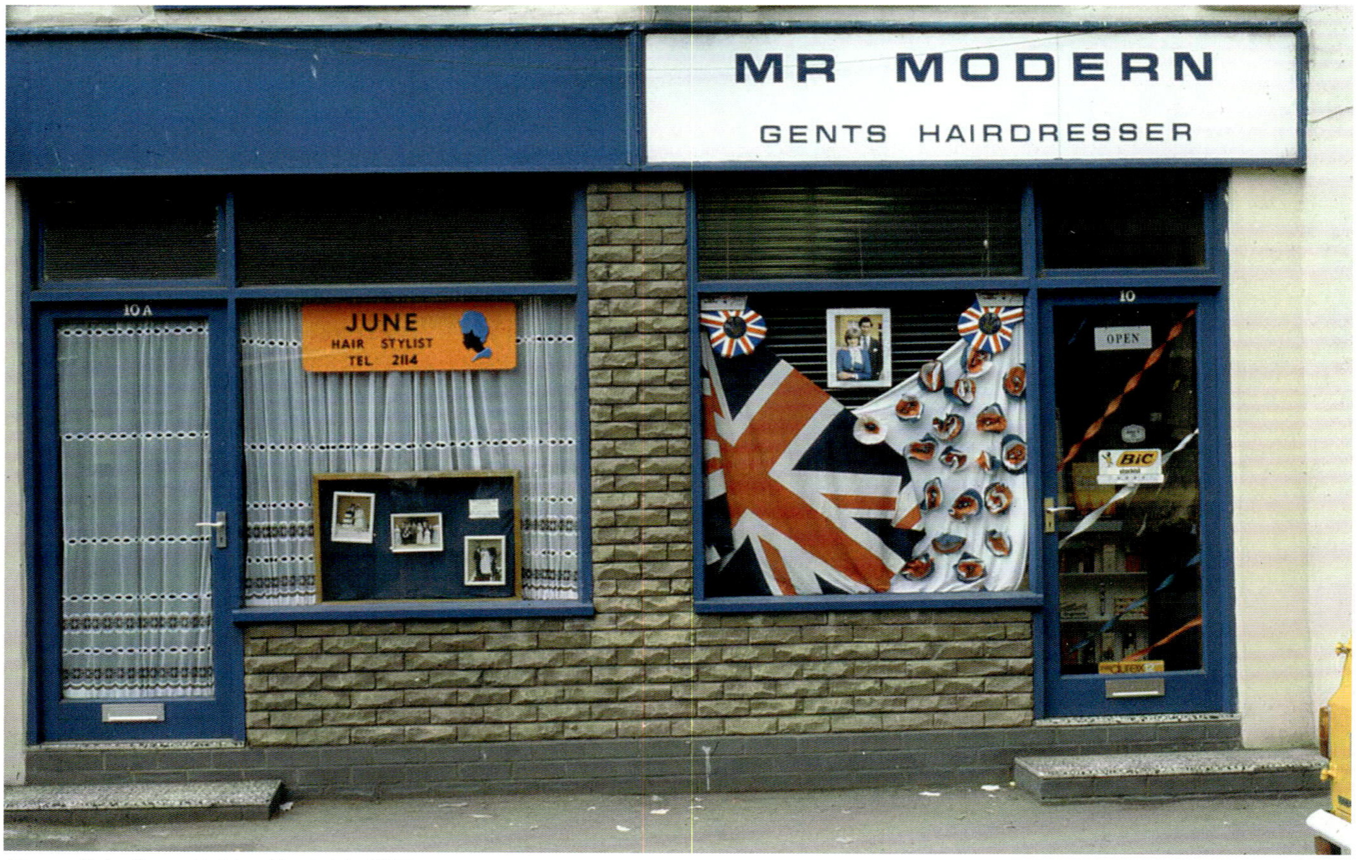

Above Twin Barge Holiday, Nantwich, 1980
Opposite Old Street, London, 1998
Pages 154–155 Bethnal Green Museum Store, London, 1959-60
Page 157 Deirdre, Silver Sands Motel, Key Biscayne, Florida, 1979
Pages 158–59 Deirdre, Cadaques, Spain, 1984 or 1985

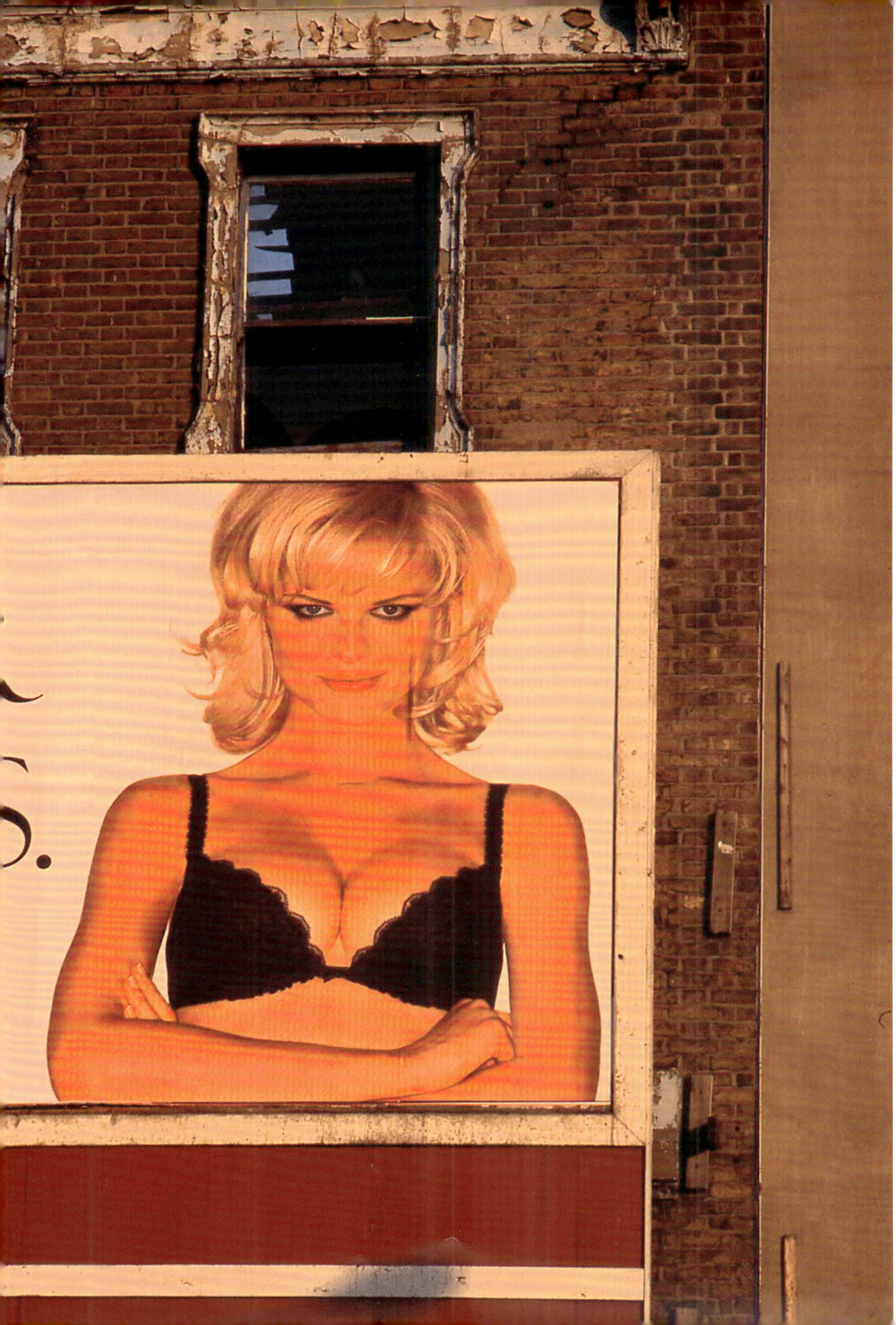

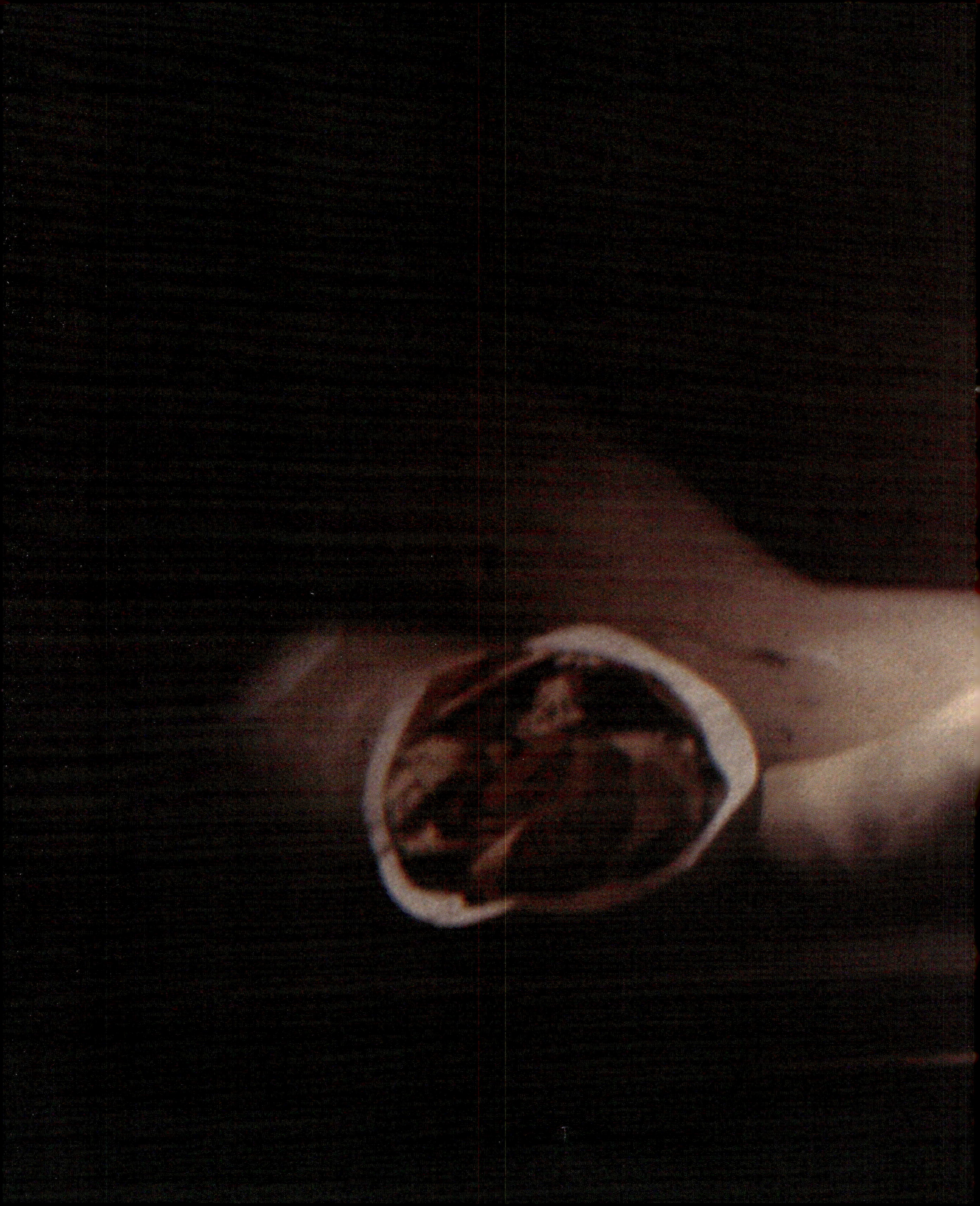

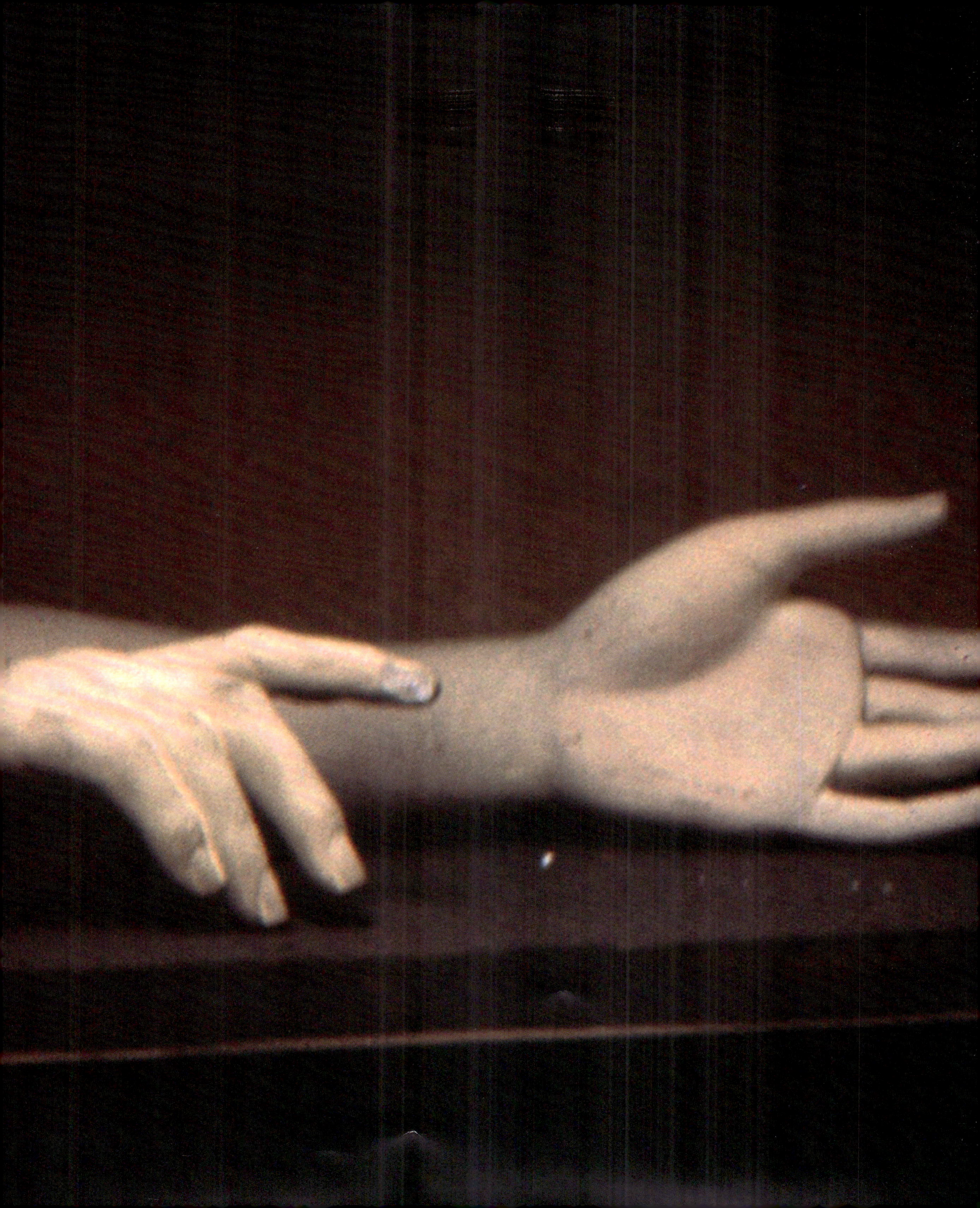

Each era establishes its own idea of beauty, and there is usually a degree of artifice in its creation. I was always drawn to a slogan in a Frederick's of Hollywood mail order catalogue from the Fifties and Sixties; "Where nature leaves off – add pads".

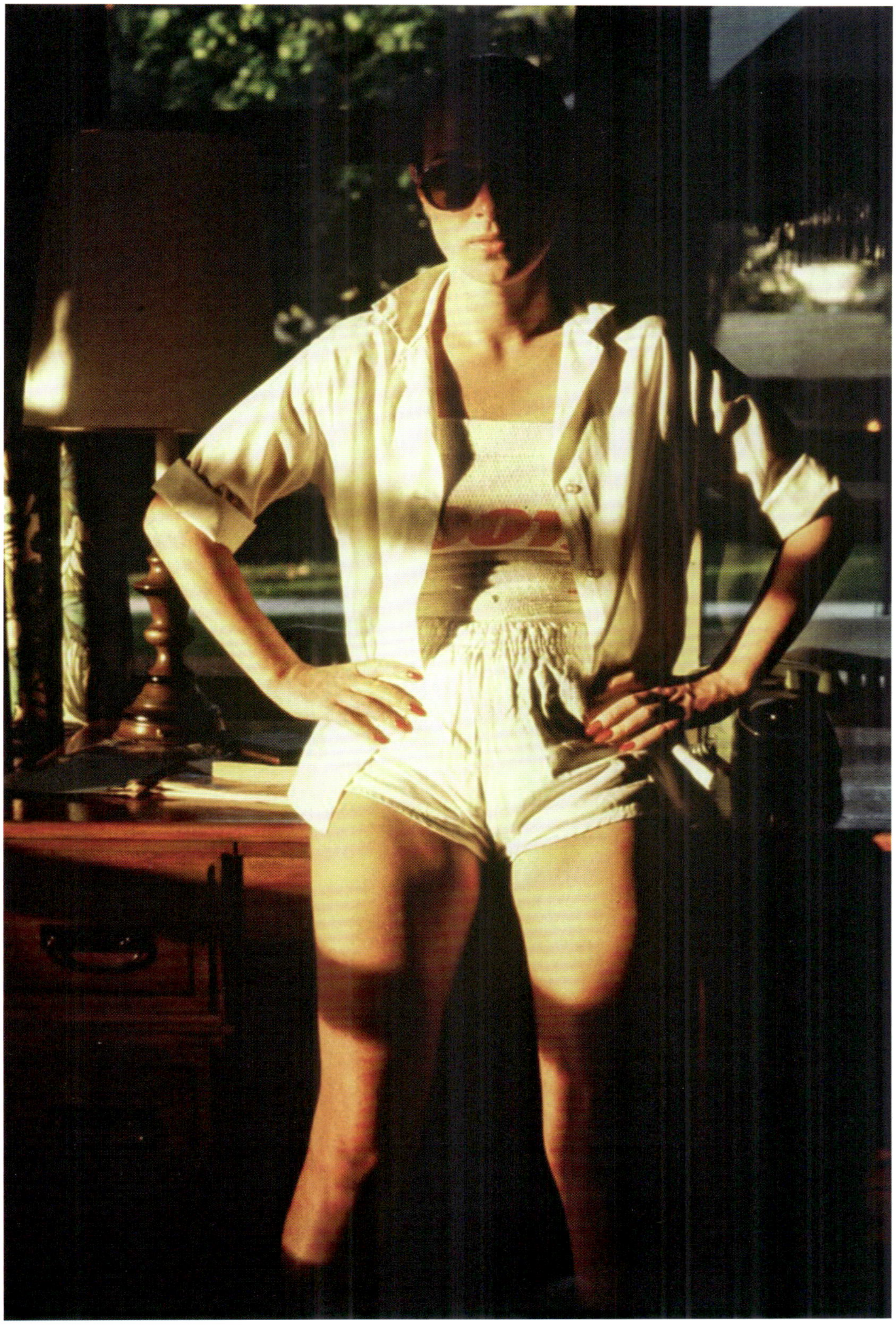

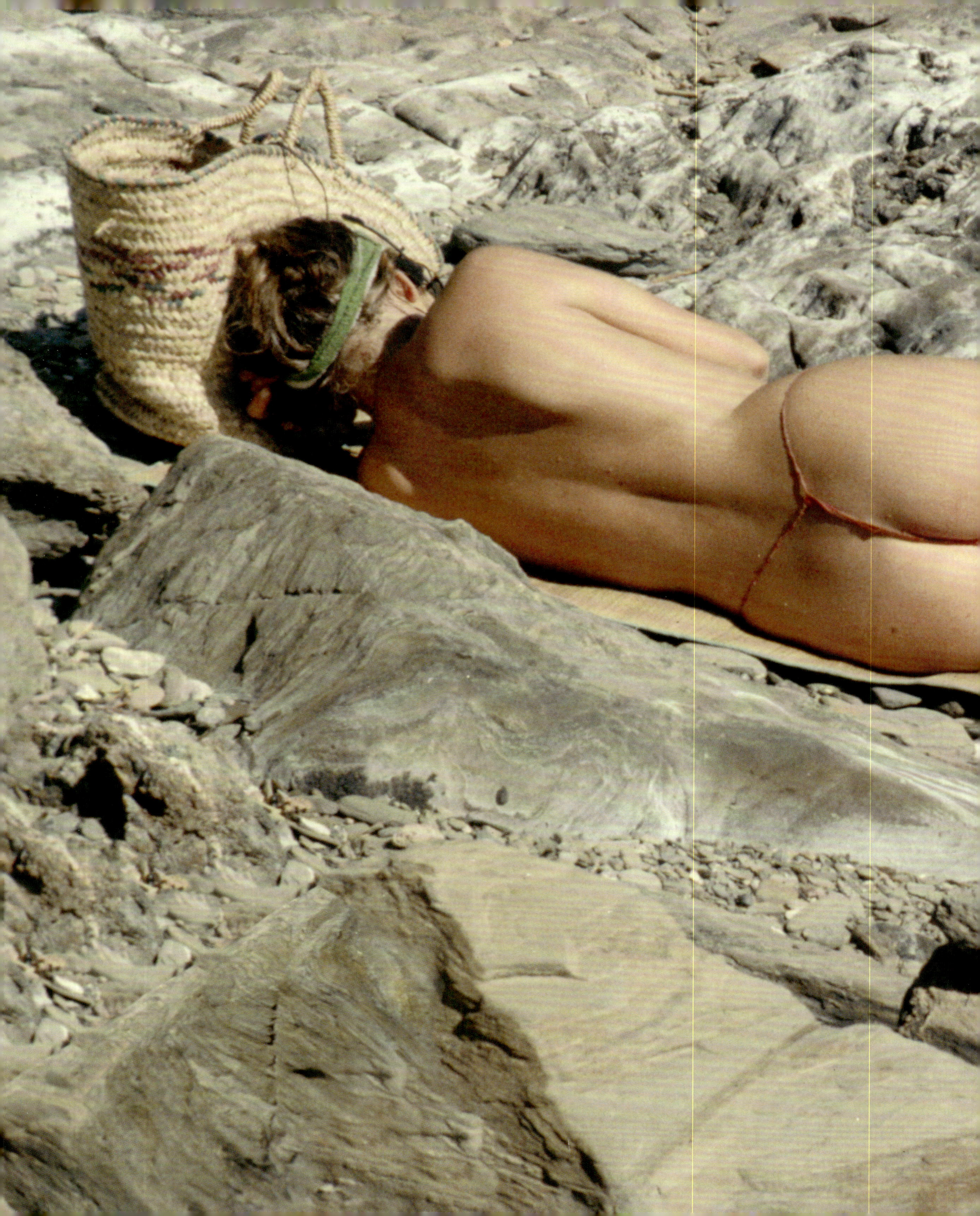

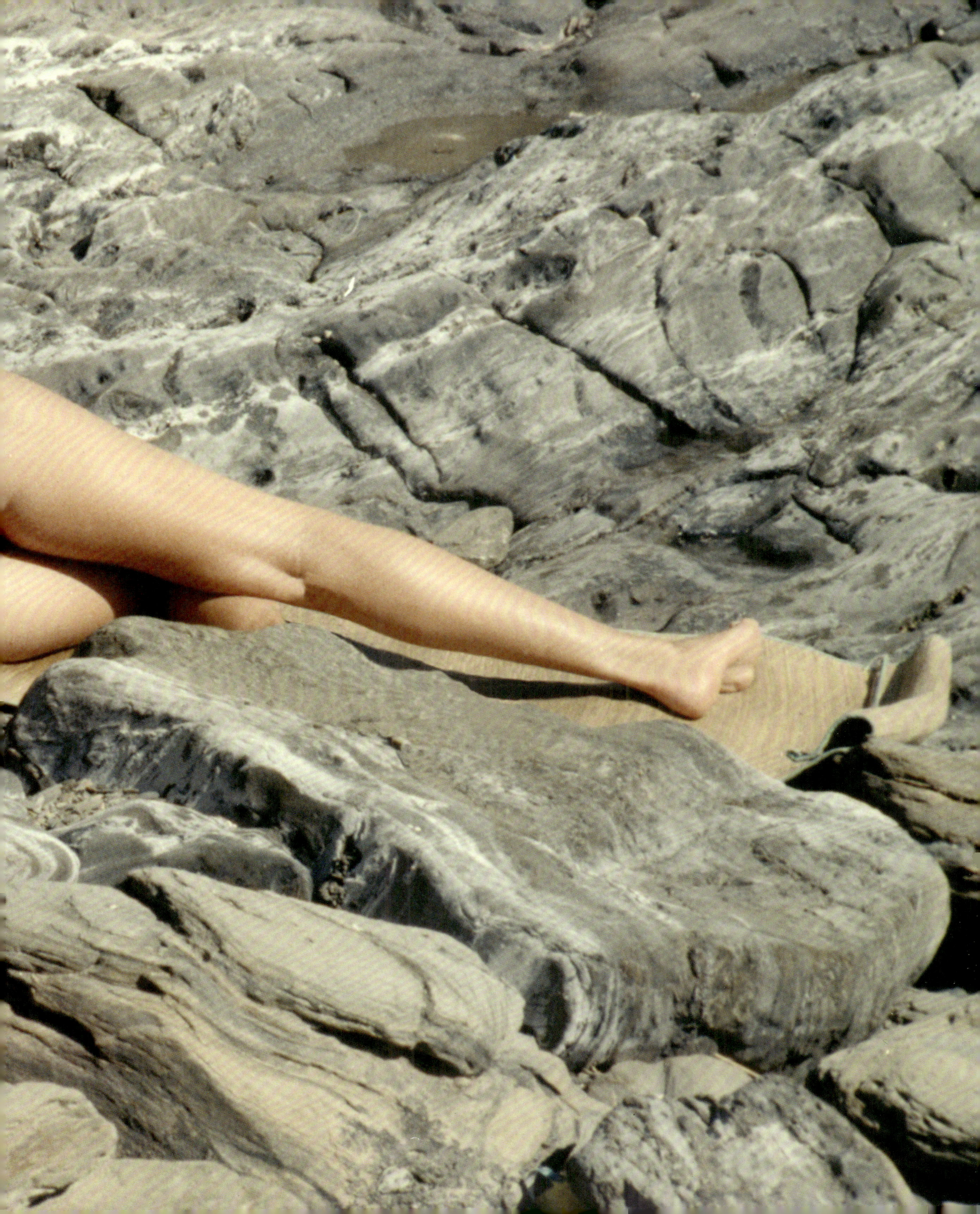

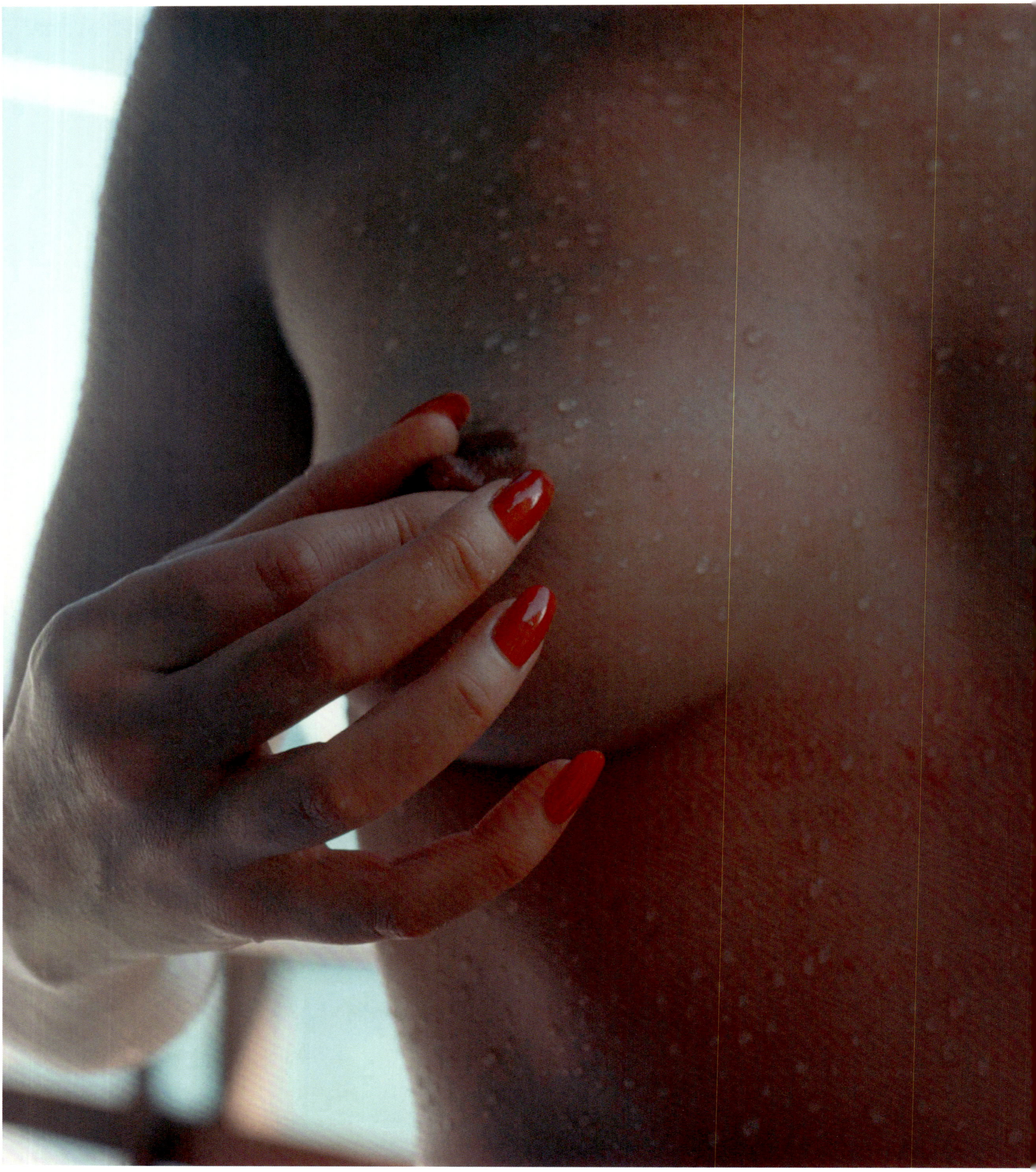

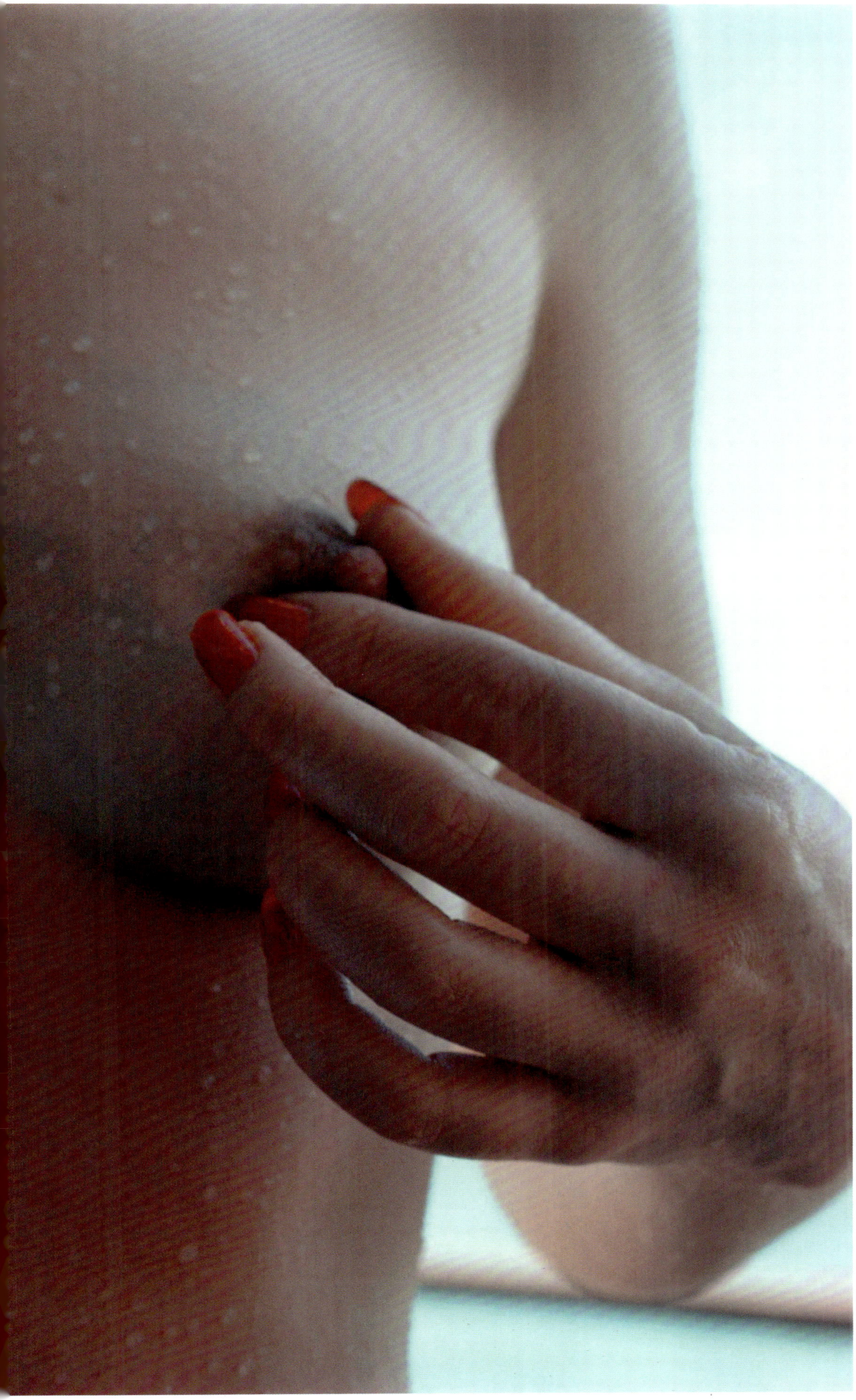

Deirdre, Silver Sands Motel, Key Biscayne, Florida, 1979
Overleaf Deirdre, Edith Grove, 1978

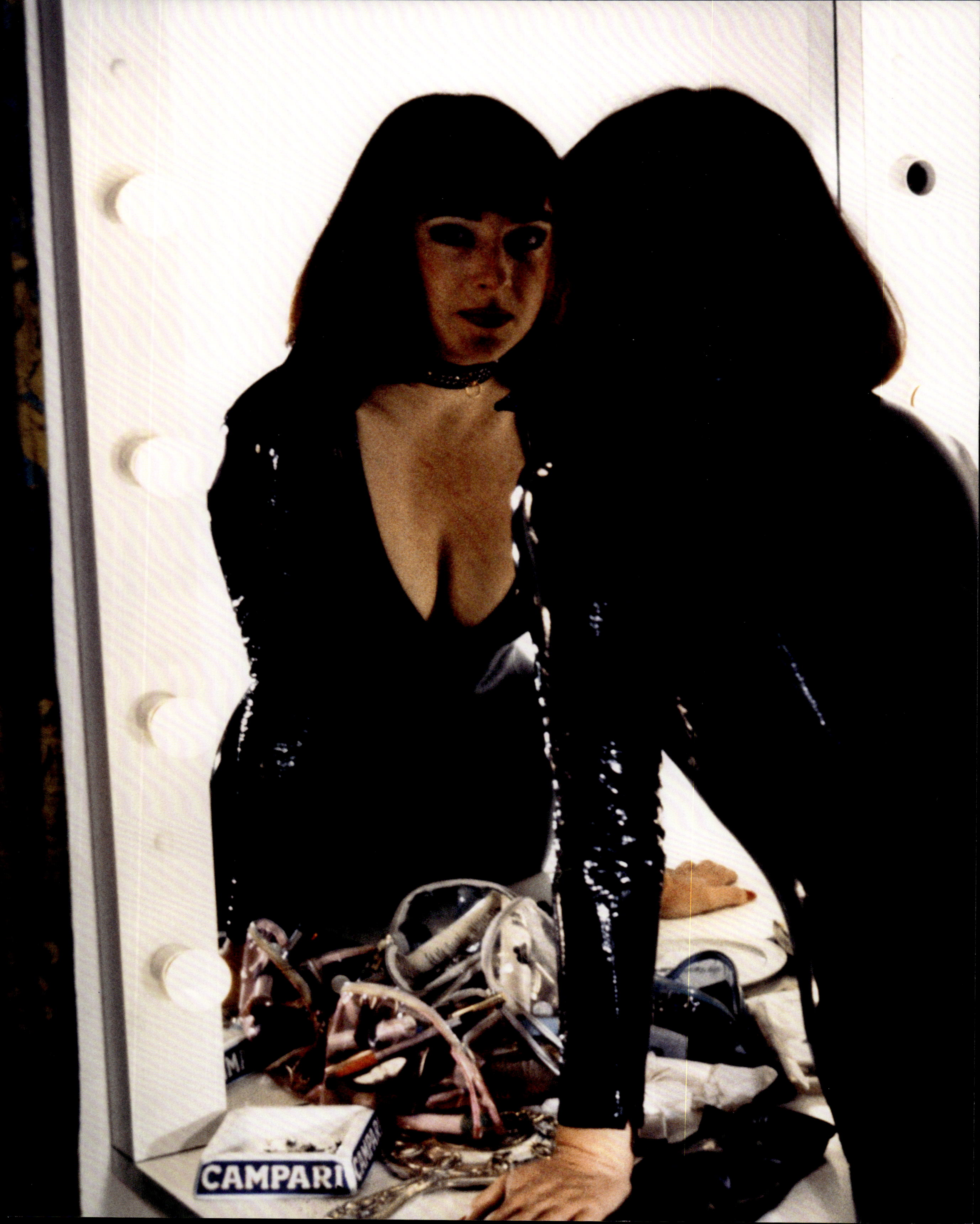
CAMPARI

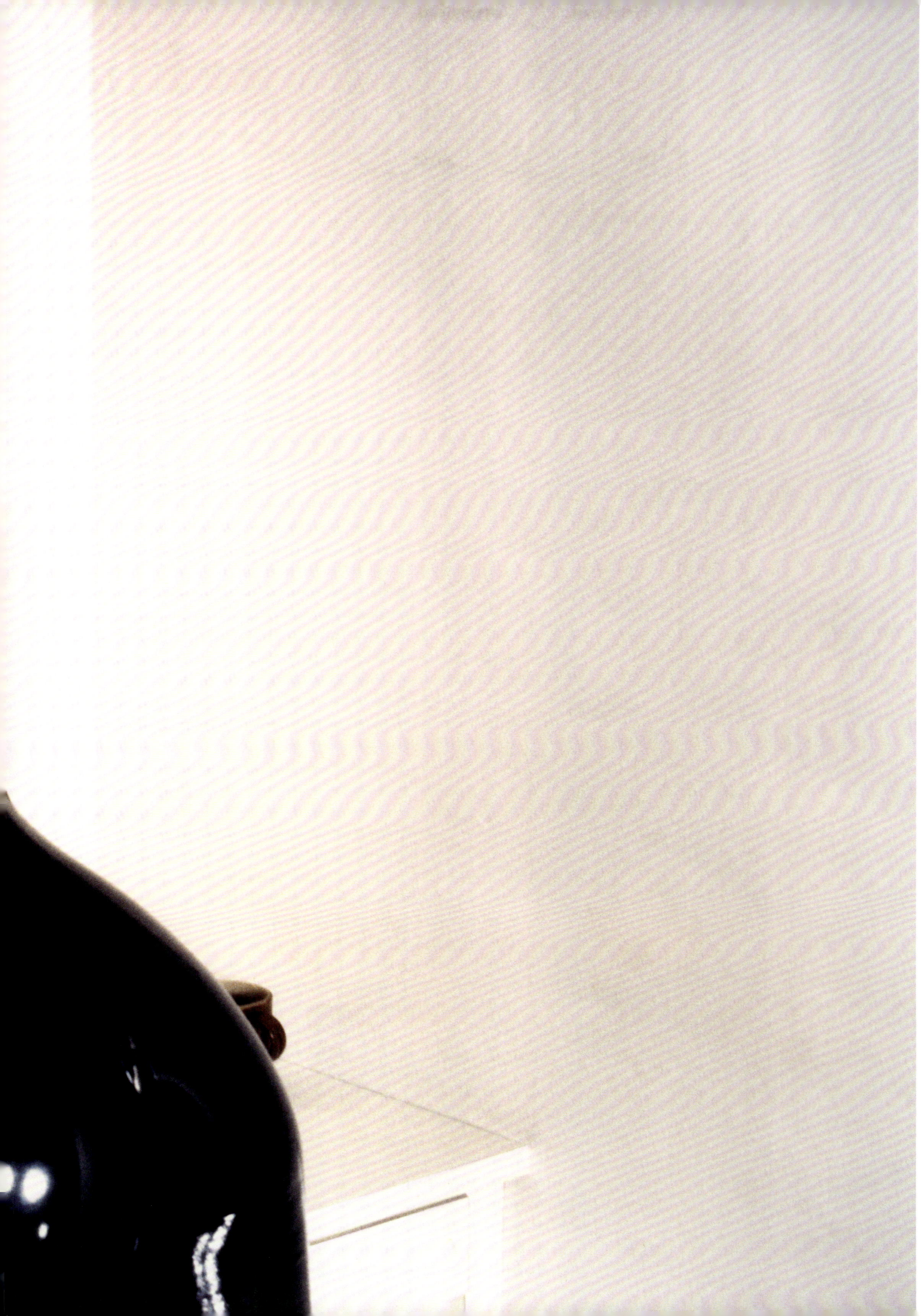

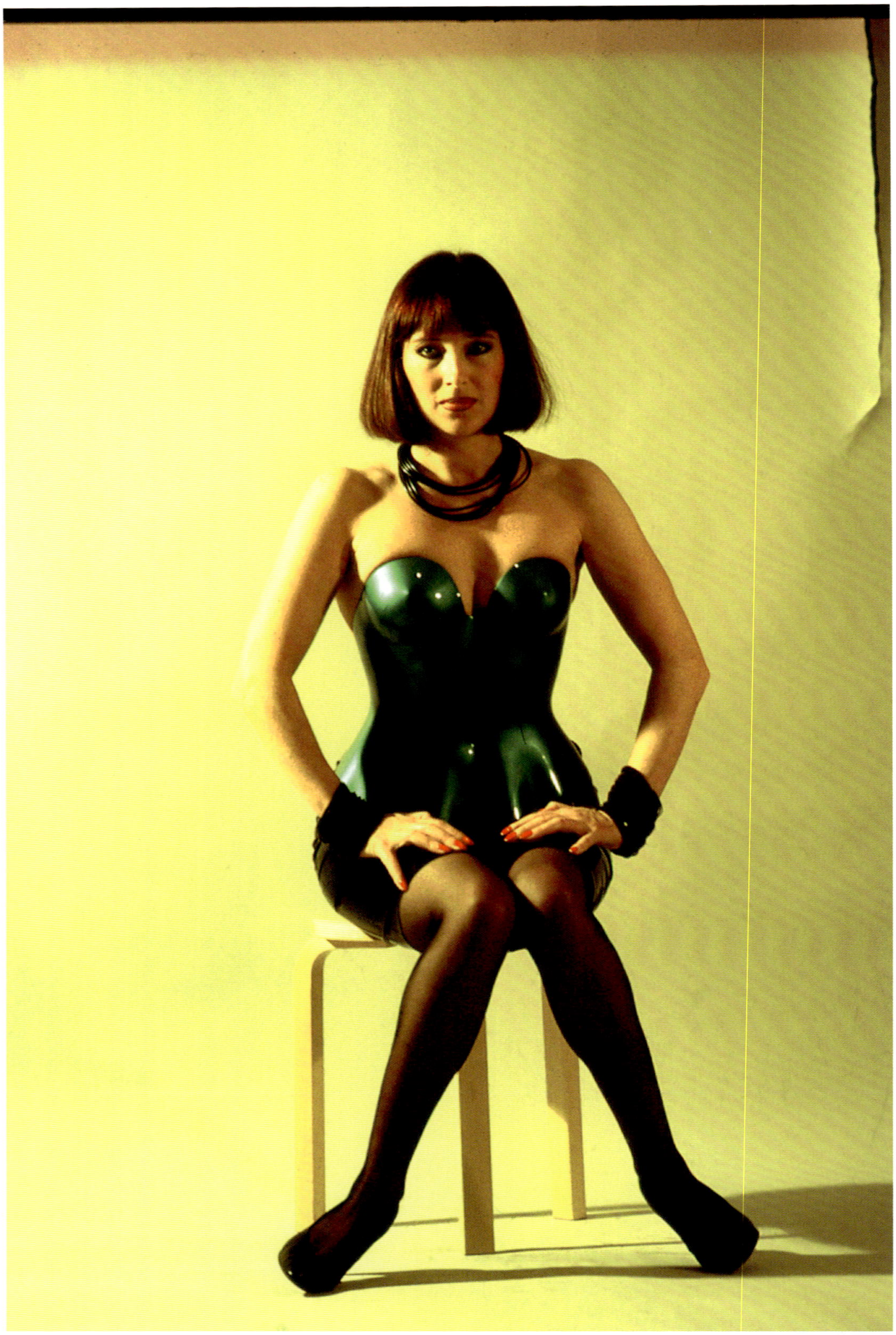

Above Deirdre in Issey Miyake bustier inspired by Allen Jones, 1986
Opposite Deirdre (1978) and 'Waiting on Table II' (1987), 2019

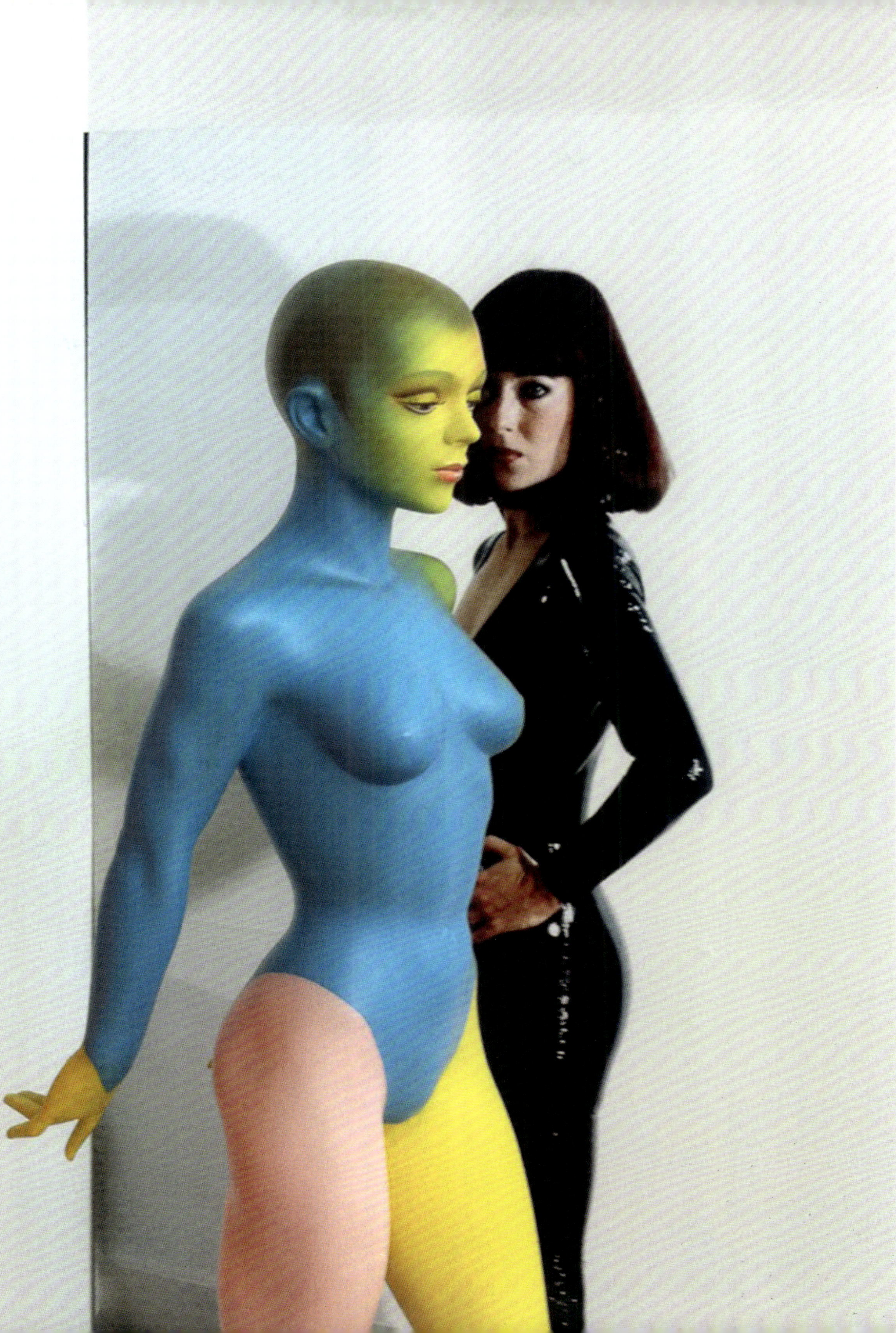

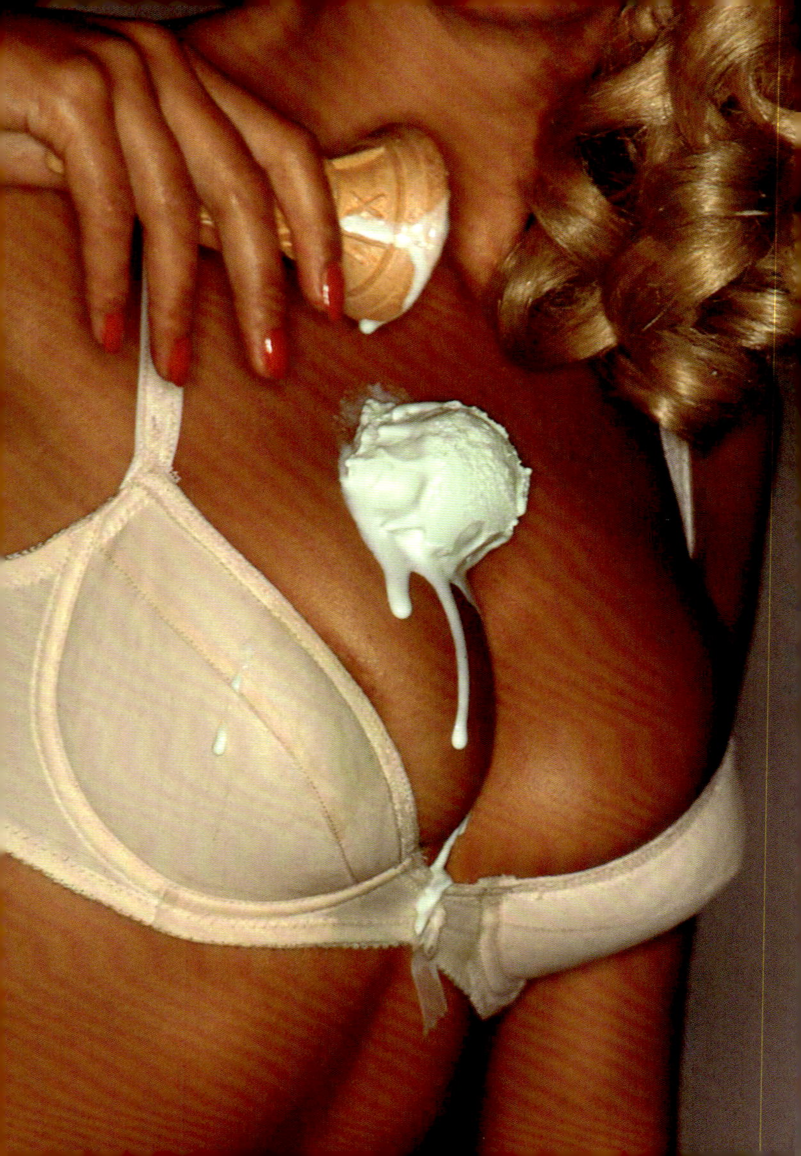

Pirelli

The people who handled the Pirelli account got in touch with me and asked if I would be interested in creating a calendar. Hitherto, these had all been made by photographers. So this was a new departure for them, and I was interested in working within disciplines other than painting or printmaking – which I had only done so far with my sculptures. I had to come up with the concept for each month – twelve images for twelve months – and basically art direct them.

My naivety helped a lot. I didn't take into account at all what the client might want, because I figured if they chose me, they chose me for what I would do and I did not want to be concerned with what Pirelli's strategy might be. I concentrated on being as original as possible within the frame of reference, and steering my collaborators who would bring their specialist technical skills to the project. Because of my printmaking past, I had experience of working with professional studios. I was comfortable working with people who would give their input from the point of view of their expertise, though I had not worked with commercial photographers.

I proposed a photographer we knew socially, John Clarke, and set up a trial run. We shot one of the images that I had suggested, which was of a hand holding an ice cream cone, tilted so that a dollop of ice cream had fallen onto the cleavage. It was collaborative and we were not so much thinking of the time involved but just working to get it right. I presented the result to the design and production team led by Derek Forsyth. He came back to me and said that this was going to take forever and cost an arm and a leg. He had a photographer in mind, Duffy, who could do it within budget, and each knew how the other worked. I accepted this, but it did distance me from the process. It became more of a case of my saying, 'Here's the image. Do your best with it.' I did actually art direct but something went out of it for me.

The idea was to use the photographic process but to straddle between photographic and graphic representation. Philip Castle was then the ace airbrush illustrator. He was a specialist, highly skilled, and bringing him in was a part of my interest in removing my own expressionist involvement with image-making, just as it had been a key impulse in my making the furniture sculpture in 1969 – which is presumably what got me onto Pirelli's radar.

Opposite Photograph by John Clarke for Allen Jones, 1972 for 1973 Pirelli calendar (not included in final calendar)

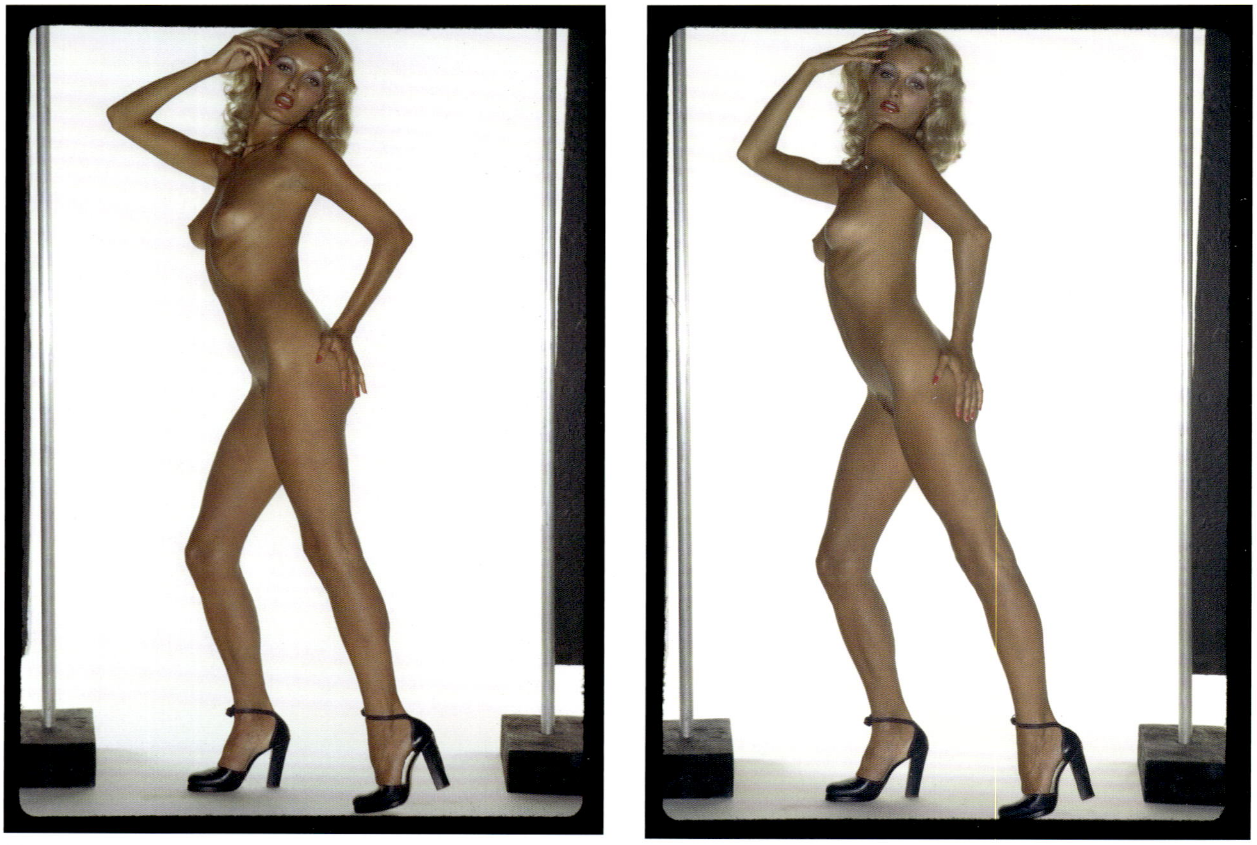

Above Photographs by Duffy for Allen Jones, 1972 (variant frames of selected image)
Opposite The Pirelli calendar page after airbrush work by Philip Castle, 1973

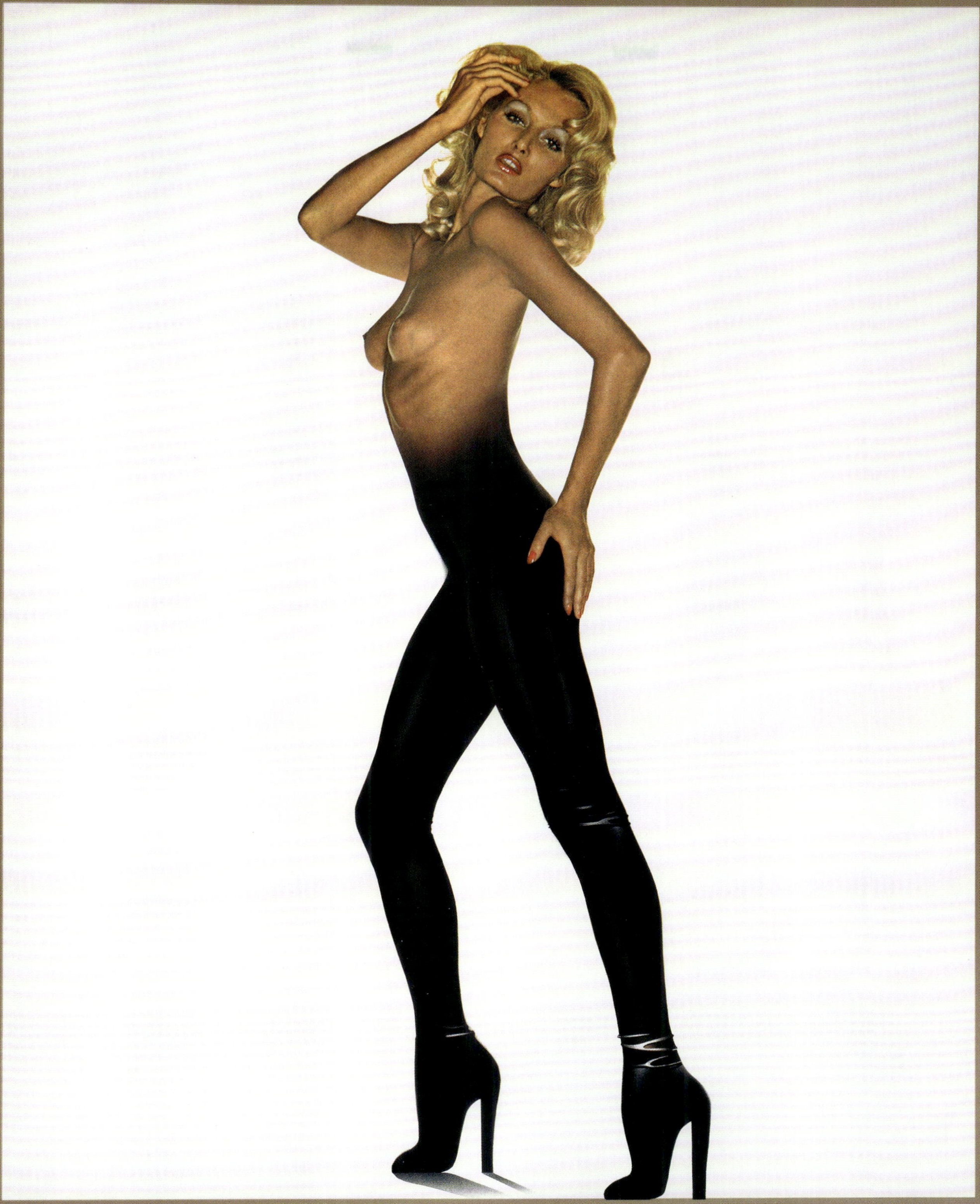

JUNE PIRELLI

Friday	Saturday	Sunday	Monday	Tuesday	Wednesday	Thursday	Friday	Saturday	Sunday	Monday	Tuesday	Wednesday	Thursday	Friday	Saturday
1	2	3	4	5	6	7	8	9	10	11	12	13	14	15	16

Sunday	Monday	Tuesday	Wednesday	Thursday	Friday	Saturday	Sunday	Monday	Tuesday	Wednesday	Thursday	Friday	Saturday
17	18	19	20	21	22	23	24	25	26	27	28	29	30

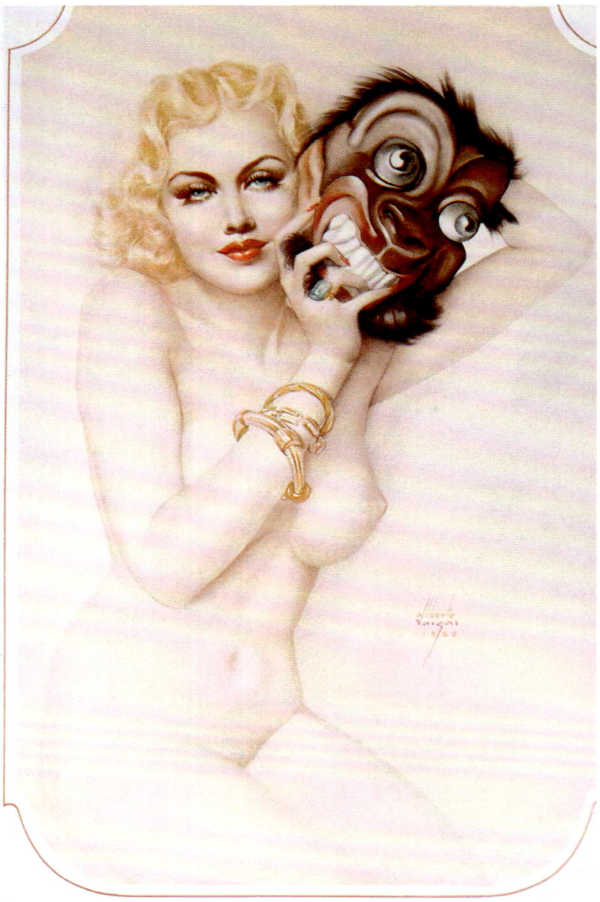

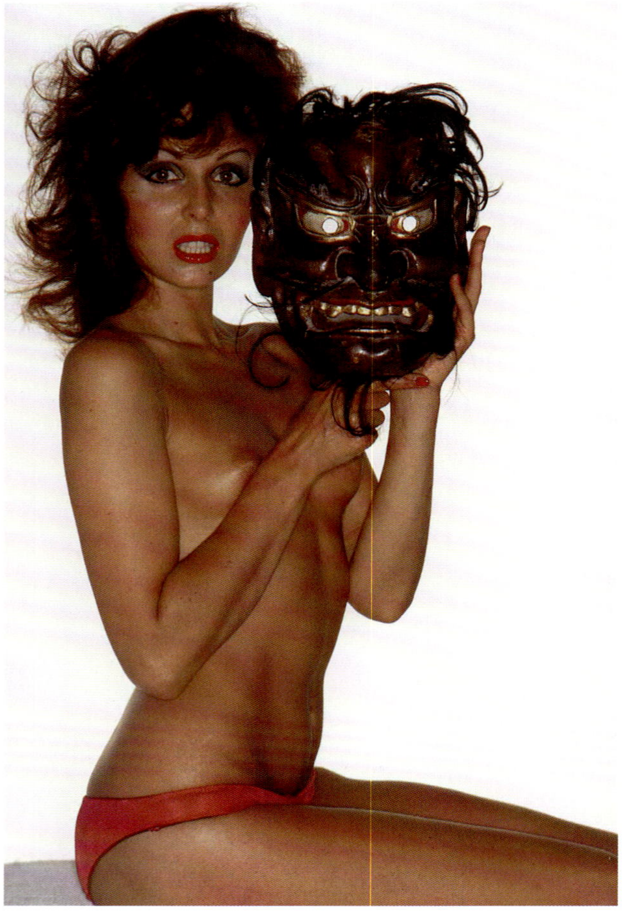

Above Source of inspiration and photograph by Duffy for Allen Jones, 1972
Opposite The Pirelli calendar page after airbrush work by Philip Castle, 1973
Page 173 Photograph by Duffy for Allen Jones, 1972

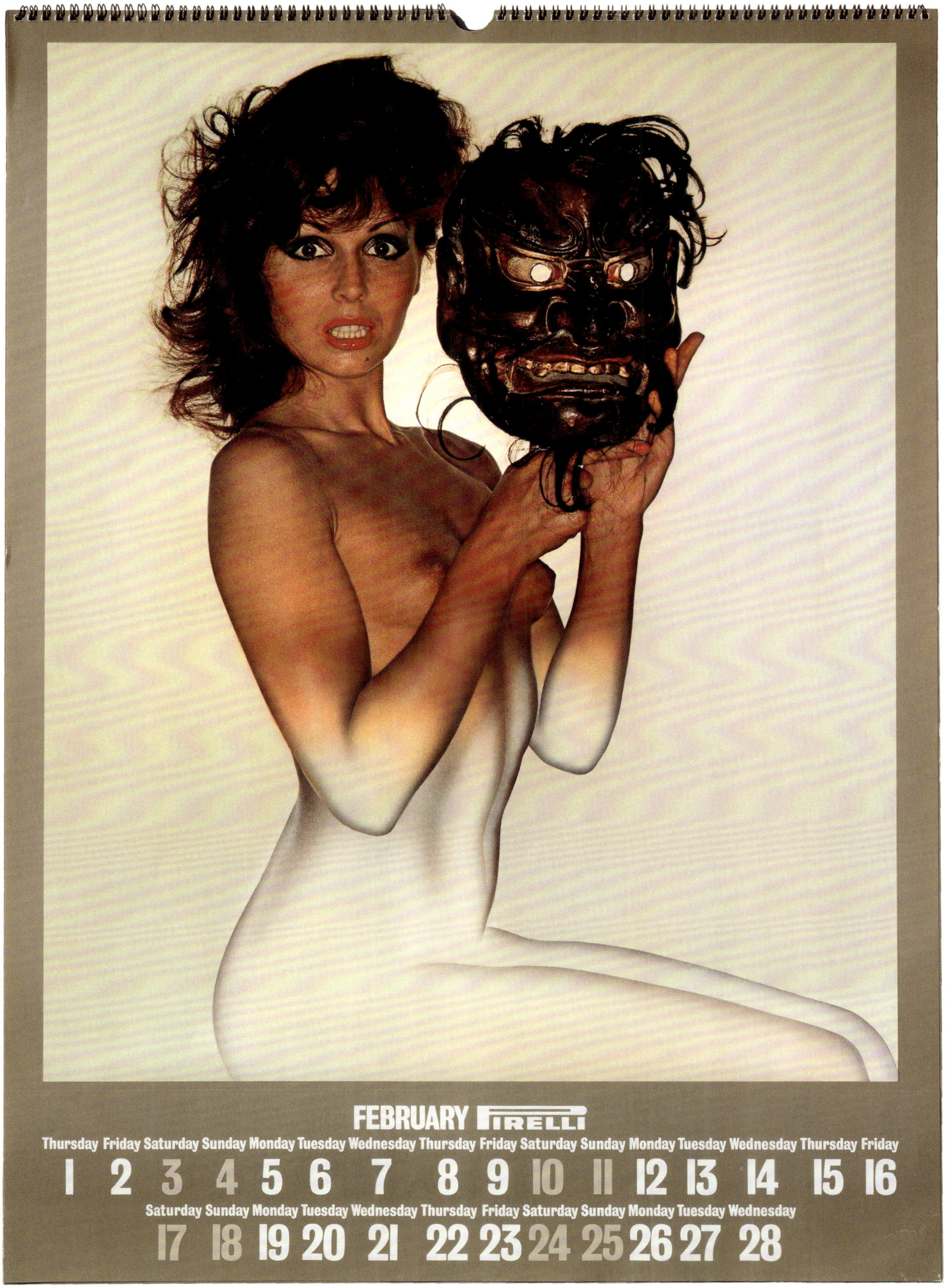
FEBRUARY PIRELLI
Thursday Friday Saturday Sunday Monday Tuesday Wednesday Thursday Friday Saturday Sunday Monday Tuesday Wednesday Thursday Friday
1 2 3 4 5 6 7 8 9 10 11 12 13 14 15 16
Saturday Sunday Monday Tuesday Wednesday Thursday Friday Saturday Sunday Monday Tuesday Wednesday
17 18 19 20 21 22 23 24 25 26 27 28

I have always been interested in "hands-on" sculpture. In the late Sixties, I had made an edition of a vacuum-formed plastic breastplate. It subsequently became the subject of a photograph for my Pirelli calendar, allowing me to echo the Pygmalion story, in which an artist's sculpture comes to life.

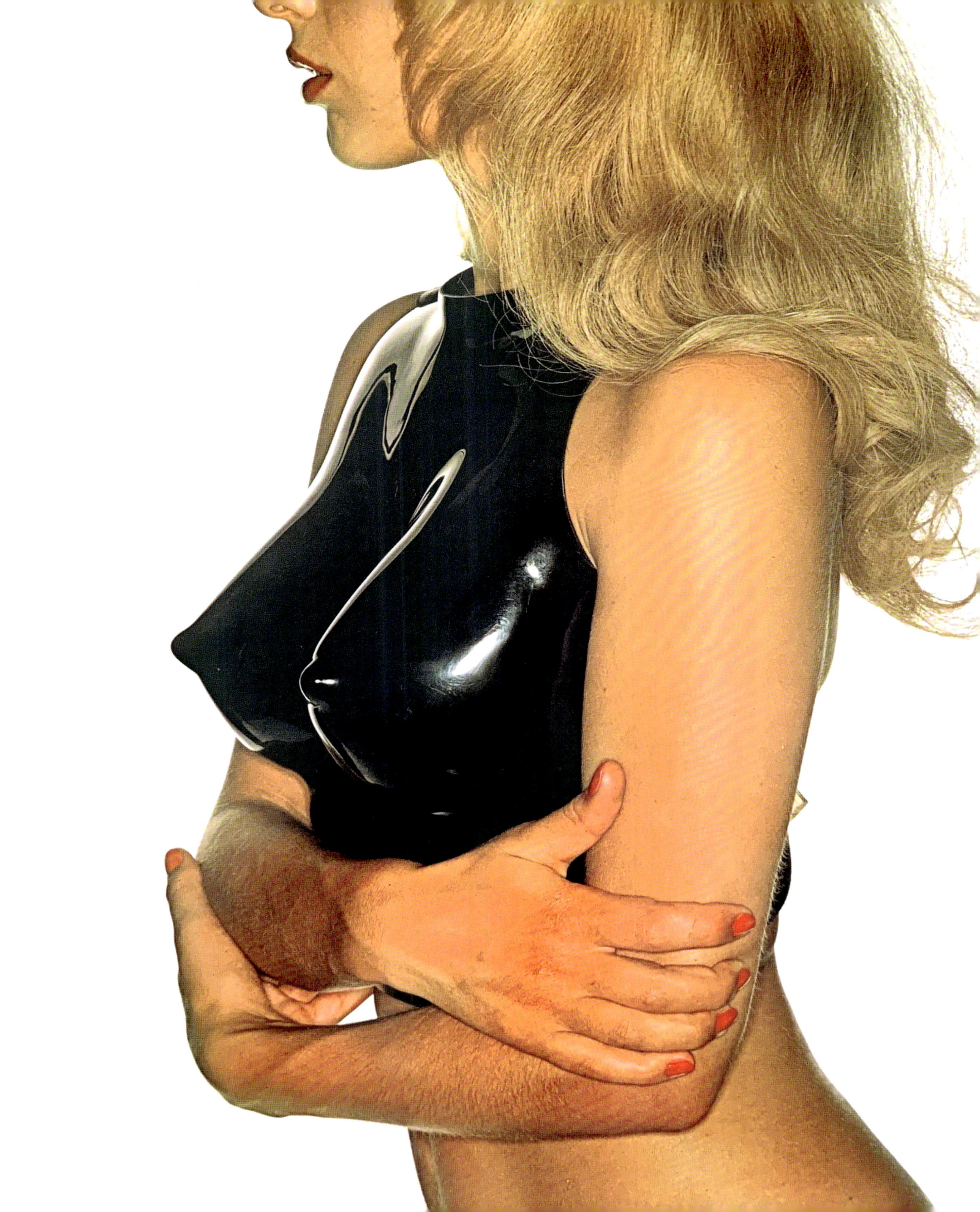

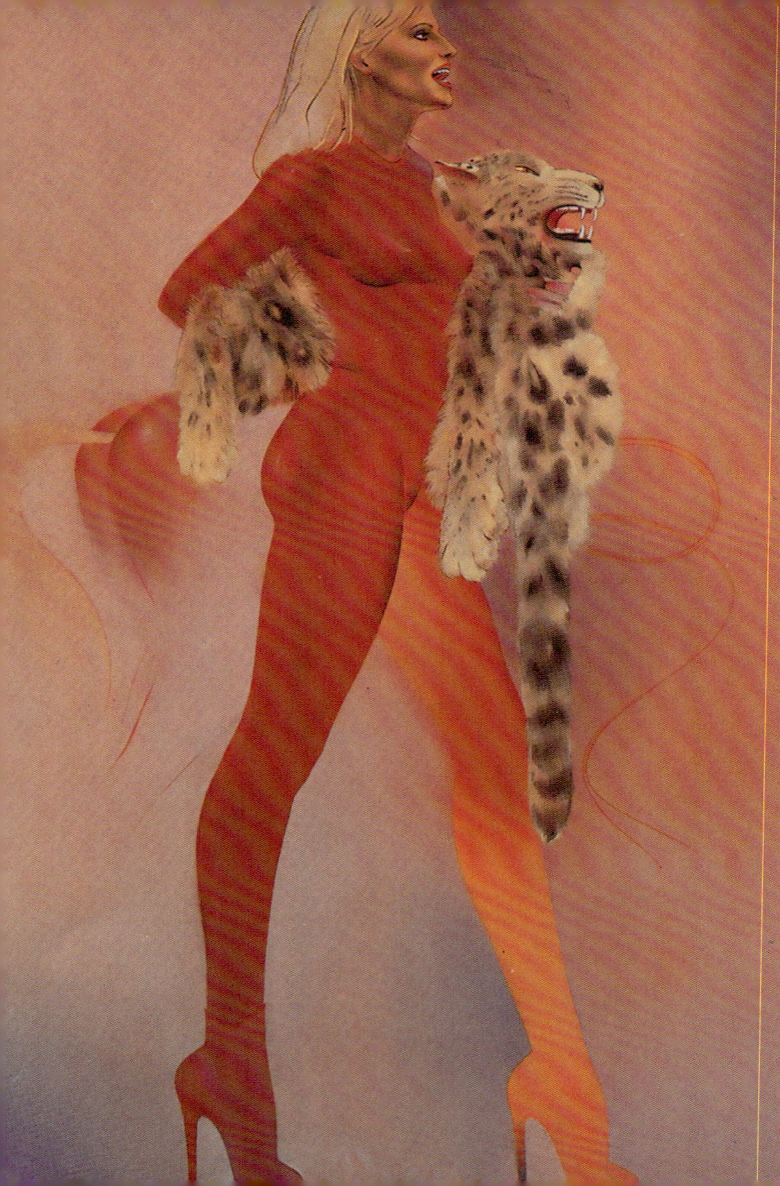

Leopard Lady

Opposite 'Leopard Lady' on the cover of *Deluxe*, issue 2, 1977
Pages 176–179 Evelyn Kuhn, Larry Rivers's studio, New York, 1976

The commission for the portrait that acquired the title 'Leopard Lady', as with my other rare portraits, came out of the blue. Peter Beard got in touch with me. I didn't know him or even know of him at that time. He rang from America and said that he had someone who was interested in my making a portrait of this particular woman, a model, Evelyn Kuhn, who was then the 'Revlon girl'. I asked questions and became intrigued when I learned that the man, who had a huge collection of photographs of this woman which he'd had people like Avedon take, had never met her and didn't have a particular interest in meeting her. That somehow resonated with my perverse nature. I was intrigued. The man's company apparently produced six percent of the gross national output of Nigeria. Beard had met him through his African connections. The girl was aware of the man's obsession and was earning quite well being photographed for him by the world's great photographers. It was a commercial deal. So, I said, 'Well, a condition is that, if I am going to make her portrait, then I do have to see her. Peter said, 'Listen, he has files of photographs of her armpits, the back of her knees…' So I said that makes it more curious and more interesting. He said, 'Well, you have to come to New York and we will pay for you to come.' I knew I could do the work in London but I had to see the woman and draw and photograph her, not because I would work faithfully from these studies, but as a means to look at her closely in preparation for creating an image. It was essential that I meet her so that I got the sense of her and could then somehow symbolise her rather than simply illustrate her.

So I went to New York, and Larry Rivers, with whom I was on nodding terms, let us use his studio downtown on 14th Street over on the East Side. My challenge was to avoid taking just one photograph and copying it in paint. Effectively, making all those photographs helped me construct a matrix from her, though I did use one particular profile photo because it seemed to characterise her head. In spite of the looking and the drawing, I was not comfortable with recreating it. There would be too much left to the imagination or to invent.

The idea of the leopard came from the African association of the client and of Peter Beard, one of whose photographs, cut from a magazine, of a girl stretched out on a crocodile features coincidentally in one of my collages [see p. 53]. I met the client only once, at his hotel, and we made the deal.

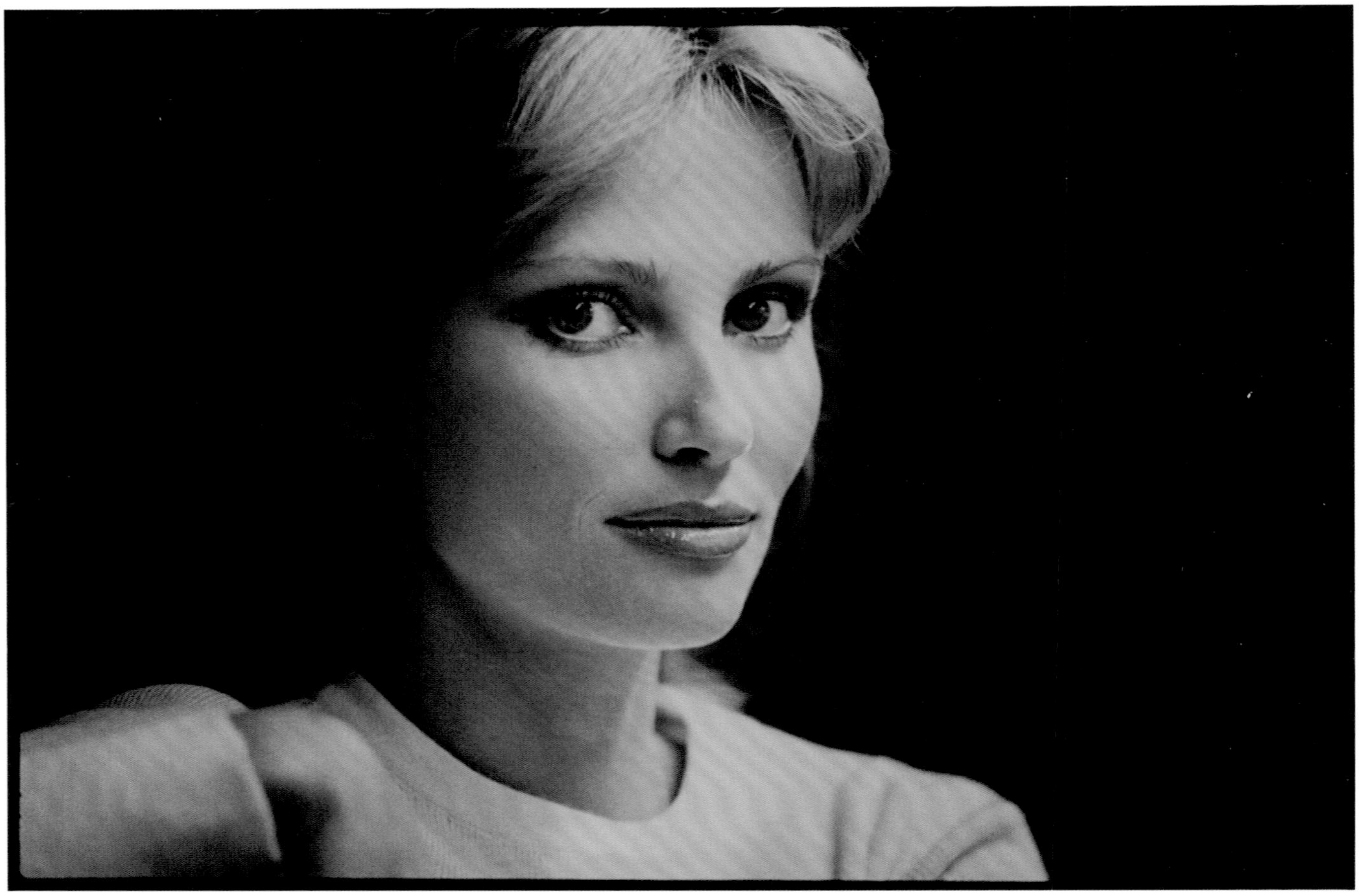

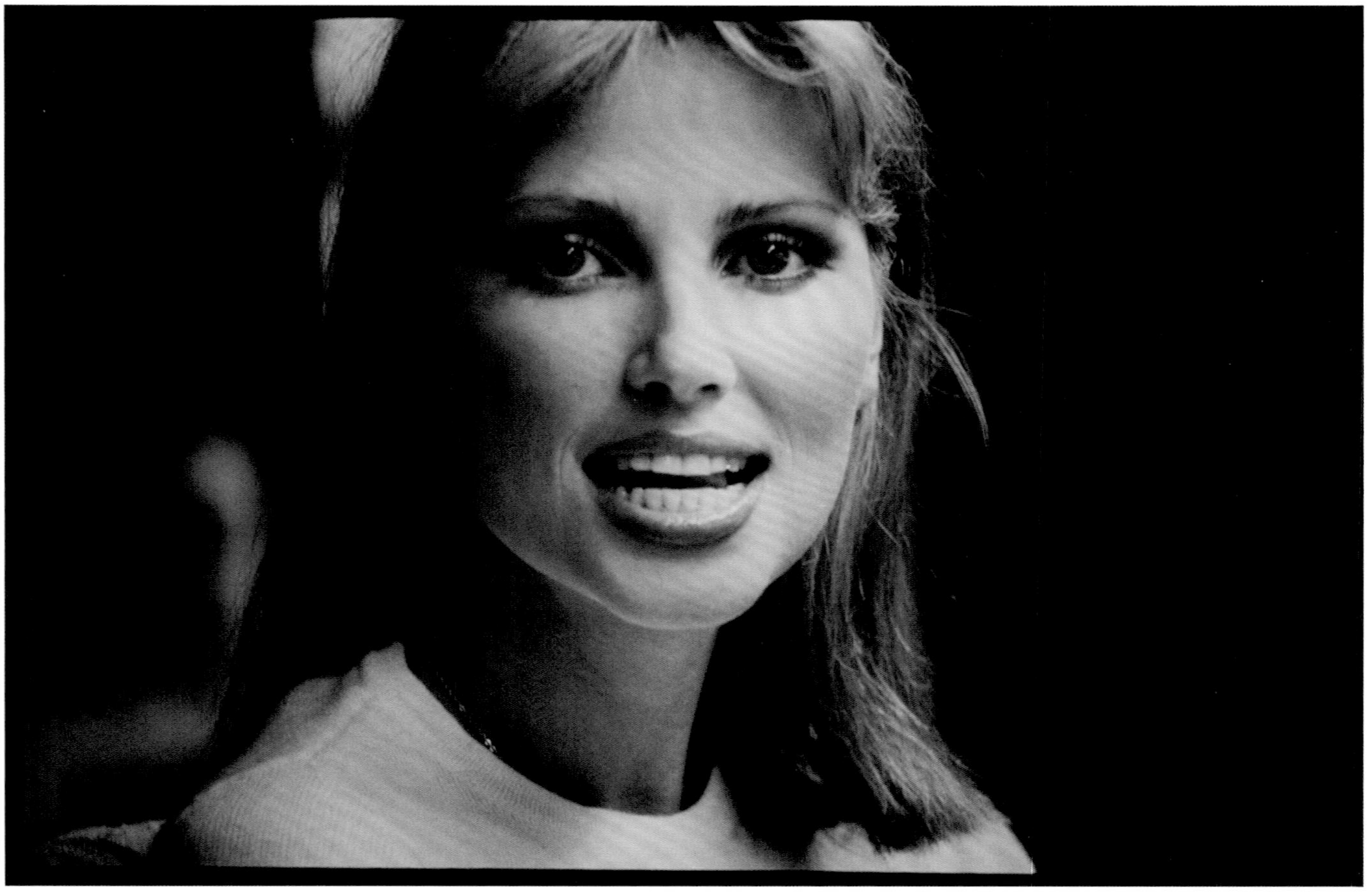

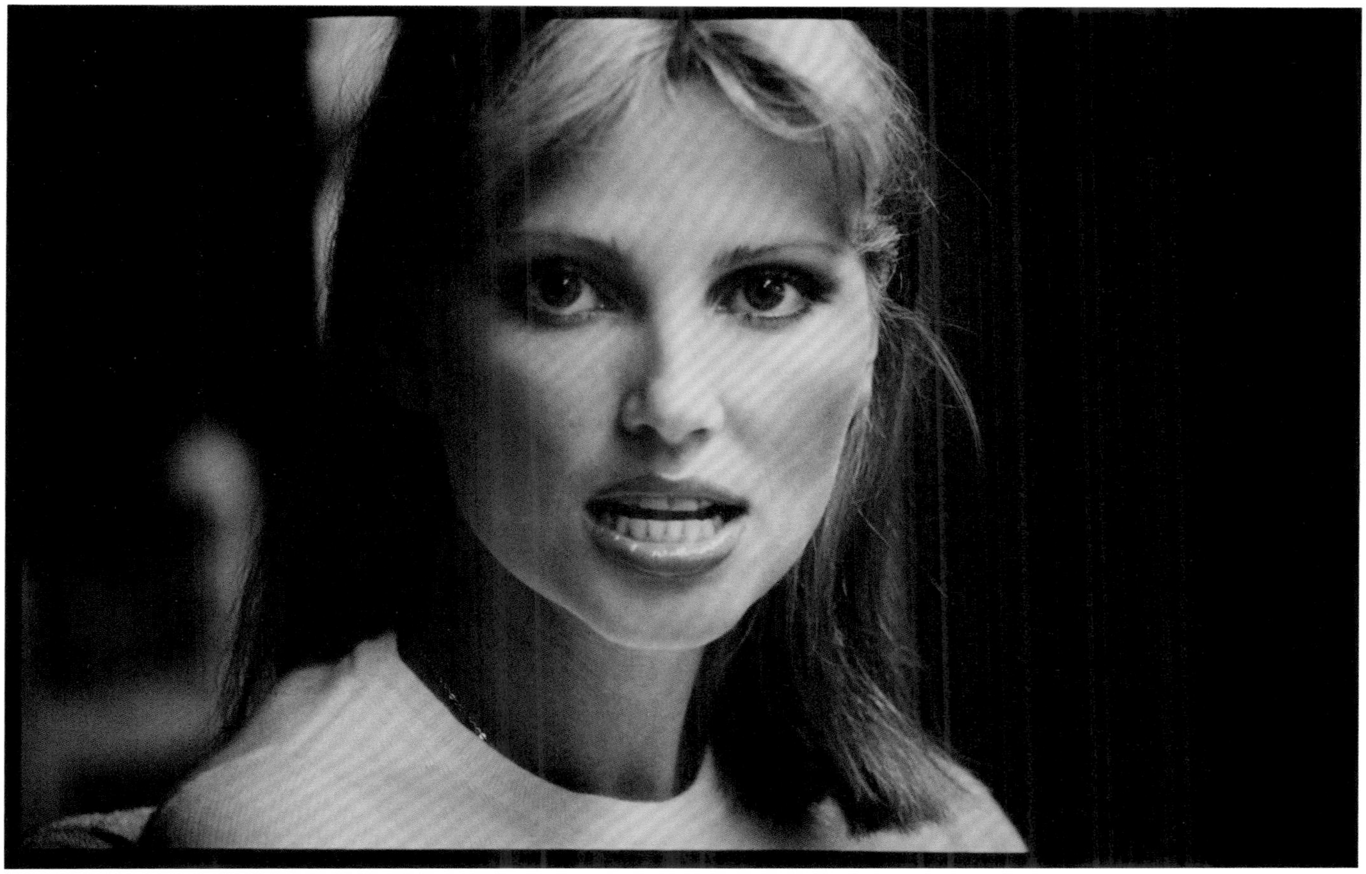

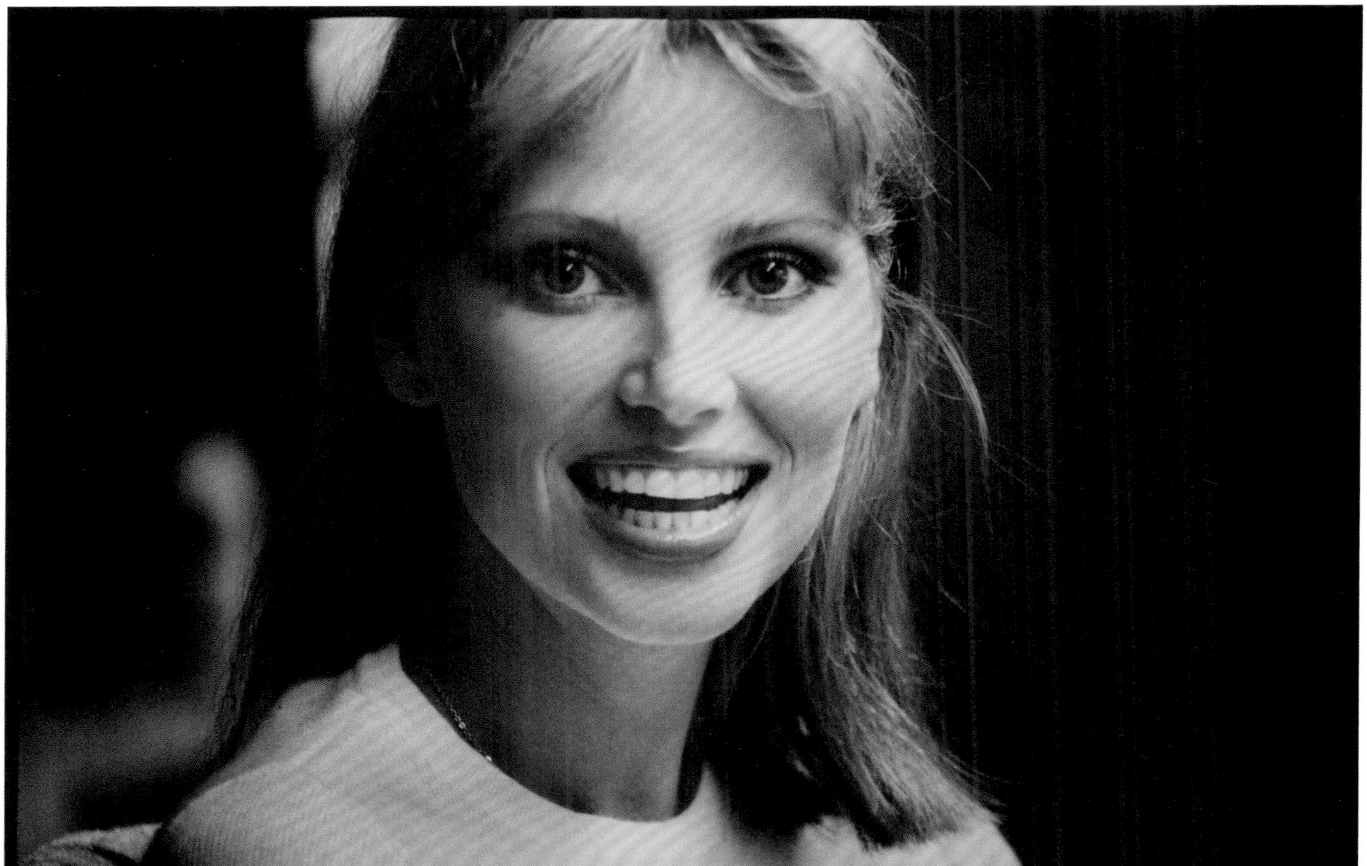

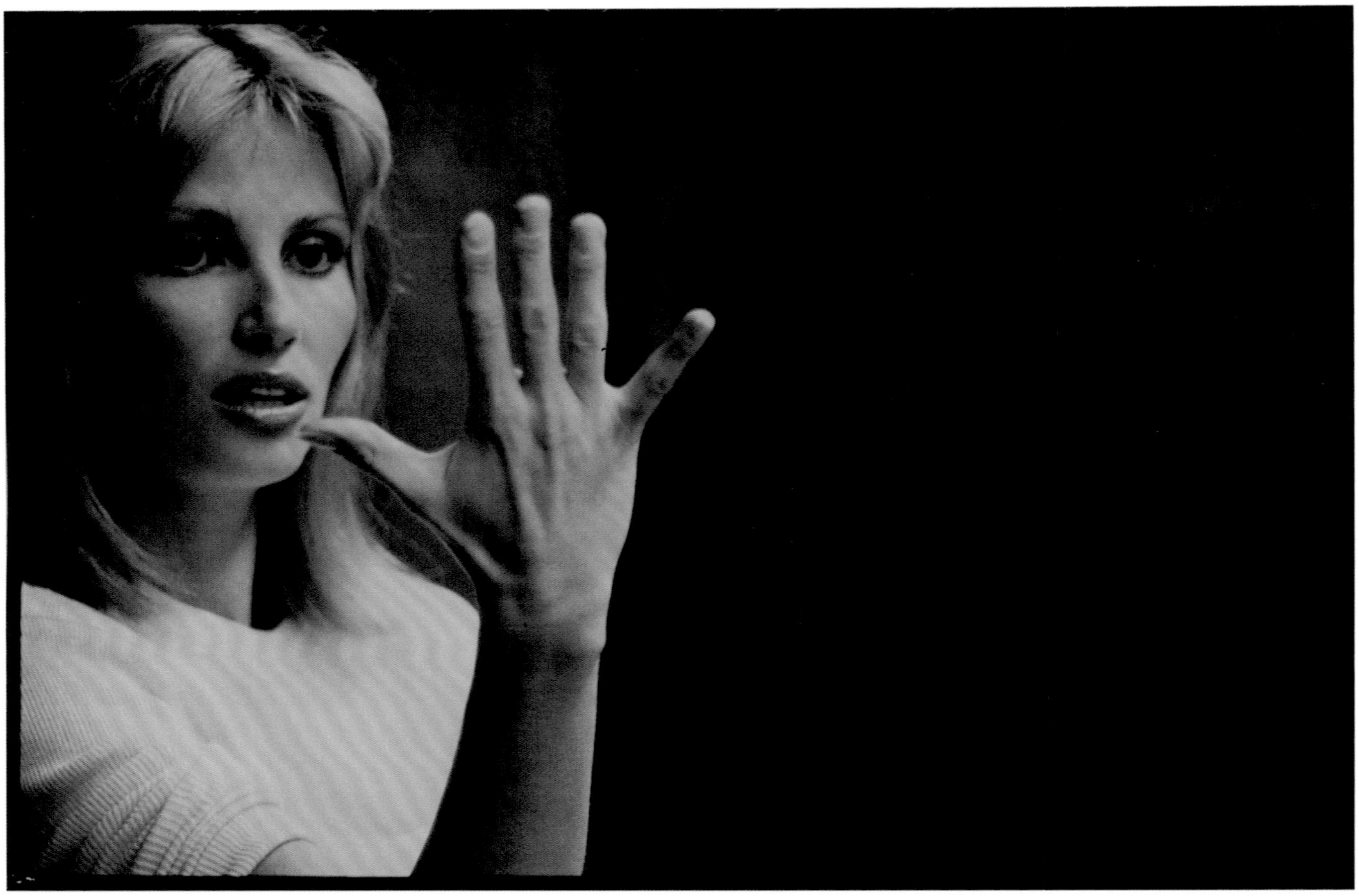

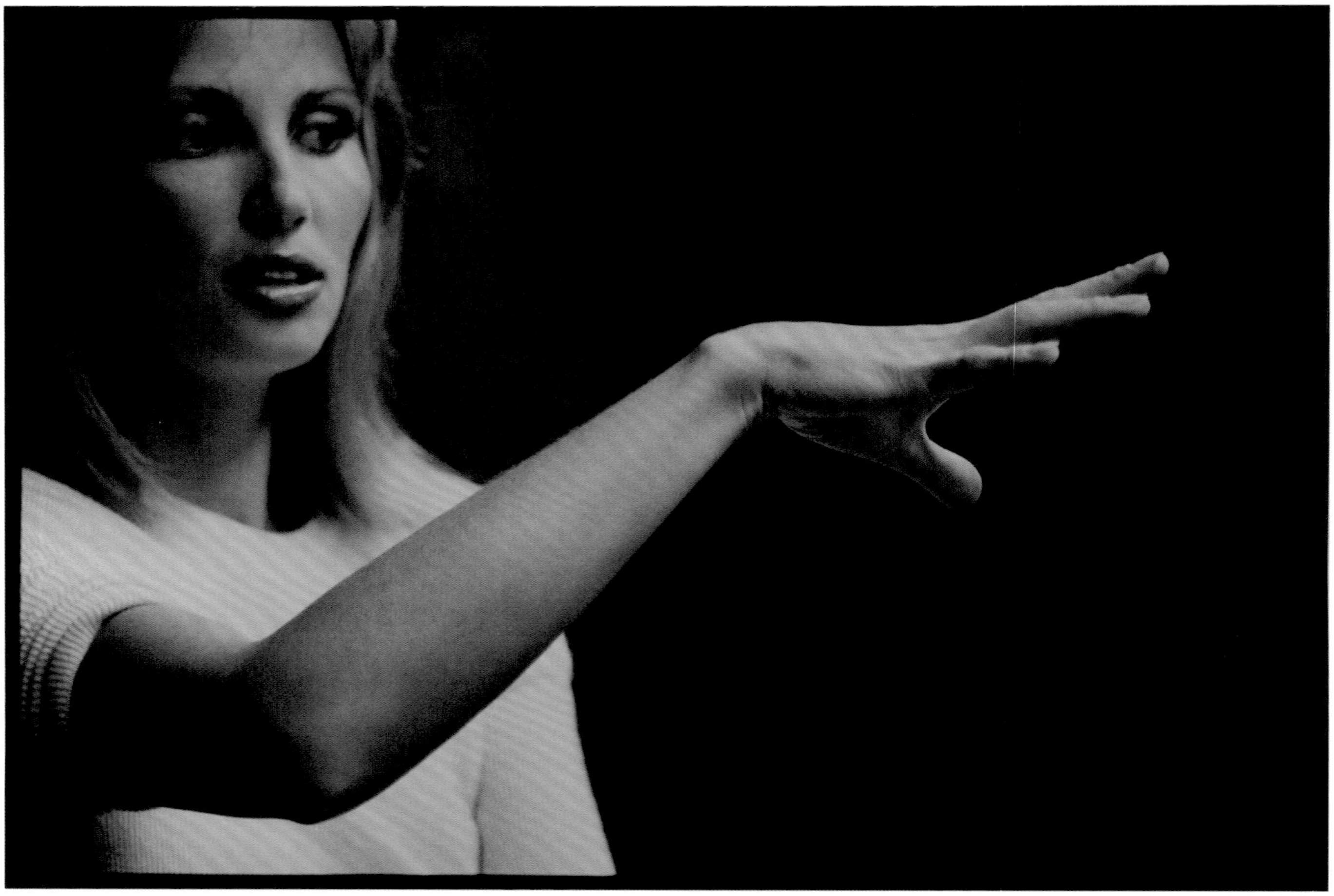

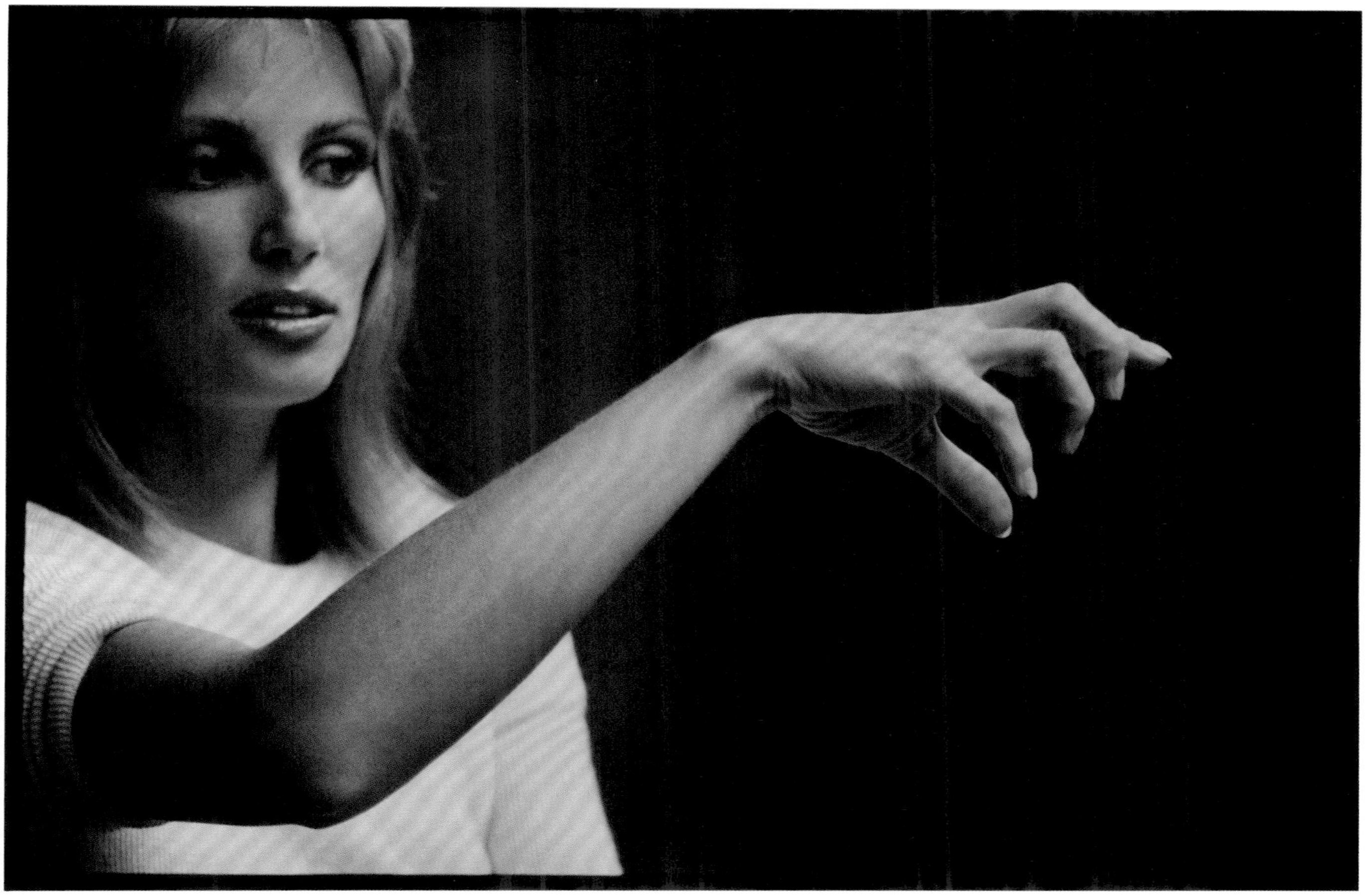

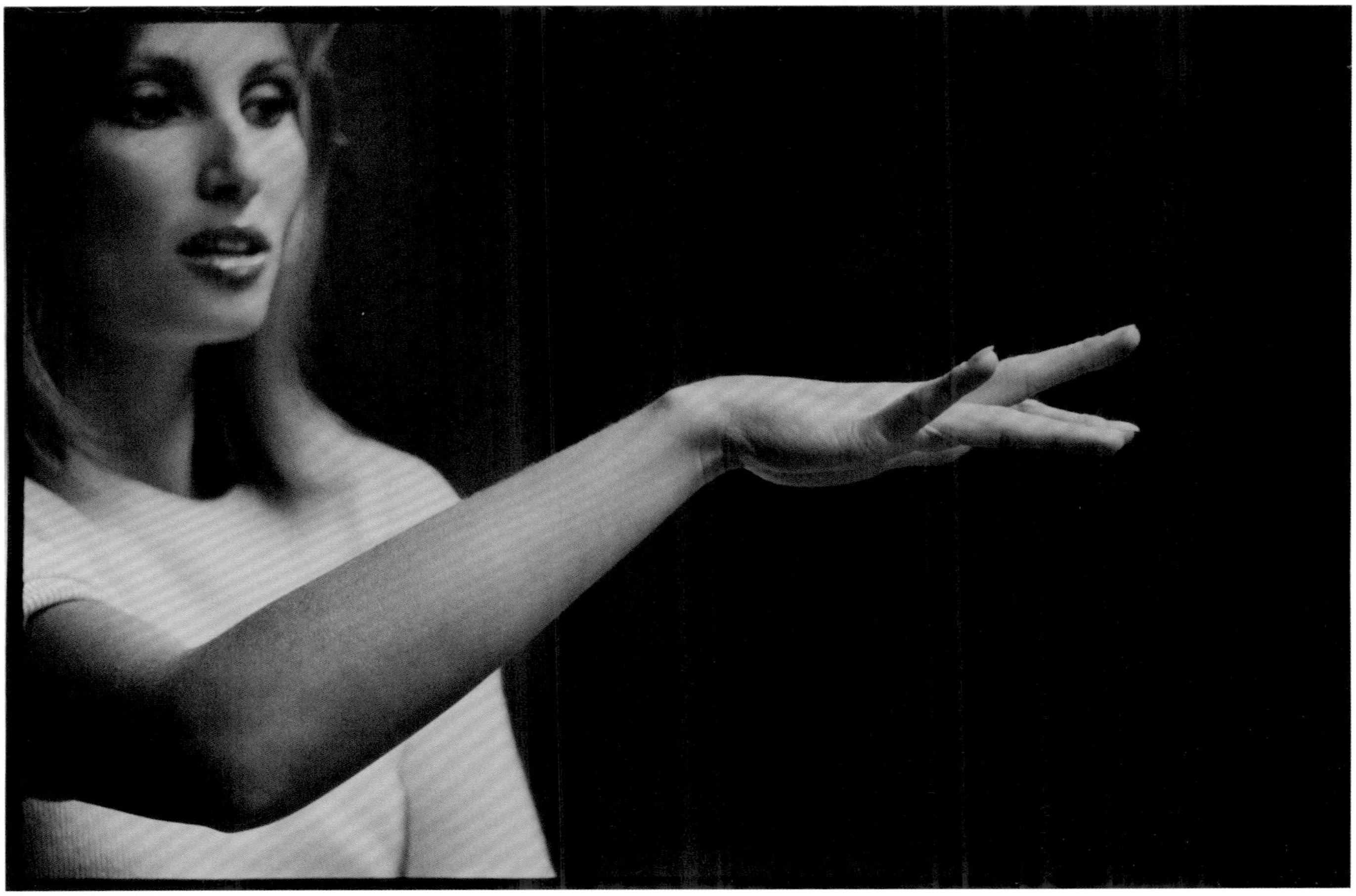

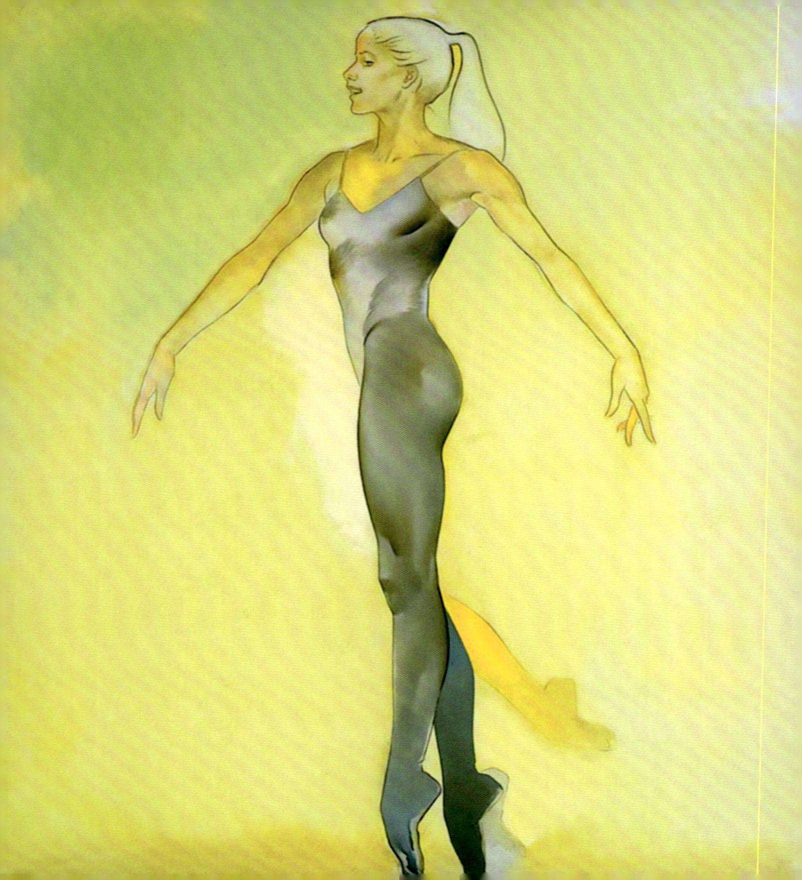

Darcey Bussell

The Director of the National Portrait Gallery at that time was a great fan of the ballet and he asked me if I would paint Darcey Bussell's portrait for them. I think that the trustees were somewhat ambivalent about it because she was barely twenty-two or twenty-three.

She was a prima ballerina, but I think that maybe it was a bit early in her career from their point of view that she should suddenly end up in the National Portrait Gallery, but either way, he was the director and that was the commission. I needed to get to know her before I could decide what I could do. It wasn't good enough to say come and sit and I will paint an illustration.

So it was agreed that Darcey should come here several times over a few weeks for me to draw her, and I went to the dance studios in Hammersmith where she was at the barre and I took photographs of her, but ultimately, the best photographs in a way were taken in my studio because I didn't feel I was impinging on her professional time.

I took a whole range of photographs of her in different positions. One of the things she was famous for was that she could stand and walk on pointe for a longer time than any other dancer. But of course you couldn't have someone stand on pointe indefinitely while you draw or paint them, but with the camera I could go 'snap' and the pose was captured instantly.

It has only ever happened with this commission that I made a deliberate photograph to specifically inform a figure painting. Painting someone's portrait has not been a part of my pictorial investigation, but painting Darcey gave me the opportunity to make a portrait that involved the authentic representation of a highly stylised figure. That is the essence of ballet, that the pose is stylised.

Opposite Darcey Bussell, Prima Ballerina, Royal Ballet, oil on canvas, 1994, second version, private collection

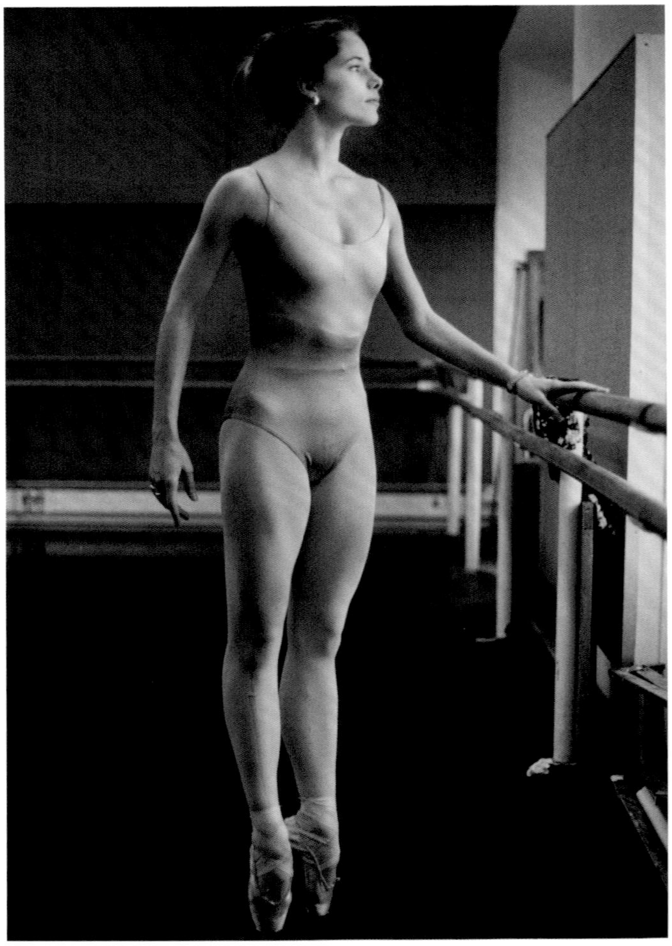

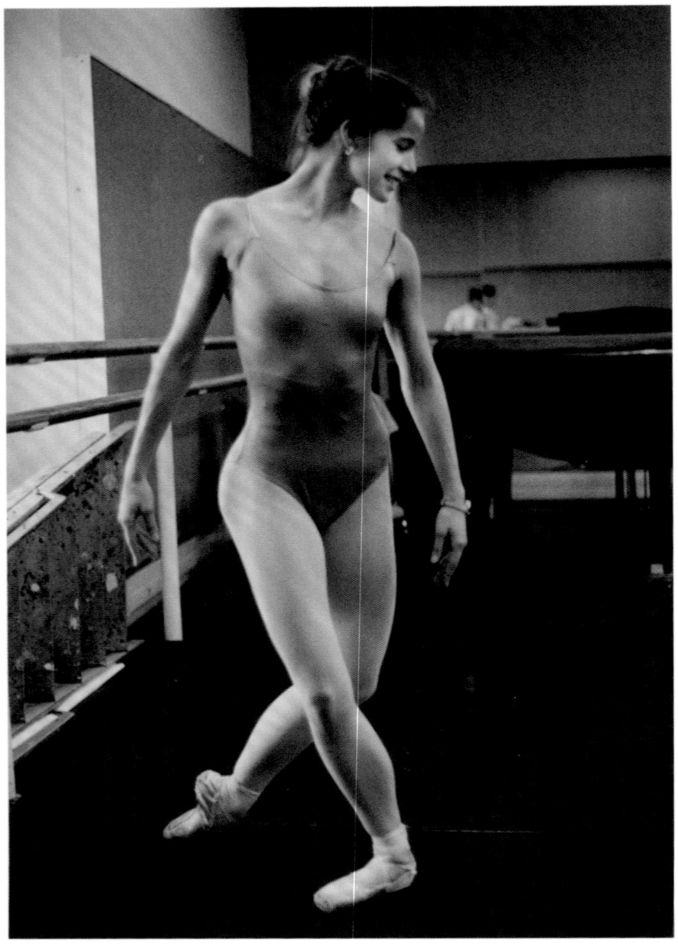

Above and opposite Darcey Bussell, Royal Ballet Company Studios, Hammersmith, London, 1994

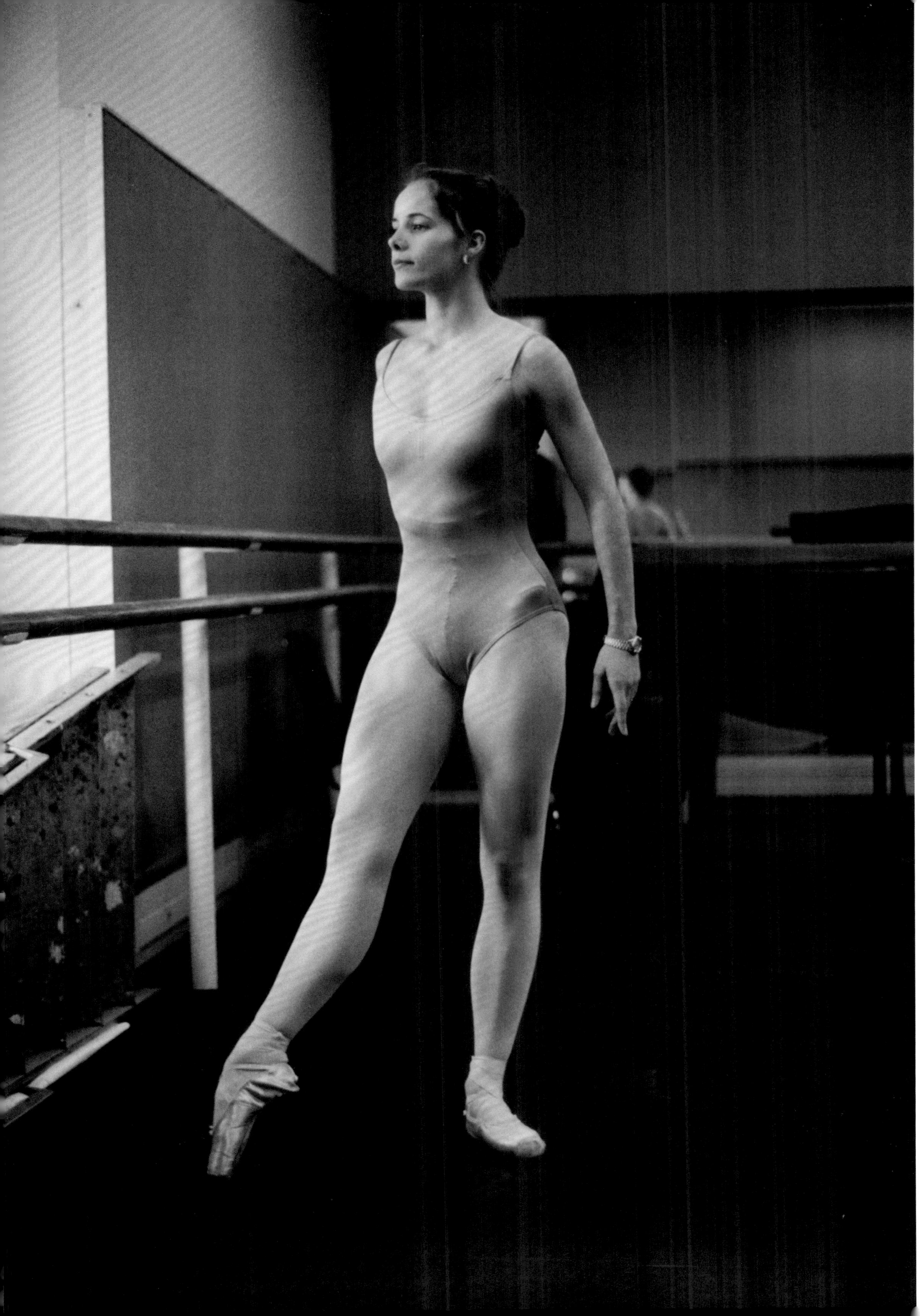

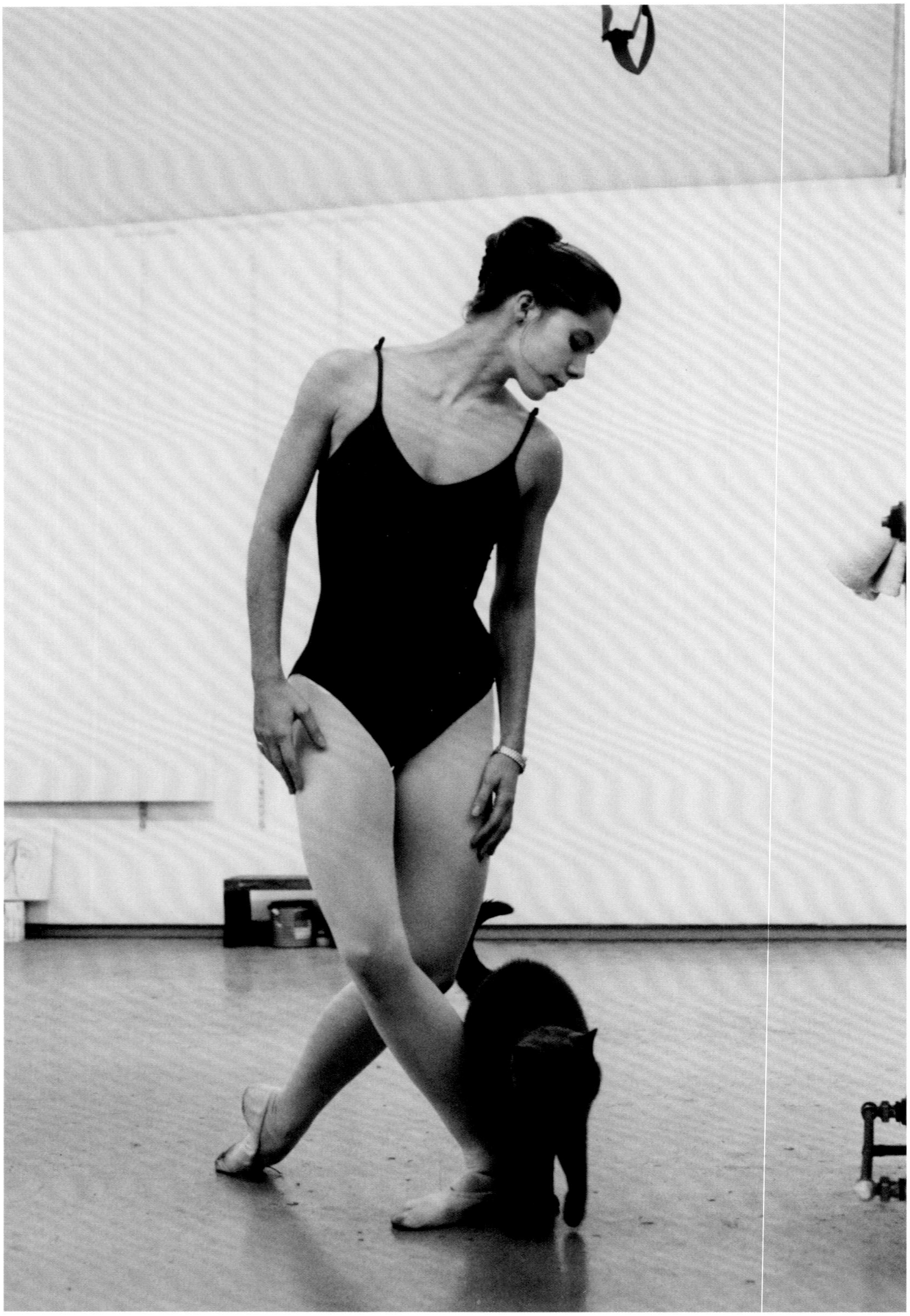

Above and opposite Darcey Bussell, Charterhouse Square, London, 1994

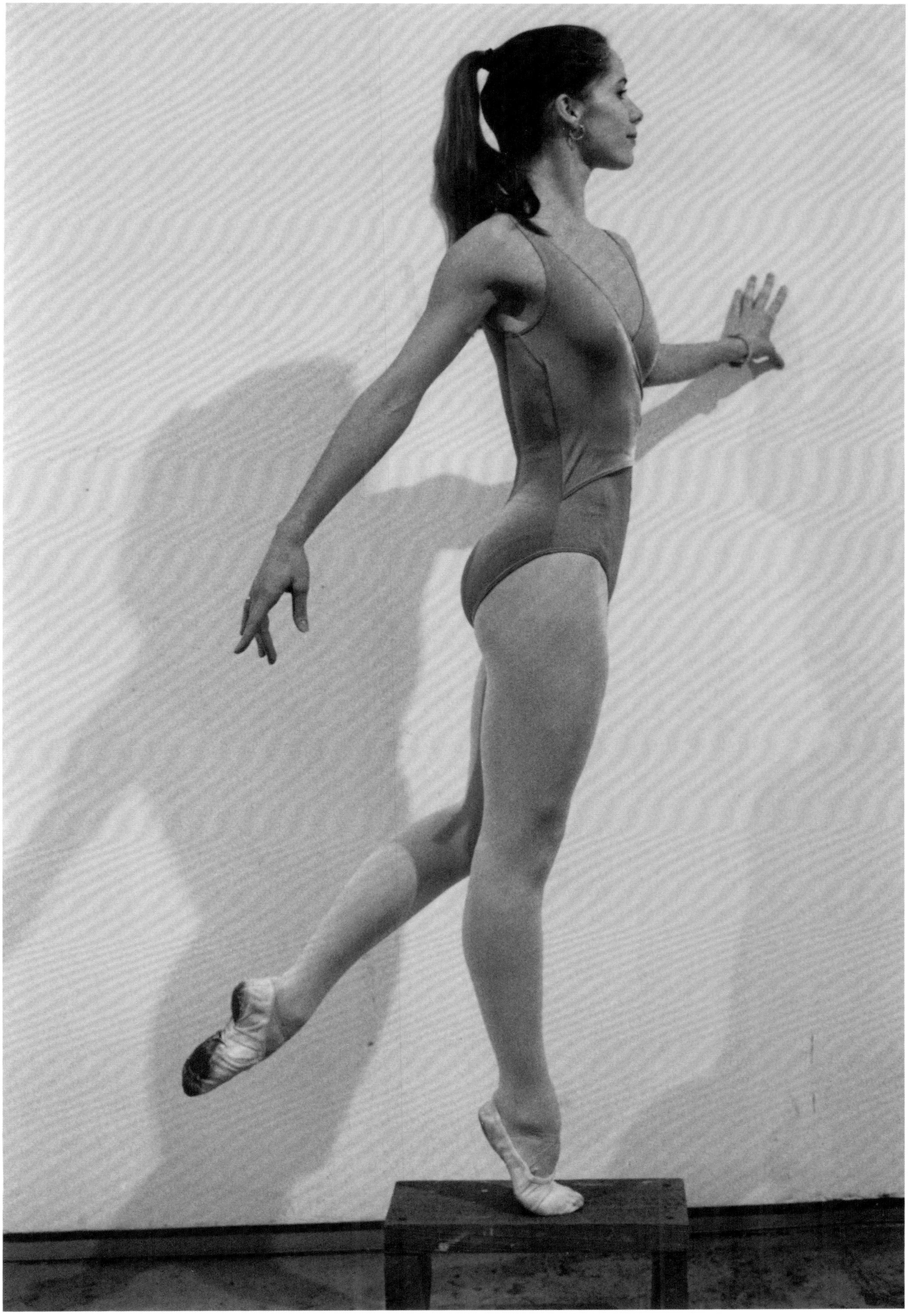

Gold body-plate

Opposite 'Cover Story', photograph by Barry Ryan for Allen Jones, 1977

Before I even thought of making what are now called my furniture sculptures, my first step in this direction was the idea of making a female breastplate. It occurred to me that throughout history breastplates were made for men, with the possible exception of Joan of Arc. I had a student in the sculpture department at Chelsea who was also in my drawing class, which I was taking one day a week. I had her make a plaster bust which I could look at and say bigger here, smaller there; and, at the time, the important thing was that the finished object need not be wearable. It was not meant to be a fashion item. Since which time I have regretted it because so many times a model has tried to put it on for a photograph but it does not go over the rib-cage; it goes in too sharply. But this was the genesis of the thing. The first version was in black plastic, commissioned as a multiple in 1968 and later featured in the Pirelli calendar. That breastplate led to my making the furniture sculptures.

Fast forward to after my making the furniture sculptures and I conceived the idea of making a film in which an aspiring model is told that she ought to go to the big city, where she has to find some photographers who will take pictures of her for a portfolio and then has to go to model agencies and get work. She duly goes to the big city and on the first assignment discovers this troubling problem – every time she steps into a spotlight, she changes into a man. But her boyfriend, who is an artist, comes to the rescue and makes body armour for her. Of course, it is my artist's licence that her head would remain the same, but I hadn't crossed that bridge. I did a storyboard for this and the film very nearly got made. I suppose the idea of the film came from my memory of the original breastplate.

The film inspired me to cut a figure in half and create a body-plate and I had it sprayed up on the Egham bypass by a motor bodywork specialist who metal-flaked it – then the big news with custom cars from America. This was a mechanical paint surface that I could order but I could not possibly have achieved myself. The gold-painted body-plate was made and finished, but the film didn't happen. Then, a few years later, I had a show scheduled for the ICA, a retrospective of my graphic work, and, looking for a poster for it, of course I already had this figure in the back of my mind. When Helmut Newton visited, we showed him the figure. Janet stood behind it to demonstrate the intention of having it photographed with a real person. The ICA opportunity pushed me to fulfil this. The photograph was shot by former singer Barry Ryan, who organised the model.

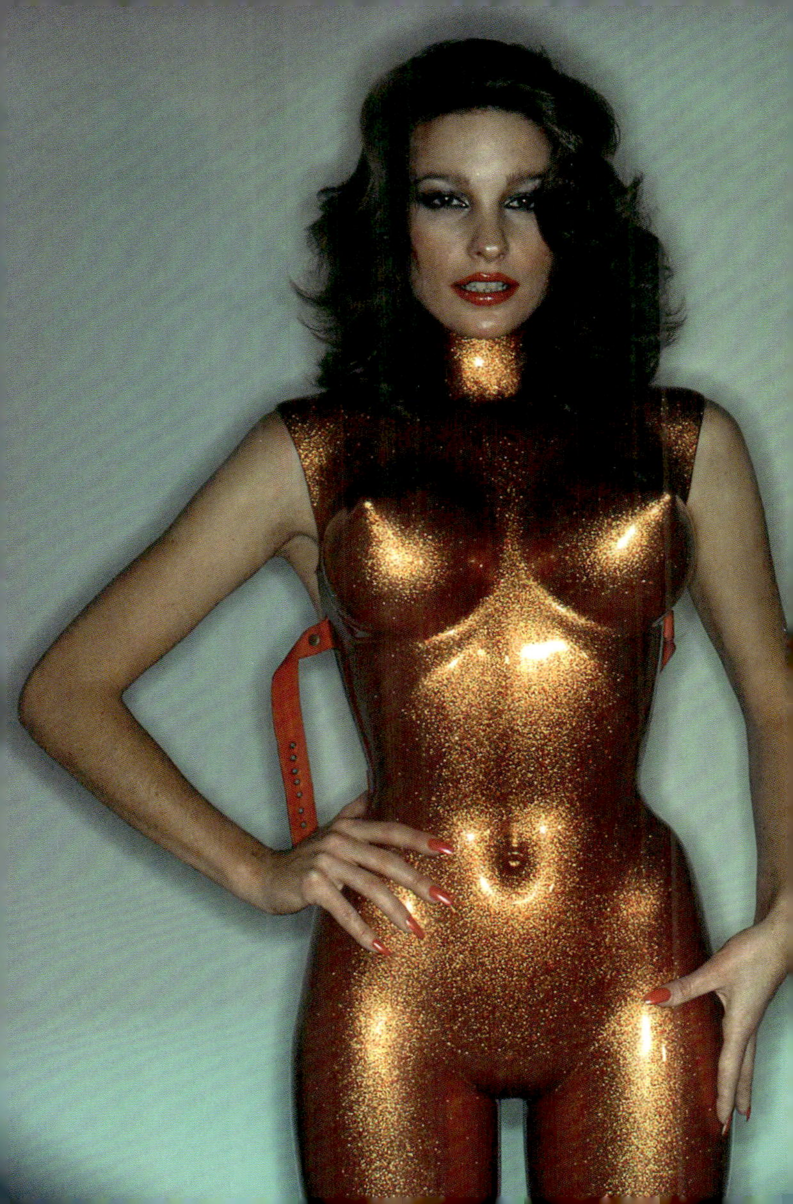

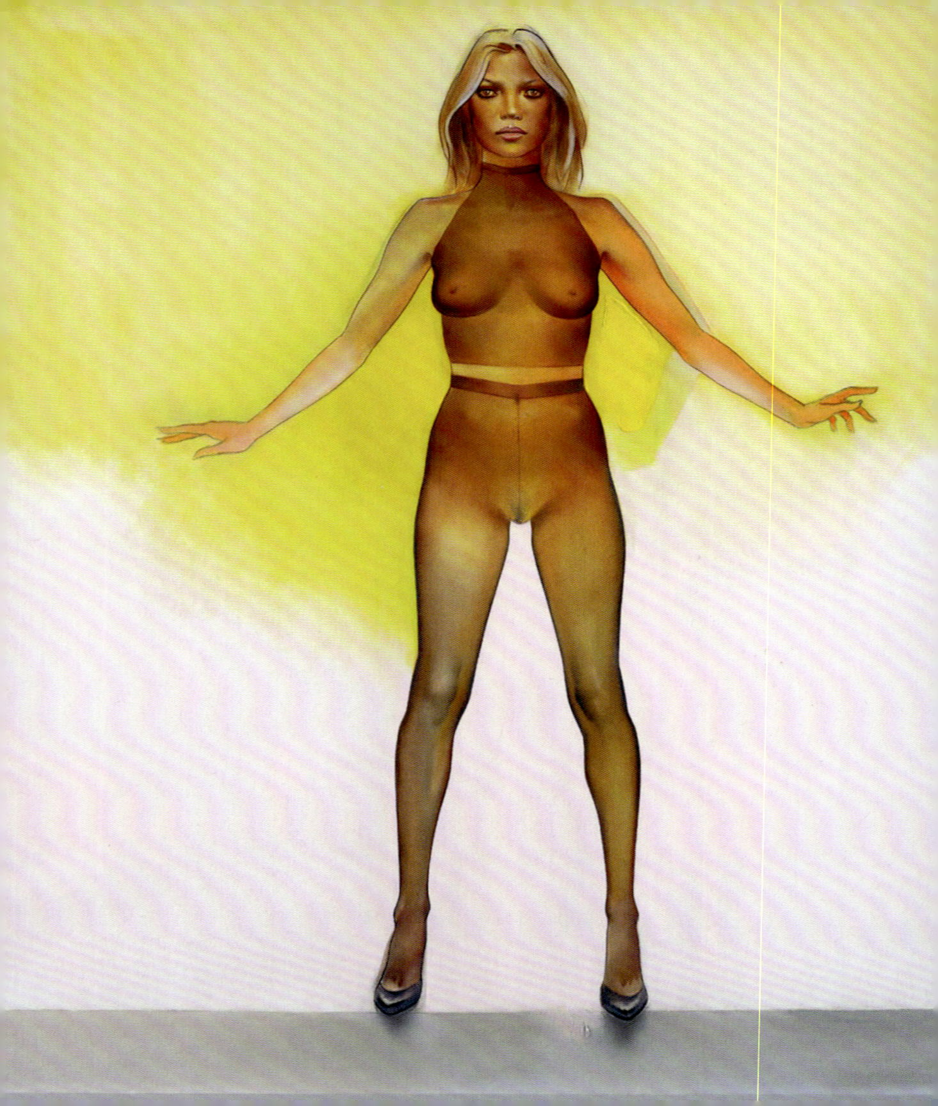

Kate Moss

I had a request out of the blue from an auction house who were going to present the collection of a man who was obsessed with Kate Moss and was buying and commissioning images of her specifically for the auction event. He wanted to know if I would accept a commission to paint her. I am not too comfortable with portrait commissions because it seems to me that your duty is to record the person and for them not to be simply a vehicle for your own capricious creativity; and so I approached it very cautiously. She was obviously a very busy supermodel but it was a part of the deal that she would come and I would draw her, but I think I only drew her for about a forty-minute session and I had no illusions about the fact that what I was drawing was going to be a part of the artwork.

Drawing is the socially acceptable excuse for actually staring intently at someone for a long time; but after a while, I wasn't comfortable doing it, so I then took a lot of photographs of her. They were not meant to be photographs which I would then copy, but they were helpful as information, and, as with the drawings, they helped me explore how things might be simplified in paint, for example the way the light falls on the cheek. They were meant to be information photographs, though looking at them now, I can see they have their own appeal, an informal, spontaneous quality quite distinct from the final works. I didn't know how it would turn out, but I wanted to know what she looked like from this angle, that angle, and so I had all this reference material. I did in fact make two paintings and kept one of them.

When I was asked to make a picture and I was contemplating it, I realised that this commission was a shoo-in for reusing the gold body-plate. And putting her in that was my initial idea. I am a painter and I just couldn't resist trying to paint her, but the body-plate definitely came first. The thing that reassured me was that I had the sense that it was in the bag with that image of her in the gold, and I knew that at least I had fulfilled the contractual obligation and that they would have something significant. So, the paintings came after; and the idea of also making a sculpture of her was irresistible.

Opposite 'Kate Moss', oil on canvas, 2013

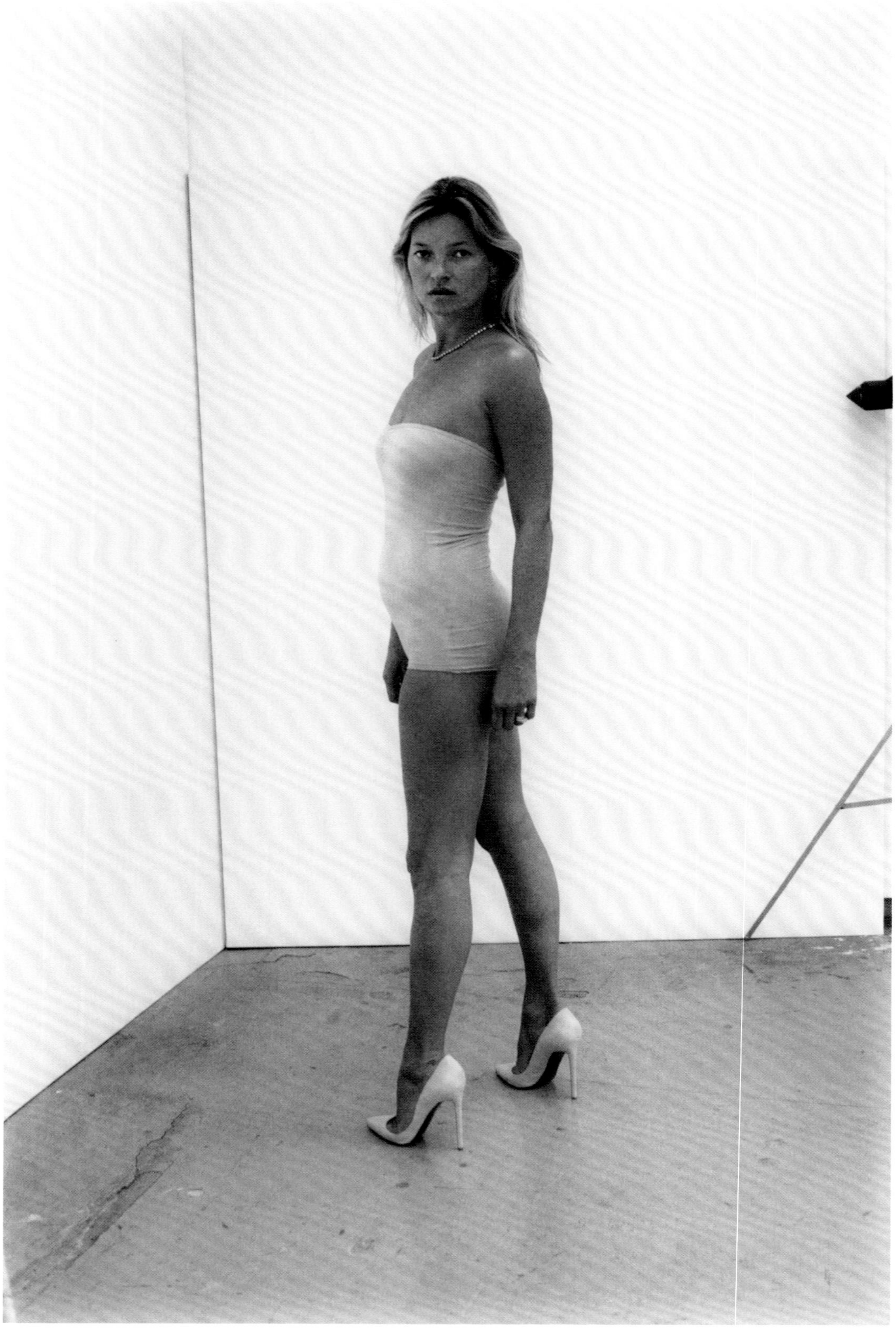

Above, opposite, and pages 192-193 Kate Moss, Charterhouse Square, London, 2013

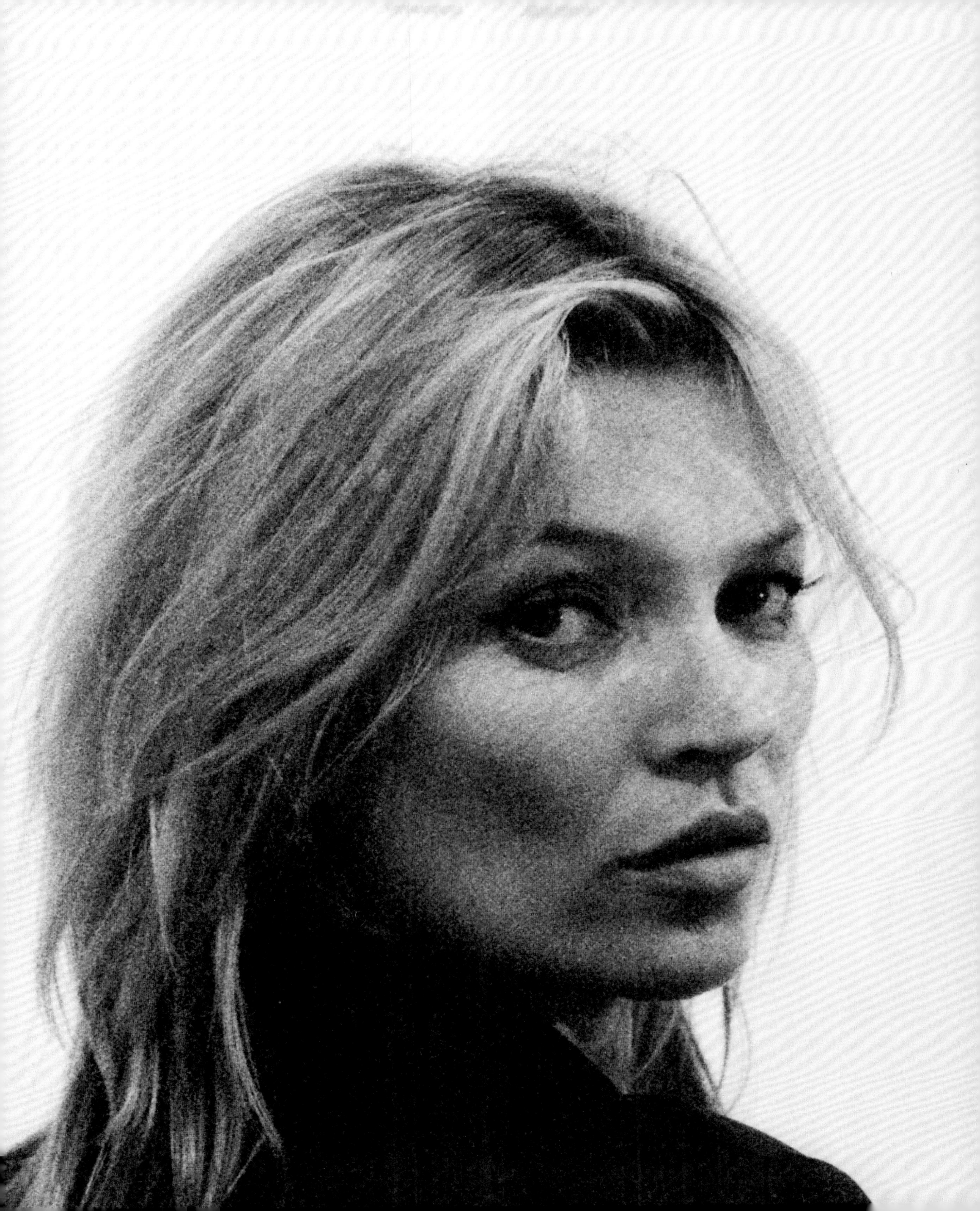

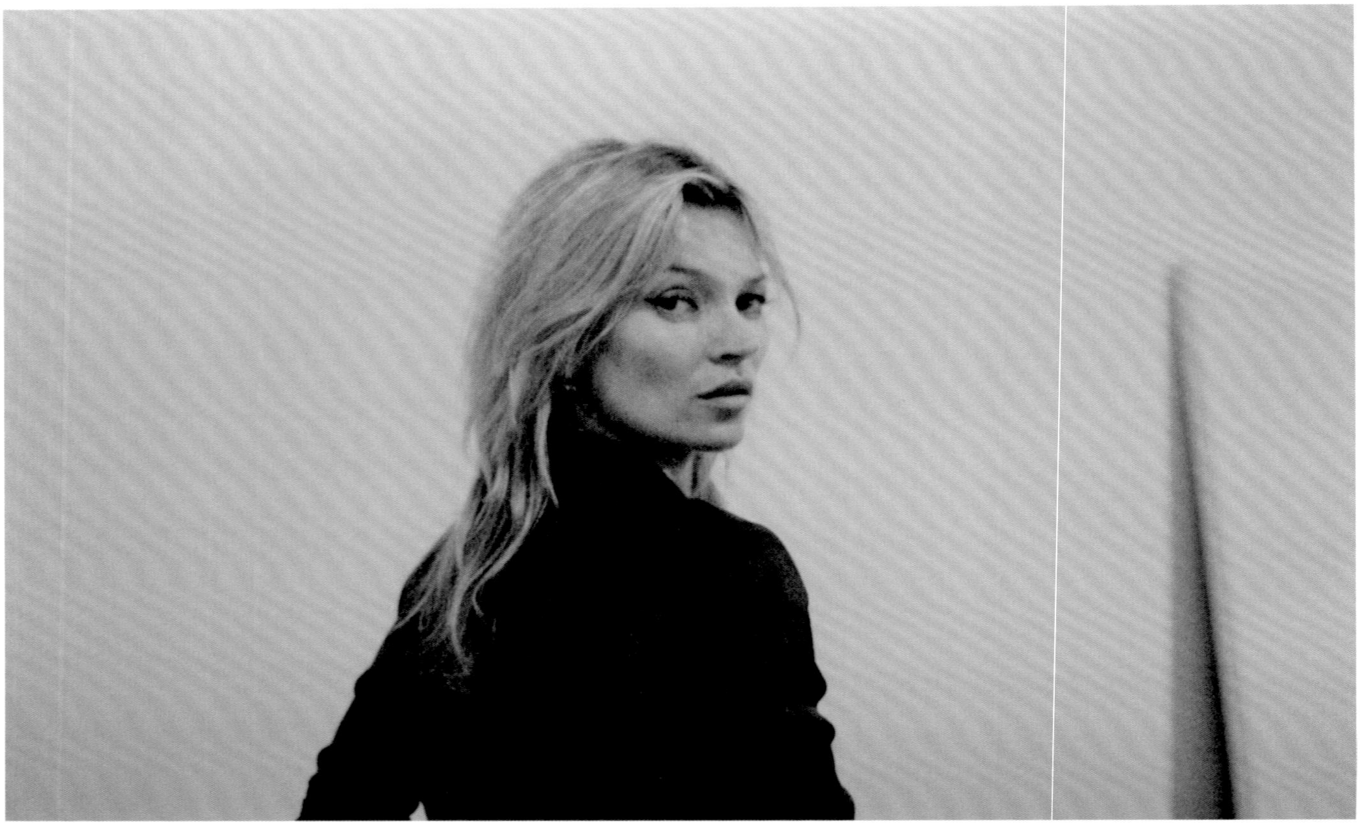

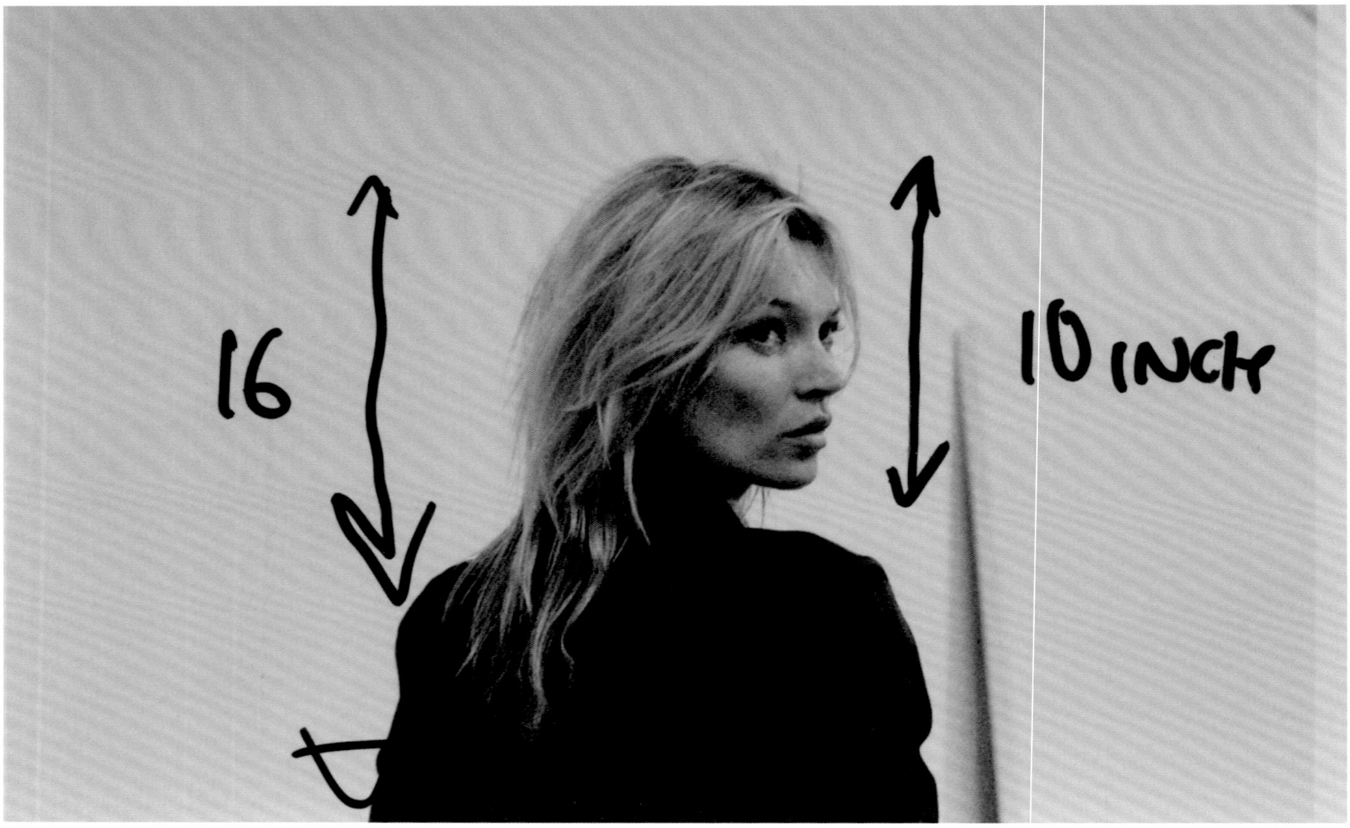
16
10 INCH

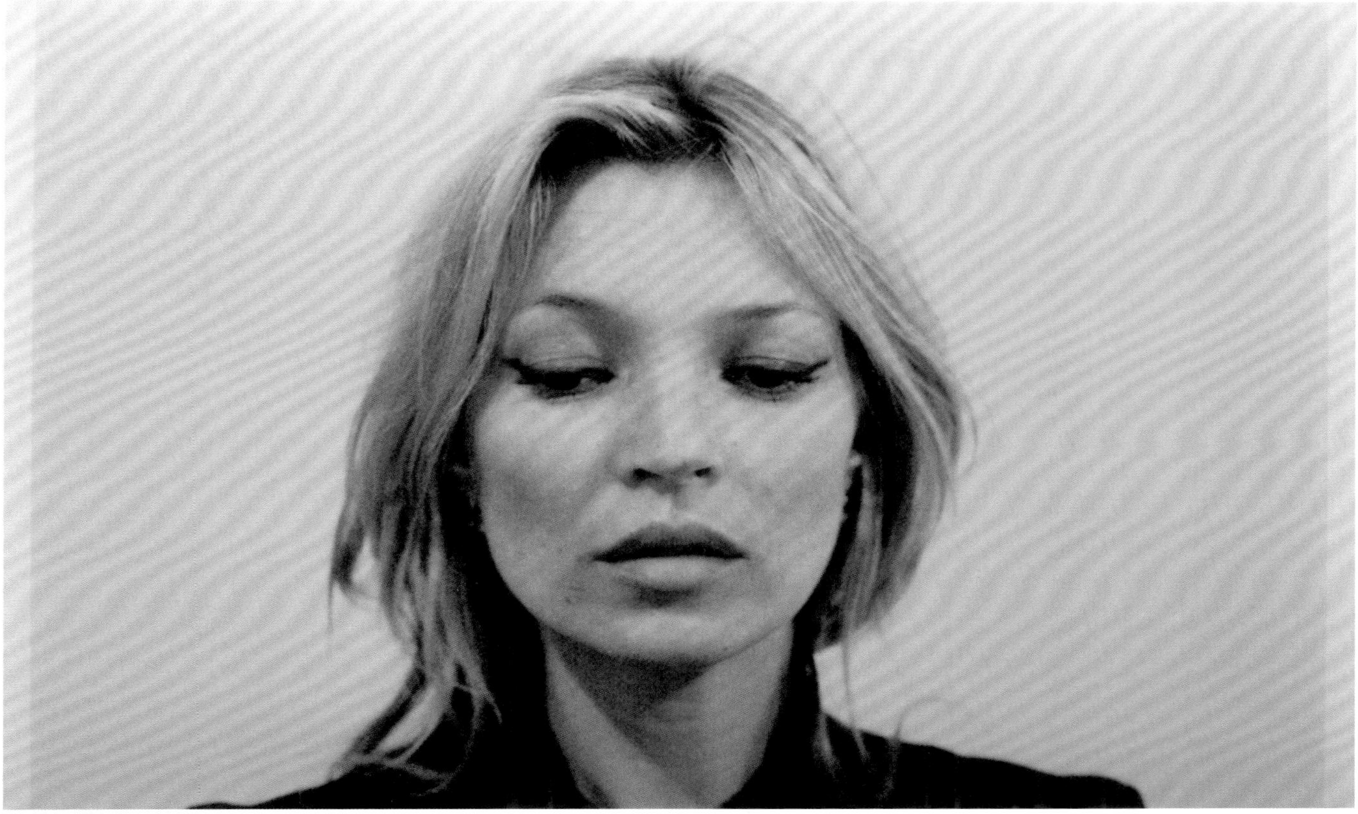

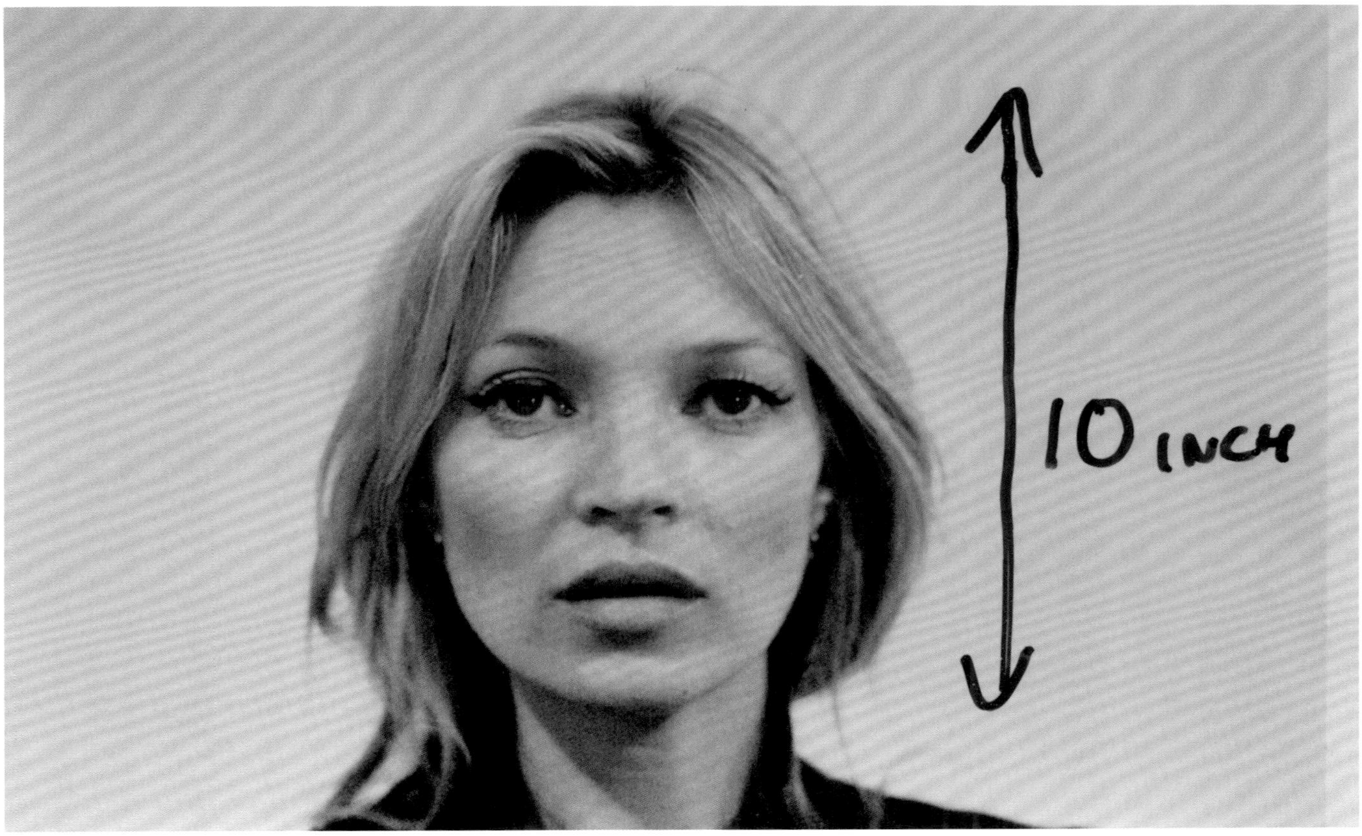
10 INCH

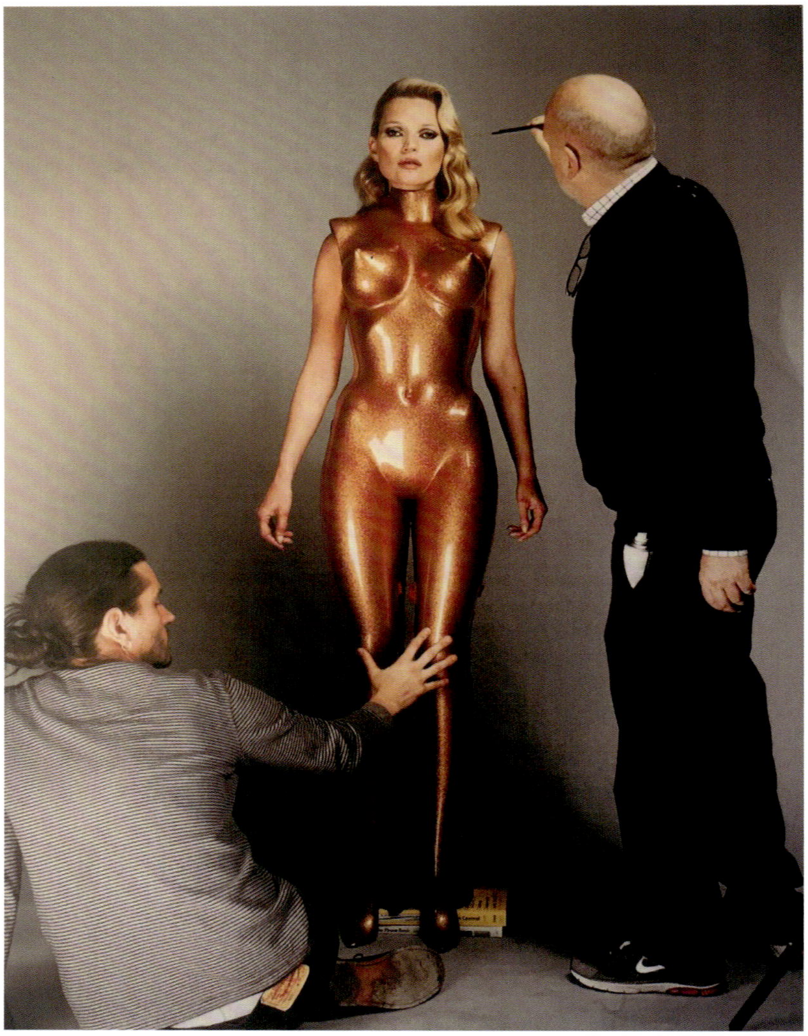

Above The photoshoot, Charterhouse Square, London, 2013
Opposite Kate Moss in the gold-flake body-plate, 2013

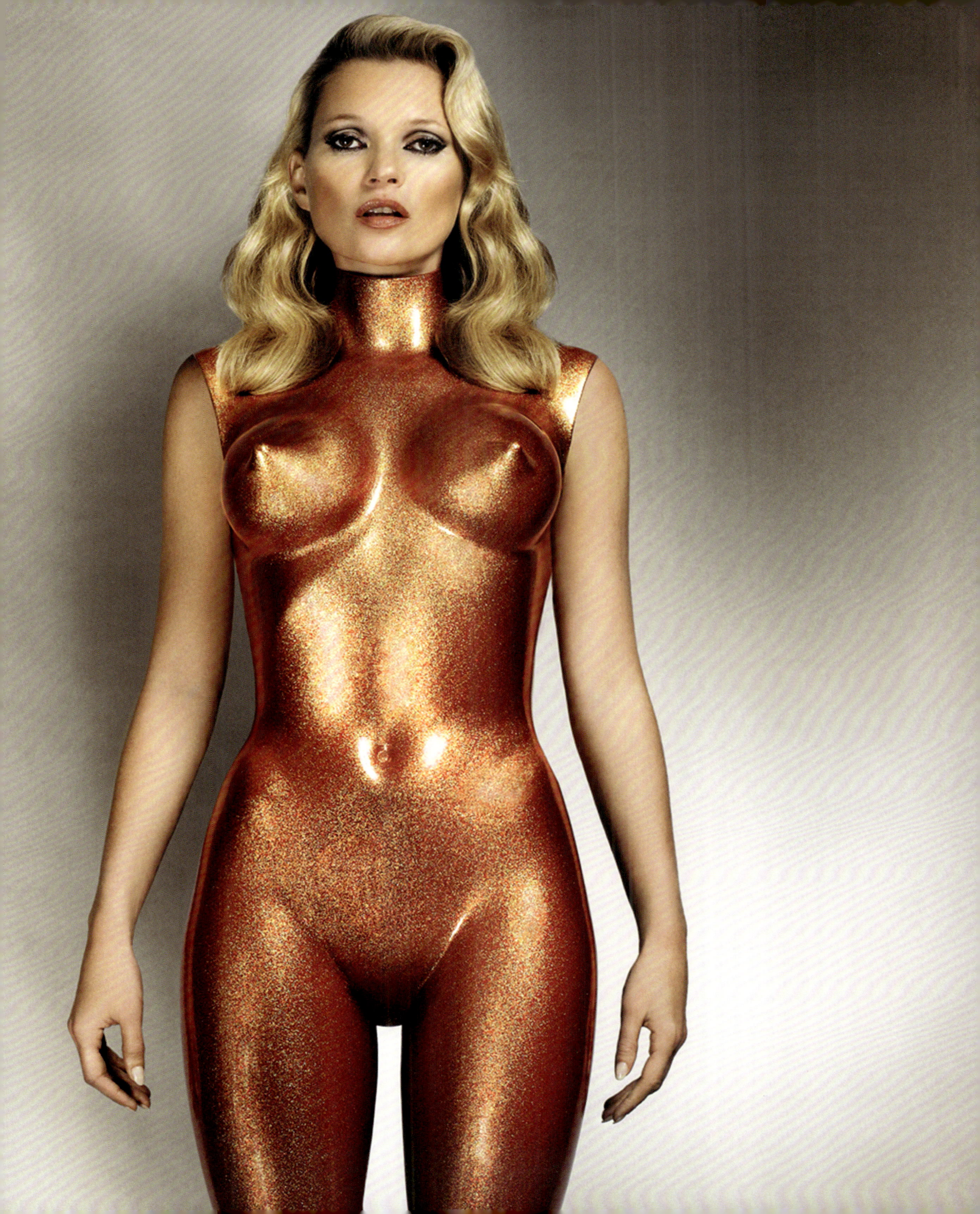

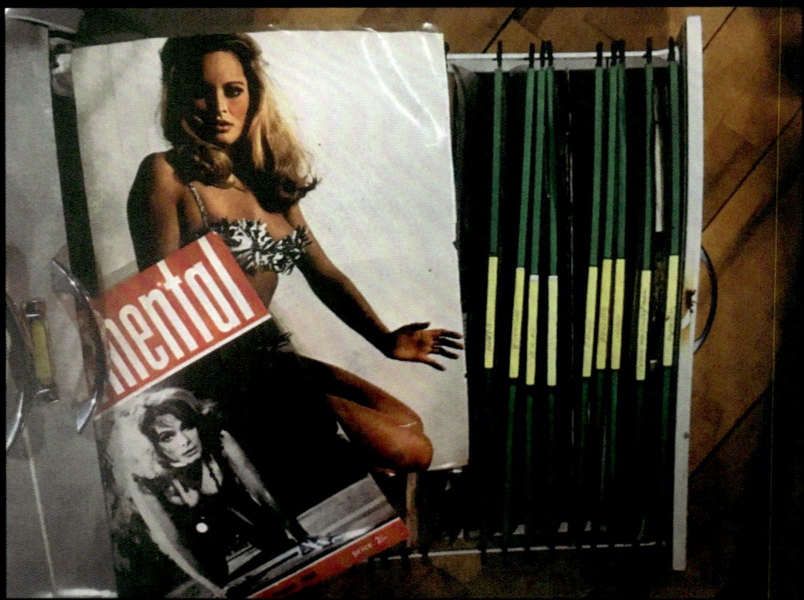

An image bank

Opposite
The 'cuttings' files, Charterhouse Square, London

I have always collected things, ever since I was a child, and so, later, when I got interested in glamour and the female figure, I would cut pictures out of the colour supplements, which were then so new and exciting. It wasn't so much the top shelf that was interesting to me but that whole explosion of visual reproduction somehow hit a nerve. I think of it as my building a kind of personal visual dictionary. I have kept adding to this over the years. I cut things out because they interested me or excited me, but when I had accumulated so many of them, I started to categorise them and so there would be files on, say, legs, cleavages, hairdos, smiling, kissing, dancing, and so on. That is one area I have collected; another is the pin-up postcards – mostly American – that I bought over the years and compiled into an album. These exemplify the things I am drawn to that might be considered kitsch, but in which I find a real intensity. There is a fascination for me in popular vernacular imagery around the compulsion of the female figure.

And I am also drawn by that business of the transgressive. An image might be seen as, at one level, say, a circus or fairground figure, but can also be an excuse to engage the viewer in a sexual way. That impulse, I suppose, is there in the things which I collected. One of the things that I was interested in was the way the pin-up was used when I was a child. In America, what I discovered in swap shops and flea markets and so on were every kind of promotional ephemera, calendars, and so forth that used glamourous pin-ups. It might have been for a Chicago tyre manufacturing company or typewriters or whatever. The glamour had been used to do everything from encouraging you to buy toilet rolls to promoting the best beaches.

It isn't that the pictures I have collected are specific sources for paintings, but they do all reflect and inform my way of looking, and so they play their part in my creative processes. They seem to fasten a moment. If you go to the theatre, you come away with a memory of the event, and obviously, if you leave the cinema, you might carry the memory of a screen goddess. The great thing about photography and the press is that these images are frozen in time and last as representations of the figure.

I realise that, taken together, this archive provides some sort of positive illumination of my work. It offers an insight into my response to ideas of glamour and seduction as mediated through photography and the printed press. A whole slice of visual history is captured there through my hungry eyes.

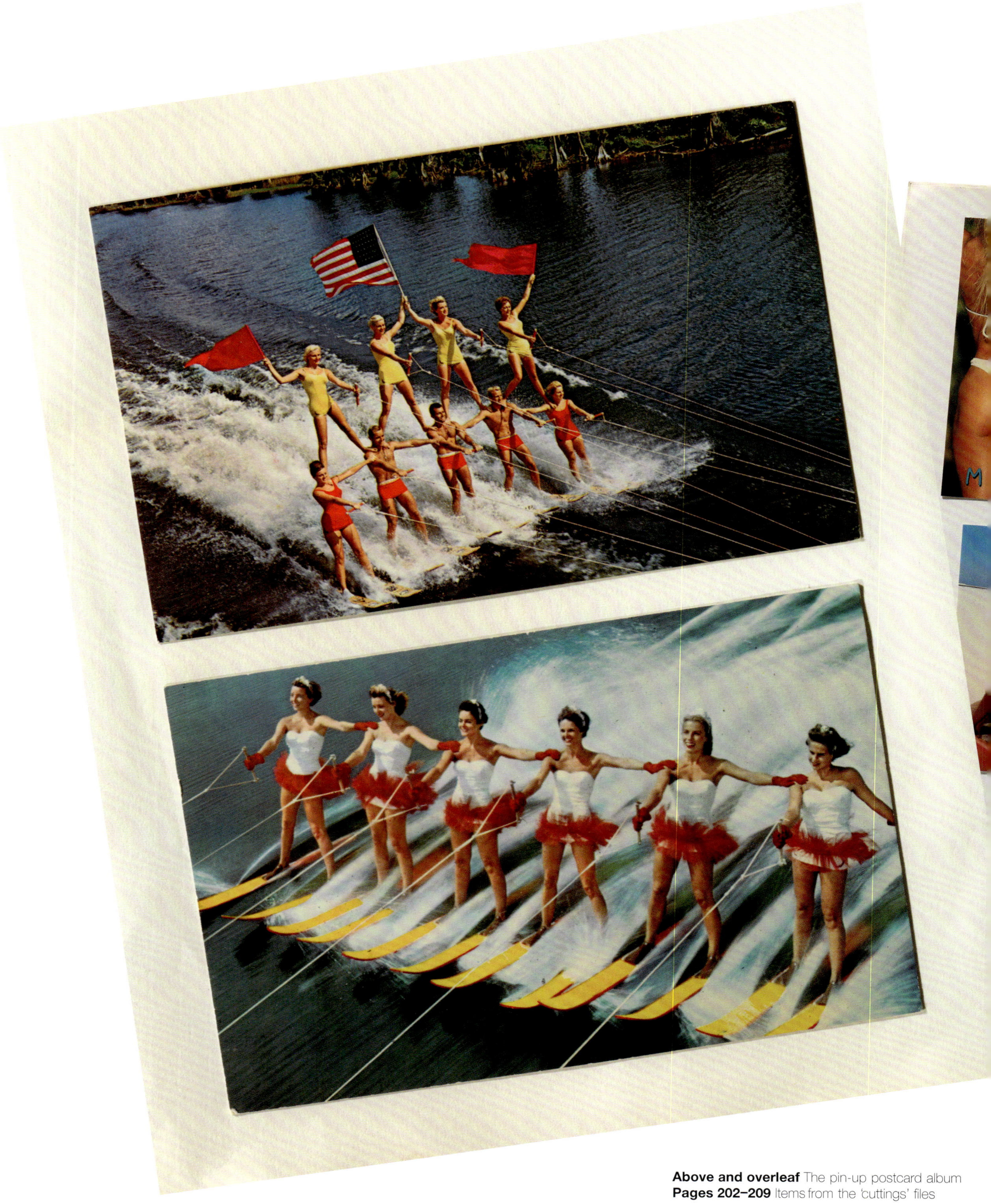

Above and overleaf The pin-up postcard album
Pages 202–209 Items from the 'cuttings' files

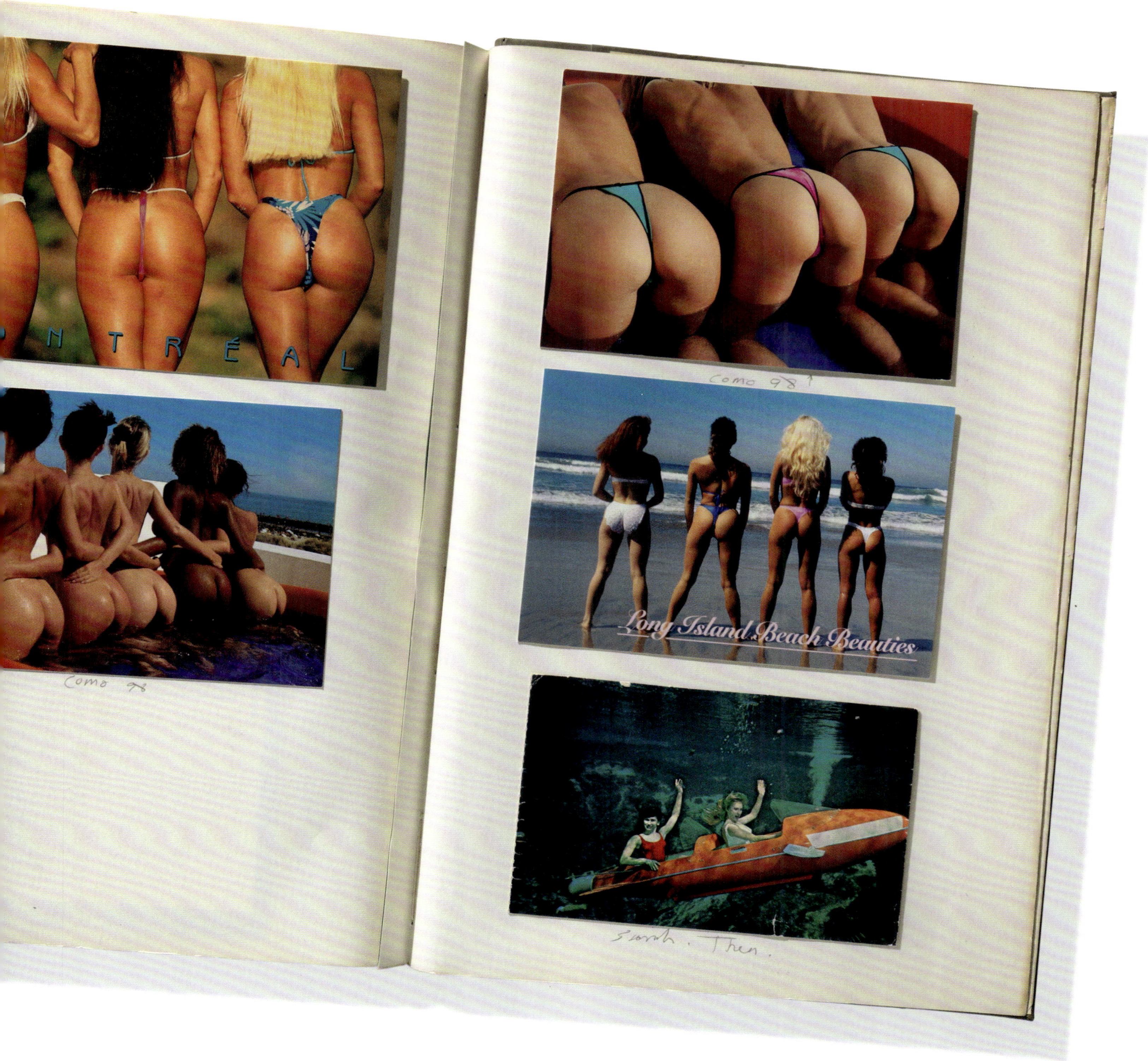
Long Island Beach Beauties

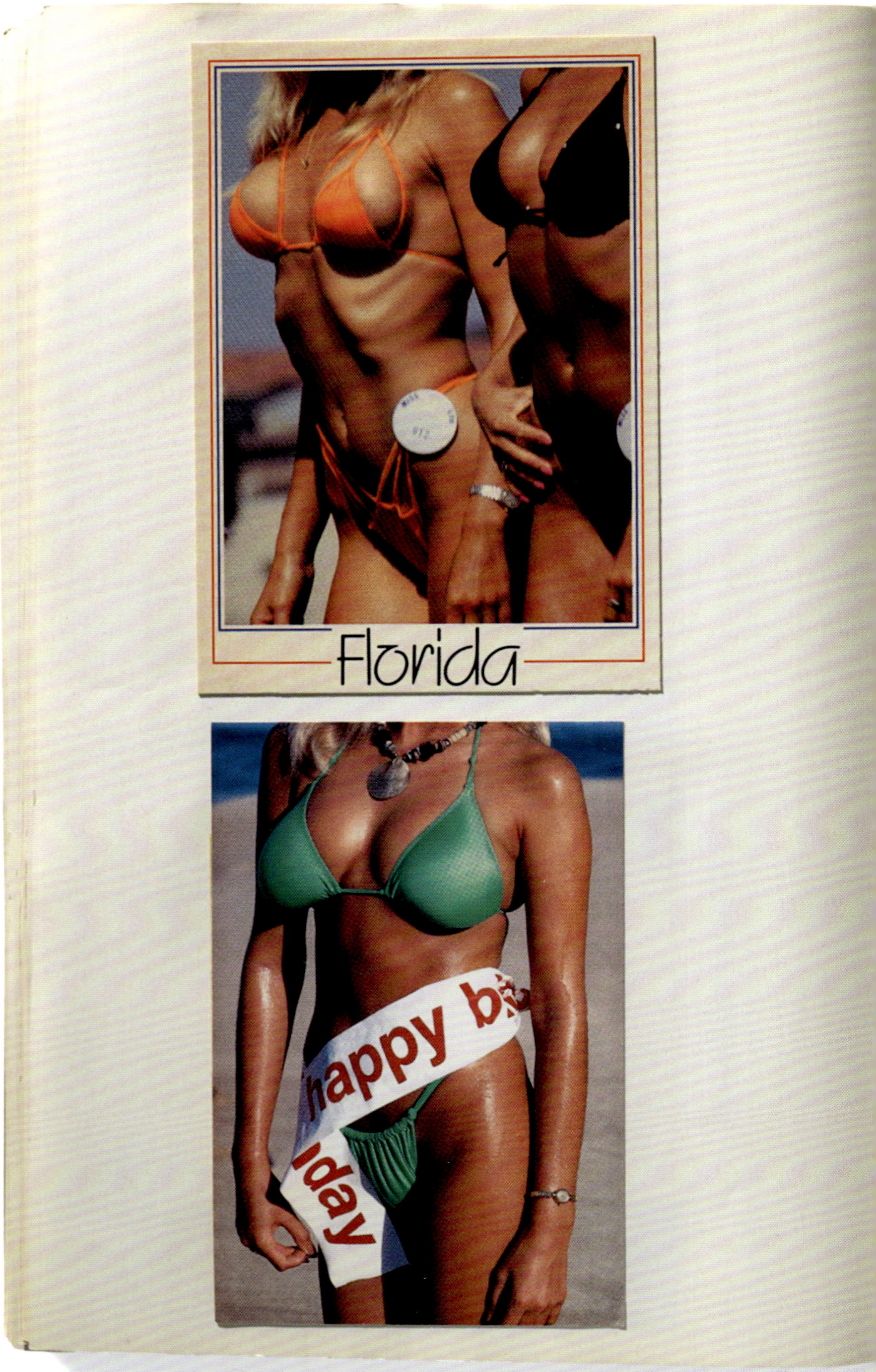
Florida
happy b
day

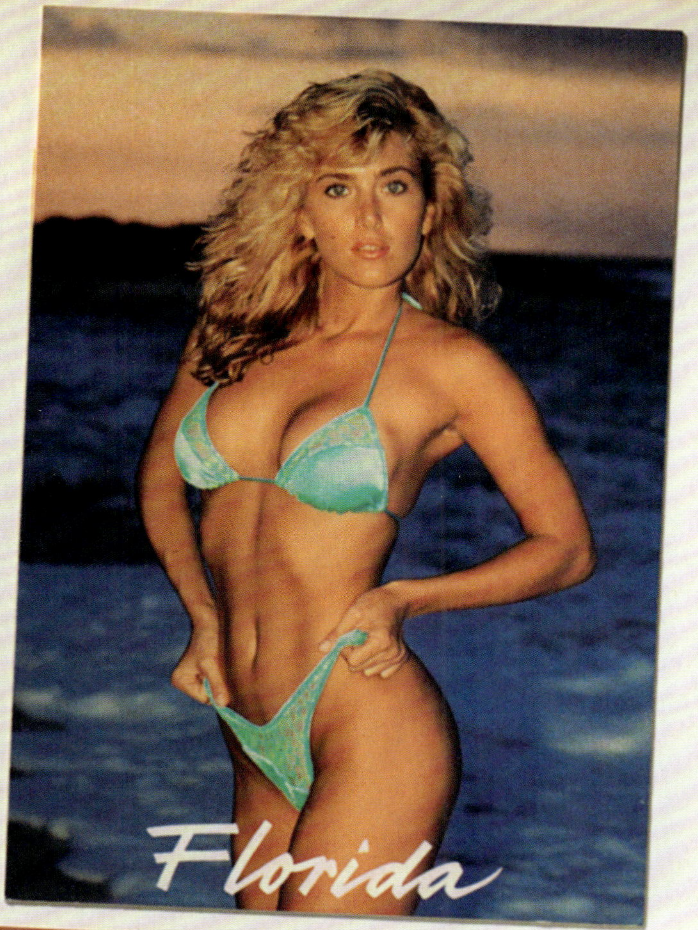
Florida

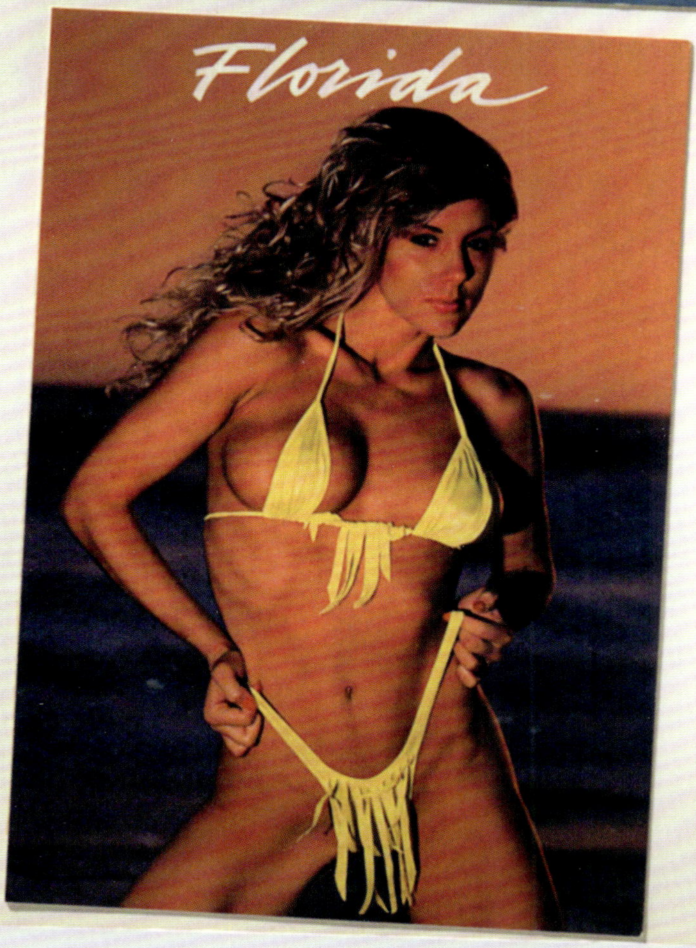
Florida

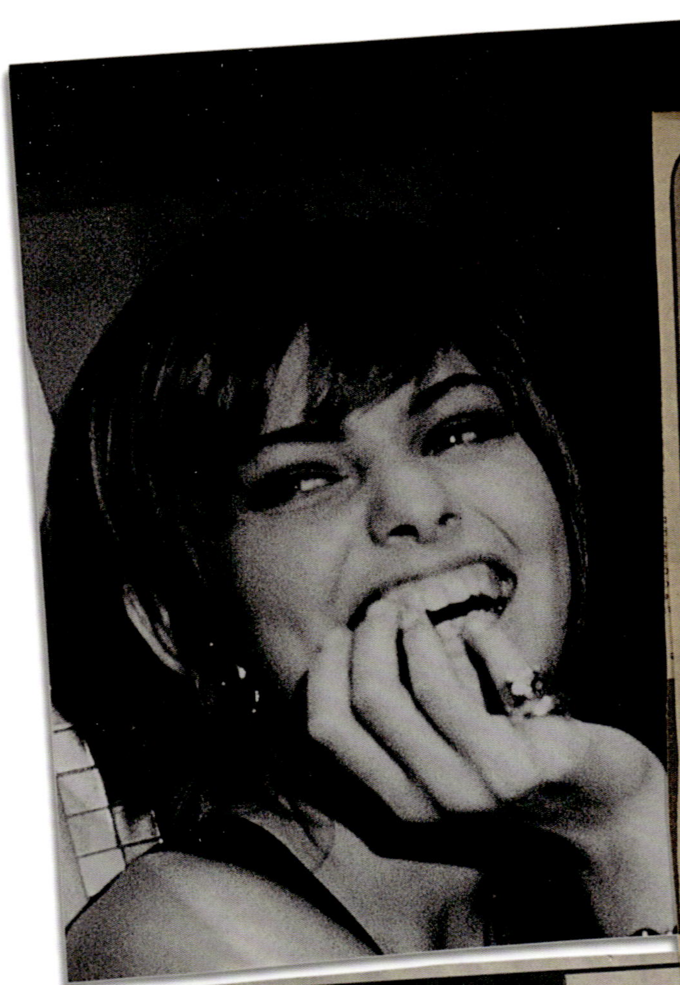

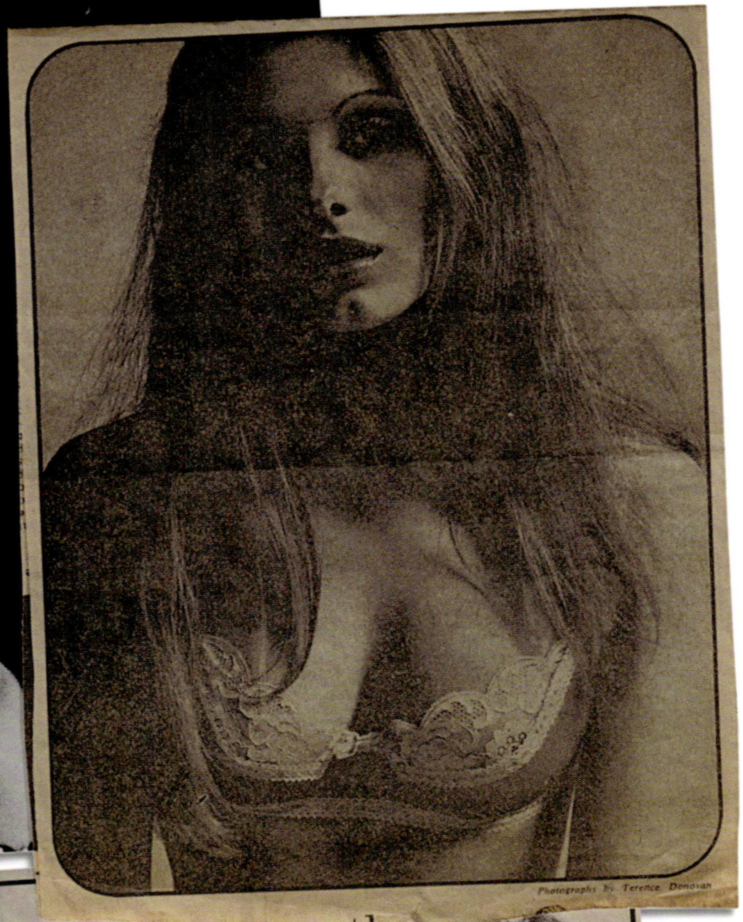
Photographs by Terence Donovan

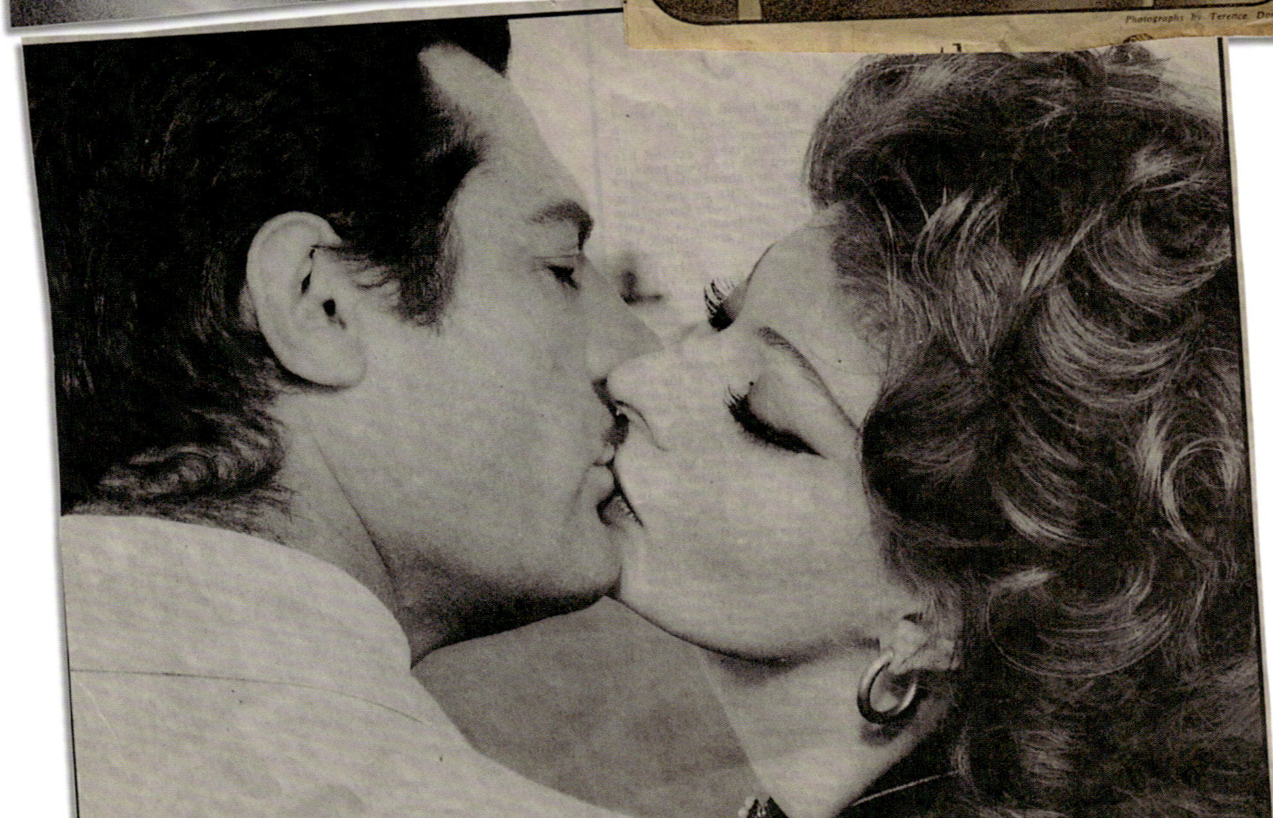

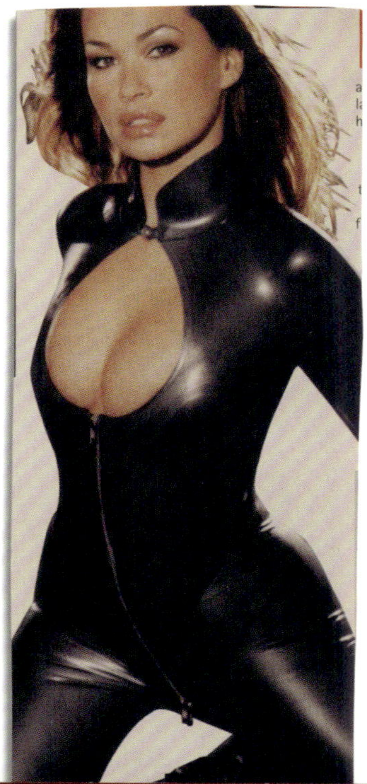

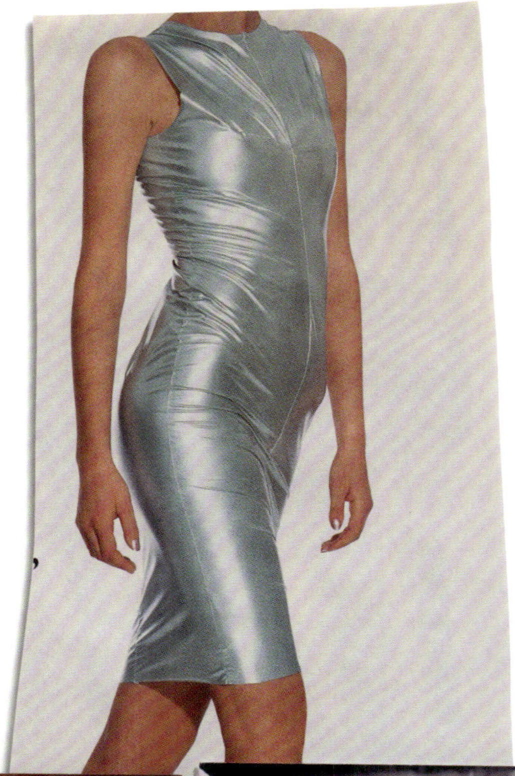

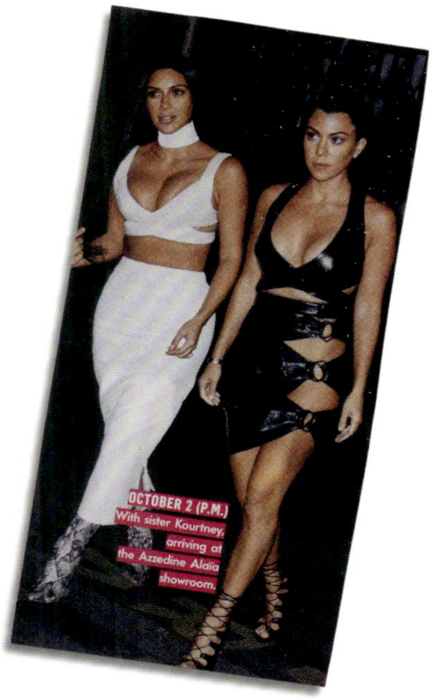
OCTOBER 2 (P.M.)
With sister Kourtney,
arriving at
the Azzedine Alaïa
showroom.

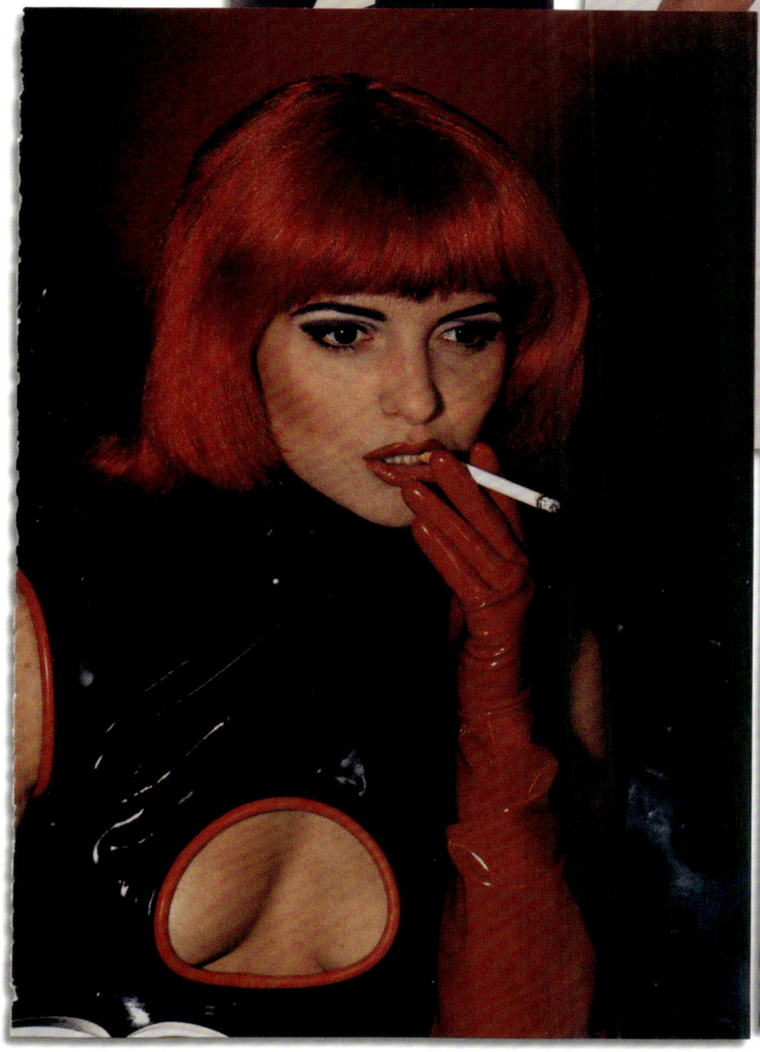

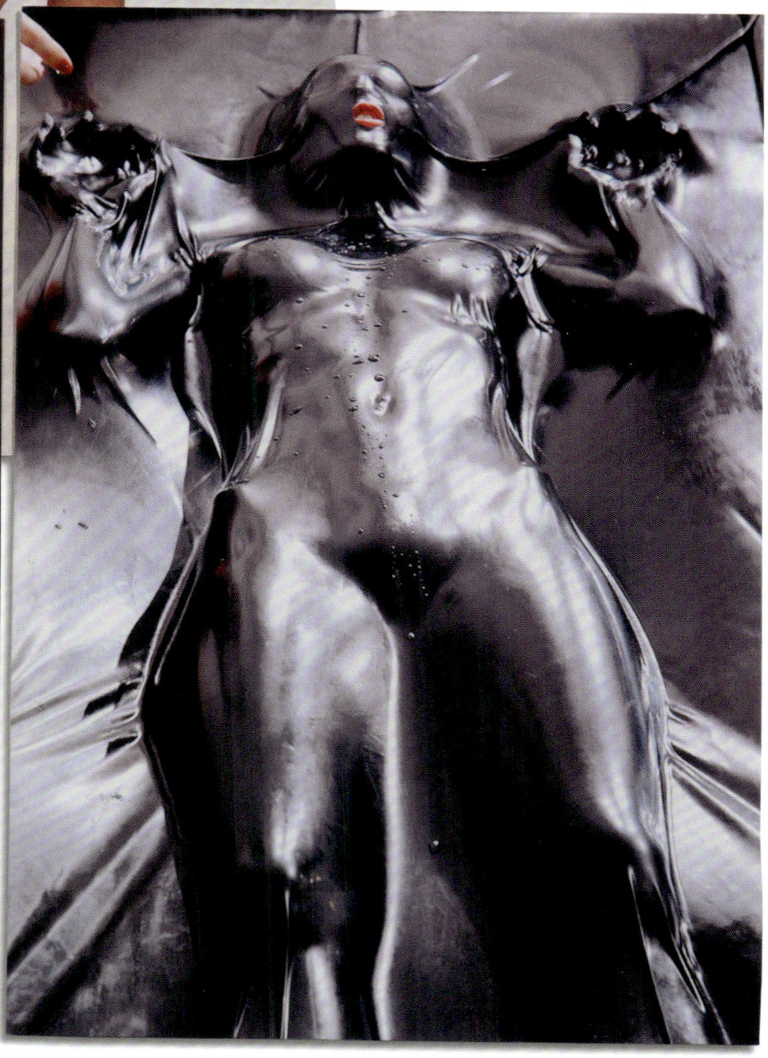

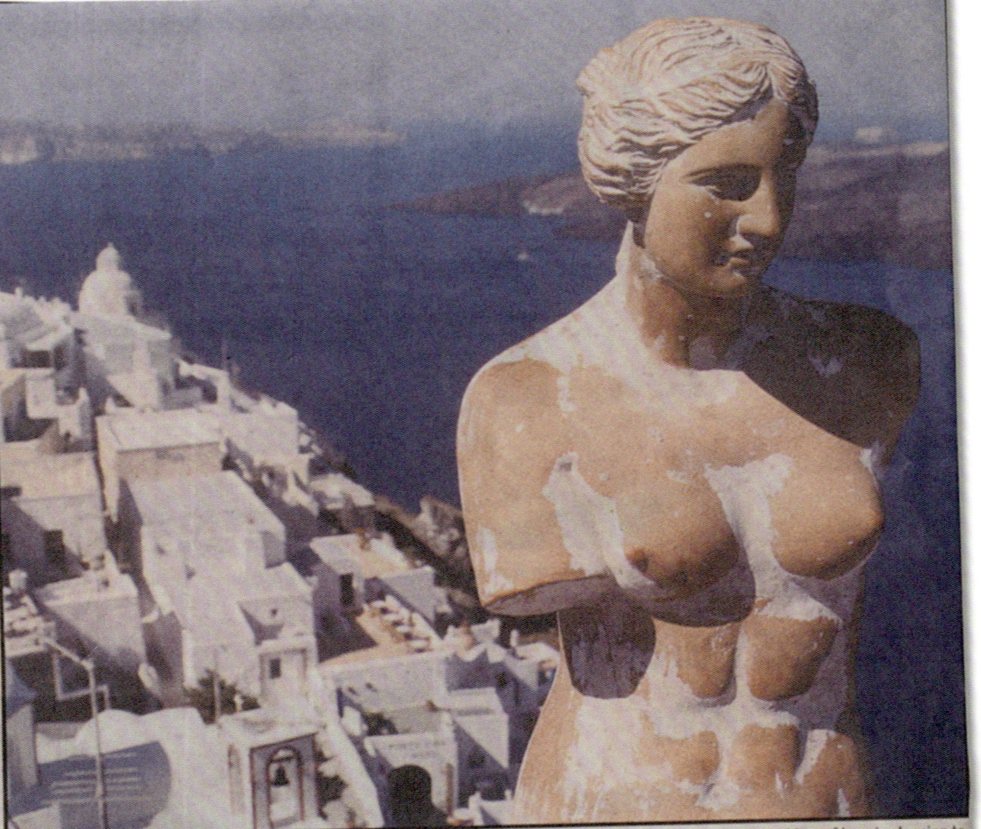

CONDOMS will be used to measure inflation in Cyprus, along with Viagra and vodka. The home of Aphrodite, the goddess of love, is planning to add the three products to its list of inflation measures because its national statistics office believes they represent an underrated but key measure of spending. Picture: ALAMY

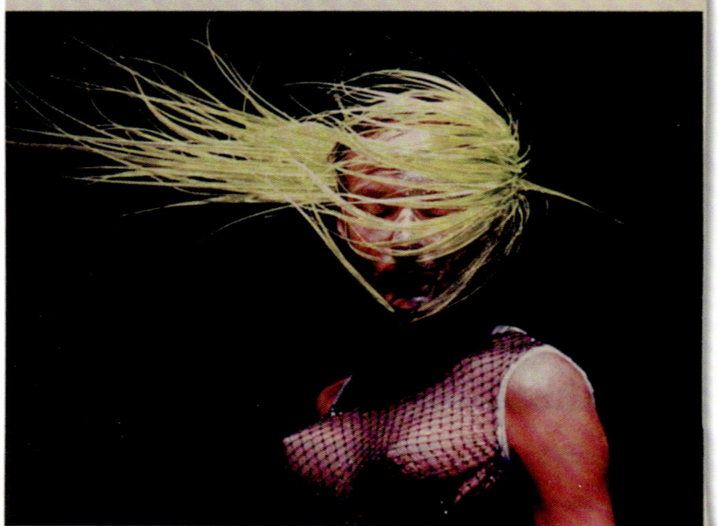

Windsbraut des Cyber-Zeitalters Kopfputz und Kleid des avantgardistischen Hutdesigners Philip Treacy

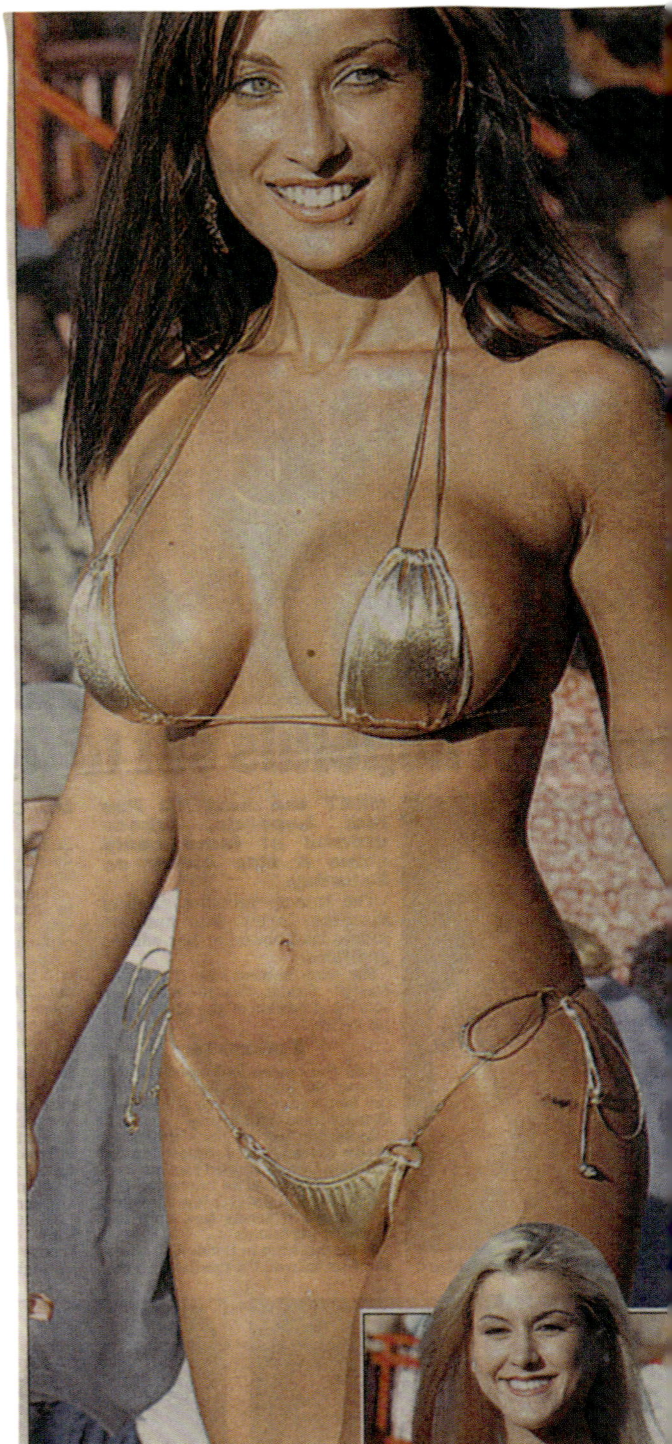

We're tops – no butts

IT WAS the brunette from Page One wot won it! The sexy lass pinched the title of Best Bod at Florida's Annual Perfect Body Competition, pipping the bikini-clad blonde.

Hundreds of women, including dancers, teachers and post office workers, competed for the title.

All the contestants had to trot across a bridge at the waterside venue near Miami for the benefit of the judges. Now that sounds like a really tough job!

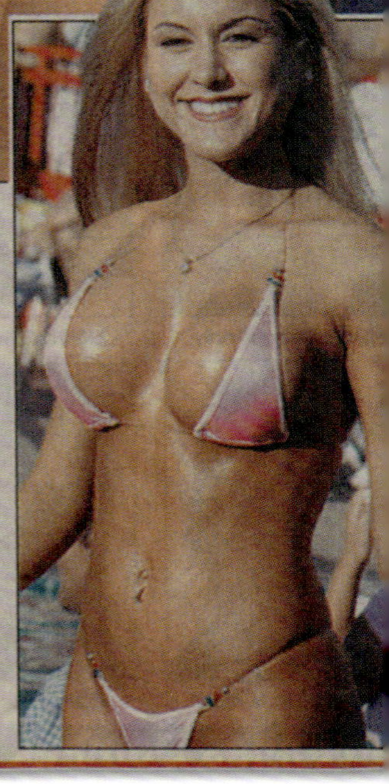

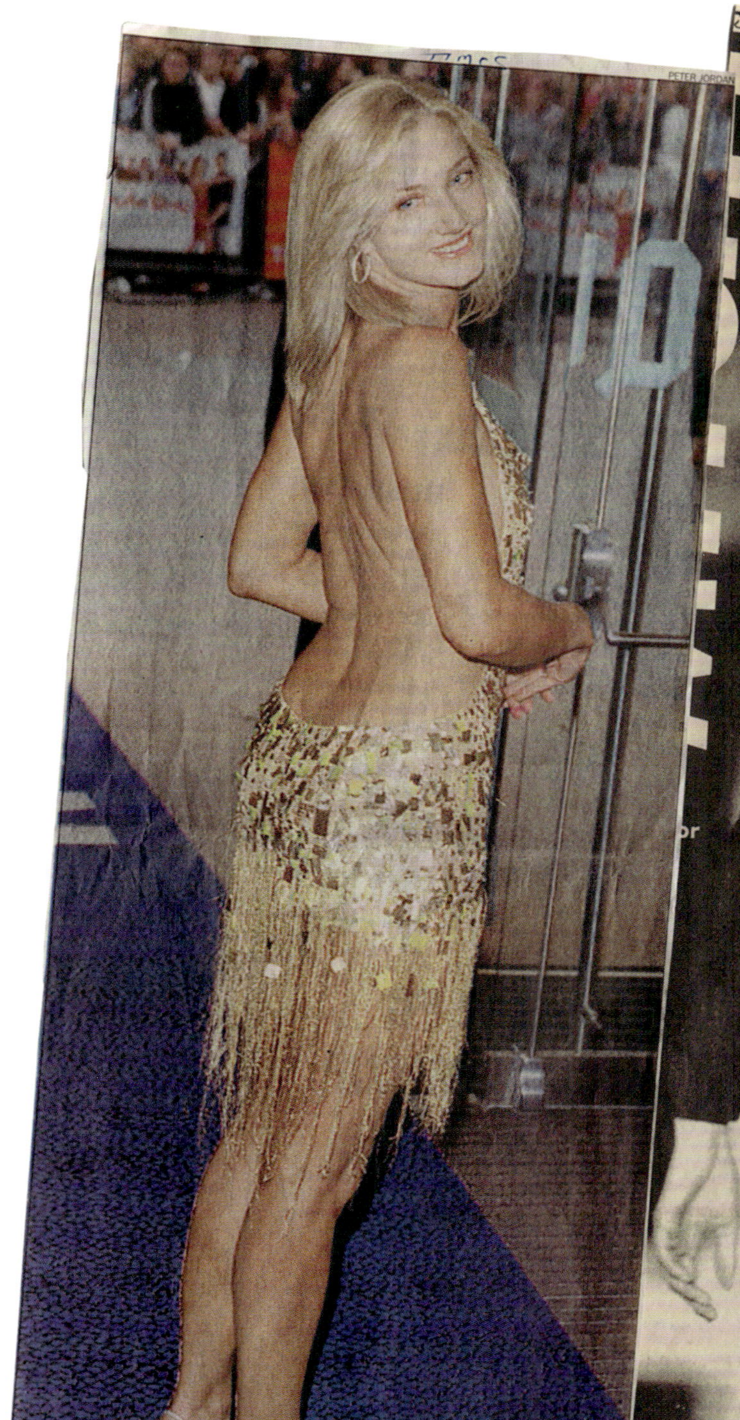

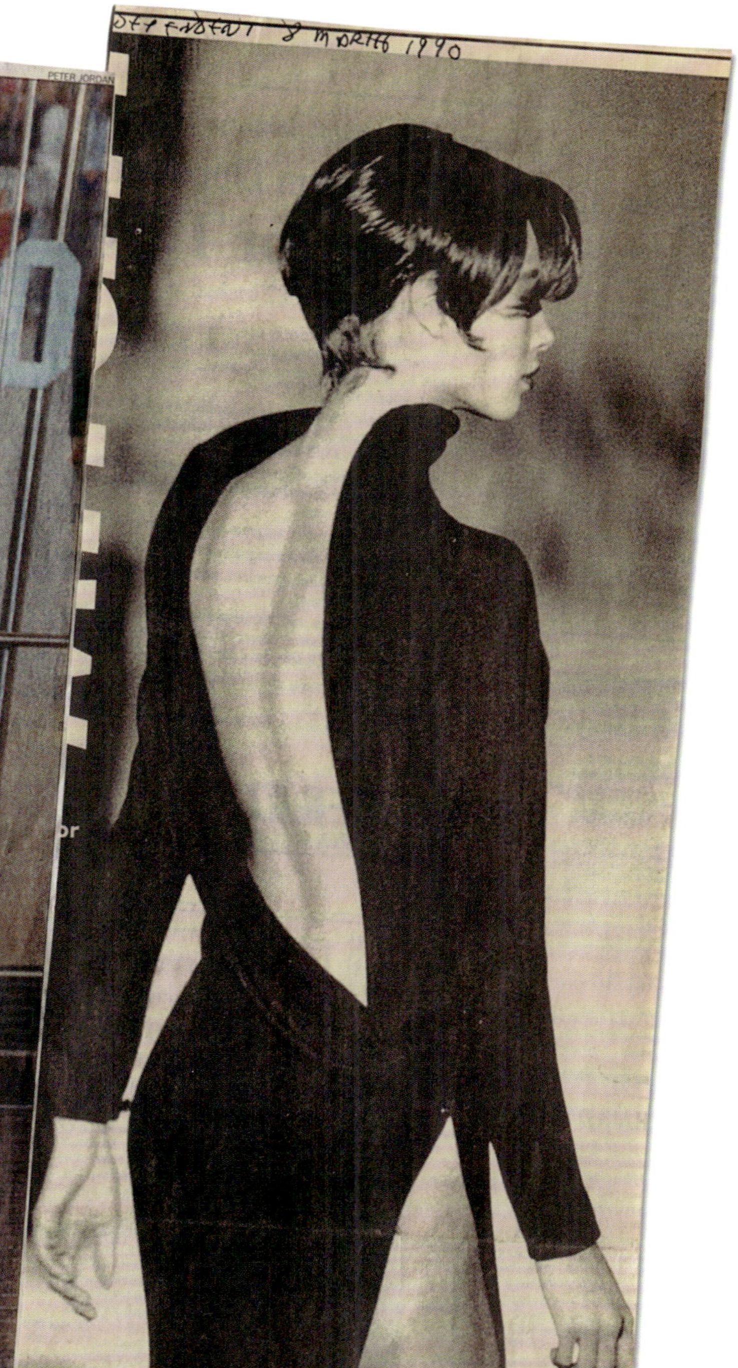

VERSACE
Black crepe dress plunging from all directions

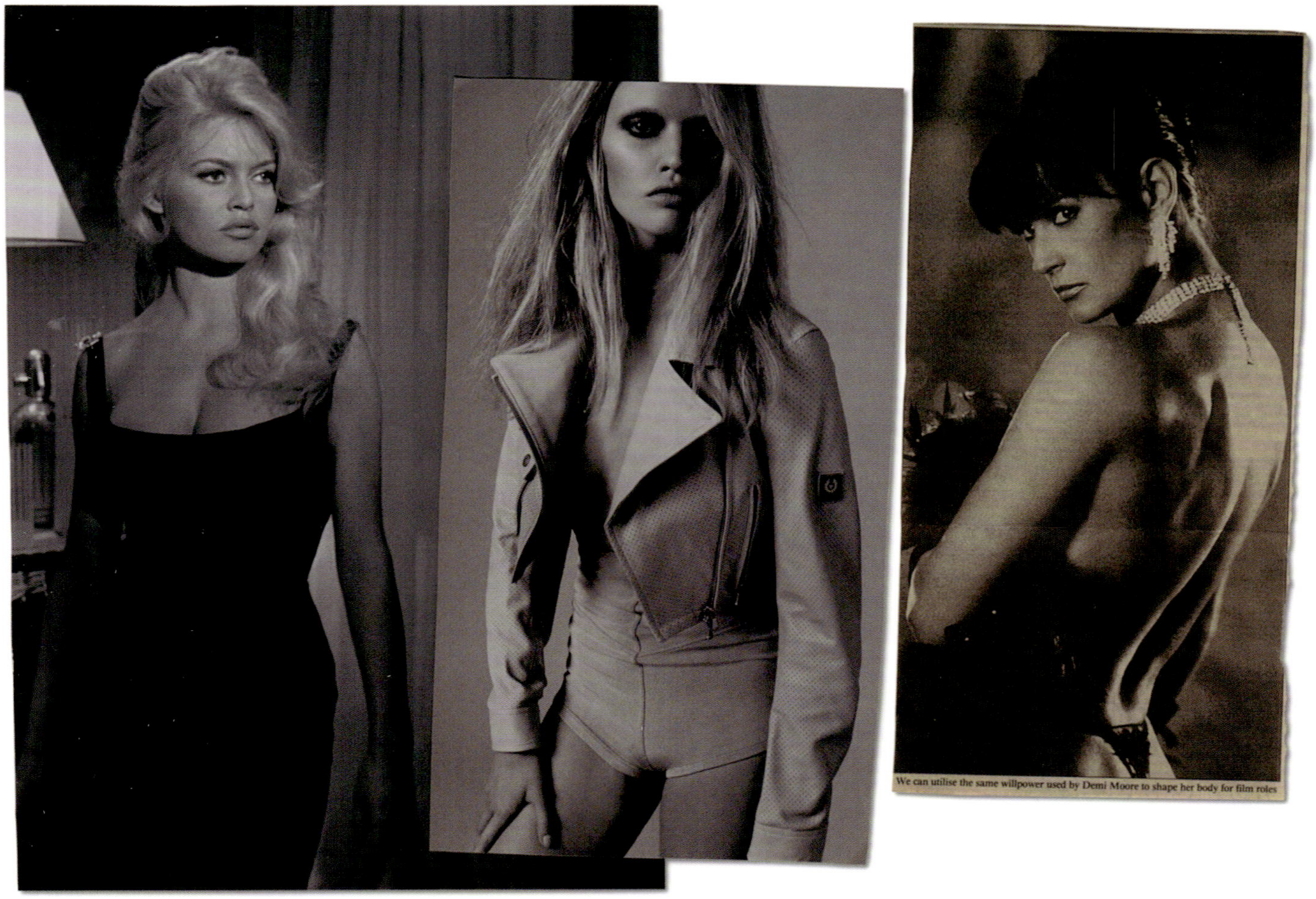
We can utilise the same willpower used by Demi Moore to shape her body for film roles

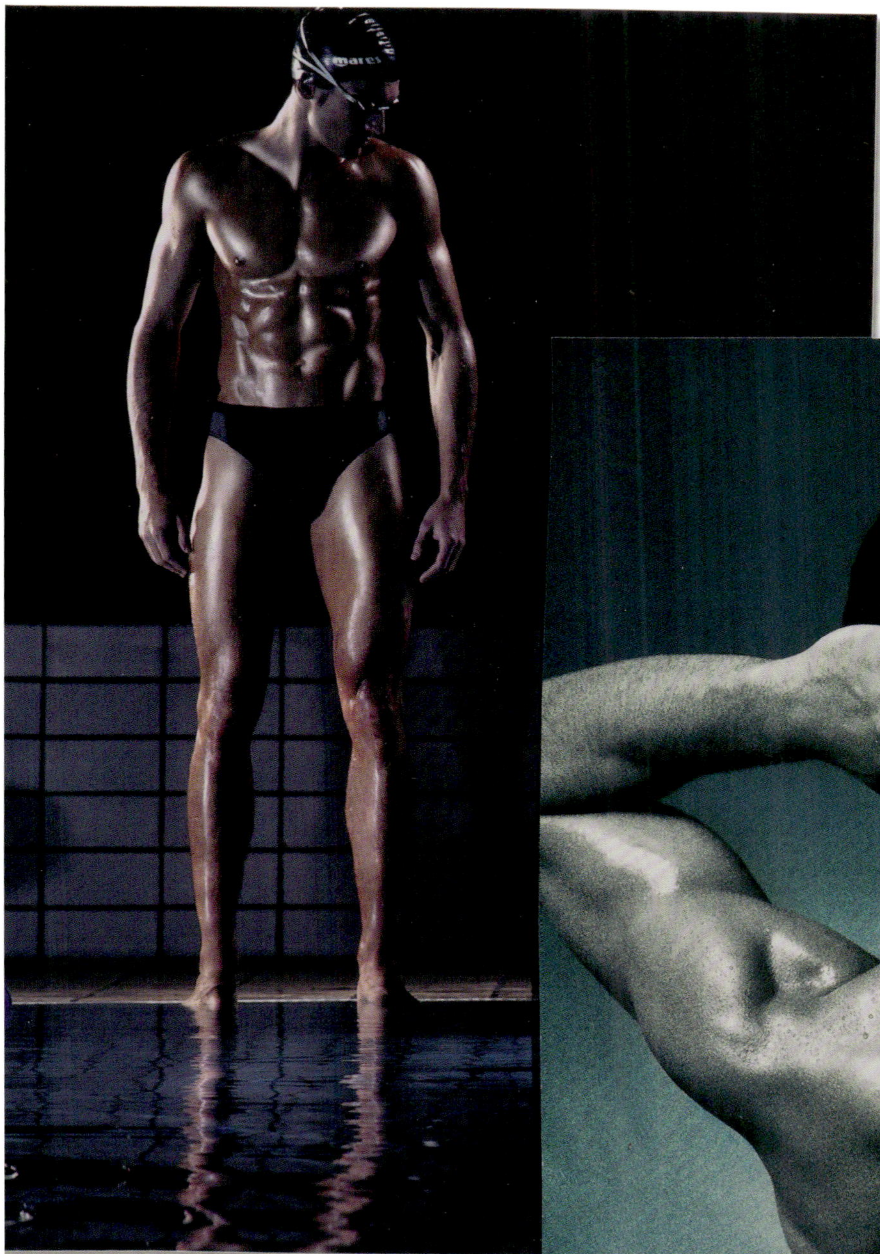
mares

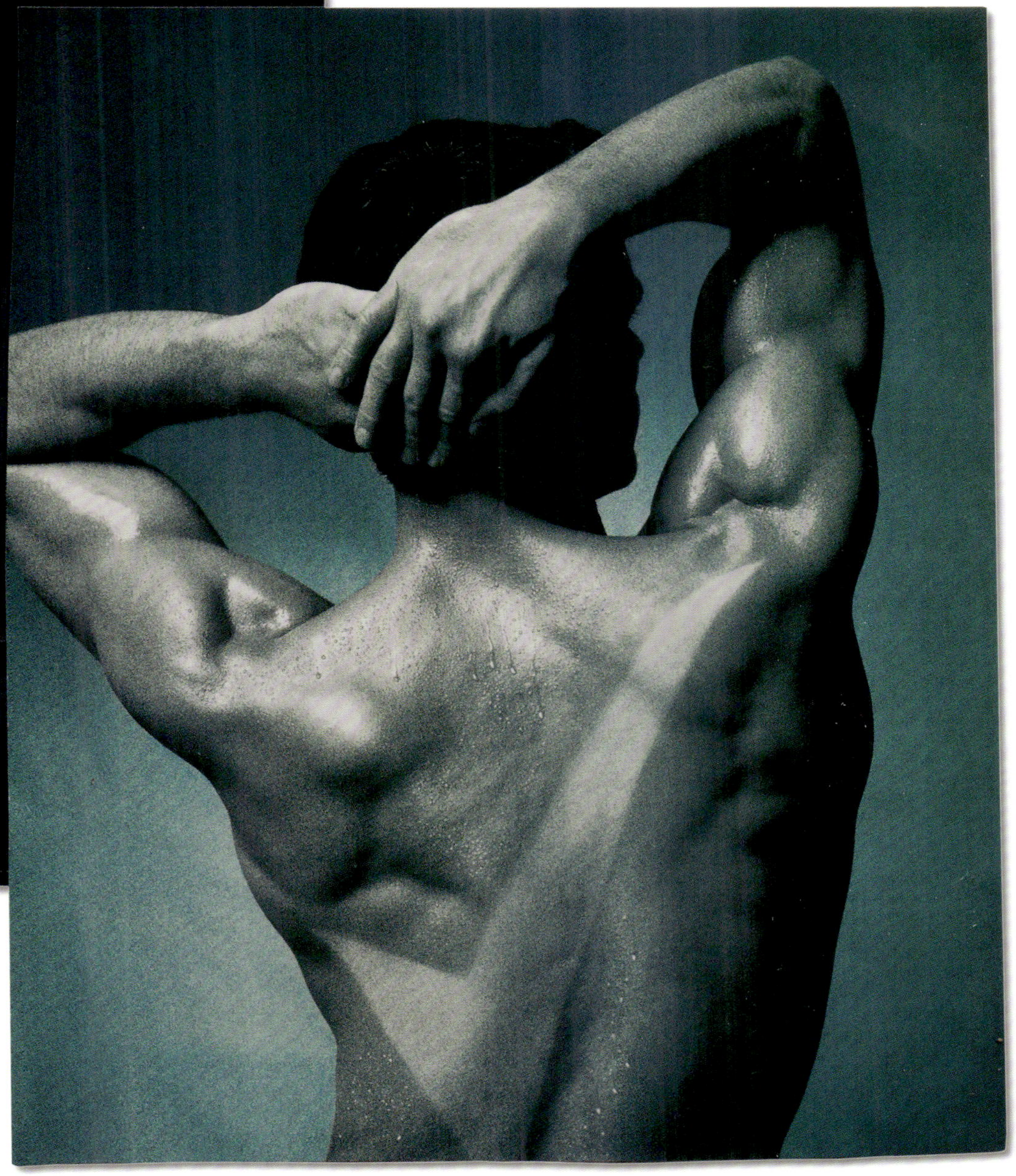

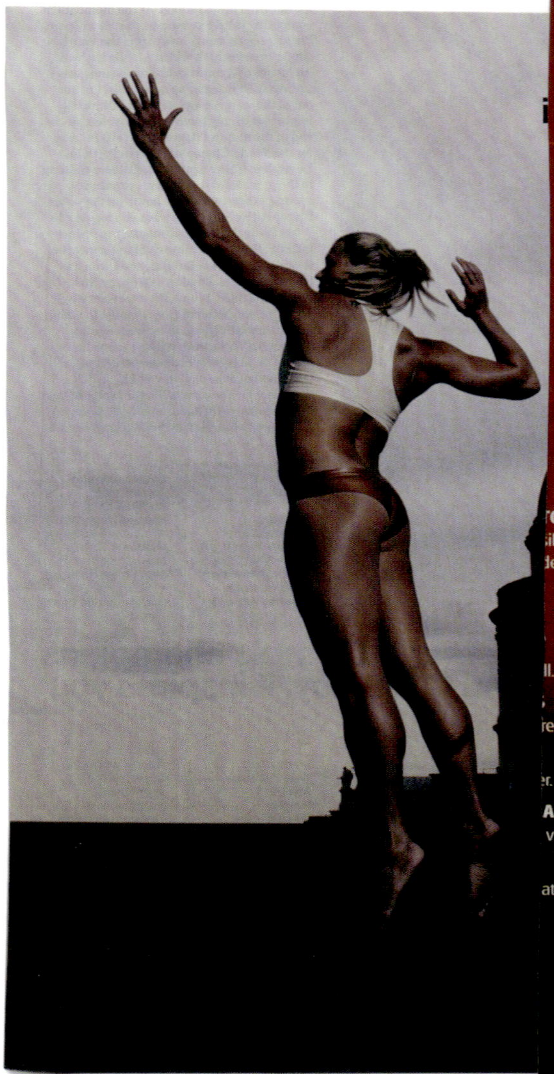

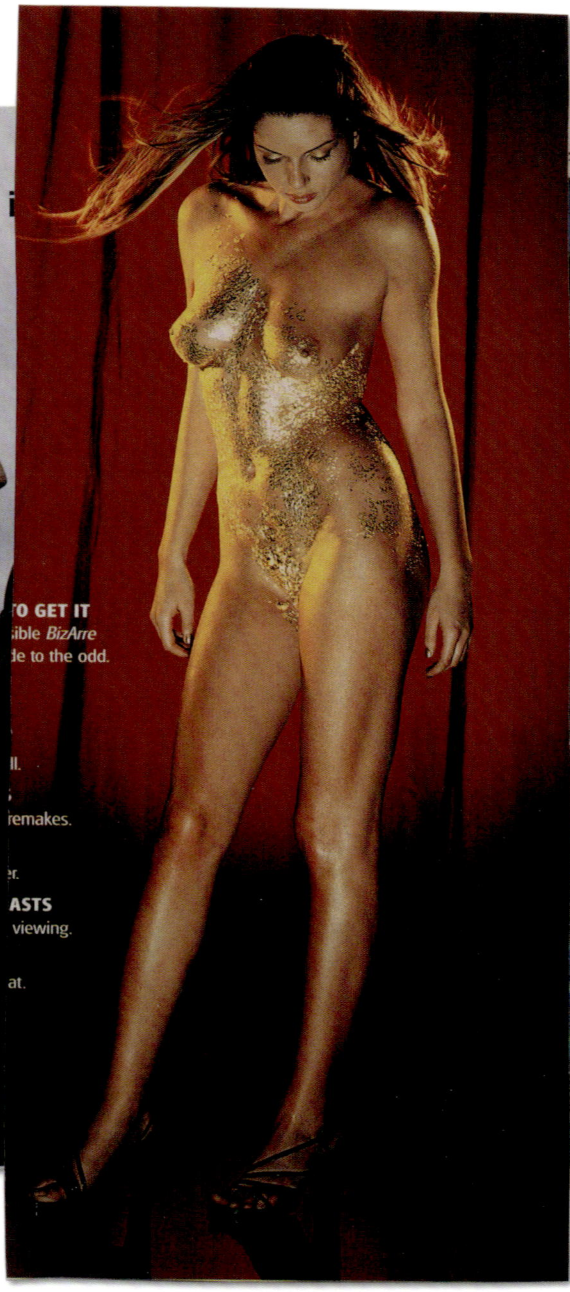
TO GET IT
sible BizArre
de to the odd.
remakes.
ASTS
viewing.

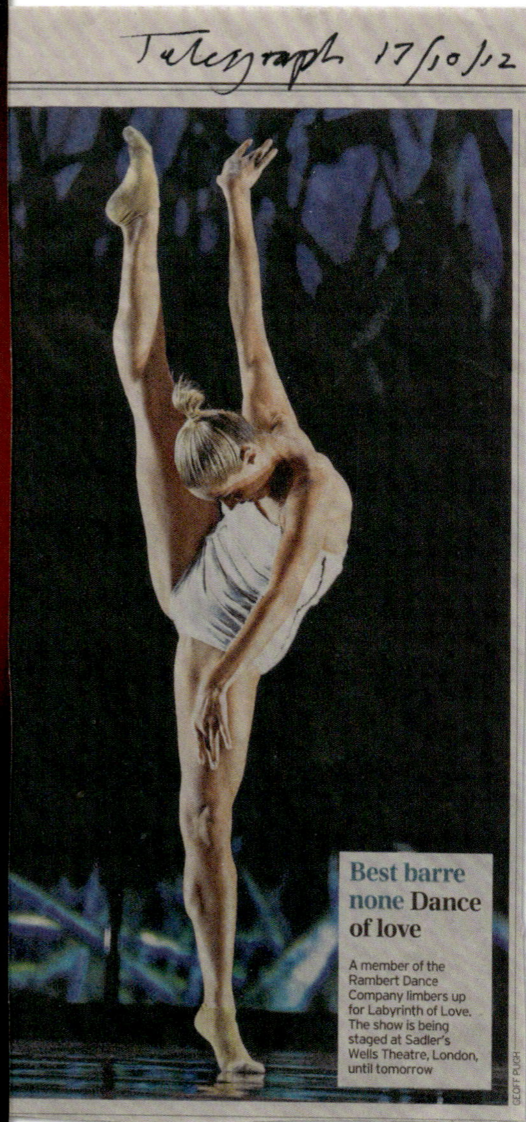
Telegraph 17/10/12
Best barre none Dance of love
A member of the Rambert Dance Company limbers up for Labyrinth of Love. The show is being staged at Sadler's Wells Theatre, London, until tomorrow
GEOFF PUGH

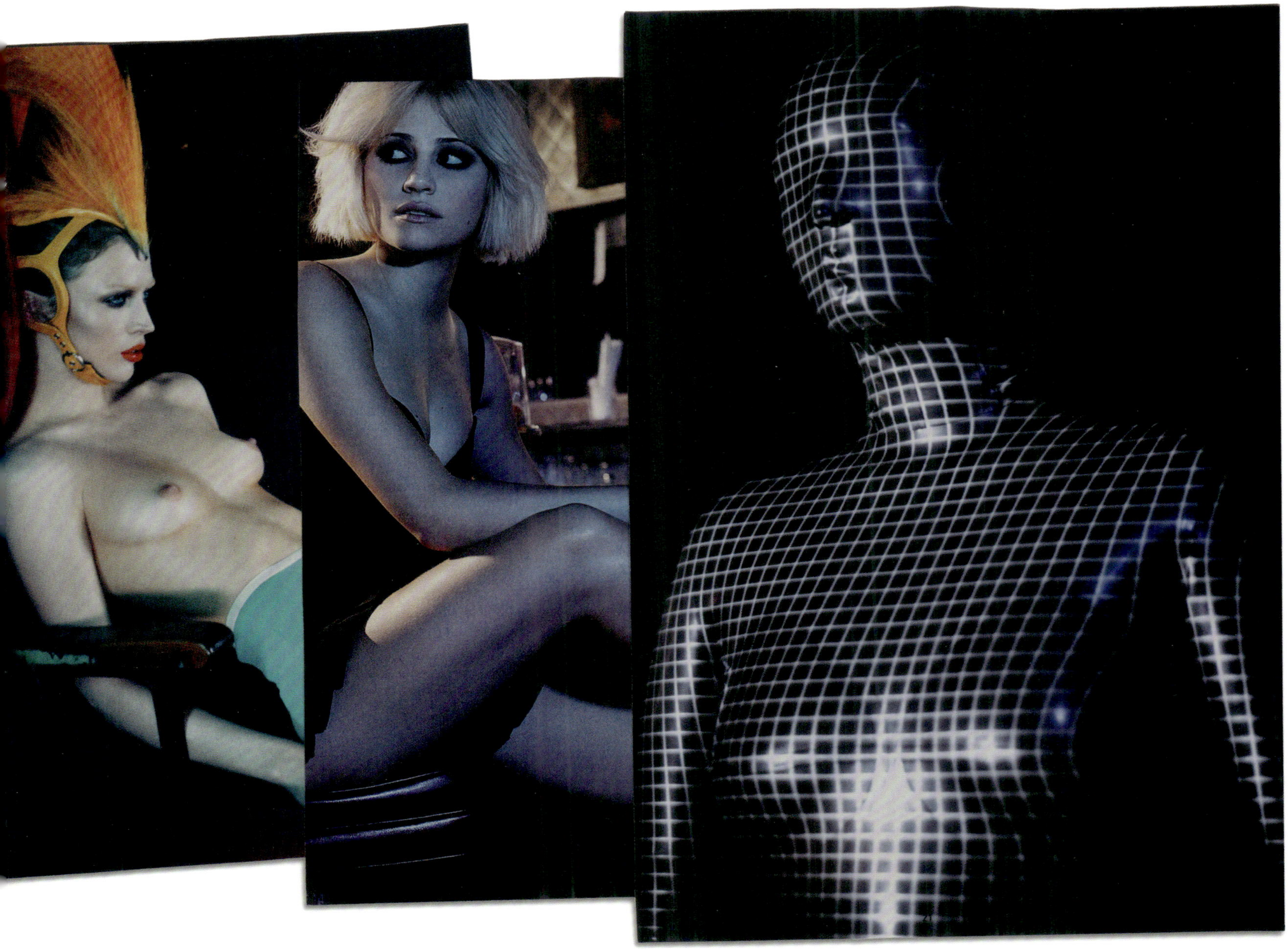

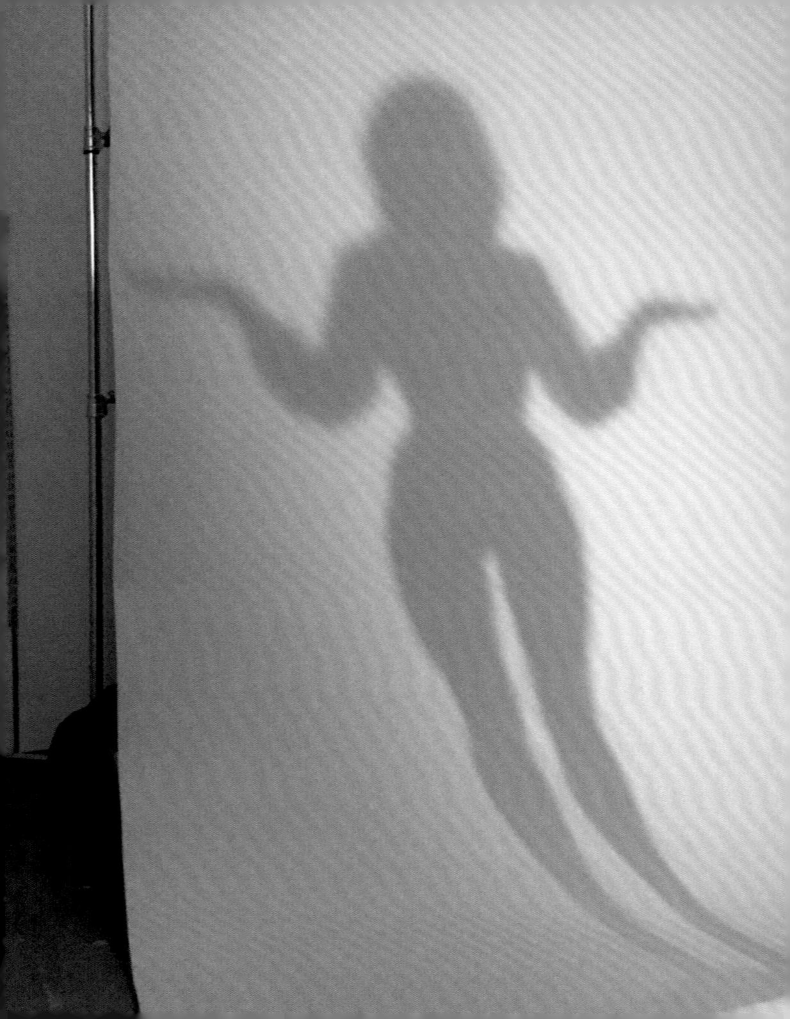

Shadowland

I started to become aware of shadows after I had installed linear sculptures in my garden in the country, notably a decorative gateway, in effect a wrought-iron drawing. I had not anticipated that the shadow it cast, while being dependant on the object, was not a replication of the object.

In a curious way it was as though the shadow was the spirit of the piece; the sculpture suddenly had another dimension, and the drawing of course varied with the time of the year. Once I recognised this fluid relationship between the object and its shadow, then, by placing the object in relationship to the passage of the sun or the moon, I realised I could make fleeting drawings which actually morph over time, creating this drawing which is repeated only once a year, weather permitting.

I then starting making photographs using my Perspex sculptures, which translate pictorially into dematerialised things. So the photographs themselves are about things that you can see through and the shadows and splashes of colour that they cast. I became aware of Perspex as a material that could be used in sculpture when I was in New York years ago with the French artist Arman. My main interest in using it is that, sited in the middle of a room, the painted colour on it stands out as if floating in the air, developing the idea of Calder's mobiles. You were not so aware of the support for the colour. It was a way of using colour and drawing in three dimensions in the air. What I then discovered was that if you paint on the surface of an acrylic sheet, the colour is diffused straight through the material to the edge. The rest of the face of course remains clear. As you walk around the object, the edge lights up and becomes a virtual drawing, and so your movement animates the figure. My photographs freeze those moments when there are elements of floating colour and shadows and transparency, all of which coalesces into a work which has its own life and that exists because of optics. The photograph allows you to fix, and makes tangible, something which is elusive and ephemeral.

Opposite
'Hatstand' shadow, Ledwell, Oxfordshire, 2014

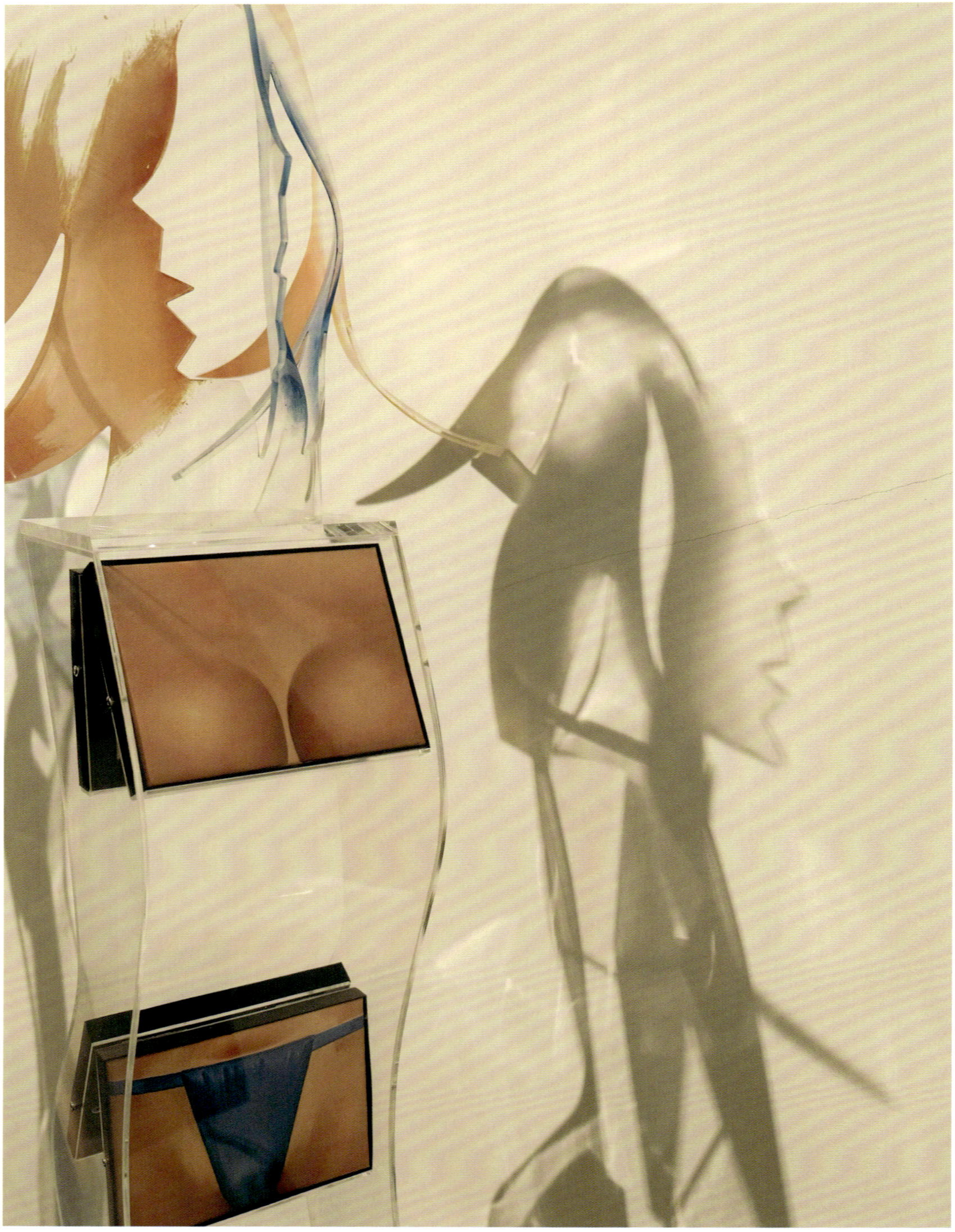

Above, opposite, and pages 214–219 Shadow studies, Charterhouse Square, London, 2018-20

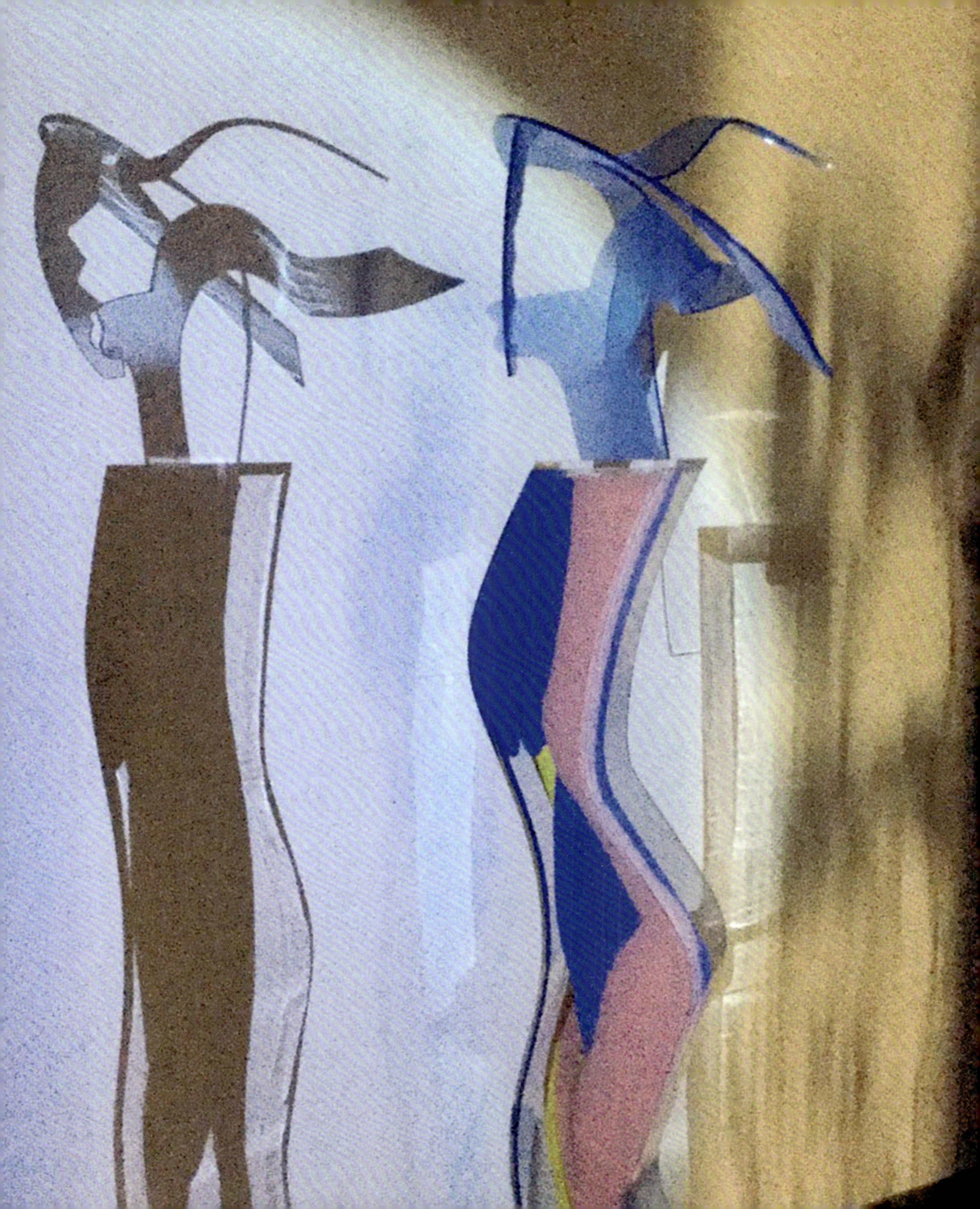

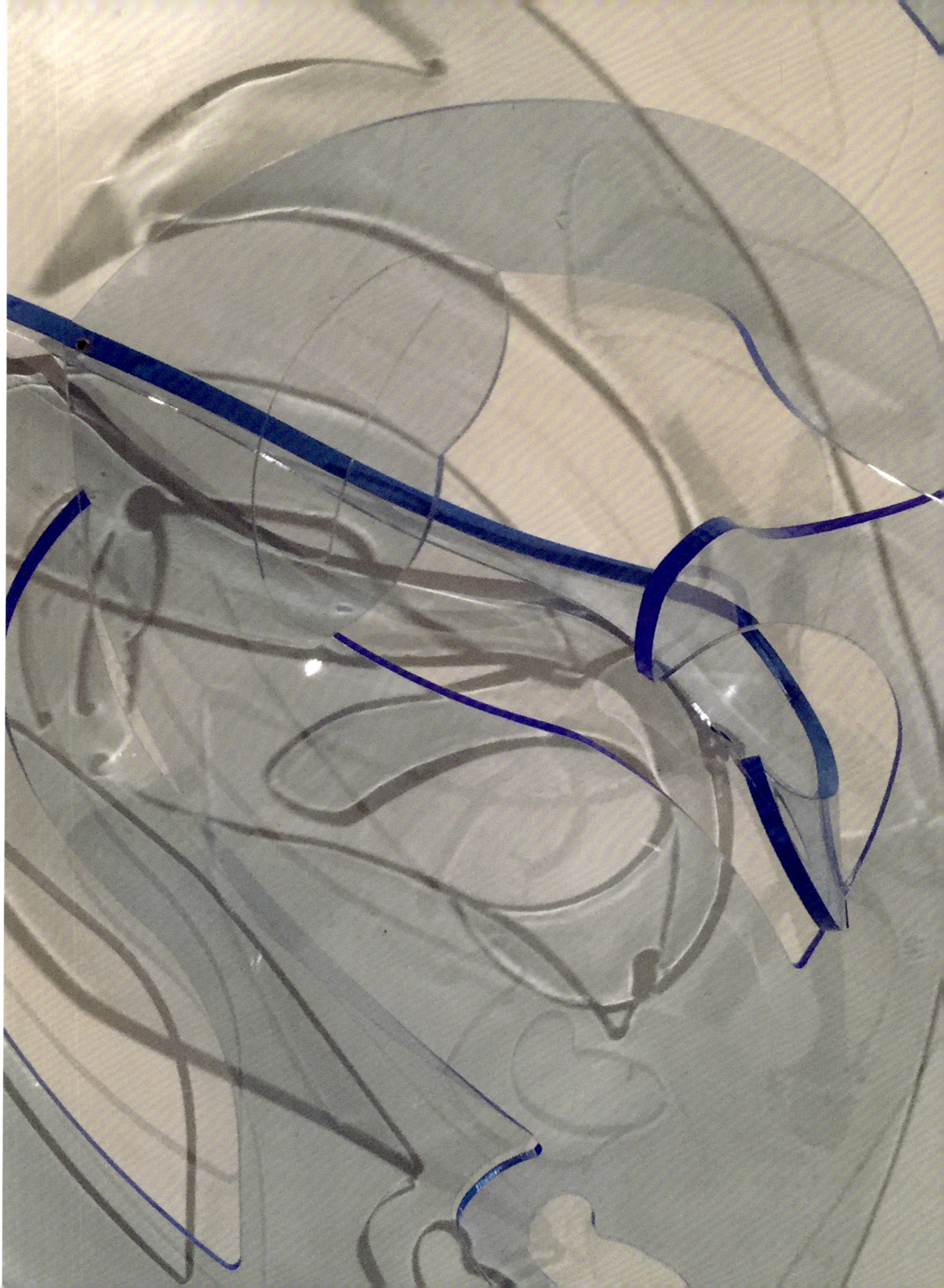

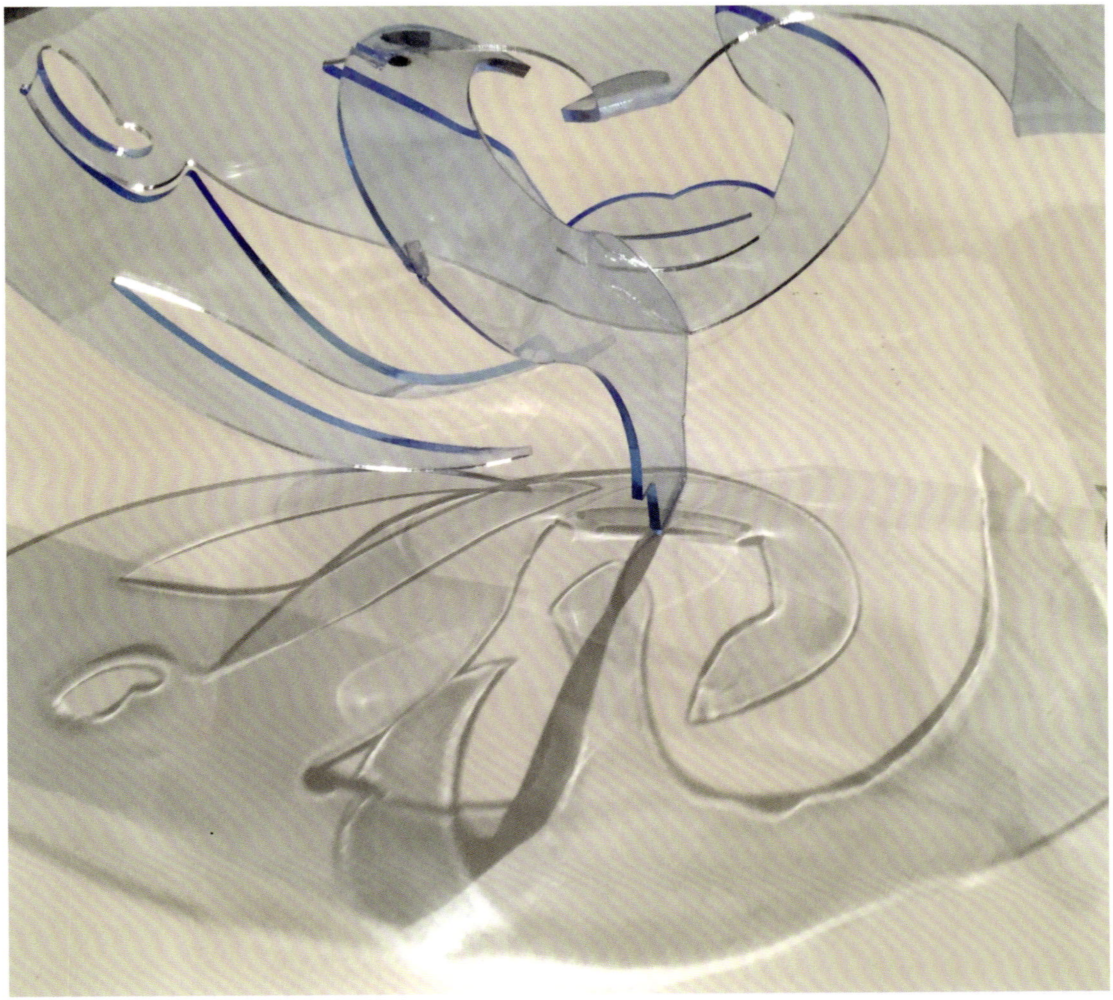

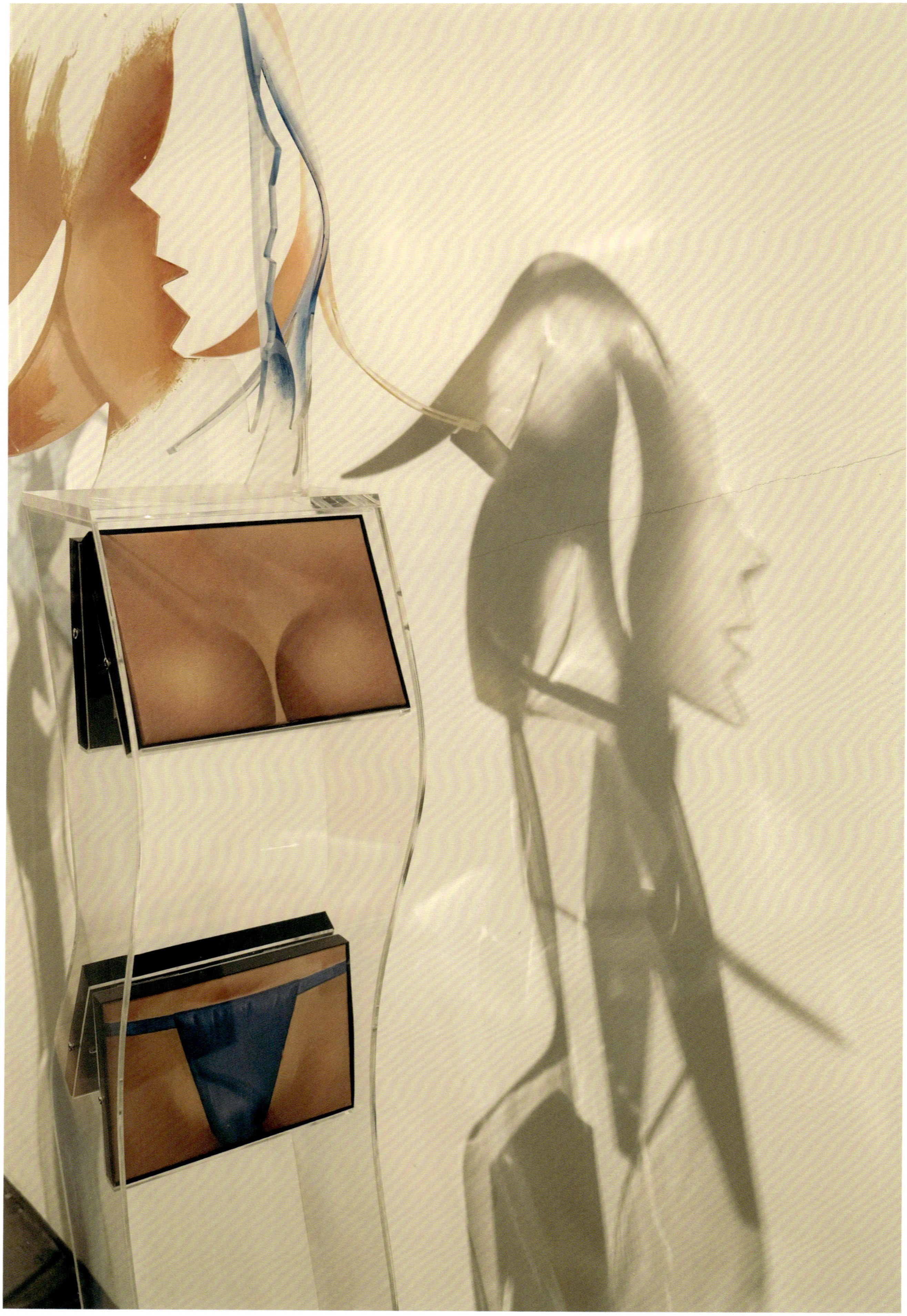

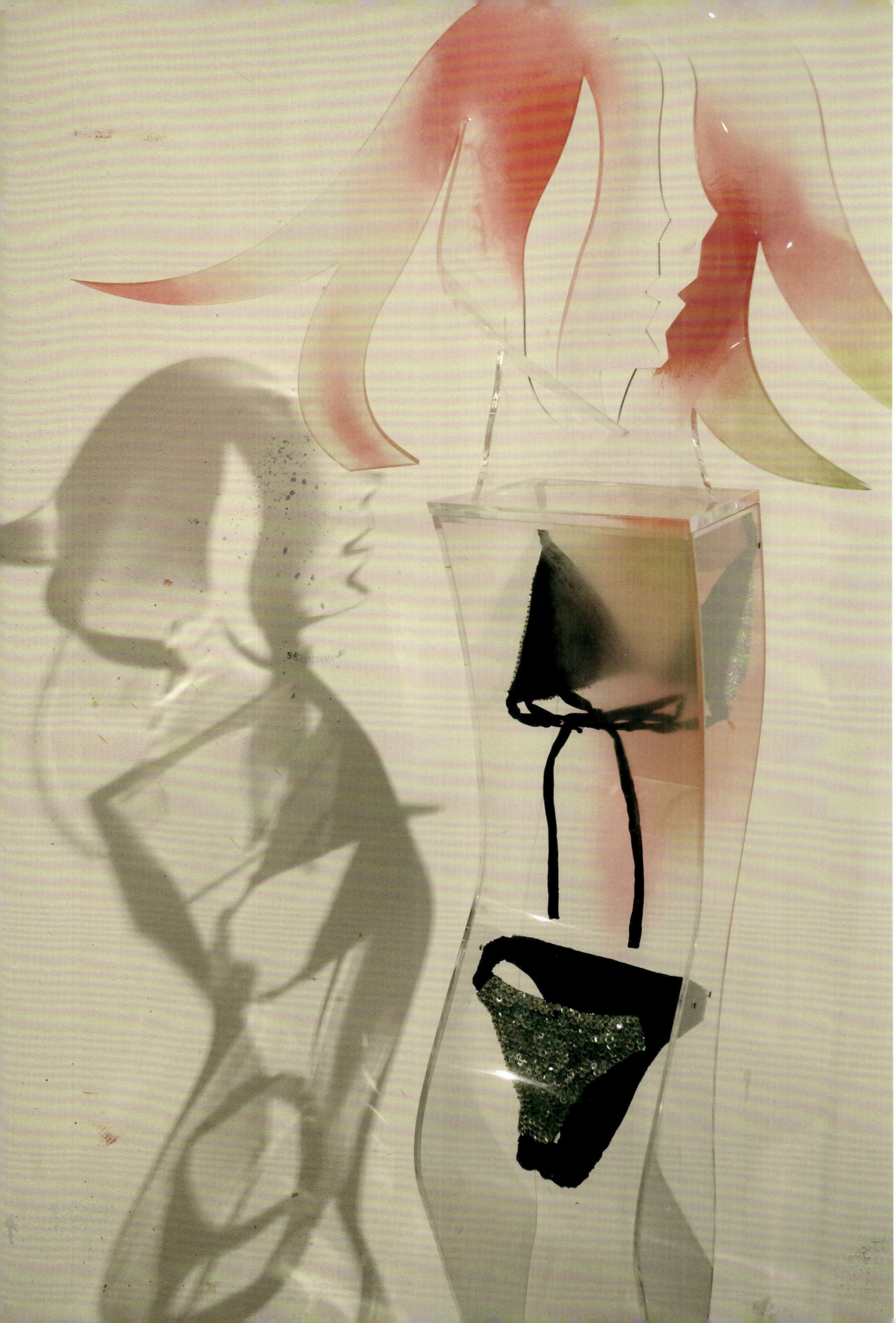

I have become intrigued by the realisation that the camera makes no distinction between recording an object and recording its ephemeral shadow. The fleeting effects of light and shade have become an engaging area of photographic exploration for me.

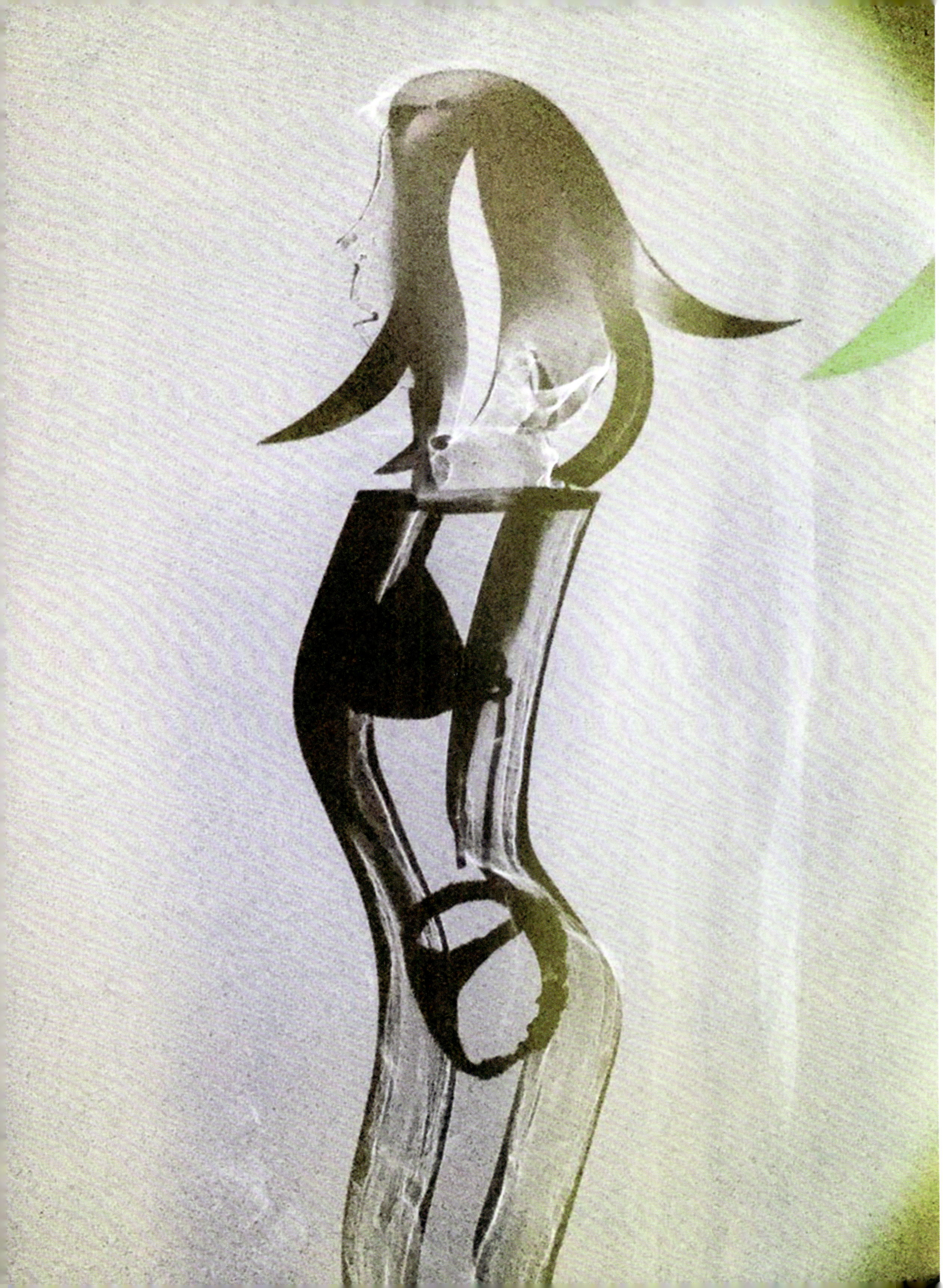

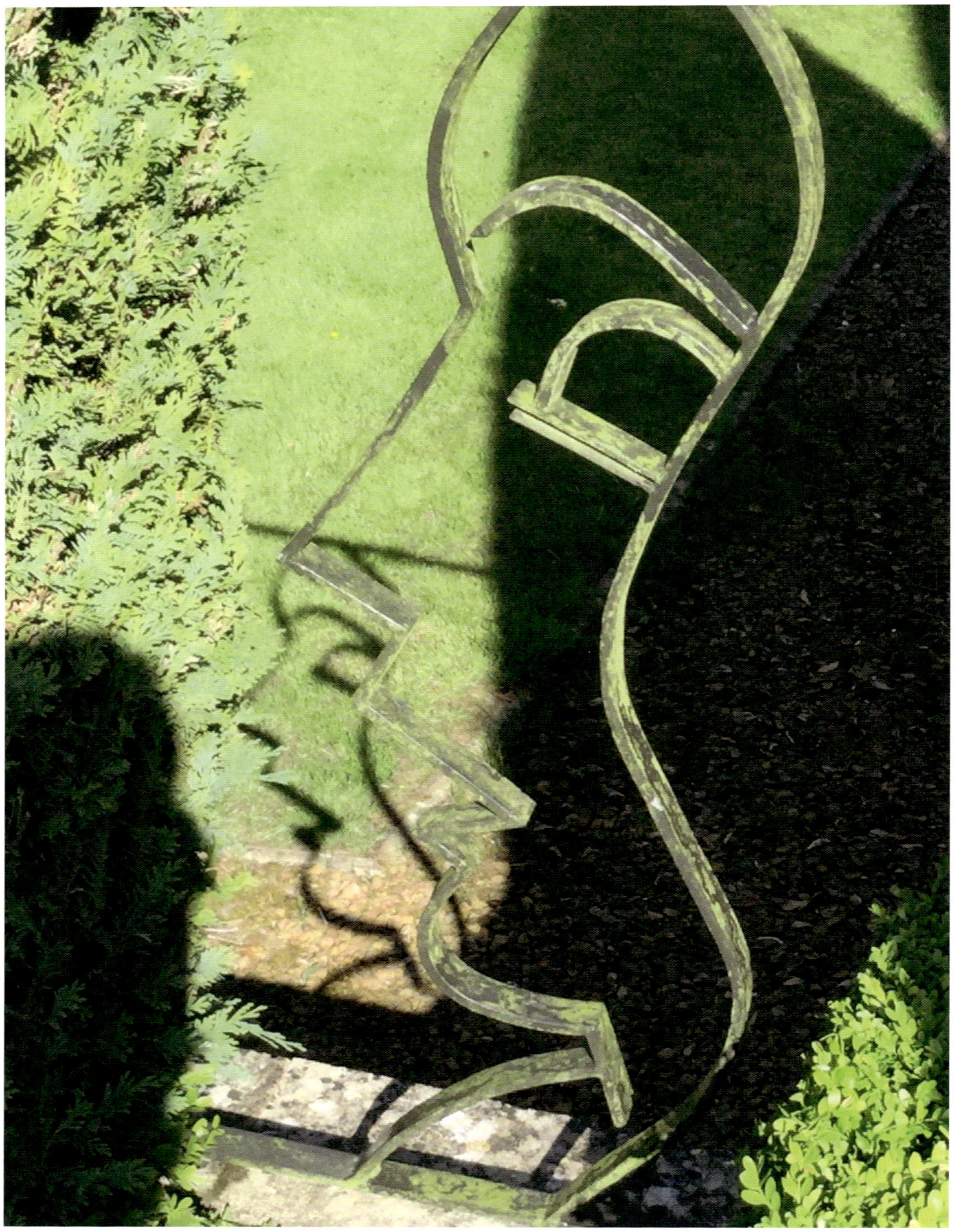

Above Sculpture and shadows, Ledwell, Oxfordshire, 2018
Opposite Shadow on American Western Red Cedar hedge, Ledwell, Oxfordshire, 2020

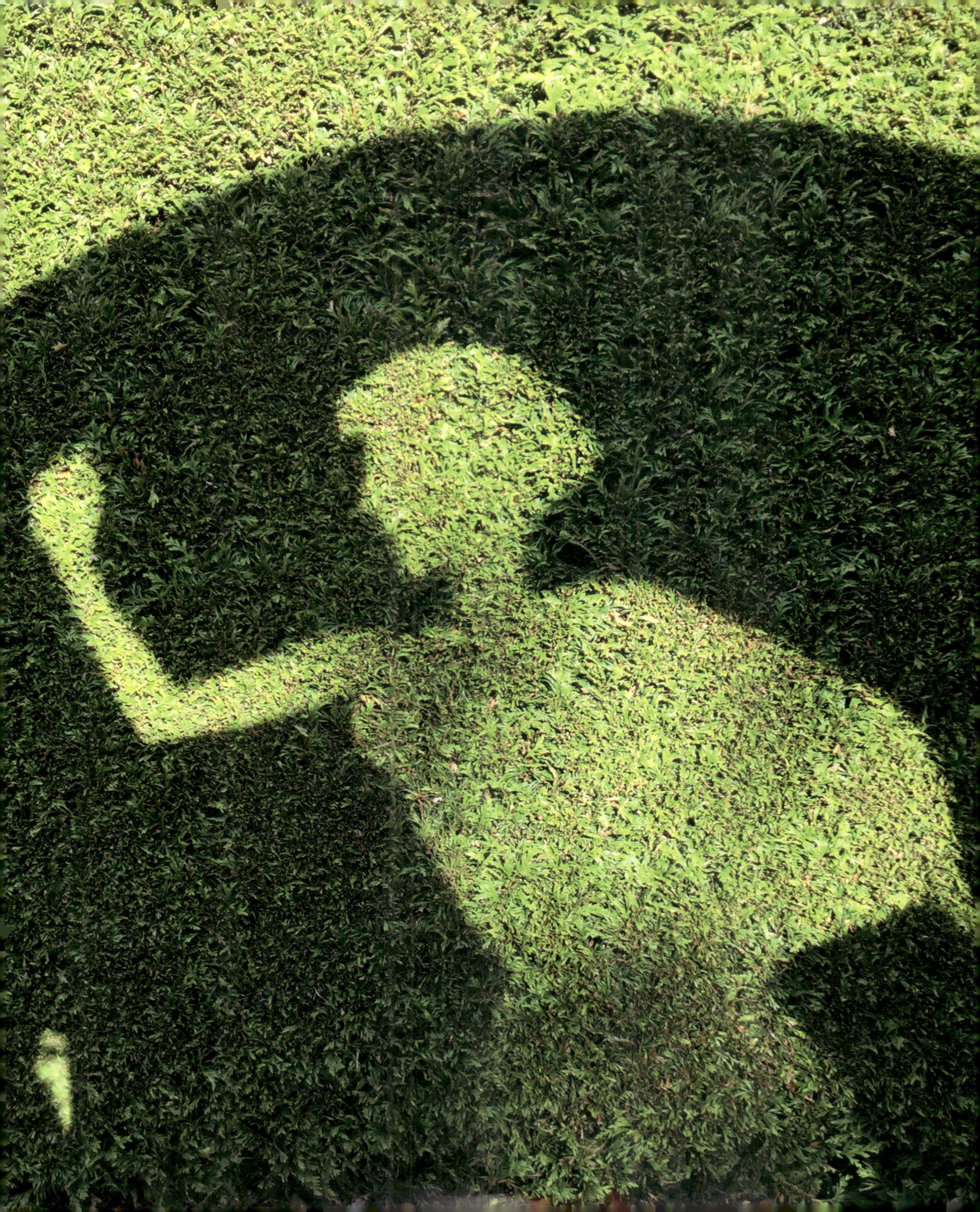

Acknowledgements

My thanks go first and foremost to Allen Jones for his openness to the idea of a book exploring the multiple ways in which photographs have been a part of his creative life. I am grateful to Allen for the wide-ranging and always stimulating conversations that the project has involved, for his allowing me a free hand to develop the structure of the book, for his constructive feedback, and for his chapter introductions and quotes that provide context and insights.

I thank David Hillman for his dynamic design, Ruby Ocean and Bridgit Getley for her invaluable practical support on multiple fronts, Tony Fisher for his impeccable scans, Sanjay Kalideen for his skill in restoring early images that had suffered over time, Christopher Gregory for his sharp-eyed checking of all the texts, Gert Elfering for a conversation that prompted me to develop this project, and James Smith and his team at ACC for publishing the end result, and last but by no means least Deirdre Morrow for her constant and steady role in ensuring Allen's freedom to focus on his work.

Allen joins me in these acknowledgements, adding to the list his gallerists, Thomas Levy in Hamburg and Bjorn Wettering in Stockholm, for including photography as a legitimate part of his work process over recent years, and artist/photographer Leon Chew for his assistance.

Philippe Garner
London, August 2022

Opposite 'A Shadow of Himself (and his artwork)', Charterhouse Square, London, 2019

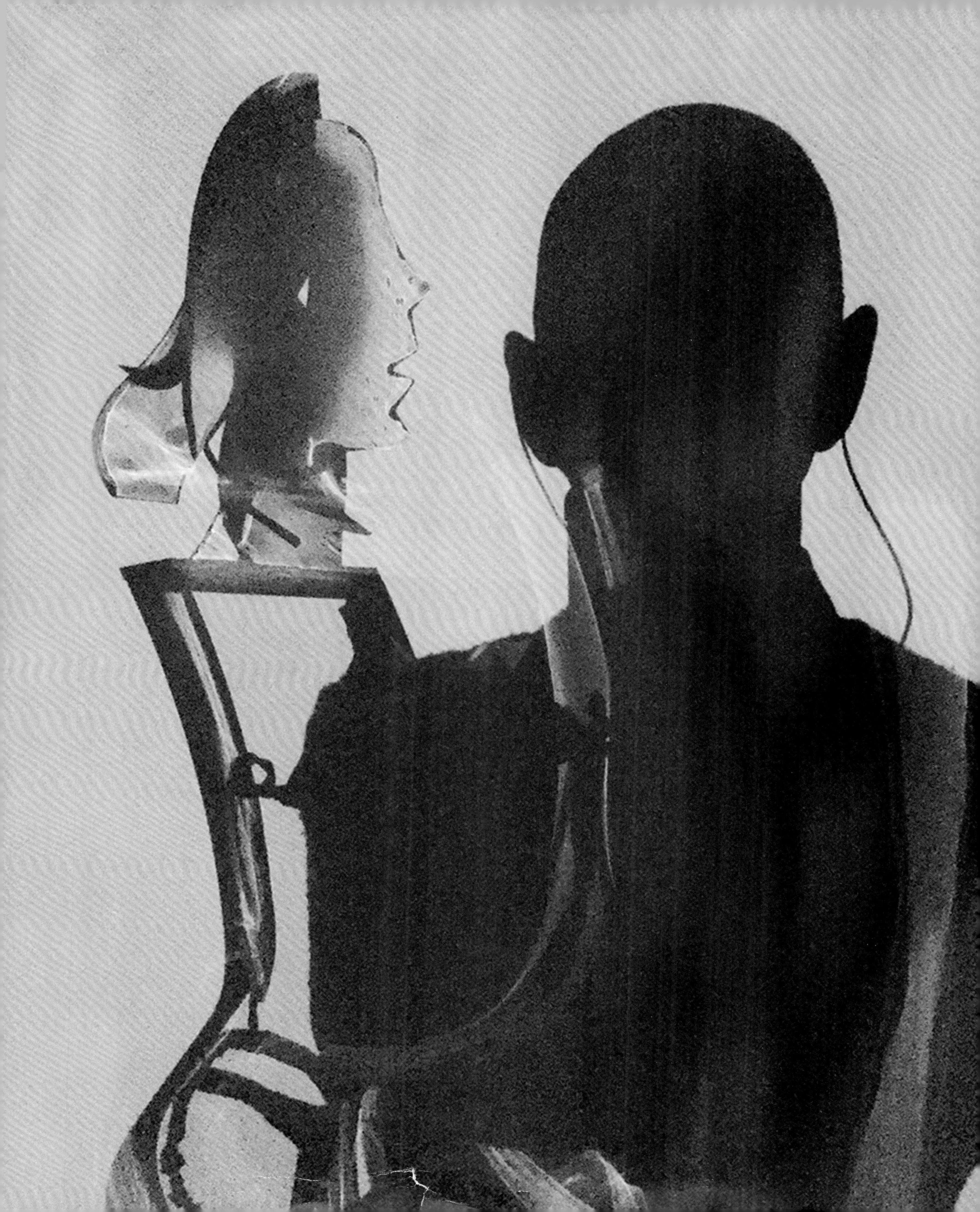

Design: David Hillman

ISBN: 978 178884 193 1

British Library Cataloguing-in-Publication Data
A catalogue record for this book is available from the British Library

The author and publisher gratefully acknowledge the permission granted to reproduce the copyright material in this book. Every effort has been made to trace copyright holders and to obtain their permission for the use of copyright material. The publisher apologises for any errors or omissions in the text and would be grateful if notified of any corrections that should be incorporated in future reprints or editions of this book.

Cover 'Hatstand' shadow, Ledwell, Oxfordshire, 2014
Pages 2–3 Billboard, London, 1988
Pages 4–5 Billboard, Miami, Florida, 1965
Pages 6–7 Waterfall, Manhattan, New York, 1979
Pages 8–9 Florida, 1965

FSC www.fsc.org MIX Paper from responsible sources FSC® C013123

Printed in Italy
for ACC Art Books Ltd., Woodbridge, Suffolk, England

www.accartbooks.com

ACC ART BOOKS